T0319354

FARM LABOR IN GERMANY,

1810-1945

FARM LABOR IN GERMANY 1810-1945

ITS HISTORICAL DEVELOPMENT WITHIN THE FRAMEWORK OF AGRICULTURAL AND SOCIAL POLICY

BY FRIEDA WUNDERLICH

PRINCETON, NEW JERSEY
PRINCETON UNIVERSITY PRESS
1961

Publication of this book
has been aided by the Ford Foundation program
to support publication, through university
presses, of works in the humanities and social
sciences, and by a grant from the New School
for Social Research.

Printed in the United States of America by
Princeton University Press, Princeton, New Jersey

To
Alvin Johnson
and
Clara W. Mayer

IN DEEP GRATITUDE

Dr. Frieda Wunderlich has been a Judge of the Supreme Court
of Social Insurance in Germany,
a member of the City Council of Berlin,
and a member of the Prussian Diet.
From 1923 to 1933 she was the editor of *Soziale Praxis*,
and from 1930 to 1933 was also a professor
of Economics at the Berufspädagogisches Institut.
Since 1933, when she came to America,
Miss Wunderlich has been a professor
in the Graduate Faculty of The New School
for Social Research.

CONTENTS

PART THREE

THE PERIOD OF NATIONAL SOCIALISM

ABBREVIATIONS

ADGB   Allgemeiner Deutscher Gewerkschaftsbund, General Federation of German Trade Unions (Socialistic)

Afa League   Allgemeiner Freier Angestelltenbund, Socialist Free Employees Federation

AOG   Gesetz zur Ordnung der nationalen Arbeit, National Socialist Labor Act

Archiv   Archiv des Reichsnährstandes

ARS   Arbeitsrechtssammlung. Entscheidungen des Reichsarbeitsgerichts und der Landesarbeitsgerichte, eds. Hermann Dersch and Others. Labor Court Decisions quoted with volume of this collection

AVAVG   Reichsgesetz für Arbeitsvermittlung und Arbeitslosenversicherung, Reich Law for Placement and Unemployment Insurance

BRG   Betriebsrätegesetz, Works Council Law

DAF   Deutsche Arbeitsfront, German Labor Front

DAZ   Deutsche Allgemeine Zeitung

Denkschrift   Das Landwirtschaftliche Bildungswesen in Preussen Denkschrift des Ministers für Landwirtschaft, Domänen und Forsten, Berlin, 1929

DGB   Deutscher Gewerkschaftsbund, Confederation of German Trade Unions (Christian)

Deutschland Berichte   Deutschland Berichte der Sopade, later Deutschland Berichte der Sozialdemokratischen Partei Deutschlands

DJ   Deutsche Justiz, German Official Law Gazette

DLV   Deutscher Landarbeiter Verband, German Agricultural Workers Union (Socialistic)

DRAnz   Deutscher Reichsanzeiger

DV   Der Deutsche Volkswirt

DW   Deutsche Wissenschaft, Erziehung und Volksbildung, Official Monthly of the Ministry of Education

Enquete Ausschuss   Publications of Ausschuss zur Untersuchung der Erzeugungs- und Absatzbedingungen der deutschen Industrie (Enquiry Committee into Production and Marketing Conditions of German Industry)

FZ   Frankfurter Zeitung

ha.   hectare = 2.471 acres

Jahrbuch DAF   Arbeitswissenschaftliches Institut der Deutschen Arbeitsfront, *Jahrbuch*

LAO   Vorläufige Landarbeitsordnung, Agricultural Labor Law

NSDAP   Nationalsozialistische Deutsche Arbeiter Partei, National Socialist German Workers' Party

M.   Mark (1870-1923)

NSBO   Nationalsozialistische Betriebszellenorganisation, National Socialist Shop Cell Organization

NS Landpost   Nationalsozialistische Landpost

NSV   Nationalsozialistische Volkswohlfahrt, National Socialist Welfare Organization

PrGS   Gesetzsammlung für die Königlichen Preussischen Staaten, 1806-1810; after 1907 called *Preussische Gesetzsammlung*, Prussian Official Law Gazette

RABl   Reichsarbeitsblatt, Official Labor Gazette

RAD   Reichsarbeitsdienst, Reich Labor Service

REG   Reichserbhofgesetz, Hereditary Farm Law

Reich Ministry for Agriculture   Reichsministerium für Ernährung und Landwirtschaft, Reich Ministry for Food and Agriculture

Reifa   Reichsanstalt für Arbeitsvermittlung und Arbeitslosenfürsorge, Federal Institute for Placement and Unemployment Insurance

Reifa Reports   Berichte der Reichsanstalt für Arbeitsvermittlung und Arbeitslosenversicherung

RGBl   Reichsgesetzblatt, Official Law Gazette

Ring   Gewerkschaftsring Deutscher Arbeiter-, Angestellten- und Beamtenverbände, Confederation of Workers, Salaried Employees and Civil Servants (liberal)

RLAB   Reichslandarbeiterbund, Federal Land Workers' Union (nonmilitant)

RLB   Reichslandbund, National League of Agrarians

Rm.   Reichsmark (1924-1948)

RMBliV   Reichsministerialblatt für die innere Verwaltung, Official Gazette of the Federal Ministry of the Interior

RN   Reichsnährstand, Reich Food Estate

RTA   Reichstreuhänder der Arbeit, Reich Trustee of Labor

RVO   Reichsversicherungsordnung, Federal Social Insurance Code

RWR   Vorläufiger Reichswirtschaftsrat, Provisional National Economic Council

SA   Schutzabteilung, Storm Troops

Schriften DLV Schriften des Deutschen Landarbeiterverbandes, Publications of the DLV

SP Soziale Praxis, Periodical

SPD Social Democratic Party

Statistisches Jahrbuch Statistisches Jahrbuch für das Deutsche Reich, Official Statistical Yearbook

SS Schutzstaffel, Elite Guard

W&St Wirtschaft und Statistik, Official Journal of the Federal Statistical Office

VdgB Vereinigung der gegenseitigen Bauernhilfe, Peasant Association of Mutual Help

VH Vierteljahrshefte zur Statistik des Deutschen Reichs, Official Statistical Quarterly

ZV Zentralverband der Landarbeiter, Central Union of Agricultural Workers (Christian)

For full citation of references given in brief form in footnotes, see Bibliography. The numerical references in the footnotes (such as Bibl. #84) refer to the Bibliography, where all entries are numbered alphabetically.

PART ONE. INTRODUCTION: HISTORICAL
BACKGROUND

ORIGINS OF THE RURAL
SOCIAL STRUCTURE

O
N THE eve of the Second World War agricultural labor all over Europe was manifold in character. In the regions where large estates prevailed, it might be part of the modern working class as it emerged from the industrial revolution; wherever landed aristocracy existed, it still preserved features of the feudal servant class. On the other hand, in regions of small farming the distinction between employer and employee was not clear-cut. The small farmer was nearer to the farm worker—and could become one intermittently—than to the big farm owner. Lack of understanding of this social structure and the attempts of industrial labor to treat farm labor indiscriminately as part of the working class aroused much discontent in rural areas and, in some cases, made the small farmer inclined to associate himself with Fascist movements. No essay about farm labor, therefore, can disregard the system of land tenure.

In Germany at the end of the First World War agricultural land was owned prevailingly by powerful squires in the east and by peasants[1] in the south and west, with only a few large estates scattered in the center, south, and west. Of the land under cultivation 62.2 per cent belonged to farms ranging in size from 10 to 100 ha. The Elbe, which separated the two parts of the country, formed an agrarian and cultural frontier. A serious labor problem existed only on the estates east of the Elbe, in the territory under colonization. But the role played by these estate owners in the political and social life of Prussia, and incidentally of all Germany, made labor conditions there a matter of national importance. The big land owners who dominated the German army and bureaucracy believed that the state was obliged to protect their privileges. Most of the agricultural population, still influenced by feudal traditions, accepted the leadership of this minority group. The preponderant influence of the feudal estate owners during the Empire was the more striking since not they, but the middle-class farmers, were the backbone of German agriculture. To understand the position of the farm

[1] According to German statistics, owners of holdings up to 100 ha. were called peasants. However, owners of large estates (Gutsbesitzer) differed from peasants more by their social status, their education, and manner of living than by size of the holding. Whereas the word "farmer" connotes an occupational status, the word "peasant" indicates a class status. According to European usage the term "peasants" is applied here to those farmers who constitute a class in the society in which they live.

worker in Imperial Germany and the Weimar Republic, one must go back to the origins of this social structure.[2]

The Lord and the Peasant

Geography and climate only partially account for the differences in land ownership and types of labor constitutions in various parts of the country. Regional diversity reflects almost every phase of medieval history. During the Middle Ages many forms of peasant tenure developed which existed for a long time beside one another. With few exceptions, the peasant had early fallen into a position of dependence upon a feudal overlord. In the fifteenth century, land in the noncolonial part of the country (west of the Elbe) was held partly by the lord, partly by the peasant. The lord collected traditionally fixed rentals through feudal dues, which were paid in goods or labor, and various fees, e.g. those received in connection with a change in tenant, a transfer of inheritance, or marriage. The dues remained limited because they served only to satisfy the needs of the crown, a lay or ecclesiastical corporation, or the lord, who was a professional soldier rather than a farmer. With the exception of some peasants in the marsh lands stretching along the North Sea, peasants as a rule were bound to the soil. If one wished to withdraw, he had to appoint a successor.

In the middle of the fifteenth century the lords began to encroach upon the common lands (Allmende), i.e. meadows on which the inhabitants of the village had the right to pasture their animals, and forests from which they gathered wood for building and fuel. This process of encroachment was supported by the property conception of Roman law which was introduced into Germany in the course of the fifteenth, sixteenth, and seventeenth centuries. Peasant revolts, which reached a climax in 1525, broke out in areas where no personal serfdom existed but where dues, taxes, and services were squeezed from the peasants and where usurpation of the common pasture, prohibition of fishing in flowing waters, of hunting, and of cutting wood caused resentment. Although the peasantry lost its wars, and the rebels were exterminated, the impact in the west was relieved by colonization in the east, which created a shortage of peasants. Thus their demands could no longer be ignored.

---

[2] A survey of feudal conditions concentrated on a few pages cannot do justice to the vast variety of conditions. The reader who wants to get a full picture may turn to the excellent description given in Max Weber (Bibl. #84); and in J. H. Clapham and Eileen Power (Bibl. #14).

From the sixteenth century on, a great change set in. "In southwest Germany . . . the rights of the lord to the land and to personal fealty, as well as the judiciary right became transformed into a simple right to receive a rental, while relatively few compulsory services and dues in connection with the transfer of inheritance remained as relics. The Rhenish and southwest German peasant thus became in fact his own master, able to sell his holding or transmit it to heirs. . . . Holdings were extremely scattered. Land holdings, judicial authority, and liege-lordship were in different hands and the peasant was able to play one against the other."[3] By the middle of the seventeenth century serfdom had largely disappeared although it was not legally abolished until much later.

In northwest Germany, where landholdings were never minutely subdivided, serfdom was abandoned as unprofitable by the landholders as soon as they saw a possibility of marketing their products after the influx of precious metals during the Crusades. They became interested in an increase in the income from the land. They emancipated their serfs and leased the land to free renters (Meier) whose property became hereditary. Services and other obligations were fixed by law or by the terms of the tenure. The lord could not dispossess the peasant except for legally demonstrable reasons.

The interest of the lords in large estates led to the law of single inheritance. Thus the land was never broken up as in the southwest and the large holding system continued. Serfdom in the northwest had disappeared as early as the fourteenth century; feudal services were displaced by money payments, while rent was paid in kind. In the northwest, west, and south, complete emancipation was the final stage in a gradual development. The lord was not interested in buying out the peasants. The Allmende (common land) remained. Emancipation was essentially restoration of unconditional property and the conversion of duties into fixed money rents. In south Germany and in the Rhineland peasant emancipation was well under way when the French Revolution and the Napoleonic government accelerated the final development. In these territories the process of emancipation was completed in 1830, with little change in the distribution of property.

In eastern Germany the land was colonized from the twelfth to the fourteenth century by peasants and squires. The peasants, originally free neighbors of the nobles, held the land on terms of a quit-rent without rendering labor services, and the native Slavs frequently had rights inferior to those of the conquering Germans. In contrast to the west with its scat-

[3] Weber (Bibl. #84), pp. 75-76.

tered estates, manorial estates of the east coexisted from the beginning with peasant villages. While serfdom disappeared in both the northwest and southwest, the position of the eastern colonist peasants deteriorated from the sixteenth century on. In this area with its poor light soil, severe climate, and long winters, towns were less numerous than in the west. The peasantry could not be used as a source of rent since there was no market near enough for their produce, but only as a source of labor. Deprived of their former occupation of fighting after the introduction of mercenary troops, the eastern nobles turned to farming and began at once to increase their territory by confiscating peasant land. Hunger for land and labor increased in this Protestant part of the country where the clergy no longer absorbed the younger sons of the nobility. The Thirty Years War hastened the process of absorption of peasant land by the lords, resulting in a system of consolidated demesne farming (estate economy, Gutsherrschaft). The fact that the rural population was decimated during the war and cultivated land turned into waste gave the lords in the east the opportunity to absorb peasant holdings into their own estates, including whole villages whose population had been swept away. When not enough waste land was available, expansion could be achieved by "relegation of obstinate peasants." With the increased extent of manorial land and the reduced number of peasants, services multiplied, and in order to secure the peasants to the land, they were made personally dependent or hereditary vassals (Gutsuntertanen). In the upheaval caused by the devastating war, earlier rights and immunities were canceled, dues increased, and menial services, which the formerly free peasants had not been obliged to render, instituted. This process of dispossessing the peasants and of transforming the free man into a vassal was greatly facilitated by the lords' prerogatives, which had been granted by the sovereigns who, in order to keep the restless knights in a peaceful occupation, sacrificed the peasants to them. The territorial rulers ceded certain rights of sovereignty to the holders of these feudal estates. Landholding, personal suzerainty, and judicial authority were identified. The landowner, who was at once sheriff, magistrate, and police chief, exercised totalitarian authority over his peasants and frequently weakened their possessory rights. Thus the peasant in the east became bound to the soil, an appurtenance of the estate. He could not marry or learn a trade without permission and his children were subject to compulsory services. There were no adequate provisions for education. At the end of the eighteenth century the amount of services varied from estate to estate, from three days a week

6

to six. In some parts those who could not prove the existence of a contradictory usage were bound to give unlimited services.[4] As a result they often had to work their own plots at night. Their possessory title was diversified. On the one hand there were good titles such as quit-rent with prevailing fees, and on the other hand hereditary or nonhereditary titles with prevailing services. An increasing number of peasants were reduced to nonhereditary ownership. A large proportion of the peasants had been forced to become cottage holders whose arable holdings consisted of only a small plot of ground. Above these lowest cotters (Häusler, Käthner, or Büdner) came the so-called Kossäth (in Silesia called Gärtner, or gardener) who tilled his own patch of land but who had no regular holding in the organized village fields (Flur). Above him was the peasant, who held land in the fields and harnessed his own beasts to the plough. He served with his plow oxen (spann-fähig), while most of the others did only manual labor (Handdienste).

The peasant of the east, a prey to the arbitrary will of his lord, had become "gloomy, discontented, coarse, slavish . . . a hapless missing link between a beast of burden and a man."[5] Thus a contrast had developed between the large produce-yielding estates of the eastern lords (Gutsherrschaft) and the rent-yielding estates of the landlords in the south and west (manorial economy, Grundherrschaft). Moreover, there was less church property in the prevailingly Protestant east than in the west where the Catholic church remained a landowner. The ecclesiastical domain showed more consideration to the peasant than did the nobleman.

After the middle of the eighteenth century a series of reforms was initiated by the Prussian kings who wished to check the process of eviction in order to protect their source of taxes and recruits.[6] Gradually they succeeded in preventing further confiscation of peasant land, but not in improving the personal status of the vassals on private estates. They helped the peasants to maintain a balance of ownership according to numbers and area and at the same time increased their numbers by means of inland colonization. Peasants on Prussian crown lands, which comprised about one-fifth of the entire area of Prussia, were granted the right to hereditary ownership in 1777, were freed from compulsory services in 1799, and became entitled to

---

[4] Georg F. Knapp (Bibl. #42), Vol. 1, pp. 39-43.

[5] *Ibid.*, p. 77. See also Thaer's description in 1806: "Present conditions let the peasant become constantly poorer, lazier, and more stupid," *Annalen des Ackerbaus*, IV, 55, quoted by Knapp (Bibl. #42), p. 75.

[6] "The fiscal interest of the state speaks in favor of the peasants, long before humanity is allowed to speak." Knapp (Bibl. #43), p. 169.

buy full proprietary rights for moderate sums. Compulsory services of children on crown lands had been prohibited as early as 1763. By a series of acts between 1799 and 1806, the freedom of domain servants was practically accomplished. On the estates of the lords, however, serfdom continued until after Prussia's defeat in the Napoleonic War, when a program of reconstruction was conceived which included the abolition of serfdom. Liberation had to come because it was overdue. In the interest of increased efficiency a change in the agricultural system was clearly necessary, but it could not be achieved with exploited and degenerated peasants. New ideas of enlightenment and of human rights, which penetrated from France, tended in the same direction. The peasant needed a threefold liberation—agricultural, personal, and political.

The Stein-Hardenberg reform, named for the two statesmen whose ideas are embodied in it, emancipated peasants and land in Prussia. It denied the monopolistic privilege of the nobility to possess large estates (Edict of October 9, 1807)[7] and proclaimed the liberty to divide estates and abrogate entails. The personal caste system was abolished.[8] Nobles were allowed to engage in civilian occupations, citizens to engage in the pursuits of peasants, the latter to choose their occupation. As a result of the Edict of 1807, hereditary serfdom was completely abolished by November 11, 1810.[9] This meant the disappearance of binding to the soil, compulsory services of children, the right of the lord to determine the heir of the holding among the children or to agree to marriage and choice of occupation. The regulation of property rights was less simple. Liberal economists who believed in the results of free ownership of land quarreled with conservatives who were afraid of possible disintegration. The first group, adherents of Adam Smith, wished to abolish state interference; the second clung to the tradition of the state supremacy in all citizen relations. The liberals carried the day. The Edict of September 14, 1811,[10] regulated peasants free owners of their land: They

[7] Bibl. #137 Supplement, p. 170. Heretofore noble estates could be held only by nobles and could be acquired by persons of civic origin only by express permission of the sovereign. In the same way peasant land could, as a rule, be held by only peasants.

[8] The strict caste system of nobles, peasants, and burghers restricted the noble to vocations within his caste. Only by special permission could he go into trade, industry, or other bourgeois pursuits. The burgher was to carry on trade and industry, the peasant to till the land.

[9] "From Martinmas 1810 every remaining villeinage in all our dominions shall cease and from that date there shall be none but freemen in our dominions." The emancipation soon followed in other German states. The main feudal right which remained was the lord's patrimonial justice, which was completely abolished only by the local government law of 1891.

[10] Bibl. #137, p. 281.

received their holdings as property, and were no longer required to furnish services or payments. But as a condition to such ownership, they had to surrender to the squire—if their land was regarded as heritable—one-third of all possessions. Those whose property was not heritable, and they were the majority, turned over one-half. The enforcement of this edict considerably restricted the liberation.

Originally it was intended to confer upon the peasant immediately the full ownership of his holding. Such settlement, however, was delayed by the resistance of the landed nobility who claimed that their economic existence was imperiled by the abolition of the forced labor system. They succeeded in getting the postponement of the small holders' emancipation, while the Edict of Frederick the Great,[11] preventing the confiscation of peasants' land, was repealed. A Declaration of May 29, 1816, which was intended as executive order to the Edict of 1811 but which changed it considerably, provided that only peasants owning teams and those of long established ownership who were registered as peasants in the tax rolls, were subject to regulation. This excluded those who rendered only manual labor, those whose land was not in the village fields, and those who had been settled during the period of peasant protection.

The redeemed peasants lost the use of the common pasture and woodland and other rights on the estate, such as assistance in emergencies and in repairing buildings. The lord sold labor and bought land, the peasant sold land and bought the freedom to work his own land. Many peasants who were unable to make a living after the reduction of their property and abolition of rights to the estate sold their entire land and became hired laborers. The lord gained considerably thereby. He consolidated his holdings, was freed from the peasants' pasture and from all obligations to help, and at the same time retained the manual labor. The team service had long proved uneconomical since the distances were too far and the animals were too wretched for productive work. It was not much more expensive for the lord to provide his own implements and teams and use merely the nonregulated peasants' labor.

Great harm was done by the wholesale enclosure of common land,[12]

---

[11] Edict of August 12, 1749 (Novum Corpus Constitutionum Marchicarum, Bibl. #137, Vol. 1, Part iv, p. 182). Another Edict of September 14, 1811 (Edikt zur Beförderung der Landkultur, *ibid.*, p. 300) and the Declaration of May 29, 1816 (*ibid.*, p. 154) removed this protection.

[12] Edict of June 7, 1821 (Gemeinheitsteilungsordnung, Bibl. #137, p. 53) provided for consolidation of farm land, in connection with division of the common pasture

which made it difficult or impossible for the peasant to keep livestock, deprived him of the free supply of turf and wood for fuel, and made many peasants inclined to sell their land to a lord.

The peasants who were liable for manual labor and not subject to regulation continued personally free, but burdened with services and dues. Where their tenures were not hereditary, peasants could be summarily evicted. When on March 2, 1850,[13] the liberation of the small holders was effected by declaring all dues and services commutable, it was too late. Most of their holdings had already been appropriated by the estate owners whose lack of capital only had prevented the complete disappearance of small holders. A class of landless agricultural laborers had been created,[14] and landholdings had become concentrated in fewer hands between 1818 and 1850. Even then many of the finally regulated landholders disappeared because they were unable to pay the compensation for their regulations which was imposed on them in the form of rent.

According to Gustav Schmoller only 45,493 farmers became independent from 1811 to 1848 in the four provinces of East and West Prussia, Brandenburg, Pomerania (without Stralsund), and Silesia.[15] About 100,000 small holdings with more than a half million ha. disappeared; 420,000 ha. were yielded as compensation; and 230,000 were bought by large estate owners. Thus more than a million ha.—one-third of the agricultural area—were transferred from peasants to large estate owners.[16]

Even then the process of encouraging large estates did not stop. In order to extend the political influence of the feudal lords who boasted that they were responsible for the greatness of the Prussian state and were its most solid foundation, the founding of entails was encouraged by the government.[17] Later, industrialists who were ambitious to become feudal lords

---

and Allmende. The peasant thus was forced into an individualistic economy. Under the same date a Prussian edict regulated the conditions of peasants with better ownership rights.

[13] Bibl. #137, p. 77. Rent banks (Rentenbanken) were set up to which the peasants paid their rent. These banks in turn gave to the estate owner a bond for the value of the capital charges. In this way the peasants could pay off their indebtedness. Law of March 2, 1850 (Bibl. #137, p. 112).

[14] The encyclopedia of Johann Georg Krünitz does not mention the word Landarbeiter (farm laborer) but speaks of Bauer, Fröner, Gesinde, Häusler (Bibl. #47, 1793).

[15] Gustav Schmoller, Bibl. #74, 1919, p. 623.

[16] Hans Jürgen Seraphim, "Neuschaffung von Bauerntum," Bibl. #160, 1937-1938, Vol. 98, p. 626.

[17] Act of June 5, 1852 (Bibl. #137, p. 319). The entailed area increased in Prussia from 1,249,300 ha. in 1850 to 2,299,800 ha. at the end of 1907. Only 44,900 of the latter

created new entails. Thus the plan of the Stein-Hardenberg Reform to displace holders of large estates by a larger number of independent peasants, was defeated. Large estates grew both in number and in size. Feudalism was legally abolished, but no social revolution achieved. The position of the aristocracy was strengthened. Later, mechanization and the introduction of cheap seasonal labor helped the big estate to retain its dominant position. The historical development explains the rural social structure of the East Elbian territory with its sharp differentiation of large estate owners and wage earners, and thus the existence of an agricultural labor problem in Germany.

Types of Labor Constitutions

I. REGIONAL DIFFERENTIATION

As the result of German agrarian history, labor conditions differed regionally, although the various labor types were not completely segregated into very definite areas. There was no uniform labor problem in Germany. The landowning worker in the west and south, the Heuerling in the northeast, the East Elbian Instmann and the Bavarian farm hand had very little in common. The Silesian deputant was far below the standard of the East Prussian deputant, the Instmann of East Holstein higher than the East Prussian, and the Heuerling higher and more independent than both. The parts chiefly to be differentiated were East Elbia (East Prussia, Pomerania, Brandenburg, Mecklenburg, Silesia), northwest (Oldenburg, Hanover, Westphalia), the west (especially the Rhineland), central Germany (especially Saxony), and the south.

Sandy soil, inhospitable climate, sparse population, and the predominance of large estates characterized the structure of the east. Estates of 100 ha. and more owned 53.4 per cent of the farmland in Mecklenburg in 1933, 44.3 per cent of the farmland in Pomerania, 33.4 per cent in East Prussia, 31.7 per cent in Brandenburg, 27.7 per cent in Silesia.[18]

---

were not owned by the nobility (F. Kühnert, "Die Fideikommisse in Preussen im Jahre 1907 und die Wanderungen in den Kreisen mit besonders ausgedehnten Fideikommissbesitze im Zeitraume 1875 bis 1905" [Bibl. #162], 1909, pp. 303, 327, 330).

[18] Bibl. #260, 1945, p. 40. Until 1937 the census gave no true picture of the concentration of ownership since it gave only the size of farms by entity but not by ownership. There was no indication of multiple ownership. According to the 1937 census 19,000 owners of estates of 100 ha. and over controlled 29,000 estates or 20 per cent of the area owned by individuals in Germany (*Statistik des Deutschen Reichs*, 1941, Vol. 549, pp. 4-5). Members of the ruling princely houses owned large estates scattered over the Reich. Prussia and some of the other states owned large demesne lands. While these estates frequently were leased, the eastern squires used to manage their estates themselves.

In northwest Germany with its favorable conditions for grassland as a basis for livestock farming, the peasant holding was maintained, but since a larger size was necessary to ensure economic independence, the larger peasant holding became the predominant type, protected in its size by undivided inheritance. While most of the peasant holdings in Germany were located in villages, a region in which isolated farmsteads (Einzelhöfe) prevailed, extended from the Weser west to Westphalia and the lower Rhine. Each family lived on its own holding separate from its neighbors. Another part of northern Germany, Lower Saxony (Niedersachsen) between the Weser and the Elbe, had a sound mixture of medium-sized and small peasant holdings. In these parts peasants were classified as full peasants, half-peasants, quarter-peasants, and cotters. The larger holdings could easily secure as workers the small owners from nearby villages.

Central Germany, the main seat of sugar-beet culture, had in its northern part large estates and large peasant farms, and in Thuringia many dwarf holdings.

In South Germany holdings of 5 to 20 ha. prevailed, the proportion of small and smallest holdings being larger in Württemberg and Baden than in Bavaria. Farming was based predominantly upon family labor. Many small farms were divided into tiny, widely scattered strips—a division which was enormously wasteful of land, time, and energy, and which consequently handicapped the best utilization of farm machinery and draft power.

Western Germany was divided into two distinct parts: an area of small peasant farms in the industrial districts (Upper Rhine to Thuringia), with prevailing holdings below 10 ha., many owners of which combined agricultural with industrial work, and a larger and middle farm area with holdings from 10 to 100 ha.

The fact that big farms were scarce in the southern and western parts was to a certain extent a consequence of natural and economic conditions, favorable climate, fertility of river valleys, and the mountainous character of the area. The smallest holdings were to be found in the western mountain regions (Eifel, Taunus, Westerwald, Sauerland) and those in the center (Thuringia and Eichsfeld). These mountain peasants had special difficulties to overcome—terrain, distance from the market, and lack of transportation. They were unfamiliar with marketing conditions and, due to irregular contact with the market, could command only low prices. In these mountain regions, far away from industrial centers, the size of farms was reduced to uneconomical units and the farm population came to depend on home industries. In the plains, on the other hand, with their good climate and soil, crowded with smaller and larger towns, the good markets for dairy products, fruit, and garden products in the vicinity favored peasant farming. Such conditions increased the number of the smallest holdings in the industrial areas and around the large cities in the Rhineland and in Southwest Germany.

Other factors which explain the diversity of land tenure were the methods of descent, inheritance, or divisibility of the land among several heirs. In some parts (Schleswig-Holstein, Mecklenburg, Baden, Lippe, and other regions) the custom, dating back to earliest times of the manorial system, prevailed in which only one son or daughter, the principal heir (der Anerbe), took over the farm and settled his brothers and sisters according to his capacity to do so. The extent to which closed inheritance prevailed in the Reich was estimated at four-fifths of all farm land.[19] Subdivision as the result of inheritance—a custom of the central and upper Rhine provinces where vine-growing made small holdings economically sound, and of Swabia (except the Alps) and Thuringia—spread by the Code Napoleon in the western territories which had been brought under French control and increased in the era of liberalism after the peasants' emancipation.[20] Due to the freedom with which land could be transferred and subdivided, the units of cultivation in some parts of the country shrank to such small proportions that they could no longer support the owner and his family. Consequently, members of the family had to find supplemental work. The labor supply thus available acted as a magnet to industry while conversely the possibility of obtaining earnings in industry proved a further incentive to the subdivision of land. In Württemberg, where the tradition of single inheritance was not widely maintained, the possible disadvantage of free division had been largely compensated by the countrywide spread of industry. This combination of farming and industry strengthened the resistance of farms to the economic depression after the First World War.

[19] Max Sering, quoted by Karl Grünberg (Bibl. #31), 1922, p. 156. Closed inheritance did not always prevent a reduction in the size of farms. See Karl Rogge, "Die Gestaltung der geschlossenen Vererbung in Westdeutschland," in Bibl. #149c, 1930, pp. 301ff.

[20] Only in some parts of the country (Braunschweig, Baden) was closed inheritance maintained by statute. The farmer himself decided whether or not his farm should become an entail even where it was provided for by statute. The introductory law to the Civil Code denied the States restriction of free decision of the testator. In some parts (Hanover, Brandenburg, Silesia, Württemberg, and others) the peasant could accept undivided inheritance by registering his farm in a farm register (Höferolle).

Division of inherited farms did not always result in disintegration. It frequently stimulated increased intensity and efficiency. Many heirs to small holdings succeeded in enlarging them by shrewd marriages or by additional leases and purchases.[21] Other heirs kept the farm undivided or paid off the co-heirs with cash or mortgage. On the basis of an inquiry, von Dietze drew the conclusion that there was a tendency in regions of free inheritance to transfer the holding intact, even if great sacrifices were involved.[22]

2. TYPES OF LABOR[23]

Any discussion of farm labor in Germany should start with the peasant,[24] the hardest working laborer. However, no generalizations can be made. There was a great range in status among peasants due to traditions, size of property, and fertility of the soil. At the one end of the scale were the proud, dignified peasants of the Schleswig-Holstein alluvial land (Marsch) who had succeeded in remaining relatively free in the period of feudalism and whose fertile soil made them prosperous. At the other, were the proletarian peasants of the sandy Geest in the same province, who in the winter might become hired men or peddlers, and the Hessian subsistence farmer—the Thuringian peasant who supplemented independent farming by home work and peddling. The dwarf holders should also be included in farm labor since many of them depended upon wages to eke out a living, and many of the migratory workers were drawn from this class.

[21] A peculiar mechanism has been described by Seiff. If the inherited holding is equally divided among the children "the son who gets the building remains the farmer. However, because the buildings are too big for the inherited farm after its division, he looks around for enlargement. Besides a clever marriage policy this is effected in the main by additional leases and purchases. A second son goes into the city to work as a laborer, craftsman, or small official until he has saved enough money for taking up farming again on his own inherited land, which he meanwhile has let to a tenant. The daughter enlarges the husband's farm with her inherited land. In this manner every division of inherited land brings many new small owners and tenants." Rudolf Seiff (Bibl. #105a), 1926, Vol. I, p. 17.

[22] C. von Dietze (Bibl. #149d), 1931, pp. 144-145.

[23] Total number of persons gainfully employed in agriculture, forestry, fishing, and horticulture, exclusive of the Saar territory:

	1925	1933	1939
Independent	2,193,700	2,179,800	1,962,300
Helping members of the family	4,790,500	4,516,200	4,764,700
Salaried employees	171,700	116,100	93,400
Workmen	2,607,300	2,530,600	2,109,000
Total	9,763,207	9,342,700	8,929,400

Source for 1925 data: Bibl. #153c, 1936, p. 19; for 1939 data: Bibl. #153e, 1940, no. 24, p. 538.

[24] This study, therefore, will consider not only hired labor, but the fate of the peasant and his family also.

The peasant farm in Germany was not a business enterprise, and farming not a profession, but a way of life. To the peasant (and to many big land-owners as well) the ancestral farm represented more than a means of earning money. He was not a man who engaged temporarily in agriculture and was willing to exchange his profession for an easier and more profitable one or to give up his land for commercial reasons. The owner felt himself closely bound to the soil by a tie amounting almost to devotion, clung to it in spite of privations, and maintained it for his family even under the unfavorable conditions. Thousands of farms were owned for centuries by the family occupying them. Sales took place in many cases only under extreme pressure. On the small peasant farm the chief laborers were members of the family.[25] In Baden four-fifths of the farm laborers belonged to owners' families. Children continued working after leaving school (for ten to fifteen years) in return for their keep and pocket money. On the large estates where the work was done by landless laborers, under the supervision of the owner, wages constituted the most important item of expenditure, whereas the main portion of the income from the family farm represented the family's wage. The peasant and his family worked harder than the farm worker and found compensation in their independence, their social status, and their attachment to the soil. Münzinger[26] found in one district (where in 1925-1927, 98.1 per cent of the farmers were peasants with holdings up to 20 ha.), that the farmer earned less than the paid laborer although he and his wife worked longer hours.

The more than two million hired workers could be grouped in several main types in 1925.[27]

Workmen without land	830,287
Workmen with own or leased land	101,683
Workmen with deputate	218,477
Farm servants	1,115,303
Milkers	65,971
Vine growers	7,855
Craftsmen, and so forth	50,754

Most numerous among them were the farm servants (Gesinde), who lived

[25] In 1925, 60.8 per cent of all farms were family farms on which only members of the family were employed, while on 22 per cent the owner worked without any help whatever. Only 17.2 per cent of farms hired workers (Bibl. #153b,3, 1929, p. 9). The percentage of hired workers grew with the size of the farm (Bibl. #104b, 1929, Part II, p. 4).

[26] Adolf Münzinger, Bibl. #59, Vol. II, pp. 873ff.

[27] Bibl. #153e, 1927, Vol. VII, No. 22, p. 926.

on the farm and worked for board and lodging plus a cash wage. They were found all over the country. Most of them were employed on family farms (except the smallest) located in western and southern Germany where the seasonal peaks of work are less sharp. Those farms were generally unable to engage the more expensive older married worker if permanent help was needed. Living conditions of small holders and wage-paid laborers were identical in those parts of the country in which small holdings prevailed. The servants lived with the family, worked with them in the stables and in the field, and ate at the same table. Peasant and servant consorted in the same room but ate at different tables in the village inn, the center of rural life. Servants came largely from the peasant class and returned to it through heritage, marriage, or settlement. Thus, no class feeling or social problem developed. Farm servants usually concluded contracts for one year, received board, a small cash wage and contractual gifts, mostly clothing, on certain holidays. Most of them were young and unmarried. Around the age of thirty, the servant had to give up agricultural work or renounce marriage unless he could either marry the heiress of a farm, or pool his savings with that of his spouse and buy a small holding. Even with such a holding, he had to supplement his income by accepting seasonal work on other farms, in brickyards, or on railroads.

In areas of single inheritance, the old patriarchal relationship disappeared, servants ate in the servants' room, and a class feeling developed which separated peasant and laborer. As a consequence the number of farm servants drawn from peasant families tended to decline in these areas. Servants were also employed on the large estates of the east.

The second largest category of farm labor was composed of wage hands, either with or without property. They were usually divided into two groups: steady workers (mostly deputatists, who lived on the estate, were bound by yearly contracts, and received cash wages and perquisites), and independent (Freiarbeiter) or seasonal workers many of whom lived in villages near the estate and went out to work during the season. A third group, migratory workers, moved from one part of the country to the other during the season.

Besides their labor contract on large farms during the year or the season, agricultural workers in all parts of the country (with the exception of eastern Germany) frequently owned the cottages in which they lived or some land to fall back on. Some, owners of small holdings which did not produce enough to give them a living, went out to work, leaving the cultivation of their land to their wives and children. Their social standing varied according to the section of the country. In small peasant districts, where members of all groups performed wage work for some time, they belonged to the peasant and small craftsman classes. There was no social gap between those who employed and those who provided labor. If surrounded by large farms, however, they were considered an inferior group.

In sections of northwest Germany (West Hanover, Wesphalia), the areas of the isolated farmstead, the Heuerling system prevailed. Heuerlings were laborers with small holdings who leased land, usually 1 to 5 ha., and paid rent partly in the form of labor (in general from twenty to one hundred days a year); frequently they owned some poultry, pigs, or a cow. The Heuerling brought his wife to help for twenty to twenty-five days a year. Due to mechanization and migration to industry the number of Heuerlings had decreased before the First World War, but migration had stopped after the war. The Enquête Commission found in 1929 that the Heuerling group (about 30,000)[28] lived at a low economic level. But since they cultivated their piece of land, practically hereditarily, and earned some cash by breeding pigs and by home work, whenever it was available, they were satisfied and considered themselves small peasants rather than laborers.

3. THE LANDLESS WORKER IN THE EAST

The large estate in the east had to rely, in addition to servants, on a class of landless farm hands created during the long-drawn-out adjustment of relations between freed peasants and their lords. In the first period following the liberation, laborers were comparable to the nonhereditary peasantry of the period before. They were married people called Instfolk, living in their own homes (in barracks in Silesia) or in employers' houses. They had annual family contracts and up to the middle of the nineteenth century received prevailingly wages in kind, such as a dwelling, a small piece of land, a share of the grinding or of the threshing, and a very small amount of money. Their income was fixed traditionally according to family needs. They could sell their surplus grain and their hogs. Thus both employer and worker had a community of interest. Both wanted high yield and high prices. The Instrelation still belonged to a barter economy. The master's lack of commercial acquisitiveness and the worker's apathy compensated each other and were the psychological basis for the traditional form of undertaking as well as the traditional position of political dominance of the manorial aristocracy.[29] This semifeudal relationship gradually disinte-

[28] Heuschert. *Das Heuerlingsverhältnis* (Bibl. #104b), 1929, p. 531.
[29] Weber (Bibl. #85), 1924, p. 474.

grated with the increased seasonal character of the work, brought about by the introduction of the threshing machine and of intensive cultures, such as that of sugar beets, and the concomitant greater expenditure of capital and rising value of the soil. The Instrelation meant greater independence and, at first, less work and equal income, but it also meant proletarization during the latter part of the nineteenth century when instead of shares of the products, laborers' wages were paid in money and definitely fixed annual wages in kind. They became deputatists. Wives and children of the deputatists and additional labor from the villages, i.e. independent workers, were employed during the harvest.

During the nineteenth century agricultural workers in the east were legally free and yet dependent. Since the early period after the emancipation, the lords had been anxious to retain control over their people. Until wages in money and in kind began partly to replace their share in the crops, the relationship was one of subjection, not of contract. As the disintegration of this "patriarchal" relationship which transformed the Instmann into a deputatist progressed, the rural laborer became more and more independent, although less well supported. The community of interest ceased, the employer was interested in low production costs which meant low wages, the worker in high wages, although neither group developed the acquisitiveness of those in industry. The custom of providing the workers with a house owned by the landowner, one-year contracts which were extremely difficult for the workers to break, the poor law, and local manorial government had made them feel personally dependent. The century-old tradition of serfdom gave the landholding class an initial claim to regard their workers as servants. The continuing institution of local manorial government (Gutsbezirke) made the owner, in effect, the government administrator in his district and thereby gave him authority over the inhabitants. Although he lost the right of patrimonial justice in 1848, he constituted the police power until 1872 and applied the poor law. He controlled the worker's daily life through the school, the church, and domination of the local and, frequently, county sphere. The squires who as a result of the grossly unequal three-class franchise system, dominated the House of Deputies of the Prussian Diet and had a stronghold in the Upper House, defeated all attempts to abolish the remnants of local government.[30]

[30] In the Upper House of the Prussian Diet large estate owners provided a bloc of life members which represented about 30 per cent of all members. Of 251 deputies in seven Eastern provinces in the House of Deputies in 1913, 58 were squires (65 of 248

Poor laws bound the worker to his place of settlement. Since residence of two years (later one) established the right to receive poor relief in case of need,[31] the estate owner was interested in keeping bad risks out and in hiring only young workers. He looked upon any newcomer as a potential recipient of poor relief and frequently refused to have laborers bring their old parents to the estate. Even after marriage restrictions were abolished, the worker who intended to marry depended upon getting a dwelling in the country and failing this, he might be obliged to move into town.[32]

The tone of the contracts was oppressive. Contracts included regulations concerning family life, and prohibited subscription to Socialist papers. Workers were expected to show extreme respect to the owner and his family. They had a secure but paltry living. Hours were long, wages not high enough to maintain a family in decent fashion. Though wages increased slowly during the period of the Empire, they lagged considerably behind wages in industry because of the importation of cheap labor from abroad. Usually the contracting worker had to put additional workers, his children or other young workers, at the disposal of his employers during the season. These subcontracted workers, so-called Hofgänger,[33] lived with the laborer whose wages were calculated to cover the board of the Hofgänger, who generally received a separate cash wage. Housing was poor, education unsatisfactory, and work very hard. Everything that makes life worth living was withheld from the farm laborer. Von der Goltz[34] and Knapp,[35] describe farm laborers of the 1870's and 1880's as unskilled, depraved, and apathetic, without social contact, separated by a wide breach from the estate owner, subservient actually and psychologically. Conditions were

in 1903). See Lysbeth Walker Muncy, Bibl. #58, 1944, pp. 217-218. Most of the large estate owners were conservative and the conservative party controlled the political situation in Prussia.

In the Reichstag, too, the strength of the squires' influence was out of all proportion to their number. This was due to the fact that the representative districts mapped out in 1871 were not changed in spite of the tremendous growth of the population in the cities. The country population, therefore, obtained proportionately more seats in the Reichstag than popular votes polled, the cities less. In 1907 the Social Democratic Party, representing prevailingly the industrial working class, won 43 seats with 3.25 million votes, the two conservative parties, 85 seats with 1.56 million votes (Fritz Specht and Paul Schwabe, Bibl. #81, 1908, p. 96).

[31] Laws of 1871 and 1908, Bibl. #140, 1908, p. 381.

[32] Theodor, Freiherr von der Goltz, Bibl. #28, 1874, pp. 50ff.

[33] The Hofgänger has no direct parallel in the agricultural system of the twentieth century. The term "subcontractor" does not quite convey the old meaning.

[34] Op.cit., Bibl. #28, p. 102.

[35] Bibl. #42, 1925, pp. 308-10.

similarly pictured in the literature of the last period of Imperial Germany. "The men must obey, work hard, learn as little as possible, be pious, and vote conservative," is a clergyman's description in a novel in which a member of the country nobility excellently portrayed his own class.[36]

Proletarian features of the eastern laborer were his landlessness and his isolation. Trains carrying urbanites to the summer resorts of the eastern coast ran right through the country, but the estates in the east were visited only by guests of the owner who belonged to the same caste. Population is rather dense everywhere in Germany as compared with rural areas of the United States, yet these workers lived as remote as if in a far-away colony. Their remoteness made it difficult to control conditions, to arouse public interest in their problems, and to enforce protective legislation. The problem of these workers was "the rural labor problem in Germany." Although the same categories could be used to characterize the employment relation in various parts of the country, the situation of the eastern laborer was different. In other parts of Germany laborers, whether they lived in villages, on middle or smaller farms, or large estates, mingled with people of similar social standards. They belonged socially with the peasants. They could visit the town in the neighborhood; they were in contact with life.

The Inferior Legal Status of the Farm Worker

During the period of the Empire, changes which could have made working conditions and life more attractive for laborers were barred not only by prejudice, but by the preservation of obsolete laws.

In the first half of the nineteenth century, agricultural workers shared with industrial workers the restriction against combination. A Prussian law of April 24, 1854,[37] corresponding to the Prussian Industrial Code, made it a punishable offense to conspire to stop or obstruct work, or to incite others so to conspire. This meant virtual prohibition of strikes. While similar restrictions of industrial workers' associations were abolished by the Industrial Code in 1869, and all attempts to hamper their freedom of coalition by legislation were refuted, the law of 1854 remained in force for agriculture

---

[36] Wilhelm von Polenz, Bibl. #62, 1903, I, p. 110. The author contrasts the domineering, authoritarian Junker who wants to keep peasants and workers in servility with the enlightened and refined noblemen who, although conscious of the unexampled "blindness and indifference" of the Junkers, still believes in their future. "We are too deeply rooted in the soil which we have cultivated for centuries to be so easily torn up and thrown aside." *Ibid.*, II, p. 259.

[37] Bibl. #137, 1854, p. 124. It was valid for the Prussian area of 1854, but not in the later acquired provinces of Schleswig-Holstein, Hanover, Hessen-Nassau.

until the revolution of 1918. There was similar legislation in the other states.

A number of special state ordinances regulated the status of work of farm servants at a level with other domestic servants, many of them including all agricultural workers. In some parts of the country they had been set up for the express purpose of allowing a continuation of many of the manorial customs which the liberation had intended to abolish. They expressed a paternalistic master-servant relationship. For breach of contract, servants on their part were liable to arrest, and, under certain conditions, even to physical punishment, imprisonment, or return by the police; whereas employers only had to pay reparations to the servant. Forty-four such ordinances were in force in Germany in 1918, twelve of which dated from the eighteenth century, thirteen from the period 1803 to 1848. The Civil Code of 1900, which included agricultural workers in its protective regulations, left the farm servant ordinances in force.

Organization of agricultural workers was hampered by a Prussian decree of March 11, 1850.[38] According to it all meetings had to be announced in advance to the police, who could send officers to the meetings and dissolve them in case the discussion incited to punishable activities. Women, students, or apprentices could not be organized. Local organizations were not allowed to affiliate with central councils. This decree was replaced in 1908 by the Reich Association Act.[39] Oppressive regulations existed in the other territories too. Mecklenburg still introduced restrictions in 1892.

The Federal Act of 1908 left untouched all restrictions concerning stoppages of work and their preparation, but marked a turning point for agricultural labor insofar as it provided freedom of coalition. But even this freedom had to endure the interference of administration authorities, who were always eager to harass trade union activities. The courts to which appeal against the administration was possible were guided by their conservative prejudice that activities in favor of better working conditions were an encroachment on God-willed dependence. Laborers who joined the first organizations, formed in 1909 and 1912 respectively, were subjected to petty tyrannies.

Though much of the oppressive legislation existed principally on paper and had fallen into desuetude,[40] it was a constant source of irritation and kept alive among the more enlightened agricultural workers the feeling

[38] *Ibid.*, 1850, p. 277. Bibl. #148, 1917, III, Vol. 68, pp. 8ff.
[39] Reichsvereinsgesetz, April 19, 1908 (Bibl. #140, p. 151).
[40] Only two suits were filed in the first twelve years of the Prussian law of 1854. (Bibl. #148, *op.cit.*, pp. 17, 28).

that they were second-class citizens. Nearly all the social legislation of the nineteenth century concerned the industrial classes only, except workmen's compensation and invalidity and old age insurance which established full equality for the rural workers.

To be sure, the estate owners did not lack paternalistic enlightenment. There were landlords who were deeply concerned over the welfare of their laborers, and loyalty and attachment were traditional on such estates. Moreover the worker's position was somewhat modified by wages in kind which he received and by many precapitalistic elements which still continued in his traditional relationship to the employer. In the nineteenth century, however, a longing for freedom, for independence, was sweeping the laboring masses and just those agricultural workers who were most vital resented patriarchalism and the almost feudal master-servant relationship.[41] They wanted higher social positions, freedom in personal life, and respect for their personalities, and they were ready to sacrifice even better food for full liberation. The less lethargic elements, attracted by the prospect of independence and social improvement, emigrated to America.[42]

Rural Exodus and Government Countermeasures

As long as agriculture was prosperous and farm hands were kept on the land by patriarchal traditions as well as by the lack of other occupational opportunities, the labor system of the east seemed to work. Germany's economic life during the eighteenth and in the beginning of the nineteenth century was centered chiefly around agriculture. The beginning industrialization in the thirties resulted in an increased demand for agricultural products, in rising prices, and in a prosperity which was due chiefly to tremendous technical improvements. Growing efficiency, largely due to the research of Liebig and Thaer, reduced the demand for farm labor. By the seventies, artificially enriched soils had to compete with virgin soil overseas, world market competition lowered prices, and industrial demands on all available

[41] Wilhelm von Polenz lets a worker, who lived in miserable conditions after migrating to Berlin, answer the former master who wants to take him back: "you and your sort are amazed that we run away. You gentlemen are responsible for it. We shall vote as the lord (gnädige Herr) wants; we shall read what the lord permits; we shall keep our mouth shut about the suppression of the people; we shall stoop under the regiment of the Mister administrator—no, times are too progressive for it; we are independent men. . . . One has too much honor to allow one's self to be treated like cattle." (Bibl. #62, 1903, Vol. 2, p. 22).

[42] From 1871 to 1900, 2.7 million Germans, prevailingly "landfolk," emigrated to the United States. See Herbert Morgan, "Bestand und Aufbau des deutschen Landvolks," in Konrad Meyer (Bibl. #218, 1942, p. 85).

supplies of labor brought many farmers into a precarious economic situation. Consequently, from the seventies on, urbanization, with higher money wages, freedom, and the attractions of city life, appealed increasingly to rural labor. The law of November 1, 1867,[43] established full freedom of migration. A rural exodus first seized those regions of smallest holdings where the surplus population found no industrial work and had no prospect of acquiring small holdings. It quickly spread to those parts of the country where large estates prevailed. The peasant and the heirs of peasant holdings held to their land even in periods of emergency while the younger children and the laborers felt free to migrate. Peasants' children and farm workers were the most mobile groups of the rural population.[44]

The exodus was felt much more in the thinly populated areas of the east than in the densely populated peasant districts. The sons of laborers did not like to follow their fathers' calling but sought their living in towns, although their situation there was no improvement at first. Industry picked young and strong workers and left the less desirable for the farm supply. Migration was a completely new phenomenon since the farm population had always been relatively fixed, conservative, rooted in the soil, with no other way of life that had meaning for them.

But the owners needed labor, cheap labor, because the fall in market prices had reduced profitability of the farms. As Germans were not available, estate owners began in the sixties to import foreign workers for a season, a process which became important after the eighties. Thus the squires who boasted that they were the bulwark against the Slavs became the very instrument of their infiltration. The main sources of manpower were Poles, who were unpretentious, docile, satisfied with poor housing barracks and low wages. They had no claim to poor relief and could be deported for the slightest insubordination. As legislation had, after 1892, limited their stay in Germany each season from April to December, they were out of the

---

[43] Bibl. #140, p. 55.

[44] M. Schönberg has shown that the shortage of manpower in East Prussia was greatest on holdings of 10 to 28 ha. The holdings of 25 ha. had a shortage of 30 per cent; holdings of 100 to 150 ha., 16 per cent; holdings of 1,000 ha., 12 per cent (Konrad Meyer, op.cit., p. 319). The widely accepted view that the flight from the land occurred mainly on large estates in the east has been successfully challenged by Peter Quante who proves statistically that the migration movement was the same in the west and east and was mainly due to the surplus of births in rural areas and to the natural process of shrinking of the agricultural segment of the population in an industrial society, and that estates over 100 ha. occupied a larger number of persons than peasant holdings (Hans Raupach and Peter Quante, Bibl. #67, passim).

way when not needed. The living conditions they accepted could not be offered to German workers. Kärger reported that on one estate men demanded 1 M. and girls 0.80 M. a day. Russians were imported who got 0.30-0.40 M.[45]

In 1886 Bismarck prohibited the immigration of Polish laborers for national political reasons, but his fall removed the barrier. After 1890 they were able to come in unrestrictedly, obliged merely to legitimization with the police and to return to their home country in winter. In 1914 one-seventh of all workers employed in agriculture were aliens (433,000); during the summer months the proportion of foreign workers on certain farms was as high as 50 per cent.[46] They were employed in the central and eastern parts of the country. A vicious circle had arisen: the employment of foreigners prevented improvement of working conditions and methods. The migration of the best workers from the rural districts was the answer.

Rural exodus aroused deep concern. The growing differential of population density in the Polish and German border districts was considered a national danger. Natural increase was greater in the Polish than in the German population. The conservative-minded groups of the population looked upon urbanization as a doubtful benefit. They argued that the country had a higher birth rate and a better standard of health than the city, that the rural sections provided a higher percentage of men fit to serve in the army, that agriculture and handicraft allowed a more all-round development of the human person than factory work. Radicalism flourished among the city proletariat, and a dense rural population seemed to be the best defense against outer and inner enemies. For decades the Prussian Upper House debated the flight from the land and measures for preventing it.

Improvement of farm workers' conditions in order to hold them on the land would have meant hardship for the large estate owners, the most

[45] Karl Kärger, "Die Sachsengängerei," Bibl. #130, 1890, Vol. 19, p. 397.

[46] Petersen in Bibl. #108, February 13, 1932, and Bibl. #139, 1914, Vol. 1, p. 580. The official figure did not indicate the total amount since the obligation to register did not hold good in all states and in the others many workers succeeded in evading registration. Recruiting and placing of foreign workers from 1905 on was supposed to be centralized in an institution set up by the Chamber of Agriculture, the German Workers' Central (at first Deutsche Feldarbeiterzentrale, then Deutsche Arbeiterzentrale). A few Chambers of Agriculture, however, continued to work in the same field. In fact, barely 20 per cent of the recruiting and placing of foreign workers was carried out by the Workers' Central. It was under employers' influence and attracted as many foreign workers as possible (Gerhard Gross, "Ausländische Arbeiter in der deutschen Landwirtschaft und die Frage ihrer Ersetzbarkeit," Bibl. #130, 1923-1924, Vol. 59, p. 6).

influential political group. The powerful heavy industries were interested in the cheap labor supply from the country. The Imperial government met the problem of rural exodus with various reforms such as protective tariffs and colonization, aimed simultaneously at the protection of agriculture and of the large estates, which were considered the backbone of national power, the surest foundation of throne and altar. The eastern nobility, who as grain exporters had been champions of free trade, reversed their stand when Germany's transition from a food-exporting to a food-importing country (in 1874) caused a fall in agricultural prices and an increase in indebtedness. Protective tariffs on agricultural products were supposed to maintain the profitability of agriculture, prevent the depopulation of the country, and increase the ability of agriculture to feed the German population, so urgently demanded by military leaders.

After 1879, the country embarked on a universal protective policy with at first moderate, then higher and higher duties, increasing land values, and raising the cost of living for the nonagricultural population. The system operated largely to the benefit of large estate owners who produced rye, wheat, potatoes, or sugar. When Chancellor Caprivi tried to change this policy in favor of industry and the urban masses by reduction of agricultural duties in commercial treaties, a Farmers' League (Bund der Landwirte) was founded in 1893. This powerful organization of economic and political agrarian interests under the leadership of the eastern nobility captured agricultural owners in all parts of the country. In their feeling of insecurity and distress the peasants followed the lords who had been traditionally their leaders and many of whom were excellent farmers. The League proclaimed: "Only as we follow class politics ruthlessly and undisguisedly can we possibly save ourselves."[47] "We must cease to complain, we must shout," said one of the founders.[48] Flight from the land was attributed to too much educa-

[47] H. Dietzel, "The German Tariff Controversy," *The Quarterly Journal of Economics*, May 1903, Vol. 17, p. 370. "Its agitation, in form and scope unprecedented in Germany, imbued public opinion with an amount of agrarian spirit which would have earlier been thought impossible." *Ibid.*, p. 371. The program of the League demanded, among other things, adequate tariff protections, tax leniency for agriculture, formation of agricultural chambers, regulation of residence requirements for local relief, rules for workers' breach of contract, revision of the laws protecting labor (F. Hohlfeld, Bibl. #38, 1934, Vol. 1, pp. 276-277). In Bavaria a peasants' association was separately organized. The Deutscher Bauernbund (The German Peasant League, at first League of Settlers) organized as opposition, under liberal democratic leadership, was not unsuccessful but never gained the importance of the Farmers' League.

[48] Ruprecht-Rausern, a Silesian tenant farmer, in an article published on December 21, 1892, quoted by Otto von Kiesenwetter, Bibl. #41, 1918, pp. 21, 335.

tion. The League defended the threatened privileges and influenced the course of domestic politics. It worked as a militant political pressure and propaganda group and tried to get its members elected to the parliaments. It soon dominated and invigorated the Conservative party, which protected agrarian interests, and controlled the political situation in Prussia. Caprivi was overthrown. Protectionism increased again as soon as the commercial treaties elapsed.

Other means to help agriculture were the development of a well planned system of credit and other cooperatives, based partly on self help, partly on government assistance. Credit associations, started by Raiffeisen in the sixties, provided loans at low interest rates. Cooperatives, with the help of wholesale societies, supplied seed, tools, and other production and household necessities at low prices. Cooperatives provided electricity, marketing, insurance. Machines were used cooperatively. Through such organized self-help the small peasant could overcome many of the handicaps he would have suffered as an individual producer.

Another government measure, land settlement,[49] was applied to the most vulnerable part of the country,[50] in which a sparse population faced growing Polish masses across the border. The Royal Prussian Colonization Commission was equipped with funds to purchase large estates in the two provinces with large Polish population and divide them into small farms for sale or lease to German peasants and laborers. In the early nineties the settlement activities were extended by law to the whole of Prussia. The settlement policy tried simultaneously to counteract the growing industrialization and to maintain an abundant peasant stock as a source of national vitality by increasing peasant holdings, abolishing the labor shortage, and establishing a bulwark of German peasants against the Poles. However, in Prussia not more than 39,900 settlements for workers and craftsmen were established by the end of 1912.[51] A Prussian high official estimated that up to the end of 1911 only 2,028 workers had been settled.[52]

The Germanization policy of the government was thwarted by Polish societies counteracting the policy and by German estate owners who pro-

---

[49] The settlement policy was successful in Mecklenburg where half the land belonged to the Grand Duke and the other half to the squires. A new peasant class was created by leasing hereditary farms of the grand ducal land to peasants.

[50] Gesetz betreffend die Förderung deutscher Ansiedlungen in den Provinzen Westpreussen und Posen vom 26 April 1886 (Bibl. #137, p. 131).

[51] *Sonderbeilage zum RABl* 1915, No. 3, p. 54.

[52] Dr. Metz, in Freiherr von Wangenheim (Bibl. #83, p. 34).

duced real or fictitious offers from Polish landowners at high prices in order to blackmail the German land settlement boards into offering still higher prices. The advantages were shared by Polish landowners and served to increase their power of resistance. In a meeting of the Prussian Council to the Crown (Kronrat) on February 13, 1906, the Minister of Agriculture reported that the fight between the settlement authorities and the Polish banks had driven estate prices up from 600 M. per ha. in 1887 to 1,200 and more in 1905.[53] The political aim to set a dam against Polonism had failed. Moreover, two-thirds of all German settlements, i.e. those in Posen and West Prussia, were lost after the First World War.

Settlement was not a success. Peasants' sons from the west who would have needed additional land did not like the inferior soil in the east. Settlement of agricultural workers met the resistance of both parties. Estate owners were afraid of losing laborers and feared that small holders would supplement their low proceeds by theft on the estates. They demanded that the nationality fight should not be made a *casus belli* against big estates. Due to their influence, the Prussian Diet restricted the right to expropriation to such a small extent (70,000 ha.) that it remained without effect.[54] Laborers found that the income they could derive from their holding was too small and feared a return of the old dependence. They were not willing to accept half-subsistence homesteads which did not offer possibilities of social advancement. The gap separating worker and estate owner remained too great.[55] No popular settlement movement arose. The exodus from eastern agriculture did not stop.

The First World War

The situation in German agriculture at the outbreak of the First World War in 1914 was acute. Due to the withdrawal of a considerable proportion of manpower, horses, and fertilizer, the shortage of coal and oil, and the decay of machinery, agriculture became less and less intensive. The crop

---

[53] Otto Braun (Bibl. #11), p. 63. The price was 1,451 M in 1906, scoring 45 per cent in the last four years (Bibl. #154, 1907, Vol. I, p. 272). The Prussian Minister of Agriculture, von Podbielski, stated that in seven years prior to 1904 Polish buyers had acquired 40,000 ha. more from German sellers than Germans had acquired from Poles in Posen and West Prussia (*ibid.*, March 3, 1904, Vol. I, p. 93). When two large estates, one owned by a German and one by a Pole, went bankrupt, the commission bought the estate of the Pole who then bought the estate of the German with the sales money (Hans Delbrück, Bibl. #18, pp. 8-9).

[54] Roman Heiligenthal (Bibl. #35), p. 10.

[55] Max Sering (Bibl. #149a), pp. 120-24, 135ff.

yields, never adequate for the needs of the population, enormously declined. The war deprived the German people of about one-third of its food and foodstuffs according to expert estimates.[56] Millions of soldiers had to be fed, yet the farm population could not be induced to curtail its consumption. The ensuing starvation of the civilian nonfarm population hampered the war effort. Regulation of the food supply was neglected at the beginning of the war because of the general belief that the war would last only a few months. The abuses which grew up in connection with the food supply weakened confidence in government authority as well as any feeling of solidarity in the community of suffering.

The growing cry for a food dictator was not answered until May 1916 when the War Food Office (Kriegsernährungsamt)[57] was established. Rationing was carried through, maximum prices were fixed. Although their shares were larger than those of the general population farmers resented deeply compulsory government measures. Black markets flourished. Government policy was "a hopeless tugging on the food cover which had become too small."[58]

The already existing labor shortage, especially of trained farmers and competent managers, increased catastrophically.[59] Skalweit estimated that nearly 2.7 million men had been withdrawn.[60] A survey of 3,000 Bavarian rural communities in the winter of 1916-1917 showed that 70.63 per cent of all agricultural workers and 37.67 per cent of independent farmers were in the fighting forces.[61] As early as 1914 (and repeatedly in 1915 and 1916) the Ministry of War ordered that conscription of qualified men in the reserves be deferred until after the harvest. From 1916 on, the military authorities granted leaves liberally for soldiers for the periods of intensive

[56] Ernst Wagemann, "Geschlossener Handelsstaat und gebundene Wirtschaft," Bibl. #110, 1917, Vol. 173, p. 200.
[57] Order of May 22, 1916 (Bibl. #140, p. 402). After the war it became the Reichsernährungsamt, which in 1919 changed its name to Reichsernährungsministerium (Reich Ministry for Food); in 1920 into Reichsministerium für Ernährung und Landwirtschaft, Reich Ministry for Food and Agriculture (Decree of March 30, 1920, Bibl. #140, p. 379), after it had been united for a short time with the Reich Ministry of Economics. The Ministry will be referred to henceforth as Ministry for Agriculture.
[58] August Skalweit (Bibl. #79), pp. 3, 164ff.
[59] Friedrich Aereboe estimated that of 5.4 million men working in agriculture (about 3.4 million of whom were in the sixteen to fifty military age group), about 2 million were serving in the armed forces (Bibl. #2, p. 25).
[60] Skalweit, "The Maintenance of the Agricultural Labour Supply during the War," *International Review of Agricultural Economics* 1922, XIII, pp. 851-852.
[61] Schlittenbauer, "Die gegenwärtigen Produktionsbedingungen der deutschen Landwirtschaft," *Süddeutsche Monatshefte*, July 1917, p. 502.

farm work. Deferred farmers and those on leave were obliged to help on other farms in addition to working on their own.[62]

It was a great advantage that the outbreak of the war occurred in a period in which masses of foreign workers were employed in German agriculture. They were detained in the country, and relieved the scarcity of unskilled labor, but not of trained farmers. At the outbreak of the war, 436,000 alien workers had been employed in Germany and 372,000 were still there in 1917-1918.[63] Prisoners of war provided another source of farm labor: 936,000 were employed in agriculture on October 10, 1918.[64] They worked in groups of thirty, and the communities arranged for their allocation. The productivity of these aliens, who were unfamiliar with advanced German techniques, was low. Organized labor complained that the employment of prisoners of war kept wages of German workers down. After the outbreak of the revolution many prisoners refused to work.

Another type of help, Juvenile Assistance (Jungmannenhilfe),[65] grew from companies of high school boys which were formed spontaneously, especially in towns, to help after school hours. By Order of March 24, 1917, the Prussian Minister of War drew up "Fundamental Principles for the Organization of Boys for the Benefit of Agriculture." They provided for an organization of strict military type. Squads of boys were placed under a leader (usually disabled war veterans) to be housed, if possible, in barracks. Farmers provided food and lodging and paid 1 M. per day to the leader. Out of this sum children were insured against sickness, accident, and invalidity, and were paid an allowance of 1.50 M. a week to meet the wear and tear of clothing. The number of boys thus employed was estimated to amount to about 75,000 in 1917. Their efficiency was estimated at about 70 per cent of the average worker. Farmers were therefore reluctant to employ them. Prisoners of war were allocated to farmers by the Ministry of War only on condition that they employ a suitable number of boys.

As early as 1915 the Bavarian military authority restricted the mobility of farm labor by ruling that the latter were not to leave their jobs before the end of the harvest without consent of the employer. Employers could engage farm labor only on presentation of a police certificate giving evidence

---

[62] Friedrich Becker (Bibl. #6), pp. 20-21.

[63] Bibl. #153c, 1915, p. 416; 1920, p. 25.

[64] Gerhard Gross (cited above, note 46), p. 9. Employers had to provide shelter and board and guard the prisoners. The authorities cared for medical treatment and clothing. A small payment was given the prisoner for work over five hours a day.

[65] Hans Fuhrmann (Bibl. #27), pp. 50ff.

of the legal termination of the worker's previous contract. Greater restrictions followed in 1917. The Auxiliary Service Law,[66] which conscripted men seventeen to sixty years of age for labor, brought no relief to the labor shortage. It provided that workers who were engaged in agriculture or rural handicrafts prior to August 1, 1916, were not to be conscripted for other work. At the beginning of 1918, persons engaged in agriculture were prohibited from passing on to nonagricultural employment without written local police authorization. In some rural districts it was ruled that young people who took jobs for the first time could accept work other than agricultural only with the consent of the authorities.

Under the pressure of the great struggle, union recognition by the government had been achieved in August 1914. On June 26, 1916,[67] an amendment to the Reich Association Law removed a great threat from organized farm labor by stating that trade unions were not to be considered political associations. The Auxiliary Service Law recognized trade unions as official representatives of labor and provided for conciliation boards, organized on the basis of employer-employee participation. The restriction of the use of foreign languages at trade-union meetings was abolished on April 19, 1917.[68]

Legislation alone was not sufficient to remove restrictions. Because of the close tie-up between the squires and the army, the military authorities continued to hamper the activities of organized labor. Meetings of the Socialist farm workers' union were prohibited on the grounds that wage discussions would create labor unrest.[69] "Estate owners in uniform" sent "labor agitators" (Hetzer) to the front.[70] The imprisonment of Karl Liebknecht for treasonous remarks evoked the first political strikes. Mass discontent, spurred by the deterioration of the food situation, increased when the peace of Brest Litovsk showed that the German government did not aim at peace without annexations.

Although agricultural workers did not suffer privations comparable to those of the city population, their standard of living had deteriorated because of the lack of clothing, soap, coal, and all the amenities of life. Dissatisfaction and war weariness as the war continued were shared by all alike. Thus the revolution in which they did not take an active part was greeted by farm workers as a harbinger of peace and a new order.

[66] December 5, 1916 (Bibl. #140, p. 1333). The inferior position of the farm worker was reflected in a clause of the law which provided that industrial workers recruited for agriculture were not subject to the farm servant ordinances.
[67] Bibl. #140, p. 635.
[68] Bibl. #140, p. 361.
[69] Bibl. #112b, 1914-1919, pp. 32-33.
[70] Ibid., p. 131.

PART TWO

THE PERIOD OF DEMOCRACY

CHAPTER I

FROM REVOLUTION TO REVOLUTION

Political Background

FOR a brief period after the military collapse and the ensuing revolution in November 1918, Germany seemed to follow the Russian example. The Socialists suddenly found themselves in complete possession of state power, a goal aimed at in their program but which came to them as a great surprise. All over the country red flags were hoisted. The masses, banded together in workers' and soldiers' councils, challenged the Provisional government, the Council of People's Commissioners which had been set up by the two Socialist parties, the moderate Social Democrats and the more radical Independent Socialists. The slogan "all powers to the Councils" fascinated the rank and file, especially in the cities. The primary aim of the revolutionary councils was to place political power in the hands of workers in big industries, which would bring about economic revolution. Although wholly unprepared for their task, the Council of People's Commissioners backed by the bourgeoisie and the majority of the working class, succeeded in maintaining their authority in the turmoil of the revolution. Officially they confirmed the claim of the Berlin workers' and soldiers' councils who assumed authority for the Reich and declared themselves the supreme political authority. Actually, however, the Commissioners prevented the councils from exercising control until the first national congress of councils on December 16, 1918, confirmed the legislative and executive power of the People's Commissioners. The Provisional government, however, had suffered internal division. The Independent Socialists, especially their left wing, the Spartakists (named after the leader of the slaves who rebelled against Rome) wanted to postpone elections until full socialization had been achieved. The Social Democratic party (SPD) aimed at establishing as quickly as possible a democratic government representing the whole of the German people. When troops were called in to suppress insurrection, the Independent Socialists withdrew their three representatives from the government in December 1918. They were replaced by another three Social Democrats.

On January 19, 1919, the Constituent Assembly was elected. The small figure of only two million (out of more than thirty million) votes cast for the Independent Socialists who wanted to follow Soviet Russia showed that the large majority of the people were opposed to a proletarian dictatorship and its program of immediate socialization. Attempts of the radicals to bring about a second revolution failed. What the working class wanted was peace, democracy, and social improvements. The German people supported the Provisional government and its successor, the Constituent Assembly, in their attempts to secure stability and democracy, and rejected the soviet system.

Thus ended the brief period of Socialist government in Germany, to be replaced by a coalition government in which, however, the Social Democratic party was the decisive group.

The Constituent Assembly, which under the most trying circumstances of peaceless uncertainty framed the Constitution, was determined to abolish the remnants of the revolutionary council system. But by a series of strikes which revealed how deeply the council idea had taken root in the masses, the government was compelled to promise to incorporate the council system in the Constitution.[1] However, of the tripartite system as outlined in Article 165 of the Constitution, with works councils, district councils, and a national council, only the bottom and the top levels were actually created, each without any trace of a once revolutionary character. The district councils were never created.

A Decree of December 23, 1918, had already set up committees—composed of representatives of the workers in their relation to the employer—for the protection of the workers' rights. Following their final regulation by law of February 4, 1920[2] (Betriebsrätegesetz, BRG) the works councils (Betriebsräte) in the shops and on the farms developed into instruments of the trade unions, whose authority the revolutionary councils had challenged. The Provisional National Economic Council[3] (Vorläufiger Reichswirtschaftsrat, RWR), the highest council body, which never became final, was an economic parliament with an advisory function. Trade-union influence was greatly strengthened by the nomination of workers' representatives to the RWR.

The revolutionary movement was essentially an urban movement. With the exception of the brief soviet episode in Bavaria, it did not stir up the rural population. Nor were revolutionary changes effected in the country.

The People's Commissioners, a conservative Socialist government after the party split, failed to break the economic power of the large estate owners

---

[1] The history is described by Emil Frankel, "The German Works Councils," *The Journal of Political Economy*, October 1923, pp. 708ff.

[2] Bibl. #140, p. 147.

[3] Established by Presidential Decree of May 4, 1920 (Bibl. #139, Vol. 1, p. 858); abolished in 1934.

against which the Socialists had struggled from the time of their rise. The critical food situation, the fact that the large estates had guaranteed the main food supply during the war, the continued blockade, and the starving population made the new government reluctant to take advantage of the confusion among the estate owners and to institute revolutionary changes which would have jeopardized the scanty flow of food supplies. Only the Communists demanded collectivization of agriculture as in Russia. The Social Democrats, who held the power, had lost the revolutionary impetus: their leadership, through close cooperation with the authorities during the war, had been drawn psychologically closer to the ruling groups. Although they had once threatened socialization of the soil and transformation of free farmers into hired laborers, they now felt that collectivization would fail in Germany, where—in contrast to Russia—the peasant was educated, organized, aware of his power, and could easily starve the large urban population into revolt. Only by guaranteeing unimpaired the continued private ownership of land could the Republic enlist the resigned support of the large middle class of peasants, without which it could not have survived the first months. The Social Democrats certainly were right in visualizing the fatal political consequences of a revolutionary program; however, they did not institute even fundamental reforms because they believed the inevitable decay of capitalism could be precipitated by economic means. According to their view, increases in wages and taxes and the abolition of political privileges were ways to weaken the power of the squires. A sweeping land reform to replace large estates by small or middle-sized farms was alien to the Marxist creed—the Socialist trade union, Deutscher Landarbeiterverband, DLV, refused socialization in its general program in 1920.[4] To aid the small landowners, and thus increase this class, would, in their opinion, perpetuate private property. In spite of Eduard David's[5] denial of the economic superiority of the large farm enterprise, the Marxists' belief in the large estate was unshaken. The economic development of the country depended on large-scale production in both industry and agriculture, and in such a program the lower middle-class group of small farmers had no place.[6] Moreover, workers on large farms, at least a considerable number

---

[4] Bibl. #112c, pp. 155-56.

[5] Eduard David (Bibl. #17), pp. 68off.

[6] "The peasants must recognize that they are lost beyond saving," wrote Friedrich Engels in 1895 ("Die Bauernfrage in Frankreich und Deutschland," *Die Neue Zeit*, Vol. 13, p. 304). Similarly the party program of Erfurt (1891) predicted the decay of the small enterprise. These views had imperceptibly changed, but the change had

of them, could be won for the Social Democratic party and unionized, while small farmers showed no inclination toward a socialism that considered them fated to lose their holdings. The fact that the Social Democrats shrank from any alliance with small farmers in the fight against the depression helped to drive the little men in agriculture into the opposition. Although fighting against the feudal strongholds of power, the Socialists were closer in their views to the Conservatives than to the Liberals, their allies in this fight.

This may partly explain the abandonment by the Socialists of their former plans to expropriate big estates, and instead to follow a policy of protection and subsidies to preserve the class foe, the archenemy of the Republic. Beginning in 1926 with the non-Socialist government of Luther, direct and indirect subsidies amounting to billions helped to maintain the *status quo* of land ownership in the east. From 1925 to 1928, agrarian protection reverted to prewar measures based on the principles of Bismarck and Bülow, and even surpassing them in protectionism during the depression. Such a policy is also explained by the necessity for making concessions in a coalition government,[7] and by pressure from the Ministry of Defense which stressed the need for large estates in the event of war.

Although property rights as such were not attacked, the Democratic government made some other serious attempts to abolish the privileges of the landed aristocracy. These privileges were part of a system under which the aristocracy controlled the monarch, the army, and the civil service. Their power stemmed in part from the Prussian election law which gave preference to the property owner, in part from a division of election districts which favored the rural area, and from numerous other precapitalistic privileges. The revolution of 1918 swept away the monarchy; the Treaty of Versailles reduced the army; the Weimar Constitution put an end to election privileges and gave impetus to the gradual destruction of the influence

---

been disguised by the continued use of the old terminology. In 1892 the Bavarian Socialists had demanded that the party recognize the family farmer as part of the working class and write into its platform measures to protect the peasants in their individual ownership (Edgard Milhaud, Bibl. #56, pp. 302ff.). However, the Congress of Breslau in 1895 with great majority declined to help the small holder and affirmed the character of the party as a class party of the industrial proletariat (Bibl. #138a, 1895, pp. 104-5). Subsequent congresses failed to take any action. Not until 1927 did the party program recognize that the peasant would be allowed to remain owner of his farm. Thus the stigma of animosity toward the farmer remained attached to the Social Democratic Party.

[7] The Catholic Center Party included owners of large estates. After 1920, the SPD did not attain to such influence as in the first eighteen months of the Republic.

of the squires on the civil service. It abolished the tax exemptions which large landowners had enjoyed. It provided for the dissolution of fideicommissa (strict family settlements)[8] because closed heritage together with the nondivisibility and inalienability of the estate had preserved not only the *splendor familias* but the nobility's position of power. The abolition of local manorial government was completed by 1928.[9] This meant the final disappearance of legal privileges, but not of political power.

How seriously insecure owners of large estates felt at the time of the revolution is implied in the statement, published by the traditionally anti-labor and antidemocratic Farmers' League in 1918, that "they entered upon the new era with wholehearted determination," ready to support "the Social Democratic government . . . and the political rights of the agricultural workers."[10] Their true attitude toward the new regime was revealed in a declaration of the powerful Pomeranian Landbund during the Kapp Putsch in 1920, the first attempt to overthrow the Democratic government: "After the pernicious activities of the previous government the new men pledge themselves to steer the Reich through the tempest of the times. . . . Their economic aims are those of the Landbund."[11]

In January 1921, as a counterrevolutionary measure, the owners of large estates rallied the farmers to the National League of Agrarians (Reichslandbund, RLB). It was formed by amalgamation of the Farmers' League (Bund der Landwirte) and a fusion of various local and district associations which had sprung up during and after the war (the Deutsche Landbund). The RLB, in effect a union embracing most of the rural population including the farm workers, was in its conception a forerunner of the National Socialist Reich Food Estate. The Christian peasant organizations and the Demo-

---

[8] In spite of various attempts in the beginning of the nineteenth century to abolish entails, they had grown in number and size. At the end of 1914 there existed 1,311 entails (1850, 519; 1918, 1,348) in Prussia, covering 7.1 per cent of the total area (C. von Dietze, "Fideikommisse," Bibl. #33, 1926, Vol. 3, p. 998). 62.9 per cent of all entails were located in the seven eastern provinces and Schleswig-Holstein. When the constitution abolished entails, enforcement was left to the individual states. Decrees of the Prussian government issued in 1916 and 1920 ordered the gradual abolition of entails at the death of current owners. Excepted only were forests, vineyards, and dike estates, undivided inheritance of which was in the public interest. As the progress of abolition was slow, a Prussian Act of April 22, 1930, ordered existing entails to cease automatically by July 1, 1938 (Bibl. #137, p. 51). Similar measures were taken in other states.

[9] Act of December 27, 1927 (Bibl. #137, 1928, p. 51). It gave full self-government to about one and one-half million persons who lived on the 12,000 manors.

[10] *Hamburger Nachrichten*, December 8, 1918.

[11] Quoted by Adolf Damaschke, Bibl. #124, 1935, Vol. 31, p. 28.

cratic Deutsche Bauernbund remained outside the RLB, in opposition to it. Affiliated with the RLB were state and provincial organizations of which those of Pomerania became the most powerful. The RLB organized the diehards who considered the labor movement a revolt and who were entirely out of sympathy with democratic ideas.

The agrarians made very skillful use of professional organizations, such as chambers of agriculture and agrarian leagues, for political purposes and for gaining political control of the peasantry, which had no clear program of its own and had failed to produce leaders from its own ranks. Family farmers in some parts of Germany had at first been not unfriendly to the Revolution and supported the parties of the Weimar coalition. They were tired of war—they had paid a heavy death toll, the rural population having provided a high percentage of soldiers. They were opposed to the bureaucratic wartime regimentation and to the rigid price control which prevented their making use of a favorable market while industry profited unrestrictedly. But the new regime had to continue the system which kept agricultural prices down in order to secure a fair distribution of the food supply. Aversion to this system of control created a community of interest between the big owners and the small. Moreover farmers were averse to being governed by workers and were antagonistic to the disorder and insecurity which are the inevitable consequence of any revolution. With the introduction of currency stabilization, they resented the heavy tax burden and high interest and social insurance rates. Their feeling of insecurity resulted in antagonism to the Republic and to the Democratic regime which seemed unable to restore security. The power of the lords, who had survived 1918 by remaining in the background, again grew unnoticed. Although they never succeeded in regaining their old privileged position, their sense of power, developed by the long tradition of domination, was not weakened. To the little man they remained the upper class, although their prestige suffered by the removal of the royal family. They had kept their positions in the higher officialdom. They had close ties with the Protestant clergy. Hindenburg, a man from their own ranks, was elected to the highest office in the Reich. The ingenious plan of presenting him with his ancestral estate in the east resulted in his support of all their economic claims.[12]

[12] Neudeck, a manorial estate in East Prussia, once belonged to the Hindenburg family, which had since become impoverished. The estate was bought with money collected by the Federation of German Industries and presented by the squires to the President in 1927 on his eightieth birthday. The gift was prompted by an astute business sense of the big estate owners. Hindenburg's neighbor, von Oldenburg-

The estate owners, however, were dissatisfied, in spite of the huge subsidies they received. They became embittered when large agricultural enterprises ceased to be profitable at the end of the twenties. Most of the estate owners had been too resentful and too inflexible to adapt themselves to the political change. They blamed the "scandalous doings in Berlin" for their economic decay. In 1928 the "Green Front" was formed by the presidents of the professional agrarian organizations for unified political action in the interest of price increases and state help. In 1930 the Reichslandbund which with its 1,700,000 members had assumed leadership in the Green Front, went into militant opposition.[18] Prior to this turn its president, Schiele, had entered the Brüning cabinet. However, under the leadership of the Pomeranian Landbund the radicals in the RLB gained control of the organization, and Graf Kalckreuth, who became president, inaugurated a new era of activist opposition. The RLB joined the National Front with the replacement of the Weimar regime by a "national" dictatorship as its aim. The Democratic Deutscher Bauernbund became less and less effective; after some of its members had gone over to the RLB in 1927, the Deutscher Bauernbund, with other peasant associations, joined the Deutsche Bauernschaft, which, however, remained weak. This situation opened the way for exploitation by the German National People's Party,[14] dominated by large estate owners and other reactionary forces—districts in which agriculture predominated soon became the bulwark of the monarchists—and later by the National Socialists, who promised panaceas for all evils. Enmity against the regime increased with growing distress. "The peasant sees in the official who attaches his corn, in the auctioneer who brings the indebted farm under the hammer the personification of the state bringing him ruin in the service of Mammon" (lässt ihn zu Grunde gehen im Dienst des grosstädtischen Zivilisationsgeistes).[15] It was not difficult, therefore, for agitators to incite

---

Januschau, a well-known conservative, counted on the President's becoming more amenable to the claims of the great landed proprietors if he himself were one of them, sharing the economic cares that weighed on them and being constantly informed by his neighbors. These expectations proved well-founded.

[18] Claus von Eickstedt, "Bauernkampf der Gegenwart," in: Bibl. #5 (*The Peasant Is No Toy*), p. 143. (The title is a quotation from a popular poem by Ludwig Uhland.)

[14] Their use of political power was all the more remarkable in view of the fact that the party, which was predominantly agrarian, was reduced from 103 seats in the second Reichstag election of 1924 to 41 in 1930 and 40 in July 1932. It did not secure more than 54 seats in November 1932.

[15] Bibl. #106, 1931, No. 5, p. 195. Eickstedt, *op.cit.*, pp. 151ff.

a kind of peasant war[16] which in Schleswig-Holstein became open revolt, but in other parts took the form of passive resistance. In the summer and fall of 1928 farmers in some parts of the country began to refuse to pay taxes because of the increase in foreclosures, to prevent forced sales by violence, and to refuse cooperation to the regime. Landbund leaders, Steel Helmets,[17] National Socialists, and members of the so-called Landvolk movement which had originated in militant opposition to the regime, heaped coals on the fire. Attacks on tax collectors and a succession of terror bombings of courthouses occurred. "Never has a nation voted itself sound (hat sich gesund gewählt); it has only fought itself sound," is the characteristic remark of one of the Landvolk leaders.[18] "The powers that be are ordained by Satan; the knife should be put to the throat of the state," said another leader.[19] A new wave of direct action followed in 1931 when the bank crash increased credit difficulties. The National Socialists made skillful use of these hostilities. By appealing to the plight of the farmer and his animosity toward the Democratic regime, especially toward the Social Democrats, by promising all that the farmers themselves had demanded— reduction or even abolition of interest rates, prohibition of importation of food which could be produced in Germany, restriction of trade profits, lowering of taxes and social insurance dues, security of tenure—the National Socialists succeeded in 1930-1932 in attracting the rural population in many, especially non-Catholic, parts of the country. Of Schleswig-Holstein, where the party obtained 63.8 per cent of the vote in rural districts on July 31, 1932 (but lost the majority in the election of November 1932), Heberle writes: "In fact, in the summer of 1932, there were only three rural groups which stood still outside; the owners of large estates, or rather the older generation of them, since the younger ones had to a great extent already become National Socialists; the richest and therefore the most respected large farmers; and finally, large parts of the agricultural working class, especially in areas of sharp class contrasts, where the Social Democratic party and the Communist

[16] Arthur Feiler (Bibl. #117), February 23, 1932. The fights have been well depicted in Hans Fallada's novel (Bibl. #24, *Peasants, Bombs, and Bosses*).

[17] The Stahlhelm, a League of War Veterans, founded shortly after the Armistice, was openly antidemocratic and became an instrument of nationalists. It cooperated with the National Socialists for a short time until the latter, after having come into power, turned against it.

[18] Quoted in the vituperative book of the attorney who defended the revolting Schleswig-Holstein farmers in the courts (Walter Luetgebrune, Bibl. #53, p. 24).

[19] *Ibid.*, p. 41.

party still had large followings."[20] The rural youth especially responded to the promises of its future leading role; the small farmer responded to the promise of security.

In 1932, when Chancellor Brüning decided finally to discontinue subsidizing a number of large estates and to make this land available for the settlement of small farmers, the squires were powerful enough to bring about his dismissal. In January 1933, when the Reichstag Budget Commission was to investigate alleged mismanagement of government funds in large estate owners' interests, Schleicher was removed through the intrigues of the same group. It was this economically bankrupt class that disorganized and overthrew German democracy and helped Hitler to seize power.[21] The Socialist doctrine that power can be acquired only in the economic sphere proved to be a costly illusion.

Economic Conditions in Agriculture

After the war, conditions of work for agricultural labor on both small and large estates became more and more dependent on economic conditions in agriculture as political power changed in favor of labor. During the war, soil mining had impaired the fertility of the soil, livestock was reduced in number and quality, plants and equipment were run down, farming methods had become obsolete. Difficulties continuing in the first two years after the war made it impossible to abolish government control. Disruption of transportation, worn out tools, decline of efficiency when the wartime incentives were gone, strikes, interference by workers' and soldiers' councils, and workers' insistence on shorter hours were disturbing factors.[22] From 1920 on, compulsory measures were gradually dropped. Inflation following the war benefited farmers in two ways. It protected agriculture from foreign competition and wiped out the heavy burden of accumulated debts. Taxes were paid in depreciated paper money, and farmers began to renew their livestock and inventory and to remedy part of the damage to the production apparatus caused by the strain of a war economy. Inflation gave agriculture the dangerous incentive to speculate instead of to produce. At the end of the inflation period, productivity was still much below the 1913 level. The

[20] Rudolph Heberle (Bibl. #34), pp. 80-81. For National Socialist votes, see the maps in Arnold Brecht (Bibl. #12), pp. 34ff.

[21] Karl Brandt, "Junkers to the Fore Again," *Foreign Affairs*, October 1935, pp. 120ff.

[22] Moreover, for several years Germany was still far from real peace. Fighting broke out in Upper Silesia before the final boundaries between Germany and Poland were drawn by plebiscites. Political unrest resulted in fights in Central and Western Germany.

German government reported to the Committee of Experts of the Reparation Commission that crops in tons per ha. had decreased in 1923, as compared to 1913, by about one-fifth.[23] As a result of wartime experience it was generally believed that the salvation of agriculture depended solely on increased production. All efforts of the government, therefore, were concentrated on increasing productive capacity.

In spite of all obstacles, the government provided funds for a campaign to increase the efficiency of labor by mechanization or other forms of modernization. There was a marked advance in mechanical equipment, in the use of electric power, and in the application of commercial fertilizers. Farm production was stepped up as a result of such measures as experimental stations; courses of instruction; and special advice on the elimination of plant and animal disease and on methods of grading, packing, and marketing. A National Board for Technique in Agriculture (Reichskuratorium für Technik in der Landwirtschaft) studied methods of improving agricultural technique, cooperated with experimental farms, schools, and institutes, and acted as semiofficial adviser to the Ministry of Agriculture. The government tried to help farmers by improving agricultural education. Attendance at vocational schools which had a distinct agricultural bias was made compulsory up to the age of 18. Agricultural schools, supported either by chambers of agriculture or by the Länder and communities, offered especially to sons of small holders such instruction as was needed for family farms, either in two consecutive years for five months each, or all the year round. There were special schools for home economics, gardening, milking, stock tending. Teachers employed in agricultural winter schools became farm advisers during the remainder of the year. Although they did commendable work, their influence was not wide enough. By way of self-help, Labor Research Rings were formed, each Ring composed of twelve to twenty farmers who engaged a trained agriculturist to investigate their farming methods and propose improvements. About two hundred farmers participated in such rings in 1930.

The farmer was confronted with a serious adjustment when consumption changed from rye (the chief bread grain) to wheat, and from wheat (the chief item of the diet) to vegetables, fruit, eggs, and milk products.

This shift was an expensive undertaking—especially in the face of shortage of capital—because the eastern lowlands were, by virtue of their climate and sandy soil, better suited to potato and rye culture than to any other crops.

[23] Bibl. #54, pp. 9, 10.

In the south, the hills and slopes were better suited to rye than to wheat. Cultivation of root crops could not be sacrificed without serious consequences to intensive cattle breeding.[24]

The years 1921 to 1923 were a period of reconstruction. Many small farmers, however, unable to understand the character of inflation, continued their custom of saving money instead of investing it. When in 1923 the meaning of inflation became clearer to them, they made investments which turned out to be failures under a stabilized currency. From the summer of 1923, when industry began to calculate prices in gold, the price situation became unfavorable for the farmer. Runaway inflation hit the farmer whose distance from markets made it impossible to spend his money income quickly enough. By the time stabilization took place at the end of 1923, the prewar debt had become insignificant;[25] nevertheless agriculture, left with increased and costly fixed investments, was unable to compete in markets with low production costs and was compelled to purchase all needed supplies in markets at high cost. Moreover, most of the harvest had been sold before stabilization and paid for in depreciated paper marks.[26] Since operating capital had been exhausted during the inflation period, farmers had to ask for new credit. The sense of careful calculation had been lost in handling astronomical inflation figures. Prices improved, but from 1927 on the price scissors which had been partly closed, opened again to the disadvantage of the farmer.[27] The inability immediately to understand the changing situation at the end of the inflation period, the heavy burden

[24] When, on the basis of international agreements, sugar-beet cultivation had to be restricted, farmers lost not only part of their income but valuable wastage for cattle fodder.

[25] Revaluation of mortgages at 25 per cent of their gold mark value obliged agriculture to assume 4 billion marks of its pre-war debts.

[26] Losses due to the paper mark sale were estimated at about 40 per cent of the harvest in 1923-1924 (Bibl. #104d, p. 88).

[27]

Year	Agricultural Prices	Industrial prices (raw materials and manufactured products)	Purchasing power of agriculture (industrial prices = 100)
1913	100.0	100.0	100.0
1924-1925	129.5	144.8	89.4
1926-1927	137.6	135.0	101.9
1927-1928	135.2	141.9	95.3
1928-1929	132.5	143.3	92.5
1929-1930	122.0	138.4	88.2
1932-1933	77.0	113.0	68.0

Sources: Ex-Minister Hermes (Bibl. #52), 1931, p. 172; and Bibl. #153c, 1936, pp. 281, 282.

of taxation resulting from defeat in war, the high cost of machine equipment and fertilizers, and the ease of getting credit which was partly used on current expenditures resulted in new debts, growing at a rate of 1½ to 2 billion Rm. a year to a total of 10.6 billion Rm. in the middle of 1932.

Although the amount was less than in 1913, an unusually large part of it consisted of short-term obligations with higher interest rates.[28] Owing to the shortage of capital and the instability of economic and political conditions, rates of interest on long-term loans approximated 30 per cent in 1924, about 20 per cent in 1925, and never went substantially below 10 per cent in the period that followed. Anyone who acquired loans at such interest rates was never again able to get out of debt because he had to borrow afresh to make his yearly payments. The Committee of Enquiry,[29] which examined thousands of farmers' accounts, found in 1924-1925 that expenses exceeded receipts in 38 per cent of the cases studied.[30] Taxes in eastern Germany had risen by 240 per cent from 1913-1914 to 1927-1928, in central Germany by 300 per cent. During the depression, surplus was taxed away in many cases. Wages and social insurance dues had increased.[31] The number of farms foreclosed multiplied as compared to the prewar period; frequently

[28] Bibl. #120a, Vol. 7, No. 4, part A, Berlin, 1933, p. 195. The interest burden was 965 million Rm. in 1929 compared to about 750 million before the war (Bibl. #120e, 1930, No. 20). Of 6.8 billion Rm. in new debts acquired from 1924 to 1928, only 2.4 had been used for new investments; the remainder made up deficits, including arrears of interest and taxation. Whereas before the war the average interest charge on a ha. of cultivated land amounted to 18 M., in 1930 it approximated 38 Rm.

[29] In 1926 an official Committee of Enquiry in Production and Sale of German Economy (Bibl. #104) was set up (Bibl. #140, 1926, 1, p. 195). It founded five subcommittees to deal with various branches of the inquiry, one of these being appointed to consider agriculture, another the effect of hours of work and wages on production (Arbeitsleistung). The agricultural subcommittee in turn worked with nine subdivisions. The publications of the Committee are a valuable source of information.

[30] Bibl. #104a, 1928, Vol. 3, p. 35.

[31] In the third quarter of 1931 the index of wages was 135-140 and that of agricultural products 103-104. Since wages amounted to 40 to 50 per cent of the costs, profitableness was endangered (I. Freiherr von Wangenheim in *Deutsche Agrarpolitik im Rahmen der inneren und äusseren Wirtschaftspolitik*, Bibl. #7, p. 542). Social insurance contributions paid by owners of farms of more than 5 ha. had risen from 2.8 per cent of operating expenses in 1924-1925 to 5.1 per cent in 1930-1931. Kurt Padberg (Bibl. #61), p. 14. Yearly expenses for cash wages including social insurance developed as follows:

1924-1925	1,342 million Rm.
1927-1928	1,755 " "
1928-1929	1,893 " "
1929-1930	1,994 " "
1930-1931	1,937 " "
1931-1932	1,681 " "

mortgages were not covered by the highest bids. The price of land went down.

The situation was different for various types of farms. The smaller and middle-sized farms were able to withstand the depression better than the big farms. The former were less indebted. They had lower percentages of sales of farm produce, and therefore suffered less from price slumps. They paid less in wages and social insurance dues. During the depression owners of small farms accomplished the reduction in costs of production simply by working harder and living more frugally than ever. With valuation based on sales price, large estates had to carry about double the amount of debts of small ones. The big estates in the east were especially hard hit. For many of them an important source of income, the breeding of cavalry remounts, had stopped with the reduction of the army. Although the prewar level of agricultural production was surpassed in a comparatively short period, the condition of German agriculture became critical in the depression of 1930 when the purchasing power of the population on which the farmer's income depended was lowered and prices sank still further. Sale proceeds declined from 10 billion M. in 1928 to 6.5 billion in 1932. Conditions were extremely crucial.

Gradually, from 1925 on, the government deserted its early postwar policy of reinforcing the effects of the blockade, of abolishing the ties that had bound agriculture in the war period,[32] and of feeding the people as cheaply as possible. From the end of 1927 on its aims were to shield agriculture from the slump in foodstuffs and to ease the debt load. A policy of import monopolies and high tariffs was followed, but it failed to raise domestic prices to exceed those of foreign products by the whole amount of the duty.[33] From 1929 on, governmental economic policy aimed at maintaining the prices of agricultural products at an existence level for the farmer. To achieve this end, maximum prices for grains and pigs were fixed, duties raised to an almost insurmountable level, import quotas set for domestic bread grains for milling and mixing. German agricultural prices were thus set apart from those of the world market and soon surpassed them considerably. However, propping of farm prices failed to eliminate the effects of diminishing demand for farm products.

[32] By 1925 the last vestiges of the war economy had disappeared.
[33] Measures for the protection of grain prices operated largely for the benefit of large landowners, but brought losses to farmers engaged in intensive hog and poultry business with purchased feed.

After 1929 the eastern regions were supported by a series of emergency measures, among which were lowering of the interest rate, of freight rates, conversion of short-term credits into long-term credits at lower rates, partial cancellation of debts, and grants of subsidies. It seemed justifiable to help those areas first which had suffered most from the formation of the new frontier. East Prussia was cut off from the main body of the Reich by the Polish Corridor, and Silesia had lost its hinterland. But the wholesale mortgage foreclosures and tense relations between debtors and creditors spread westward so rapidly that agricultural assistance had to be extended to the entire Reich. A few months after the bank crash of July 1931, a moratorium was declared and a system of debt conversion and cancellation for agricultural concerns established. Interest rates were compulsorily reduced by 2 per cent to a minimum of 4 per cent.[34] Taxes were relieved, foreclosures restricted. That the measures to help agriculture had definite therapeutic value was only later recognized.

[34] Reduction of taxes and interest rates by legislation in 1931-1932 decreased the total tax burden by about 200 million Rm. and the interest burden by about 400 million Rm. And yet the share of taxes, interest rates, and social insurance dues had increased from 17 per cent of sales money in 1926-1927 to 24 per cent in 1931-1932 (Willy Neuling, Bibl. #225, pp. 100ff.).

CHAPTER II

LABOR IN TRANSITION

THE REVOLUTION brought the immediate realization of many long-cherished desires of labor. November 12, 1918, the day after the Armistice was signed, saw the beginnings of a new social order for the German farm worker. That day, by proclamation,[1] the Council of People's Commissioners abrogated the Farm Servant Ordinances, those strange survivals of feudal times, incompatible with the spirit of postwar Germany. It abolished all exceptional laws concerning rural workers and all restrictions of the right of association.[2]

When workers' and soldiers' councils, modeled after the Russian soviets, spontaneously sprang up during the revolution, the agricultural population, too, was aroused. On November 11, two days after the revolution, all farmers' organizations which were united in the Kriegsausschuss (later Reichsausschuss) der Deutschen Landwirtschaft (War—later Reich—Committee of German Agriculture), offered to form together with farm workers and with district and local committees in order to secure their services to the new government, and immediately began to form peasants' councils.

On November 12, 1918, a call was issued by the People's Commissioners[3] to form peasants' councils to secure the food supply for the population, and to restore order in the country. The appeal referred only to "peasants,"[4] not to farm workers. Organized labor protested. On November 19, 1918, the agricultural associations and the trade unions met for the first time and discussed the formation of councils. In compliance with the demand of the trade unions to include workers in the councils, the Reich Food Office on November 22, 1918,[5] issued a regulation for election to "peasants' and workers' councils" which were subscribed to by all agricultural associations. The regulation provided that local councils, composed of three employers and three employees, be directly elected in every community; it provided also for the election of district councils. The subscribing associations

---

[1] Bibl. #140, p. 1303.

[2] Later, Article 159 of the Constitution guaranteed the right of combination.

[3] Bibl. #102, 1919, Heft 1, pp. 44ff.

[4] The expression "peasant" instead of farmer was used because it suggests the small farmer. Thus it concealed the fact that owners of big farms participated inconspicuously.

[5] Bibl. #113, November 25, 1918, No. 278. On January 16, 1919, the Reich Food Office repeated the demand that councils be elected, pointing out that their function was to be economic, not political (Bibl. #102, 1919, No. 1, p. 47).

(agrarian, peasant, cooperative, trade union) united in a Reich Peasants' and Workers' Council (Reichs-Bauern-und Landarbeiterrat). The functions of the local councils were, among other things, to assist the government in all attempts to secure the food supply, to promote agricultural production, to cooperate in re-employing demobilized soldiers, in allocating dwellings, and in concluding collective agreements in cases for which no other bargaining agency existed. The Reich Council was to advise the local and district councils and to cooperate with the federal government. Actually the councils were formed partly by election, partly with the aid of industrial workers or political parties: the Social Democratic party was very active in forming councils in order to gain a footing in agriculture; right-wing organizations joined councils in order to prevent their becoming radical.

Thus the agricultural councils distinguished themselves from the industrial workers' and soldiers' councils by the official character of their formation and by their inclusion of employers and, frequently, representatives of other groups of the rural population.

In Bavaria, for instance, the local and district councils included mayors, craftsmen, and civil servants as well as peasants and farm workers.[6] Although nearly one-half the membership in the Central Bavarian Peasants' Council (Zentralbauernrat), appointed by one revolutionary leader, were agrarians without other occupations, the journalists and teachers in the membership made their influence felt. Since workers are usually more concerned with local problems their proportion was smaller in the councils for larger areas. For example, in the community councils they represented one-tenth; in the district councils, where mayors exerted great influence, one-fiftieth; in the central representation, one or none. Those who owned no land at all were represented only in the community councils. The Bavarian councils were built up on principles other than those underlying the councils in other parts of the Reich, and were out of contact with them.

Although the councils in Bavaria represented 90 per cent of the agrarian population, many of them remained inactive since their chief purpose was to prevent the growth of Socialist organizations. Some local councils cooperated with the government in black-market problems; the district councils cooperated in matters of demobilization; the Central Council received complaints and demands of the agrarian population (in connection with the return of soldiers, prisoners of war, and the distribution of war horses).

The agricultural councils did not gain influence comparable to that

[6] Wilhelm Mattes (Bibl. #55), pp. 94ff.

exercised by the councils of industrial workers and soldiers. On the whole, the agricultural groups lacked a revolutionary spirit. Only in Bavaria was a striking alliance formed between radical workers' and peasants' councils during the brief period of a soviet venture in 1919, and only in Lower Bavaria had peasants become revolutionary. The council idea had no appeal for the majority of peasants. With the breakdown of the political council system, the Bavarian council movement came to an end, and in March 1920 they were transformed into peasant chambers—semiofficial, bureaucratic bodies.

The Reich Council turned its attention to discussion of an agricultural labor law which was urgently needed to fill the gap left by the repeal of the old statutes and also because it was certain that the eight-hour day provided for in the Joint Agreement and promised by the government, could not be applied to agriculture. As early as December 20, 1918, the Reich Council drafted a bill which, with only slight additions, went into force[7] on January 24, 1919. The Reichstag passed it without discussion, as a provisional regulation, to be replaced as quickly as possible by a definite statute. In view of its origin, the "Provisional Agricultural Labor Act" (Vorläufige Landarbeitsordnung, LAO) may be considered a collective agreement, endowed with the force of a law.

A cooperative venture of utmost importance had been launched by capital and labor in the first days of the revolution—a dangerous time for capital as well as for organized labor, threatening the former with socialization, the latter with being swept away by the workers' councils. On November 15, 1918, a "Joint Agreement"[8] was reached between the employers' associations and the trade unions, securing recognition of trade unions and of collective agreements,[9] establishing works councils and conciliation bodies, introducing the eight-hour day, and the joint administration of employment offices. It provided for the establishment of a joint association of employers' associations and trade unions for cooperation on all economic and labor questions. On December 4, 1918, the Joint Industrial Association was founded, including all trade union federations as well as all the employers' associa-

[7] Bibl. #140, p. 111.

[8] Bibl. #113, November 18, 1918, No. 273.

[9] The right to bargain collectively was established by an order of December 23, 1918, which also made it obligatory to elect workers' committees on estates and establish conciliation committees (Bibl. #140, p. 1456). The Orders of the Provisional Government were recognized by the National Assembly by law of March 4, 1919 (Bibl. #140, p. 285).

tions. The desperate situation which gave rise to this "peace treaty" after decades of class struggle was described in the terms of an employer: "When the wave of revolution transferred the powers of government to the workers' and soldiers' councils—when all orderly demobilization had become impossible; when millions of troops returned suddenly to civil life; when the fall in the exchange, the rise of prices, the dearth of raw materials, the lack of foodstuffs, the weight of debts, the lack of will to work, the absence of orders, and political difficulties prevented all ordered transition from wartime economy to peacetime economy; when insufficient transport, strikes, *coups d'état*, the reign of terror and the disastrous financial policy of the new leaders threatened to convert the country into a heap of ruins—in this hour of utter distress, when the country knew neither government, authority, nor respect for the state, morality, or laws, the great associations . . . set to work to find an independent solution. . . ."[10]

In agriculture, employers' organizations did not exist and accordingly were formed; their uniting in the National Federation of Agricultural and Forestry Employers' Associations (Reichsverband der land-und forstwirtschaftlichen Arbeitgebervereinigungen) on November 11, 1919, made a joint association in agriculture possible. However, the stratification of agriculture where no clear division of employers and workers existed created great difficulties. The estate owners demanded a division into three groups, the third to be composed of small holders who employed labor only part of the year. Moreover, they tried to restrict collaboration to labor questions and to exclude economic discussions. But labor was firm in its demands for full participation on equal terms. Finally, aided by strong government pressure, on February 20, 1920, the employers' federation combined with the trade unions of farm workers to form the Joint Association of Agricultural Employers Organizations and Trade Unions (Reichsarbeitsgemeinschaft land-und forstwirtschaftlicher Arbeitgeber- und Arbeitnehmervereinigungen) with district and local suborganizations. Small landholders were not included, and labor was given equal representation. The purpose of the Reich organization was to promote the conclusion of collective agreements, to build up a conciliation system and to act in an advisory capacity to the government. The Joint Association issued regulations for work rules on farms, gave suggestions for the employment of foreign workers and prisoners of war. The Socialist trade unions emphasized the fact that they considered the Joint Association merely

[10] W. Krüger, "Employers' Associations in Germany," Bibl. #121a, September 1926, Vol. 14, pp. 332-33.

an instrument by which resistant employers could be induced to bargain collectively; that they would adhere to it only as long as it was in their interest.[11] In fact the Joint Association in the first years after the revolution was very active in promoting collective bargaining; but it existed only for a short time. The suborganizations restricted their activities to collective agreements and conciliation questions and were not in contact with the National Association.

When the storm of revolution had passed, peasants' and workers' councils, which had concluded district collective agreements because of lack of employers' and workers' organizations, very soon dropped out of existence. Works councils, established on farms employing twenty or more workers according to the Works Council Act of February 4, 1920, were concerned merely with labor-employer relations on individual farms, and were subordinate to trade unions. A Socialist and a Christian trade union had been founded in 1909 and 1912 respectively, but they had made little headway before the war. During the revolution and the consequent general upheaval the trade unions, which seemed to stand like a *rocher de bronze*, had gained tremendously in membership. On the other hand they suffered from the sudden influx of new members and from the attempts of the Communists and rival organizations to undermine their influence. They lost part of their gains when the political excitement subsided.

The revolution was followed by a flood of labor laws and regulations which were intended partly to organize demobilization, partly to carry out the provisions of the Joint Agreement. They expanded the existing laws, frequently by abolishing discrimination against farm labor, and entered new fields, such as the protection of farm labor, collective agreements, unemployment relief. During this period, the chief gains made by agricultural labor were:

(1) The recognition of the right to combine.
(2) The recognition of trade unions as the competent representative of labor, and their cooperation in joint bodies which were gradually built up, such as employment offices, conciliation and arbitration bodies, labor courts.
(3) Recognition of collective bargaining and collective agreements.
(4) Recognition of works councils.
(5) Protective legislation.
(6) Establishment of self-government in social insurance.

[11] Bibl. #112f, p. 28.

Based on this new legislation, collective bargaining, heretofore almost unknown in agriculture, became widespread, despite resistance on the part of some employers' organizations.[12] After centuries of patriarchy it was not easy for the estate owner to negotiate with outside representatives of labor. Nor were the workers, elated with the success of the revolution, always inclined to negotiate peacefully. They were filled with a new sense of power and accustomed through years of war to violent action and unaccustomed to collaboration.[13] They expected some Socialist utopia with a high standard of living without much effort of their own. Demands for higher wages and shorter hours were frequently supplemented by wildcat strikes, which broke out partly in response to the autocratic behavior of estate owners, partly as a result of efforts by political agitators who recommended harvest strikes to stir up revolution. Farmers' organizations and trade union leadership alike tried to prevent stoppages which endangered the insufficient food supply of the nation and aroused resentment against labor. In the summer of 1919 the Farmers' League, cooperatives, and trade unions jointly appealed to farmers not to discriminate against trade union activities and to workers not to strike.[14] When conflicts arose in Pomerania where employers refused union recognition, the military authority proclaimed martial law (Belagerungszustand) with compulsion to work. The workers reacted with great excitement, which resulted in a general strike in Stettin to which the citizens responded with a strike of their own (Bürgerstreik). The Prussian government settled the conflict,[15] and the state of martial law was abolished. Pomeranian squires remained adamant in their refusal to conclude collective agreements and rejected arbitration awards which proposed such agreements.[16] Conflicts resulting in thousands of notices to farm workers in 1920

[12] On January 24, 1919, the East Prussian Chamber of Agriculture resolved that no agreement should be concluded (Bibl. #102, 1919, Heft 1, p. 14).

[13] "On both sides the understanding for the collective contract is lacking," said the President of the Socialist farm workers' union (Bibl. #112b, p. 56).

[14] Bibl. #150, July 24, 1919, p. 756. A similar appeal was issued by the Joint Association in the spring of 1920 (ibid., April 7, 1920, p. 626).

[15] Bibl. #150, July 24, 1919, p. 755. During the harvest, however, danger of strike induced the Prussian Minister of Agriculture to decree that in case collective agreements were refused by an employer or employers' organization, the demobilization authority was entitled to regulate conditions of work for the county (Kreis) after hearing agricultural experts and to enforce the decision if necessary—i.e., if the performance of important work was endangered, even to the point of depriving the owner of the administration of his farm. The legality of the decree was attacked and it was withdrawn on January 4, 1920 (Bibl. #137, p. 29).

[16] Bibl. #150, June 15, 1921, p. 626.

induced the military authorities for Pomerania to void the notices and to decree that a dismissal of agricultural workers was valid only in urgent cases.[17] The unions claimed that estate owners tried to employ foreign workers and that they introduced extensification in order to avoid paying high wages. Antagonism increased so much that the Society for Social Reform appealed to the government to establish immediately agricultural labor courts and to adapt the conciliation committees to the requirements of agriculture.[18] The Kapp Putsch of 1920 which intended to restore an authoritarian state and which was followed by Communist agitation for a counter-revolution of the left, brought labor unrest to a pitch.

In addition to the attempt to improve the social and legal status of agricultural labor, another tremendous problem had to be tackled, the reorganization of the labor market during and after the period of demobilization in order to secure the food supply. The continuance of the Allied blockade after the Armistice—a prolonged war in the midst of a so-called peace—condemned the German people to further hunger and misery. The revolutionary masses flooded the big cities where unemployment increased; in the rural districts scarcity of farm labor hindered efficient cultivation, thereby aggravating the urban food problem. The entire thought of the German people was dominated by the urgent need to abolish the food shortage.

[17] *Ibid.*, February 11, 1920, p. 449.
[18] *Ibid.*, January 28, 1920, p. 402.

CHAPTER III

THE LABOR MARKET

AFTER the end of the war a tremendous political migration movement took place during which 700,000 prisoners and most of the 350,000 foreign civilian workers returned to their home countries,[1] creating at first a serious labor shortage. Of the hundreds of thousands of Germans in the lost parts of the Reich who pressed back into their fatherland, many migrated to rural districts. This influx, coupled with the disinclination of labor to join the starving masses in the cities, restored a rather sufficient labor supply of married workers for agriculture as soon as the revolutionary upheaval had abated. Unmarried servants, however, remained scarce.[2]

Following final lifting of the blockade—it was partially lifted at the end of March 1919—the food shortage continued because of the impossibility of securing imports during the inflation which lasted until the end of 1923. After the stabilization of the mark the food supply for the urban population was secured and a new exodus to the cities began. The east with its sparse population suffered most by these losses.[3] Two of the basic causes underlying migration were the inequalities between urban and rural occupations, and the farm worker's own feeling of inferiority, partly reminiscent of his former serfdom, partly due to the real lack of prospect of improved social position. The hunger to live after years of deprivation became indomitable. The farmer was restless under the hardship of strenuous, dirty, and disagreeable work, poor housing conditions, long and irregular hours, and the lack of educational opportunities, of sociability, of entertainment, of communication. The impoverishment of farmers, and the consequent delay in the transmission of the farm, implied for the heir a postponement of marriage and prolongation of uncompensated farm service—or the alternative of migration. The country housewife was much more burdened than the woman in town; amenities in the daily life of the city housewife promised liberation from drudgery.

---

[1] Gerhard Gross (cited above, footnote 46, Part 1), pp. 9ff.

[2] This shortage of young workers with an ample supply of married workers characterized the period of currency inflation.

[3] From 1925 to 1933, Eastern Germany without Berlin and the district of Potsdam (East Prussia, Pomerania, Grenzmark, Silesia, Brandenburg, Mecklenburg) lost 342,000 persons by migration. East Prussia's loss—95,000 persons—was more than one half of its surplus of births, which was far above the Reich's average. At the same time Berlin gained 357,000 through immigration (Bibl. #153e, 1934, No. 1, p. 30).

Moreover, young women who felt their marriage chances too slim in the country tried to escape: peasant daughters who witnessed their mothers' drudgery were not inclined to become peasants' or farm workers' wives.

Other factors which helped to continue the exodus during depressed periods were East Prussia's isolation from the Reich following the creation of the Polish Corridor, and industry's preference for workers newly arrived from the country.

Country workers were considered physically stronger, more modest in their claims, often unorganized, and less politically radical than the urban worker. After a short time, however, such differences disappeared and country workers were treated like the unskilled city workers and were exposed to the same risk of unemployment. The shortage of agricultural workers gradually began to be felt, reaching a climax in 1928-1929.

The depression marked a new turning point in the migration movement. Beginning with 1930 the country-to-city exodus stopped, and 1931 marked a counterexodus from city to country. This trend coincided with the full effect of technical changes in agriculture. Increasing modernization and mechanization of agriculture, and fixing of shares for the cultivation of sugar beets limited the labor demand. The deplorable condition of the farmer obliged him to dispense with the services of all except the most essential workers. The small and middle-sized farmer dismissed outside help and increased family labor; former farm workers who had migrated to the cities returned to the country. Unemployment of farm laborers, formerly only a winter phenomenon, in 1929 began to extend into the summer. For the first time in German history, the labor market became unfavorable for the agricultural worker. An official inquiry counted 103,746 unemployed farm workers on April 30, 1931, i.e. 4.34 per cent of all farm workers (women 3 per cent) as compared with 20 per cent in all occupations at that date. In the middle of May 1932, 213,464 agricultural workers were unemployed.[4] It should be noted, however, that the demand for young workers remained in some places unsatisfied and that unfavorably located farms always complained about shortages.

Insecurity increased with the tendency of estate owners to replace the

[4] Unemployed applicants in agriculture and forestry in public employment offices:

July	1929	20,049
"	1930	53,835
"	1931	96,663
"	1932	165,600

Fourth Reifa Report (Bibl. #139, 1933, Sonderbeilage, No. 7, p. 10).

deputatist, a year-round worker, by temporary workers, thereby reversing a former trend toward an increase in the number of permanent workers at the expense of casual workers. The new tendency was due to the owners' need to reduce his wage costs, to technical changes, and to the disappearance of the patriarchal relationship. It was encouraged by the abundance of the labor supply, unemployment insurance which provided some subsistence for dismissed workers, and the improvement of the employment service which could be relied upon to provide extra hands when needed. (On the other hand, the unemployment insurance law provided an incentive for long-term contracts by allowing exemption of workers with a year's contract.)

Labor Market Policy

I. DEMOBILIZATION

On October 4, 1918, the imperial government established a Reich Labor Department (Reichsarbeitsamt)[5] which in March 1919 became the Reich Ministry of Labor. By Order of November 7, 1918,[6] the Reich Chancellor had been authorized by one of the last acts of the old regime, demanded by trade unions, to provide for regulations "to prevent and abolish disturbances caused by economic demobilization." Consequently on November 12, 1918,[7] the revolutionary government created a Reich Office for Economic Demobilization (Reichsamt für wirtschaftliche Demobilmachung).

Its purpose was "to carry over the German economy to peace conditions," a characteristic change from the aim to "maintain the economy" which the Decree of November 7 had expressed.[8] Commissioners of demobilization were appointed for each state or for large administrative districts by the state governments and committees formed in all urban communities and country districts.[9] The legislative powers of the demobilization authorities—functioning in addition to the ordinary process of legislation—in a revolu-

[5] Bibl. #140, p. 1231.

[6] Bibl. #140, p. 1292.

[7] Bibl. #140, p. 1304. For the description of the demobilization authorities cf. Oberregierungsrat Bernhard Lehfeldt, "Der Stand der Demobilmachungsgesetzgebung mit besonderer Berücksichtigung der Sozialpolitik," Bibl. #139, 1921, Vol. II, p. 760.

[8] Oberst Koeth (Bibl. #44), Vol. IV, pp. 163-64.

[9] In order to promote agricultural production the Reich Commissioner of Demobilization on November 9 ordered the formation of agricultural committees in the district of every demobilization commissioner. They were to be composed of two farmers and two workers, the latter either nominated by the unions or where none existed by the sick fund organizations under the chairmanship of the commissioner or a person nominated by him. The committees had to discuss all affairs concerning demobilization in agriculture (Bibl. #150, January 9, 1919, p. 243).

tionary period of uncertain competence were so large that most of the great reforms achieved in the first postwar years were based on it. The Ministry of Demobilization itself, whose president could issue orders with the force of law, was dissolved on May 1, 1919,[10] and its powers transferred to the respective Ministries. The committees continued to work until March 31, 1921.[11] The commissioners, the center of the whole system, continued until April 1, 1924.[12]

The labor market policy of the government corresponded to the needs of the market. In anticipation of discharged soldiers streaming back to the country, a government proclamation (December 19, 1918) ordered farmers to re-employ the returning soldiers at their former working place and to provide work for the unemployed. However, since agriculture did not receive an oversupply of labor, the government decree which established the legal obligation to rehire pre-war wage-earner veterans[13] and which forbade the discharge of workers before hours of work were shortened, was not applied to agriculture. The order which obliged enterprises to employ severely injured war veterans applied only to large estates. A campaign was started to induce workers to accept employment in agriculture. An amendment to the Unemployment Relief Order of January 15, 1919,[14] gave the authorities the power to direct former farm workers back to agriculture. It stipulated that persons who had changed their residence during the war were entitled to receive relief at their new residence only for four weeks if they were able to return to their former place. Relief could be withdrawn if workers refused to accept a job, even at a different place and in a different occupation—unless they were unfit for it, wages were too low, or housing conditions objectionable. An Order of February 17, 1919,[15] obliged all employers who needed five employees or more to report the demand to a nonprofit employment office. Still further went the Order of March 16, 1919,[16] which obliged

[10] Decree of April 26, 1919 (Bibl. #140, p. 438). The demobilization orders expired on October 31, 1923 (Order of March 23, 1923, Bibl. #140, Vol. I, p. 215); however, a few survived, based on a new legal authority.

[11] Decree of February 18, 1921 (Bibl. #140, p. 189).

[12] Decree of March 25, 1924 (Bibl. #140, Vol. I, p. 375).

[13] Order of January 4, 1919 (Bibl. #140, p. 8). The Orders of January 25, 1919 (*ibid.*, p. 100), which concerned salaried employees and the redrafting of all orders in one of September 3, 1919 (*ibid.*, p. 1500), and February 12, 1920 (*ibid.*, p. 218) applied to agriculture.

[14] Bibl. #140, p. 82.   [15] Bibl. #140, p. 201.

[16] Bibl. #140, p. 310. It was supplemented October 28, 1919 (*ibid.*, p. 1833) and March 25, 1920 (*ibid.*, p. 520); rescinded together with the Order of February 17 on March 31, 1922 (*ibid.*, p. 285).

employers in agriculture to report at once all vacancies to a nonprofit employment office and to inform the office immediately when these vacancies had been filled. Employers were not allowed to employ agricultural workers in nonagricultural occupations nor were employment offices allowed to place them in other than agricultural positions[17] as long as there were such vacancies. Exemptions were admitted for persons who were no longer available to do farm work. Unemployed workers, formerly employed in agriculture, were encouraged to return to the country by grants of traveling expenses and of benefits for their families from whom they were separated. Further stimulus was provided by granting all agricultural workers the right to provide themselves, without rationing, with food from the farm for which they worked (Selbstversorgung)—an enormous privilege in a time of starvation. Another Order of March 28, 1919,[18] empowered the demobilization committees to order nonfarm employers to dismiss workers who had been farm workers at the time of the outbreak of the war or later. The underlying purpose was twofold: to free working places for those who needed work and to provide workers for agriculture. Farm labor, however, resented the impairment of their mobility and employers were not always willing to employ "radical" city people. All these restrictions expired in 1922, and after that no measure infringing upon the mobility of labor was taken. Government policy in the following period concerned itself especially with the improvement of the placement service and the training of young industrial workers for agriculture.

2. THE PLACEMENT SERVICE

The placement service in agriculture produced special difficulties since workers usually did not live in the vicinity of their new position and every change of work involved a change of residence. Farmers frequently were situated at considerable distances from each other and from an employment office. Traditionally, employment service in the country had been for profit. There were many abuses. The applicants for work were housed and fed by agents who sometimes charged exorbitant sums for board. Registration fees were high. Only a few nonprofit employment offices were run by communities, special associations, chambers of agriculture, welfare organizations, the Dairymen's Union, and the German Farm Workers' Central which

[17] By decree of October 28, 1919 (Bibl. #140, p. 1833) the demobilization commissioners were empowered to admit exceptions.
[18] Bibl. #140, p. 355. An Order of March 5, 1921 (*ibid.*, p. 222) restricted the vacating order to large cities. The Orders were rescinded on March 31, 1922.

placed foreign seasonal workers. During the war the existing public offices had been improved and new ones established.

An Order of December 9, 1918,[19] empowered the central state authorities to oblige communities to establish employment and vocational guidance offices[20] and to set up a clearing system for all nonprofit offices. On May 5, 1920,[21] a Federal Employment Board (Reichsamt für Arbeitsvermittlung), was established for the purpose of watching the labor market and regulating the procedure of employment offices. The board had, among other duties, that of regulating the recruiting and placing of foreign workers. The Federal Employment Office Law of July 22, 1922,[22] which provided for a complete network of local and state public employment offices, with a federal office at the head, started to bring the placement and vocational guidance service under more centralized direction, with the cooperation of employers, unions, and community representatives. In 1927 this law was replaced by another[23] which gave complete jurisdiction over placement, vocational guidance, unemployment insurance, retraining of unemployed persons, and other controls of the labor market to the Federal Institute for Placement and Unemployment Insurance (Reichsanstalt für Arbeitsvermittlung und Arbeitslosenversicherung, Reifa), operating as an autonomous public corporation under the supervision of the Federal Minister of Labor.[24] At every stage in the administration those directly concerned took a share in the responsibility. Joint bodies composed of equal numbers of employers' and workers' representatives and representatives of public authorities governed all offices. (Bodies to decide questions of unemployment insurance were composed only of representatives of employers and workers.) The forty-eight-member governing body (Verwaltungsrat) of the Reifa which was composed of sixteen representatives

---

[19] Bibl. #140, p. 1421. It was followed in 1919 by ministerial decrees, obliging Prussian cities and rural districts to establish public employment offices, and centers for vocational guidance (Decrees of March 18, 1919 and September 12, 1919, Bibl. #131, 1919, pp. 108-9). Similar regulations were introduced in other states.

[20] In Germany vocational counselling was not considered a school problem, but attached to the public placement service. However, data collected in the vocational guidance offices included school grades and opinions of teachers and school physicians.

[21] Bibl. #140, p. 876.

[22] Arbeitsnachweisgesetz (Bibl. #140, 1922, Vol. I, p. 657).

[23] Placement and Unemployment Insurance Act (AVAVG), July 16, 1927 (Bibl. #140, Vol. I, p. 187).

[24] The system included a headquarters office, 13 district offices, and 361 local employment offices. Every commune was covered by a local office. A central clearing system for applications for employment and for workers was set up. The headquarters office was largely a planning and supervisory agency, not an operating unit. Most of the control of local activities was exercised by the district offices.

each of employers' organizations, unions, and public authorities, included four agricultural employers as representatives (and four alternates) and two farm workers' representatives.[25] The law of 1927 prescribed the establishment of a section for agriculture and forestry at the headquarters of the Reifa. The section promoted efforts to improve the organization for placing of agricultural workers. Farm sections were established in local offices supervised by tripartite committees, and the staff of placement officers with agricultural experience was increased considerably. Both the law of 1922 and that of 1927 ruled that profit-making agencies had to end on January 1, 1931. This practical placement monopoly involved the serious obligation of building up an efficient public service since profit-making agencies heretofore had been placing 27 per cent of all farm workers placed by employment offices in 1927.[26] At the end of 1930[27] 323 such offices were still in existence. Non-profit agencies continued to work. No coercion was exercised in the hiring of workers. Farmers were not obliged to register vacancies, nor workers to apply for work at the offices. The fact that the unemployment insurance act obliged the unemployed to report regularly to the employment offices was an indirect compulsion for workers to use the public placement service.

Beginning in 1926, the absurd contradiction of a labor shortage in agriculture despite thousands of unemployed in the towns, many of whom had come from agriculture, forced the employment administration to improve the placement service. One notable improvement was the employment of field

[25] *First Reifa Report*, October 1, 1927, to December 31, 1928 (Bibl. #139, 1929, Sonderbeilage, No. 6, pp. 80-81).

[26] Regierungsrat Ehmke, "Aufhebung gewerbsmässiger Stellenvermittlung," Bibl. #139, 1931, Vol. II, p. 30. In 1927, 520,000 farm workers were placed by public offices, and 50,000 by non-profit private agencies. According to statistics published in Bibl. #139, 1930, 1932, 1933, and 1935 (*second, third, fourth, and sixth Reifa Reports*), the placement by public offices in the following years developed as follows:

1927	520,600
1928	561,900
1929	589,100
1930	478,000
1931	401,800
1932	355,300
1933	739,295

The decrease of placements from 1929 to 1932 was due to the depression. Since about a million more workers were usually employed on farms during the season than during the winter and the number of other workers fluctuated, the figures show that public offices succeeded only in getting a fraction of all placements (Petersen, "Der Aufbau der landwirtschaftlichen Arbeitsvermittlung der öffentlichen Arbeitsnachweise," Bibl. #139, 1928, Vol. II, pp. 285ff.).

[27] *Third Reifa Report for the Year 1930* (Bibl. #139, 1932, Sonderbeilage No. 7, pp. 31-32).

officers who visited farms in the district to find out which workers were needed and to investigate conditions, especially in housing.

3. DIRECTION OF YOUTH AND TRANSFER OF CITY WORKERS TO AGRICULTURE

During periods of rural exodus serious attempts were made to induce former agricultural workers who had migrated to the cities to return to agricultural work and young boys from the western mining districts who were not yet legally allowed to go into mining to accept jobs on farms.

In the first period those attempts met with no success because the workers were not yet selected according to their qualifications for the job and the conditions on the farm. Young people returning from the trenches were hungry for city life and not inclined to stay in rural solitude. Neither were farmers ready to accept city people, whom they suspected of being radicals. The employment offices were not yet qualified to overcome these difficulties.[28] It was estimated in 1921 that 60 to 80 per cent of transferred city workers did not remain on the job. With improvement of the placement service the task could be handled more efficiently. The vocational guidance service gave information on farm work and tried to direct children leaving school to agriculture. In some farming districts several employment offices jointly ran a vocational guidance department. In others, teachers were employed to give advice in addition to their regular school work.[29] Workers were carefully selected from among those who had grown up in the country; lower age groups were preferred and retrained. Public subsidies were granted, with the obligation to carry through instructions of the President of the Reifa[30] and the Federal Ministry of Labor.[31] In the provinces of Saxony and Anhalt, employers' organizations, farm workers' unions and miners' unions came to an agreement with the local employment office in 1924. Every vacancy was carefully investigated in order to check up on food, housing, and the willingness of the employer to train the workers. The latter were accompanied by

[28] A high official wrote: "It is disastrous—as was done in the beginning—to let a crowd of unemployed loose in the country without selecting, preparing, guiding, and supervising them adequately. The result was that, after a few days, they returned to the city without having done any work but taking with them all kinds of articles." Bardow, "Erwerbslosenfürsorge durch Ueberführung grosstädtischer Erwerbsloser auf das Land," Bibl. #139, 1921, Nichtamtlicher Teil, p. 850.

[29] In 1926-1927 the figure of boys and girls seeking advice for agriculture was 15,561 boys, 6,445 girls; in 1927-1928, 12,936 boys and 4,655 girls. "Die öffentliche Berufsberatung in Deutschland nach der Berufsberatungsstatistik von 1926-1927," Bibl. #139, 1928, Vol. II, p. 256, and Bibl. #153c, 1929, p. 277.

[30] Circular of January 25, 1922 (Bibl. #139, pp. 66ff.).

[31] Circular of April 10, 1923 (ibid., p. 283); and of March 3, 1924 (ibid., pp. 121ff.).

an official of the employment office to their working place, received clothing and food during transportation. There was also a continued observation of workers after they had been placed.[32]

Retraining was done in either of two ways. Frequently boys were placed on selected peasant farms, the holders of which received special compensation for the training (Anlernzuschuss). Conditions of the grant after 1930 were that no agricultural workers were available and that a contract of employment for at least six months had to be concluded. Although it was not easy to overcome the family farmer's prejudice against the city population, this method proved very successful. The second method consisted of short practical courses in special estate schools established either by charity organizations, by the German Farm Workers' Central (as Fliegerhorst at Frankfort a.O.), or by the public authorities.[33] When in 1930 unemployment began to penetrate agriculture, retraining and placing of industrial workers in agriculture had to be stopped.

4. VOLUNTARY LABOR SERVICE

Of the measures to fight unemployment, voluntary labor service was especially important for agriculture. The labor service of German youth—originally an educational experiment designed to teach young people from all social strata to live and work together—was used during the depression to acquaint youth with labor and to give them a feeling of doing useful work. From June 5, 1931[34] on, the Reich government and the Reifa financed management and upkeep, leaving it to public authorities and nonprofit associ-

[32] In 1923, 14,000 urban workers were placed in agriculture, of whom 30 to 35 per cent left. In 1925, 23,000 urban workers were placed in agricultural work (among them 10,000 young people); in 1926, 28,900 (especially from Rhineland, Westphalia, and State Saxony); in 1928, 116,700; in 1929, 90,400 (Bibl. #139, 1927, Vol. II, p. 153; ibid., p. 4); Second Reifa Report (Bibl. #139, 1930, No. 12, p. 25); Third Reifa Report (Bibl. #139, 1932, No. 7, p. 25).

[33] In Fliegerhorst unemployed young workers (twenty to twenty-five years of age) were trained for farm work in courses lasting from four to six weeks. Upon completion of the course the students were sent to selected peasant farms. The scheme seems to have worked successfully since in 1929 only 306 out of 1,599 students left the school before completing the course; 1,050 were brought into farm work, about 40 per cent on larger estates (Second Reifa Report, Bibl. #139, 1930, No. 12, p. 26). In 1930, 1,000 students were provided by Fliegerhorst, 130 by a Protestant school (Third Reifa Report, Bibl. #139, 1932, No. 7, p. 26). In 1932, the Reifa stopped supporting the schools, which then had to close.

[34] Bibl. #140, Vol. I, p. 279, and Decree of June 23, 1931 (Bibl. #140, Vol. I, p. 398); Decrees of June 14, 1932 (ibid., Vol. I, pp. 273, 283); July 16, 1932 (ibid., Vol. I, p. 353); August 2, 1932 (ibid., Vol. I, p. 392).

ations to provide the work, and to charitable, educational, and youth organizations to provide education. Most of the young people lived in camps. On October 31, 1932, 81,890 worked on land improvements; 25,427 in forestry; 25,169 in land colonization and small gardening.[35] Girls did household work. Boys and girls worked half a day and spent the rest of the day at lectures, sports, and games. They received pocket money and could elect to have a portion of it credited toward a future purchase of a small holding or homestead.

Migratory Workers

At the end of the nineteenth century a migratory movement started which may be considered as a late offspring of the Industrial Revolution. When commercial goods replaced home-made goods on the farms, when the threshing machine was introduced, the farm could no longer occupy all its workers all year round. The seasonal character of farm work was augmented by the extension of sugar-beet cultivation which required from three to five times as many hands from April to November as were needed in the normal grain culture. Saxony was the first province to which migratory workers from the eastern parts of Germany were attracted;[36] later as beet culture spread to other parts of central and eastern Germany, the movement also spread. In the east, with its unfavorable climate, it was still more difficult to distribute operations over the year. Outside eastern Prussia and the sugar-beet districts, the migratory laborer was of small importance. The chief reasons for the migration of German workers, who could often have found employment near their homes, were that wages were higher in other parts of the country, and that they were disinclined to work under known patriarchal conditions. When the volume of migration of German workers to agricultural work in other parts of the country decreased as a result of the attraction of Rhenish Westphalian industry and the progress of agriculture in the eastern provinces, foreign labor was introduced.[37]

[35] President Syrup, "Der freiwillige Arbeitsdienst für die männliche deutsche Jugend," Bibl. #139, 1932, Vol. II, pp. 382ff.; *Statistische Beilage zum RABl* 1932, No. 34, p. 12. The movement which started with 106 volunteers in 1931 had increased to 235,000 in April 1932 (Bibl. #153e, 1936, No. 4, p. 134).

[36] In the nineteenth century migratory workers were named according to the part of the country from which they came or to which they migrated: Landsberger, Hollandgänger, etc.

[37] In Mecklenburg-Schwerin the percentage of foreign workers among all those seasonally employed increased from 30 per cent in 1902 to 62 per cent in 1906 (Hermann Wenkstern, "Landwirtschaftliche Wanderarbeiter in Mecklenburg 1902 und 1906," Bibl. #159, 1906, p. 425, quoted by Werner Radetzki, Bibl. #66, p. 31).

Four main groups of migratory workers existed in postwar Germany:[88] 1) German agricultural workers who left their homes during the season and returned to them in the autumn, and who often owned a plot of land; 2) migratory German workers who had lost their homes and lived nomadic lives—on farms in summer, in shelters for the homeless, charity institutions, or huts in winter; 3) foreign migratory workers who returned to their homelands after the harvest; 4) industrial workers who in times of unemployment sometimes accepted seasonal employment in agriculture.

Recruiting German workers was done by employment offices, agents of the employers, wildcat agencies, or as a rule by workers who tried to provide their employer of the previous year with as many hands as he needed. The employer paid the traveling expense of all who did not break the contract; he also provided food and housing as part of the remuneration. The workers were generally crowded in large dormitories in cheaply constructed barracks, many of which had no lavatories; vermin were not infrequent; and moral conditions were at a low level. Migratory workers, therefore, became a floating population of a very low type.

No figures exist on the nomadic worker. In the winter of 1928-1929 Berlin was faced with the great problem of caring for about 2,000 such persons,[39] of providing decent shelter for families, education for the children, and, if possible, winter occupation for the men.

Foreign migratory workers were employed mainly on large estates and in sugar-beet cultivation. Unemployment after the war, the resentment of German labor over the practice of undercutting wages, and the obvious fact that low working standards of foreigners contributed to the rural exodus of German workers forced the government to reverse the policy of the open door which had been pursued until the war. Although the Joint Association of Agricultural Employers' Organizations and Trade Unions in 1919 had resolved to limit employment of aliens to estates which could not get German

---

[88] There are no reliable official statistics of the number of German migratory workers. A study by Radetzki, carried through with the help of the district employment offices, found 16,826 workers, 13,004 of whom were women, who migrated in 1927 from five eastern Prussian provinces (*op.cit.*, Bibl. #66, p. 35). The complete figure for that year has been estimated at 25,000 to 30,000 migratory workers. An inquiry by the Reifa from October to December 1929, which may not have been complete, got a total of 20,636 for Germany, 9,000 of whom were women (*Erhebung der Reichsanstalt für Arbeitsvermittlung und Arbeitslosenversicherung* von October 10-December 15, 1929).

[39] Frieda Wunderlich, "Die Not der Kinder wandernder Landarbeiter," Bibl. #150, January 8, 1930, pp. 45ff.

workers, employers renewed their efforts in the next two years to obtain foreign workers, claiming inability to meet the more exacting demands of German labor. Since the food situation made an increase of agricultural production necessary, the intended complete prohibition of foreign work was not enforced. Instead a system of annual quotas was established. The government had a twofold aim: to re-establish the seasonal character of migration, which had disappeared during the war, and to return to their own countries those foreign workers who had settled in Germany during the war. Whereas heretofore only police measures, such as the issuing of identity cards, had been used, the government began to exercise certain controls, the chief principle of which was that foreign workers should be employed only where no German workers were available. Recruiting and placing of alien workers were gradually brought under control of the public employment offices until by decree of January 23, 1933,[40] it was reserved for the Reifa. Workers could be employed only between February 15 and December 15. Foreign seasonal workers at first came from Poland, later also from Czechoslovakia, Yugoslavia, Austria, and Hungary. The German government cooperated with foreign governments under special agreements. On November 24, 1927,[41] a treaty was signed which regulated emigration of Polish workers to Germany and stipulated that it should be seasonal. The treaty was deemed to be tacitly renewable from year to year.

Only those workers who had entered Germany and settled there before January 1, 1919, and those for whom repatriation would have caused undue hardship, were entitled to remain in Germany on the basis of an exemption certificate. Agricultural workers who had arrived between January 1, 1919, and December 31, 1925, were to be progressively incorporated in the seasonal movement by the annual repatriation of a certain number from 1928 to 1932.

The Treaty accorded Polish agricultural workers the same treatment enjoyed by German workers in all matters pertaining to their protection, freedom of association, public assistance, and the regulation of the conditions of work, including arbitration and labor court procedure. They were exempt from income tax, entitled to accident and sickness insurance. Invalidity insurance was granted only to those in possession of an exemption certificate. They were not included in unemployment insurance.

The incentive to replace German by foreign workers was reduced when

---

[40] Bibl. #140, Vol. I, p. 26.

[41] Bibl. #121b, 4, pp. 148ff. Law of March 31, 1928 (Bibl. #140, Vol. II, p. 167). Treaties with Czechoslovakia and the Serb, Croat, and Slovene Kingdom followed.

the unions succeeded in having included in the contract worked out by the agricultural committee of the Reifa the provision that cash wages and hours of work were to correspond to those of German workers under collective agreements, the same rates for overtime, and piecework applying to both. Thus savings could be effected only through housing conditions which German workers, accustomed to a higher standard of living, refused to accept. One of the chief obstacles to attracting German workers was the lack of service dwellings. The government exerted every effort to substitute German for foreign workers by improving conditions and encouraging the building of decent dwellings.

The authorities compelled farmers to employ German instead of foreign workers, refusing permits in stages—first for nonseasonal work, then for estates producing crops other than beets, then for small- and medium-sized farms producing beets—reducing thereby the immigration quota. The quota was fixed annually and was determined on the basis of the estimated need for foreign labor.

The maximum quota of 436,736 foreign workers, reached in 1914, decreased from year to year until it reached zero in 1932 (except for those having the exemption permit).[42] Thus a development which had started in the seventies seemed to have come to an end.

Around 1924 a youth movement known as the Artamanen (guardians of the soil, Hüter der Scholle) got under way. Young people who yearned

[42] Foreign workers admitted:

Year	Quota	With Exemption Certificate
1913-1914	436,700	
1921	293,900	
1924	107,200	2,400
1925	136,800	2,200
1926	124,000	10,800
1927	118,500	18,800
1929	115,300	25,500
1930	100,300	32,400
1931	44,100	35,500

Source: Bibl. #153c. In 1930 the full quota admitted was not required. As clandestine work could not be prevented, the figures are underestimates. The Workers' Central reported for Prussia:

1924	140,707
1925	207,058
1926	185,711
1927	197,317

Source: Friedrich Zahn. *Wirtschaftsaufbau Deutschlands* (Bibl. #33, p. 964). About 90 per cent of the workers admitted were Poles, 80 per cent women. Foreign workers were chiefly employed on large estates with more than 100 ha.

to transfer from mechanical to nature work went into the harvest fields to displace foreign agricultural workers. Their number increased from 125 in 1925 to about 600-1,014 in 1927,[43] and 2,000 in 1928.[44] After having been harvesters for one or more years, they returned to their work in the cities.[45] Each group consisted of from four to twenty boys and one girl. Members had to pledge themselves not to smoke and not to drink. Friends of the movement hailed it as a reversal of the flight from the land, a flight "from mechanics to eugenics."[46] From 1931 on, when the National Socialist Artam League in Mecklenburg was founded, the National Socialists tried to gain a foothold in the movement.[47] They used it for preparing the revolution.[48]

[43] Bibl. #104b, pp. 21, 181; Bibl. #136, erstes Artamanenheft, 1927.
[44] Bibl. #136, viertes Artamanenheft, November 1928.
[45] E. Wilke, "Die Artamanenbewegung," Bibl. #101, Vol. 1, Nos. 4-5, January-March 1929, pp. 41ff. Members of the movement were united in the League Artam.
[46] Dr. Schiele-Naumburg, ibid., pp. 46ff.
[47] Albert Wojirsch in Bibl. #272, September 15, 1934, p. 17.
[48] Rudolf Proksch, "Zurück aufs Land," Bibl. #327, April 1937, p. 824.

CHAPTER IV

PROTECTIVE LEGISLATION

For a short period after the proclamation of November 12, 1918, agricultural workers were subject only to the provisions of the Civil Code. Then labor laws following one another in rapid succession to carry out the Joint Agreement of Employers' Associations and Trade Unions (concerning collective bargaining, arbitration, labor courts, works councils, compulsion to employ disabled war veterans) included agricultural labor on an equal footing. The Provisional Agricultural Labor Act of January 24, 1919 (Vorläufige Landarbeitsordnung, LAO), was supposed to provide protection for farm labor similar to that provided for the factory worker in the Industrial Code. It covered all undertakings and employees (German and alien workers and salaried employees whether permanent or temporary) in agriculture, forestry, and their subsidiary enterprises. The LAO contained only minimum requirements which were to be adhered to in the conclusion of contracts. In contrast to the Ordinance it replaced, no oppressive duties of workers were mentioned. It remained for contracts to fix more favorable conditions.

The enforcement of the LAO was largely in the hands of the employers' organizations and trade unions as no special machinery had been provided for its administration. Though intended only as temporary, the LAO remained the only special law governing agricultural labor.

Wages

In order to prevent misunderstandings concerning the quantity and nature of wages, which easily arise where wages in kind are fixed for a long period, the law provided that in the absence of collective agreements, contracts concluded for a period of more than six months had to be drawn up in writing in cases in which remuneration in kind was stipulated. Wages paid in kind had to be of average quality. Dwellings, the use of land, and other services which have no market value had to be definitely stated in writing at their money value. In cases of yearly contracts the remuneration had to be fairly distributed over the different seasons. (Former contracts sometimes provided only one-third pay during the winter.) Retention of wages as security for the payment of damages in cases of breach of contract was not to exceed a certain percentage. Pensions for disabled soldiers or survivors of war victims could not be counted as part of wages.

Housing

Housing was required to be acceptable with respect both to moral environment and health conditions, and, in the case of married people, to be adequate in relation to the sexes and the number of children. Rooms for the unmarried had to be heated, provide locks, and to contain adequate furniture.

Hours of Work

Hours of work were to be restricted to a daily average of eight during four months, ten during four months, and eleven during the remaining four. This meant a total of 2,900 and an average working day of 9⅔ hours. Overtime was to be at least time and a half at the rate of one-tenth of the local daily rate. Regular working time included time of travel to and from the farm to the place of work; however, workers who were under contract for animal feeding did not receive overtime pay for this work. Feeding and care of animals performed by workmen who did not undertake it by contract was calculated as overtime. For other pressing Sunday work at least double the local wage had to be paid. At least two rest periods of an hour each per day were required during the summer months and were not included in working hours.

Periods of Notice

Since the LAO did not prescribe periods of notice the provisions of the Civil Code[1] had to be applied. According to the latter the legal term of notice depended on the period for which the remuneration was fixed.[2] Other periods could be agreed upon. Under certain circumstances the worker could be dismissed or could quit without notice. As important reasons for premature (immediate) termination of contract, the LAO mentioned deeds of violence, gross insults, immoral proposals to the other party to the contract, constant refusal to perform the work required or gross neglect of work, repeated delay in the payment of wages, continual bad food, and unhealthful dwelling places. In cases of premature dissolution of contract, the products of the land granted to the worker were to be allotted to him in proportion to the services rendered on the basis of the average production of the area in question. The employer had to allocate to workers with their own households a rent-free dwelling for three weeks after the expiration of the contract, provided that

[1] Section 621.
[2] If wages were fixed by the day, then one day's notice could be given; if by month, notice had to be given on the fifteenth to take effect at the end of the month, and so forth.

it was terminated prematurely through no fault of the workers; in case the latter were at fault, only a fortnight was required with payment of rent.

The right of the employer to dismiss was further restricted by the right of the works council[3] to protest if there was ground for suspicion of sex, political, religious, or trade union discrimination, if the dismissal seemed to be unjust and involved hardship not occasioned by the behavior of the employee or the condition of the undertaking, or if it took place without statement of reason or because the worker refused to undertake regularly some work other than that agreed upon at the date of his employment. If the council considered the appeal justified, it tried to bring about an understanding. Failing this, the council or employee could appeal to the labor court. If the court considered the protest justified, the employer was obliged either to reinstate the employee with back pay or to pay one month's compensation for each year of service the employee had worked on the farm, not to exceed six months. The economic situation of the employee and the farmer had to be taken into consideration. Accident and war invalids (Schwerkriegsbe-schädigte)[4] could be dismissed only with the consent of the authority.

Work Rules

Work rules were to be issued in agreement with the works council and posted in a conspicuous place. They had to contain provisions with regard to hours of work as well as to penalties and the use to be made of fines which were to be applied only for the benefit of the workers in a particular undertaking.

Safety Rules

Safety rules were not included in the LAO, but were issued by the workmen's compensation associations.

Protection of Women

The LAO completely neglected the protection of women. The main provision concerning women's work was that women who had the care of a household had to be released from work early enough to allow them to reach home at least one hour before their main meal. They could not be required to work on the days before Christmas, Easter, and Whitsuntide. Women who had the care of a large household, especially those who had to provide meals for laborers in addition to their own family, were required

[3] BRG, Section 84.
[4] Gesetz über die Beschäftigung Schwerkriegsbeschädigter of January 12, 1923 (Bibl. #140, I, p. 58), section 13 and amendments.

to work only insofar as this did not seriously affect their household duties. Thus "protection" was given to household work, but not to women. No restrictions on work were provided for the time before and after childbirth.[5]

Child Labor

It is remarkable that the only law drawn up by labor itself neglected to protect the weakest group, children. And yet child labor had always played an important role in German agriculture. It was prevalent not only on the family farm but in the cultivation of root crops, which depended on the labor of the family. Child labor increased as the size of the estate decreased.[6] A considerable number of children lived with peasants without belonging to them by any natural tie, e.g. orphans or children from reformatories, placed out by the municipal authorities. According to the occupational census of June 16, 1925,[7] 390,412 children under fourteen years of age (202,098 boys and

[5] The sickness insurance law provided the same maternity benefits before and after childbirth for women in agriculture as for industrial workers.

[6] While in Central Germany 3 per cent of all labor was performed by children in holdings of 5-20 ha. in 1925, the percentage fell to two in holdings from 2-100 ha. and to one in estates of more than 100 ha. (Bibl. #104b, 1929, p. 333).

[7]	1907	1925	1933	1939
a) Children working for their own families				
Permanently	103.256	201.267		122.971
Temporarily	288.364	148.121		
Total	391.620	349.388	61.470	122.971
b) Children employed by strangers				
Permanently	48.034	21.457		
Temporarily	72.674	19.367		
Total	120.708	41.024	20.258	13.329
Total number of working children (a and b together)				
Permanently	151.290	222.724		
Temporarily	361.038	167.688		
Grand total	512.328	390.412	81.728	136.300

Source for 1907 data: Bibl. #153e, 1907, No. 19, pp. 803ff. The figures of the census of 1907 (Bibl. #153b,1. pp. 606-607) have been calculated above for the smaller Reich territory of 1925. Children in forestry and on farms below 5 acres, included only in the 1907 census, have been deducted.

Source for 1933 data: Bibl. #153b,6, pp. 4-5. The figures for 1925 and 1933 are not

188,314 girls) were employed in agriculture. A comparison of these figures with those of 1907 shows a decrease of 121,916 in contrast to the increase in the total number of persons of all ages in agricultural occupations during the same period. The proportion of children to the total number of persons fell therefore from 4 per cent to 2.7 per cent (mostly in peasant holdings from 20 to 100 ha.). The absolute decrease in all agricultural child labor was nearly 25 per cent made up of an absolute decrease of 66 per cent in child labor in the employment of strangers (including an absolute decrease of over 50 per cent in the number of children permanently in such employment) and an absolute increase of over 90 per cent in the number of children working permanently for their parents.

The decrease of child labor from 1907 to 1925 was due in part to a reduction in size of the five- to ten-year age group in consequence of the decrease of births during the war, and in part to the displacement of children by other workers, e.g. on very small holdings, by their fathers who, owing to the shortened working day, could themselves cultivate their plot after their day's work. Unemployment, the introduction of machinery, efforts of employment offices to transfer unemployed to farm work were other causes.[8]

The census of 1933 showed another large decline to 81,700 employed children (43,160 boys and 38,560 girls) under fourteen years of age; 265,612 children between fourteen and sixteen years (137,129 boys and 128,483 girls) were employed.

The need for safeguarding the child was realized very late. Life in the open air and the manifold interests of country life were considered to be valuable factors of education. It was not easy to distinguish occasional help from regular employment. As it was, parents, especially those who needed their children on the farm, often ignored the fact that such an occupation

---

quite comparable since the former are taken from the census of personnel on farms (Betriebsstatistik), the latter from that of occupations (Berufsstatistik). However, a considerable decrease is certain.

Source for 1939 data: Bibl. #153e, 1941, No. 11, p. 209. Not counted were children who helped as family members (Bibl. #310, 1938, Vol. 1, p. 353).

Census figures never give a complete picture of child labor. The restriction of counting to one day (June 16), a date on which those children working only during the early spring and harvest were not included, as well as the inclination to conceal child labor, tend to make the census figures unreliable. How huge the gap between census figures and actual work may become may be judged from the fact that the official inquiry of 1904 revealed 1,769,800 children employed by strangers, while the census of 1907 counted only 137,291 such children (Hanna Marcuse, "Landwirtschaftliche Kinderarbeit," Bibl. #150, March 29, 1928, p. 291).

[8] Hanna Marcuse, ibid., April 5, 1928, pp. 313ff.

might not be reconcilable with the health and the educational needs of the child, and that children might be robbed of their childhood by excessive work.

The German revolution which gave the agricultural laborer his proper place in the social order "may be said to have forgotten the children."[9] The LAO referred to children only in connection with provisions for housing accommodations for the worker which had to be adequate for his children. Collective agreements generally did not provide for children. Organized labor was convinced that the improvement of its own conditions of work would make all other protective legislation unnecessary.

The resolution of the International Labor Organization in 1920 to discuss child labor in agriculture stimulated the German Association for Child Protection (Deutscher Kinderschutzverband) to undertake a nationwide inquiry (from January to May 1922). Ten thousand questionnaires were sent to all kinds of organizations and to persons such as clergymen, teachers, and others. The Ministry of Labor which sponsored the work appointed Helene Simon, an outstanding scholar, to evaluate the data. She compared her findings with German and Austrian government inquiries of 1904[10] and 1908 respectively. Her study is the only comprehensive source of information available in this field.

The study of 1922 covered only a small part of the occupied children but provided a typical picture. It covered 400,000 children who were employed by their own parents and 100,000 employed by others. The study revealed that children of all ages were working for their parents, in a few instances even at four years of age. The most frequent age for admission to outside employment was twelve; in the immediate family six to nine. Hours of work varied from two to twelve a day with the season; during school vacations children not working for their parents began at ten years of age to work the same hours as adults; while school was in session, they worked from four to five hours a day.[11] The amount of work done per week was considerable.

Work before school hours and immediately after impaired education; insufficient sleep impaired health. Much of the work—leading and driving of animals, machine work with sharp tools, carrying of loads—was heavy, dirty, and precarious. Moreover, it involved risk of accident to the children,

[9] Helene Simon (Bibl. #78), p. v.

[10] The inquiry of 1904 which covered 1,769,800 public school children employed in agriculture, excluded employment of children by their own parents.

[11] Helene Simon, *op.cit.*, pp. 329ff.

dulled their intelligence, and, because of contact with adult and sometimes degraded companions, was dangerous morally. Overwork and exploitation of children were considered by many of the persons questioned as a reason for the rural exodus. Children who acquired a distaste for agricultural work were inclined to migrate to the cities as soon as they were old enough.

The study by Helene Simon gave rise to discussion of necessary protective legislation, e.g. fixing an age for admission to employment, regulating hours, prohibiting dangerous work. The Association for Social Reform[12] in co-operation with the Association for Rural Social Welfare (Verein für länd-liche Wohlfahrts-und Heimatpflege) established a committee composed of representatives of employers' and workers' organizations to deal with these problems.

The discussion revealed that in the opinion of the employers child labor was unavoidable for certain light agricultural operations, e.g. weeding, as such work required a physical adaptability which adult workers had lost. Both employers and labor representatives agreed that child labor should be limited to light operations.

The Social Democratic party introduced a motion in the Reichstag[18] which included the committee's recommendations as well as a recommenda-tion that the same restrictions be provided for children employed as hired labor in agriculture as were provided for children in nonindustrial occupa-tions by the Act of 1903. This would have meant twelve years as the age of admission. The socialist trade unions of farm workers accepted a similar resolution in its fourth general assembly in 1926. In spite of all such resolu-tions, however, organized labor was afraid to risk tampering with the LAO and refrained from pushing legislation in this field.

Children in agricultural work therefore were protected merely by the indirect operation of school laws. Article 145 of the Weimar Constitution put compulsory attendance up to fourteen years of age on a nationwide basis, but this was not immediately adopted by every state. As fixed by the Bavarian law the age limit was reached at the end of the school year following the child's thirteenth birthday, if the prescribed standard of knowledge was attained. Moreover, exemptions could be admitted for agricultural seasonal work for short periods (in Prussia two months a year; a whole year for children thirteen years of age in cases of poverty of parents. Similar exemp-tions were permitted in other states). The yearly minimum period of

[12] Bibl. #150, May 6, 1926, p. 442ff.
[18] On February 16, 1926 (Drucksache No. 1894, III, 1924-1926).

attendance was 40 weeks. As afternoons were free, much farm work could be done after school hours. In Bavaria the school day was shortened during the summer to enable children to assist their parents in the fields or to help the school principal in cultivating his plot of land. The larger Bavarian cities made school attendance compulsory up to fourteen years. The farmers therefore used to retain their children in agriculture for a year before sending them to the cities for industrial work. In Prussia Polish children were not included in the compulsory school attendance laws. Some state regulations tried to prevent exploitation of children.[14]

Tenant Protection

Workers whose contracts of labor provided tenancy—the Heuerlings in Westphalia and Hanover—were protected, together with other tenants, by the order protecting leaseholders. Although tenancy did not form the basis of the agrarian structure—only 10.7 per cent of the agricultural area was on lease in 1936[15]—it was an important addition to independent ownership of land not sufficient to provide a livelihood and a means of climbing the agricultural ladder to independent ownership. Small tenancy as well as the Heuerlings' constitution was threatened shortly after the war when the better food supply of the farm population and the insecurity of money values induced owners to withdraw land from tenants. They gave notice to their Heuerlings in order to raise the price or to till the land themselves. Moreover, the period of currency inflation disturbed the relation of the landlord to the tenant who paid his rent in cash. In order to check evictions and an immoderate increase of rental rates, the Reich Tenant Protection Order was enacted on June 9, 1920.[16] It authorized the Laender to establish

[14] In 1928 the Baden State Youth Welfare Office (Badisches Jugendwohlfahrtsamt) issued a regulation to all youth offices concerning selection and employment of children in cattle tending in the pastures. They prescribed a medical certificate for each child and the exclusion of all children with physical ailments. They stipulated minimum requirements for accommodation and board, guarantee of night rest and school attendance, The Youth Offices were obliged to supervise these children as they did foster children (Bibl. #150, June 14, 1928, p. 570).

[15] Bibl. #153c, 1936, p. 77. The proportion of leased land rises to 16.6 per cent if considered in relation to the agricultural area after deduction of forest land. Pure tenancy was only important among the very small and the very large holdings. Only 6.2 per cent of all farmers were tenants proper. There was no share tenancy. One third of the rented land consisted of the smallest types of holding under 2 ha. and was partly horticultural or vineyards, partly ground held by people who were not primarily agriculturists.

[16] Pachtschutzordnung (Bibl. #140, I, p. 1193). The provisions of the Act were renewed and extended from time to time and reduced in certain particulars. The states made use by special rules of power given to them.

tenancy offices (Pachteinigungsämter), composed of representatives of owners and tenants with a judge as chairman to settle rent disputes. They were entitled to supervise the fixing of rents for all farms. In cases concerning small farms (at first those up to 2.5, later to 10 ha.) and of all Heuerlings, they had the power to permit postponement of a notice for two years (later, one year); they could void an eviction notice and authorize the breach of a rent contract before completion of the term. In almost all cases landlords were compelled to procure other accommodations for evicted tenants. Originally intended as a temporary measure, the legislation was renewed again and again.

CHAPTER V

TRADE UNIONS OF AGRICULTURAL WORKERS[1]

Types and Membership

ONLY AFTER the Reich Association Act of 1908 had removed some of the worst handicaps was the formation of farm workers' unions possible. In 1909, free trade unions in cooperation with the Social Democratic party founded a union of agricultural and forestry workers which in 1913 adopted the name "German Agricultural Workers' Union" (Deutscher Landarbeiterverband, DLV). Prior to its formation, some agricultural workers had been organized in the free factory workers' union. However, the interests of the unskilled industrial workers and farm workers were too divergent and the dues in the factory workers' union too high to attract many members from agriculture. The DLV affiliated with the federation of free (Socialist) trade unions, then known as the General Committee of Trade Unions. The organizers began in Central and South Germany because they expected violent resistance from the eastern squires. However, they soon learned that it was very difficult to organize the worker

---

[1] The German trade union movement, which had been in existence since the sixties but had gained momentum only since the nineties, comprised three distinct organizations. The Socialist "free trade union," which included 78 per cent of all organized workmen in 1925, federated after the World War into the General Federation of Free German Trade Unions (Allgemeiner Deutscher Gewerkschaftsbund, ADGB). Socialist salaried employees' unions formed their own head federation, the General Federation of Free Trade Unions of Salaried Employees (Allgemeiner Freier Angestelltenbund, Afa League). A second group, the Christian trade unions which included 9.5 per cent of all organized wage earners, had formed the Federation of Christian Trade Unions (Gesamtverband christlicher Gewerkschaften) which united after the war with unions of salaried employees in the Deutscher Gewerkschaftsbund (DGB), Confederation of German Trade Unions. A third branch, the liberal minded Hirsch Dunckers Unions, remained relatively small and did not make any headway among agricultural laborers. They united with a large salaried employees union in the Gewerkschaftsring Deutscher Arbeiter-, Angestellten- und Beamtenverbände, Confederation of Workers, Salaried Employees and Civil Servants. The trade unions gained tremendously in membership after the war but declined from 1923 on and began to recover again in 1927. The free trade unions had some 4.9 million members in 1929, the Christian wage earners unions 673,000, the Hirsch Dunckers 169,000. In the Joint Agreement of November 1918, the employers' associations had pledged themselves not to patronize any non-militant (so-called yellow) unions. In addition, there were some independent unions (for instance, a Polish union) and organizations of civil servants.

on small holdings who had no "class" consciousness. Much more response was found among workers on big estates. The organizers, therefore, turned to the east. As expected, the squires resisted. Police were sent to union meetings. In 1911 the Farmers' League demanded the union's dissolution because of its political character and because it advocated strikes.[2] On April 1, 1914, the union was notified by the president of the Berlin police that it was considered a political association,[3] but the old service ordinances were not used against it. In spite of all difficulties unionization proceeded. By the end of 1913, the DLV had a membership of 20,260 (among them 884 women), one-half of 1 per cent of all agricultural workers in Germany.

In 1912 a Christian trade union of the Vineyard, Forestry and Agricultural Workers was founded which adopted the name "Central Union of Agricultural Workers" (Zentralverband der Landarbeiter, ZV).[4] Like the DLV it was organized from above and did not spring up spontaneously. Its members were recruited principally from the vineyard workers of the Rhine and the forestry workers of Bavaria and the Harz. It affiliated with the Christian Trade Unions' Federation, had a membership of 3,776 at the end of 1913, of about 4,100 in 1917, and 6,900 in 1918. In addition, there existed a few small technical organizations: the Dairymen's Union (Allgemeiner Schweizerbund), founded in 1909, with 8,800 members in 1914, which after the war joined the ADGB, the same head federation as the DLV. A Catholic rural servants' organization was restricted to Bavaria and lost importance after the war.

The end of the war brought at once a loss of membership, because of the loss of German territory (especially Upper Silesia, Posen, Memel, West Prussia) and a tremendous gain, due to the greatly heightened spirit of class consciousness and sense of power of the workers, and the abolition of coalition restrictions. In the trenches the farm worker had learned about the labor movement. The soldiers were strongly resolved not to return to the old dependence. The first two years after the war brought a phenomenal

---

[2] Bibl. #112b, p. 3.

[3] President Schmidt at the fifth convention of the DLV (Bibl. #112l, p. 135). Unions as political organizations were prohibited to organize workers under 18 years of age. They had to provide the authorities with their statutes and membership lists and had to get the consent of the police for open air meetings. German was the only language permitted at public meetings.

[4] In 1929 the ZV changed its organization and name to Reichsverband ländlicher Arbeitnehmer, National Union of Rural Employees.

increase of membership: the DLV rose to 700,000, the ZV to 100,000 in 1920.[5] The sudden increase in the DLV from 8,000 at the end of the war to 624,935 at the end of 1919 almost upset the organization. The new members were inexperienced, exacting, and an easy prey of political radicals. There were not enough old officials to cope with the task, nor was it possible to select new officials carefully. If, up to this point, it had been the aim of the union to strengthen the self-confidence of the worker, it was now obliged to appease the craving for power of the masses. Moreover, the Communists worked for the dissolution of the unions, and in a circular of August 28, 1919,[6] they demanded the secession of local groups from the unions. When, from 1920 on, the "conquest" of unions by "boring from within" became the slogan, they tried to stir up strikes and to discredit union leadership. Although they met with little success, their attacks did weaken the DLV. When a district leader in Central Germany transformed his district into an independent syndicalistic union, the DLV lost more than 30,400 members, none of whom rejoined when the independent union disbanded[7] shortly afterward.

A decided drop in membership followed in the years of currency inflation (1922-1923), the DLV by 77.7 per cent, the ZV by 19 per cent, Catholic servants' union by 75 per cent. Inflation ruined the finances of the unions. Every attempt to adjust dues to currency depreciation resulted in loss of members. Officials spent their time in useless wage negotiations. No time was left for the education of members.

After the stabilization of the mark, the trade unions consistently consolidated their organization. Officials were instructed not to promise more than the union could fulfill. Those who had collaborated with the Communists were removed. From 1924 on, membership increased slowly but steadily,

---

[5] In 1921, at the peak of the union power, *Der Landarbeiter* (Bibl. #127, February 1, 1921) made the following estimate:

Unions	Members
DLV	780,000
ZV	130,000
Non-militant	50,000
Dairymen's	15,000
Communist	15,000
Gewerkverein der Deutschen Landarbeiter (Hirsch Duncker)	1,000
	991,000

[6] Bibl. #112a, pp. 6ff.
[7] Bibl. #112f, p. 6.

but reached only about one-quarter of the former size, with 167,444 members in the DLV in 1929. Gains were smaller than in industrial unions because of the exodus of farm workers to the cities. In 1927 the DLV had about 7-8 per cent, the ZV 3-5 per cent of all agricultural workers organized. The Dairymen's Union had succeeded in organizing 15,000 of 40,000 dairymen. The influence of the unions, however, extended far beyond their membership. The network of collective agreements was maintained. Noncovered employers frequently observed union standards in order to prevent their workers from organizing, sometimes granting even better terms to unorganized workers. In 1929, the DLV was able to report that "the time of toilsome construction is passed." The depression brought a slight decline beginning in 1929.

The two unions covered the entire Reich with their focus in Eastern and Central Germany. They included especially the deputatists on large estates.[8] Farm servants were less inclined to organize. In 1925, 12.4 per cent of the membership of the DLV and 16.7 per cent of the ZV were women. In 1928 71.26 per cent of the members of the DLV were farm workers, 24.24 per cent forest workers and 4.5 per cent below 18 years of age.[9]

Communist unions were set up at three different times. An association of family farmers and workers in 1919 (the Verband kommunistischer Landarbeiter und Kleinbauern), which rejected collective bargaining and recommended the expropriation of large estates by workers' councils and the abolition of mortgages on small holdings, developed into a family farmers' organization and disbanded. When the DLV expelled many Communist members in 1921, a Communist union (Verband der Land-und Waldarbeiter) was founded. In 1924 it proposed fusion with the DLV and, after the latter's refusal, dissolved. In 1931, another Communist union was set up, after the fifth Congress of the Red Trade Union International in Moscow in 1930 had officially sanctioned dual unionism. However, the Communists failed to win over employed workers and there were not enough unemployed farm workers to make a success of the Communist fight against what they termed the "Social Fascist" unions.

A more serious threat were the Landarbeiterbünde which had been founded with the help of employers. Local groups were organized in 1919 in Pomerania, others followed in Mecklenburg and Grenzmark. In 1920 they united

---

[8] On estates of more than 100 ha., about one third of the male and one sixth of the female workers were organized in 1929 (Bibl. #104b, p. 33).

[9] Bibl. #112l, p. 13.

into the Federal Land Workers' Union (Reichslandarbeiterbund, RLAB) which affiliated with the National League of Agrarians. The Pomeranian League of Agrarians, the model for the other leagues, was a coalition of all persons interested in the promotion of agriculture on a Christian and national basis. The League was formed horizontally by local and district groups as well as vertically by an employers' group and a workers' group, the last two forming a joint association. The regional joint associations were the wages and arbitration bodies whose decisions could be appealed in case of differences about principles.[10] The movement spread to other parts of eastern Prussia, but suffered a setback in 1928 when two of its organizations seceded and joined the ZV. The RLAB had a foothold in Pomerania and Mecklenburg-Strelitz. It gained during the last years of the Republic when the political parties of the Right, which backed the leagues, increased in power. Two estates under the administration of the Federal Minister of Defense which had had collective agreements with the DLV for ten years refused to negotiate in October 1932 because the estates had joined the Pomeranian Landbund which dealt only with its own organizations.

Philosophies and Programs

Although cooperating in practical policy, the DLV and the ZV stressed the fact that they represented different philosophies. The DLV, strongly influenced by unions in industry, clung to the ideas of class struggle and socialism. It was its aim to equalize conditions in city and country, in industrial and agricultural work. Patriarchal relations were to be replaced by free contracts. The agricultural worker was to receive cash wages and to have them raised to the level of the industrial worker. Hours were to be shortened, not in order to give the worker time to work on his plot of land, but to give him leisure. Independent living accommodations were to be provided. The DLV did not aim to convert the agricultural worker into a family farmer. It did not wish to eliminate all opportunities of this type of advancement, but considered it a concession in exceptional cases, reserved for the few—for cottagers and small land holders—not for laborers, although many of the rank and file were in favor of becoming independent landowners.

The ZV, whose members were conservative and more deeply rooted than

[10] On October 1, 1920, the total membership of the Pomeranian League was 120,000, of whom 35,000 were workers. The DLV at that time claimed 60,000 members in the province, the ZV 1,000. The total number of workers in Pomerania was 187,000 (Bibl. #21, 1922, p. 82).

the Socialists in national and religious traditions, though accepting the principle of workers' solidarity, emphasized the interest of the nation as of greater importance than that of the class. They considered a common interest in agriculture to have a stronger claim than the community of industrial

Average Membership of Agricultural Wage Earners in Trade Unions by Years[11]

	DLV		ZV		RLAB	Gewerk-verein HD
	Total	Number of Women	Total	Number of Women	Total	Total
End of 1913	20,267	884	4,116	....	....	. . ...
End of the war	8,000[a]	.... .	....	....	. . ..	....
End of 1919	265,862	63,602	55,775	9,403	....	......
1920	695,695	173,543	89,108	16,304	. .. .	. . ...
1921	636,414	155,480	103,722	28,482	. .. ...	......
1922	555,864	137,089	102,820	26,466	111,393	.. ...
1923	237,714	60,905	87,786	21,871	. . . .	. ...
1924	147,650	37,140	77,903	19,365	......	.. ..
1925	155,299	27,014	78,256	18,363	83,720	... ..
1926	138,154	18,376	..........[c]	..........[c]	78,000[d]	. .. ...
1927	131,181	14,682	77,387	17,920	82,000[d]	1760[e]
1928	151,273[b]	14,604	79,599	17,803[11]	84,000[d]	1891[e]
1929	167,444[b]	15,696	80,536	17,235[11]	....	.... .
1930	161,579[b]	15,091	72,749	....	... .	1789

[11] Bibl. #123, Nos. 25, 30, 36, 52.

[11a] Bibl. #112c, p. 46.

[11b] Bibl. #122, 1929, p. 340; 1930, p. 366.

[11c] No figures because of cleavages and dissolutions.

[11d] Information given by the president, Johannes Wolf. Latest figures published are from the beginning of 1926.

[11e] Mauricy Bergmann and Others, Bibl. #9, 1931, p. 256.

and farm workers. They demanded that a special rural culture be fostered in collaboration with teachers and clergy, that rural folk develop their own specific life pattern. They encouraged land ownership and considered the deputat and the leasing of land as rungs in the agricultural ladder, giving opportunity gradually to become a self-supporting farmer. The ideal of the DLV was the "free" worker; the ideal of the ZV, the independent land-owner. The DLV fought for abolition of Heuerlings' contracts, which the ZV considered as a step in the direction of land ownership. The Christian

Union considered wages in kind as a special advantage which might lead to ultimate independence. The free trade union saw in it a feudal remnant. The DLV demanded abolition, the ZV restriction, of the system under which members of the family or alien workers were called upon to offer their services under the farm workers' contract. Both the Socialist and the Christian trade unions would have impressed an American trade unionist as working-class movements, concerned not only for the welfare of their members but for the welfare and reform of society; only the Hirsch Duncker unions would have been recognized as business unions. Yet all German unions were, in addition to their political reform aims, real unions. They exercised their main functions in a way similar to that of unions in other western countries, but differed from American unions' in relying strongly on legislation rather than on collective bargaining in some fields. In practical trade union policy the course of the three German movements was the same. They were agreed in their demand for higher wages, shorter hours, workers' representation in chambers of agriculture, and abolition of foreign labor. Wherever the interests of workers were concerned, they were a united front, both with a high sense of solidarity. In the spring of 1918 the DLV and ZV issued a joint program demanding among other things the abolition of all discriminatory legislation, rural conciliation bodies, recognition of collective bargaining.[12] The program was carried out by the revolution of 1918. The joint program later included the improvement of the labor law and regulation of labor conditions by legislation and collective agreements, improved housing and education. Both recognized the strike as a weapon, but only as a last resort.

Both unions united in opposition to the RLAB, which refused to use the strike. The RLAB reflected the fact that class antagonism was less pronounced in agriculture than in industry and that rural life was determined by patriarchal relations. The union stressed the fact that no class division existed in agriculture where many small land owners were nearer to the worker than to the large estate owner. Not solidarity of labor, but solidarity of agriculture was claimed. Their philosophy was Christian, nationalistic, anti-Socialist, nonmilitant toward the employer. Although related in their philosophy, ZV and RLAB cooperated merely in cultural matters. Both bona fide trade unions accused the RLAB of lack of solidarity and independence. The bona fide unions pointed to the RLAB's pamphlet, "Landvolk wohin gehst Du?" ("Whither, people of the land?") published in 1926 in

---

[12] Bibl. #102, No. 2, pp. 113-14.

which employers were admonished to grant higher wages and better dwellings unless the Reichslandbund were to lose its worker members, but in which very little was said about the function of workers' organizations. The unions considered the tenor of the pamphlet submissive. "We protest against these eunuchs who cannot take care of themselves," said the president of the DLV.[13]

Functions

The functions of both *bona fide* unions were collective bargaining,[14] the legal protection of their members, advice as well as aid in the courts in all questions concerning work and social insurance. They gave benefits in case of victimizations, strike, death, and sickness (the ZV gave maternity aid and unemployment benefit in addition),[15] and aid in economic emergency.

Periodicals were used for educational purposes.[16] Both unions provided leisure-time cultural activities. In 1929 the ZV founded the Christian National Agricultural Workers' School in Berlin, which provided courses for workers. The institutions of Catholic cultural organizations were open to the Catholic members of the ZV, the socialist schools to those of the DLV. Functionaries of the unions—such as assessors in labor courts, members of works councils—and union officials were trained in schools or courses set up by the head federations (ADGB and DGB). Care was taken to prepare them in such a way as to make it possible for them to get employment in social insurance offices, public employment offices, wherever vacancies occurred, and thus strengthen union influence in these institutions. The DLV held seventy courses for works councilors in the winter 1928-1929, in which twenty to seventy members participated.[17] Common to all these schools and

---

[13] Bibl. #112c, p. 71.

[14] Activities of the DLV Involving Wage Actions:

Year	Total cases	Number of workers involved
1923	3,022	1,714,993
1924	492	2,371,719
1925	345	1,711,439
1926	280	2,749,398
1927	260	2,474,725
1928	219	2,123,110

Source: Bibl. #112g, p. 27; and Bibl. #112l, p. 24.

[15] The unions were financed by dues, in the DLV in 1927, to an average of 18.49 Rm. a year. The initiation fee in the DLV was 60pf., in the ZV 50pf., and for women 30pf. The unions were financially weak in comparison with the industrial unions. The DLV had a per capita income of 19.78 Rm. in 1927 as compared with 58.71 of the free building workers and 53.08 of the metal workers (Bibl. #122, 1927, pp. 258-59). Per capita expenditures amounted to 19.05 in the DLV (40.30 building workers, 32.23

courses was their two-fold aim: education in economics, labor law, and administration on the one hand, in the respective philosophy of the movement on the other. Residential schools of the head federations were not merely institutions of learning; they were meant to bring the workers into

metal workers). Both agricultural workers' unions received subsidies from their head federations.

Expenditures of the Trade Units

	DLV (1926) (138,100 members)		ZV (1926-1927) (77,300 members)	DLV (1929)	ZV (1929)	
	Rm.	Per Cent	Rm.	Per Cent	Per Cent	
Administration	1,384,900			66.0	39.2	
Organizing	333,600		251,900	17.4	13.0	Other
Wage increase agitation	136,000		145,100	5.1	19.0	Expenses
Benefits (friendly)	154,900	6.6	64,100	3.8	13.8	
Meetings	79,800		10,600			
Legal protection	47,000		55,000			
Victimization benefit	16,300	0.7				
Strike benefit	8,600	0.4				
Press	114,500		37,900	7.7	7	
Education	41,500		67,000		8	
Total	2,361,700		631,354	100	100	
Per member				21.28 Rm.	11.51 Rm.	

Source: Bibl. #123, 1930, pp. 139ff.; 145ff.; 153ff. A comparison of expenditures in the DLV with other free trade unions shows the difficulties which confronted the farm workers' unions. Since they could not rely on voluntary help but had to pay all functionaries, their administration costs amounted to 62.6 per cent of the total in 1927, while building workers paid 34.2 per cent, metal workers 30-37 per cent. On the other hand only 4.8 per cent could be spent by farm workers for friendly benefits (44.9 per cent by building, 38.8 per cent by metal workers). For organization work the DLV had to spend 12.3 per cent, the two others 4.5 per cent and 4.2 per cent respectively.

[16] The chief publication of the DLV was the weekly (since 1929 bi-weekly) *Landarbeiter* (1930 total edition of 170,000), with supplements *Landarbeiterin* and *Landarbeiterrecht*. Further, the DLV published district papers (with a total edition of 100,000 in 1928) and the *Landarbeiter-Archiv*, a "scientific" periodical which appeared every two months with a circulation of 1,700. A periodical for Polish workers appeared four to six times a year with a circulation of 20,000. A press service informed Socialist newspapers. With exception of the *Landarbeiter-Archiv* all publications were delivered without charge. The chief publication of the ZV was *Die Rundschau* with a total edition of 45,000 in 1930. Another periodical, *Der Berufsschweizer*, was issued for the Dairymen's Union. The Hirsch-Duncker's unions published *Der deutsche Landarbeiter*, with a circulation of 1,300; the RLAB, *Der Reichslandarbeiterbund*; the Communists issued *Der Land- und Forstarbeiter* (Franz Hering, Bibl. #112k, pp. 34, 59; Bergmann and others, Bibl. #9, pp. 343ff.).

[17] Bibl. #112l, p. 52.

close contact with the driving force and the aim of the movement and to strengthen working-class solidarity. Moreover, advanced education for union leaders was carried on in three schools financed by the Prussian State to which the unions could send their most promising officials. For the rank and file, films showing the work of the union and other matters of importance to the membership were presented at the local union offices.

The two unions cooperated in the nomination of representatives to all self-governing bodies. They were recognized as official representatives of agriculture wherever public functions had been delegated to joint bodies of employers' and employees' organizations. They nominated delegates to the National Economic Council; they provided lists of assessors for labor courts and arbitration bodies. Social insurance (except workmen's compensation) and the placement service were built upon the principle of self-government by employers and the insured. In sick funds, for example, they provided two-thirds of the delegates in all bodies; the placement service was practically run by the unions since employers restricted their cooperation to important questions and occasional nomination of officials. Functionaries were either elected, as in sickness and invalidity insurance and works councils, or nominated on the basis of organization lists. Labor representatives in the latter case were distributed according to a code agreed upon between the trade unions.[18] Wherever possible trade unions used their political power to replace elections by appointments, because this was an easy method of excluding outsiders and of suppressing opposition from the rank and file. Although the high standard of integrity of trade union functionaries prevented misuse of benefits or services, the monopoly established by appointments rather than elections was widely resented and gave the unions an erroneous impression of their power.

RLAB members were not admitted as assessors or representatives of labor in the public institutions of self-government. Within the RLB the county workers' associations (Kreisverbände) bargained with county employers' associations. The RLAB paid benefits to members and maintained its own employment office in Pomerania. Joint associations of workers' unions and

[18] In the Agricultural Committee of the Reifa, for instance, trade unions had seven seats and seven proxies, distributed as follows: 4 DLV (plus 3 proxies); 2 ZV (plus 2); one Union of Agricultural Salaried Employees (plus 1); Dairymen's Union one proxy (Bibl. #139, 1932, 1, p. 155). In 1928 the DLV had 280 representatives in all Reifa committees (including local and district), 180 in labor courts, 33 in chambers of agriculture, 3,190 in the sick funds, 700 in invalidity insurance, 430 in accident insurance bodies, 250 in other bodies (Bibl. #112l, pp. 7ff.).

employers' organizations within the RLB had an extensive program embracing all problems in the employer-worker relationship. Actually, however, they do not seem to have been concerned with more problems than the other collective agreement associations.

Political Influence

Political influence was exercised by union representatives in parliaments[19] or through their head federations. The unions wanted their officers to hold political offices in order to exercise political influence. In parliaments the delegates of various parties who were union officials formed blocs whenever union interests were concerned.[20] The Christian Union had ties with the Catholic Center party, the DLV was closely connected with the Social Democratic party, although in times of a Socialist split, "neutrality" had to be maintained. Union members who belonged to the Communist party were expelled only when their work in the union was controlled by party policy, i.e. when they joined Communist cells. Whenever the other Socialists were unified in one party, the DLV backed it openly in elections. The SPD weekly press helped the union to inform the rural population.[21] On the other hand "union meetings were frequently used to make up for the lack of party organization."[22]

Greater even than their indirect influence in parliaments and the RWR was the influence exercised directly on the government for which trade unions frequently provided Cabinet members. The unions were consulted when bills were being drafted which affected their interests. No important political, economic, or labor decision was made without their advice. Pressure was exerted by union petitions and memoranda usually in conjunction with the head federations. Zwing, the editor of the Gewerkschafts Archiv (of the free trade unions), wrote: "The parliament today is no longer the decisive arena it was, but an executive committee (Vollzugsausschuss) of the wishes

[19] In the Reichstag and diets the DLV had 13 representatives in 1928, in district and provincial parliaments 210, in municipal parliaments 2,540 (*ibid.*, p. 9). In the Provisional National Economic Council the workers' seats were distributed among the trade unions of various orientations according to their membership.

[20] The president of the DLV, Georg Schmidt, became a member of the Reichstag as a representative of the Social Democratic party. The president of the RLAB, Johannes Wolf, as well as the president of the ZV, Franz Behrens, were members of the Reichstag for the German National People's Party; Franz Behrens, however, resigned from the party when, under Hugenberg, party leadership was assumed by heavy industry.

[21] Bibl. #112f, p. 35.

[22] President Schmidt at a meeting of union officials in November 1921 (Bibl. #112, No. 12, p. 17).

and needs of the autonomous groups of interests."[23] The small and rather weak farm workers' unions alone never could have exercised great political influence if they had not been backed by the powerful industrial unions and their head federations. A DLV report was right in stating "We are a power which extends its range far beyond the aims of trade unions proper."[24]

Agitation and Organization

While, in general, activities of trade unions in agriculture fell in line with those of unions in industry, in their organizational work, which had to be concentrated in a few winter months, special difficulties had to be overcome. There was greater identification with the employer than in industry: there was no "class" front since many felt more akin to the small holder than to the landless worker. Workers were scattered, they lived in small groups of co-workers; they were less cultured and less aggressive; they were conservative and disinclined to any change.[25] Shortly before the foundation of the free farm workers' union in 1909, it was doubted in Socialist circles whether it would be possible to organize workers of different districts with such a diversity of interests into one trade union, and the formation of regional unions was proposed.[26] Even after unionization had succeeded the rural exodus caused the loss of the most energetic groups in the rural population. Wages in kind made it difficult to pay dues. Employers, in personal contact with their workers, were hostile to trade unionism. Speakers had to be carefully trained, and house to house visits were necessary. Even after joining the union, the rank and file frequently lacked understanding.[27]

The organization of the unions was built up on three levels: local, district, and national. Due to the farm workers' lack of education, officials could not be drawn from their ranks. The ZV, which had organized many rural craftsmen, made them into leaders of the local group. The DLV, with no

[23] Bibl. #118, May 1926, p. 275.

[24] Bibl. #112l, p. 9.

[25] There was a distinct hierarchy on the large estate, characterized by petty social distinctions which harassed the union organizer. Forelady (Mamsell), first and second maid, and goose maid felt that they did not belong to one class. Neither did the Grossknecht und Kleinknecht (chief and lesser laborer).

[26] Arthur Schulz, "Der landwirtschaftliche Arbeiter," in Bibl. #151, 1908, Part III, pp. 1578ff.

[27] The DLV leadership complained that some of the membership did not identify themselves with the organization as a body of workers, but looked upon it merely as something to which they could carry their grievances without having to work for it. Löhrke at the fourth Convention of the DLV (Bibl. 112g, p. 129).

rural craftsmen among its members, had to borrow officials from other, usually industrial unions.[28]

The local of the ZV and the county office of the DLV paid benefits[29] and gave legal advice. The leaders were assisted by an elected board. The next unit was the district (Gau, Bezirk). Their leaders, appointed by the center, had to help in collective bargaining, to supervise organization, and to safeguard union aims against local interests. Special district leaders' conferences were supposed to educate these officials and secure uniform action.

The DLV was highly centralized in its organization, all decisions being handed down to district and local organs by the central organs. The central organs were the Executive Committee of eight members, an Advisory Council of seventeen district representatives, and the General Assembly (convention), which met every three years, in which there was one representative for every 5,000 members. The ZV was similarly organized and centralized in its organization (three members of the board appointed all officials) but gave more autonomy to the seven technical groups affiliated with it, such as dairy workers, gardeners, and forestry workers. The general assemblies of the unions were not always an expression of the rank and file because officials who were dependent on the center formed a large proportion of the representatives.[30] They were better informed than the man on the farm, and likewise better orators. As the other delegates were for the most part trusted members of long standing, opposition had little possibility of success. Leadership in the DLV was exercised by members of the Executive Committee. Officials were appointed and dismissed by the committee.

The lack of female influence in the organization was reflected in the small number of women delegates in the assemblies of the DLV: 5 out of a total of 95 in 1920, 3 out of 70 in 1923, 2 out of 60 in 1929. There were no women among the officials.

The DLV was affiliated with the International Agricultural Workers' Federation, founded in 1920, the ZV with the International League of Christian Agricultural Workers' Unions, founded in 1921.

[28] The intermediate body of unpaid, small officials in industrial unions, who discussed the daily problems with the members, was not present in the agricultural workers' unions.

[29] The locals of the DLV became offices to which members paid dues (Zahlstellen) and were administered by "trustees" (Vertrauensmänner), but they were not permitted to administer the funds (Franz Hering, Bibl. #112k, pp. 51-52).

[30] Hering, op.cit., p. 49.

The RLAB, as distinct from the DLV and ZV, was decentralized, its head-quarters having the single function of making contacts with parliaments.

Organization of Foreign Workers

Most of the foreign workers remained unorganized although the German-Polish Treaty of November 24, 1927, provided the right for Polish workers either of belonging to the German unions or of forming independent unions. The mobility and dispersion of the workers and the instability of their employment, however, were obstacles to organization. In 1925, the DLV had concluded an agreement with the Polish Agricultural Workers' Union by which members of the latter automatically became members of the DLV during their stay in Germany with all the rights and obligations of German members. The DLV published a propaganda paper in Polish and distributed it among the Polish workers. The DLV, however, did not succeed in organizing many Polish workers, partly for the above-mentioned reasons, partly because the DLV, with its ardent fight against admitting foreign labor, did not attract Polish workers. A "Union of Polish Agricultural Workers in Germany" was active, too, but did not build up a large membership.

CHAPTER VI

EMPLOYERS' ORGANIZATIONS AND
COLLABORATION WITH TRADE UNIONS

UNTIL the revolution of 1918 employers had been represented only in Chambers of Agriculture. Employers' organizations were not founded because there was great fear of encouraging counter organization among workers. The first employers' organization for the purpose of collective bargaining was formed in January 1919 in the province of Saxony, an industrialized area, where a Provincial Agricultural Labor Act (in the form of a collective agreement) was passed even before the LAO. Other employers' organizations sprang up, each covering a province or a smaller state, and united in the National Federation of the Agricultural and Forestry Employers' Associations. Only a few associations, for example the Bavarian, remained outside the Federation. The Pomeranian association was dissolved and its membership formed the employers' group of the Pomeranian Landbund.

The Federation of the Agricultural and Forestry Employers' Associations,[1] as its name indicates, was decentralized. To the provincial or district organizations was left the responsibility of concluding collective agreements. They also represented their members in legal and arbitration proceedings, while the Federation presented their interests before government and parliaments. The Federation cooperated with the agricultural entrepreneurs' organization and in 1926 joined the RLB corporatively.

The variety of committees on various technical questions (such as wages, social insurance, efficiency, finances) indicated the activities of the associations. Their official publication was the weekly "Land-und Forstwirtschaftlicher Arbeitgeber." Employers' organizations were especially powerful in the districts of large estates in central and eastern Germany.[2]

Agricultural employers exercised their political influence through parties and even more through economic organizations and chambers of agriculture. In parliaments their representatives, for the most part, belonged to the

[1] Chief organs of the Federation were the annual general membership meeting and its Executive Council. Members contributed to the association, and associations, in turn, to the Federation.

[2] The Enquiry Committee found that out of 466,018 agricultural estates included in the 1925 census, 164,478 (35 per cent) were organized in employers' associations in eastern and central Germany (Bibl. #104b, p. 204). There existed twenty district organizations within the National Federation in 1928 with 180,000 members (Bibl. #123, 1930, pp. 7ff.).

German National People's party, but there were scatterings among other parties of the Right and the two Catholic parties, the Center party and the Bavarian People's party. While in the north and east the German National People's party controlled the agricultural vote, in the south and west control was largely Catholic. The Christlich Nationale Bauern und Landvolk Partei (Christian National Peasant and Country Folk party), created by the Thuringian and Hessian Landbünde after secession from the German National People's party did not gain importance.[3] The RLB, the most

[3] After the revolution of 1918 the farmer representation, especially of large estate owners in the Reichstag and the Prussian Diet, had considerably decreased (especially in the Prussian Diet where the two conservative parties had, owing to the three-class election system, held 62 per cent of all seats in 1913 and were reduced to 17.7 per cent in 1919.

Farmer Representatives in the Reichstag

	1912 Absolute	Per cent of Total Parliament	1919 Absolute	Percentage
Large estate owners	41	10.3	4	0.9
Middle estate owners	37	9.4	9	2.1
Small estate owners	14	3.5	21	4.9
Total	92	23.2	34	7.9

	1924 (second Reichstag) Absolute	Per cent	1928 Absolute
Large estate owners	10	2.0	8
Middle estate owners	12	2.4	} 24
Small estate owners	37	7.5	
Total	59	11.9	32

Farmer Representatives in the Prussian Diet

	1913 Absolute	Per cent	1919 Absolute	Per cent	1925 Absolute	Per cent
Large estate owners	97	21.89	3	0.74	11	2.44
Middle estate owners	42	9.48	10	2.49	19	4.22
Small estate owners	7	1.57	5	1.24	13	2.88
Total	146	32.94	18	4.47	43	9.54

Farmer Representation According to Factions
(in the second Reichstag 1924)

Parties	Absolute	Per cent of Total Representatives of the parties
German National People's Party	31	27.9
German People's Party	4	7.9
Catholic Center Party	14	15.9
German Democratic Party	1	3.1
Social Democratic Party	–	–

Source: Walther Kamm, Bibl. #152, 1927, pp. 11, 19, 28, 37.

powerful representation of agrarian interests, presented its own election slates in various parts of the country for reasons of propaganda. These slates were allied with those of the German National People's party candidates so that the latter received the surplus votes. Moreover, representatives elected from the RLB slates joined the German National factions in parliament. Although the organization included many small farm owners, its program was of greater benefit to the owners of large estates, e.g. in questions concerning tariffs, tenure, and taxation.

After the Joint Association had ceased to exist, free collaboration between employers' organizations and trade unions continued in collective bargaining, and in joint bodies such as those established for employment offices, social insurance associations, arbitration authorities, labor courts. The employers' associations nominated representatives to these bodies.

The highest legal body for collaboration, the Provisional National Economic Council, was originally intended to make proposals on economic and labor questions for the government but remained restricted to opinions on all bills pertaining to economic and labor questions before they were presented to the Reichstag and to advice to government departments. Of the 326 seats of the RWR, agriculture and forestry held 68 (25 representing farmers, 25 workers, 18 experts). However, the horizontal division of the industrial groups was abandoned in favor of a vertical grouping of employers and employees. The government increased the number of the third group to equal each of the other two. Conceived as a body reflecting the unanimous opinion of all members of the economic branch, the council developed into a parliament in which employers and workers opposed each other with divergent interests. After June 30, 1923, the Council worked only through committees,[4] of which the two principal ones dealt with economic and social-political matters.

---

[4] Subcommittees dealt, among other matters, with land settlements, housing, works councils, export duties.

Collective Agreements

Collective agreements were virtually an achievement of the postwar period,[5] although some agreements had been concluded for vineyard workers before the war. In 1914 they affected only 500 workers. After the war collective agreements became the accepted method of regulating conditions of work on large estates. They were common in almost every part of Germany, but much less so where peasant farming prevailed.

Collective agreements could be established in either of two ways: by free agreement between the contracting parties or by awards of official arbitration bodies, if both parties had accepted the award or the authority declared it binding.

According to the decree of December 23, 1918,[6] collective agreements had to be made in writing. Three important principles were established, the first that on the worker's side only *bona fide* trade unions were capable of concluding a collective agreement. Secondly, the norms of collective agreements were binding on the contracting parties. They established minimum conditions. Deviating labor contracts were valid only if their norms were more favorable to labor or the deviation was provided for in the agreement. Less favorable conditions were automatically changed. Workers were thus protected against conditions of work inferior to those fixed in the collective agreement. Thirdly, if the latter obtained preponderant importance in the district for which it was concluded, the Federal Minister of Labor on request

[5]   Number of Agricultural Workers Covered by Collective Agreements

		Total	Women	Forestry
December 31,	1912	4,243		
	1913	4,056	2,800	
	1919	90,577		
	1920	49,128	11,927	
	1921	1,643,780	547,459	
	1922	1,996,917	634,146	
January 1,	1925	1,500,690	625,843	
	1926	1,313,750	578,973	242,256
	1927	1,435,446	537,456	274,949
	1928	1,668,059	691,008	281,358
	1929	1,498,607	520,523	284,957
	1931	1,715,848	650,252	249,803

Workers in horticulture, forestry, and fishery are included in figures for 1912 through 1925.

Source: Bibl. #139a, Nos. 7, 1912, p. 25; 10, 1913, p. 17; 26, 1920, p. 30; 27, 1921, p. 31; 31, 1922, p. 16; 35, 1925, pp. 13, 15; 40, 1926, p. 15; 47, 1928, p. 2; 55, 1929, p. 22; 58, 1931, p. 13.

[6] Bibl. #140, p. 1456. It was newly edited by the decree of March 1, 1928 (Bibl. #140, I, p. 47).

of either party could declare it generally binding for all outsiders in the area who belonged to the occupational groups covered by the agreement. In this way the conditions of work of a larger proportion of farm workers than were organized were covered by collective agreements. Underselling by outsiders, farmers as well as farm workers, could thus be prevented.

The question as to which trade unions should be entitled to conclude collective agreements was seriously contested. The DLV and the ZV were recognized by the government as the only *bona fide* trade unions and therefore entitled to conclude legally valid collective agreements. The employers' organizations of the RLB tried to conclude agreements only with their own workers' associations and fought in the courts "agreements" imposed by arbitration. Some groups of the RLB imposed fines on employers who concluded collective agreements with others than RLB organizations or who granted higher wages than approved by their wage committee. They demanded official recognition of the RLAB unions. DLV and ZV denied the latter's financial independence because contributions to the RLAB were only a small percentage of its income.[7] According to the statute the union was financed chiefly by its journal. The *bona fide* trade unions were suspicious that employers financed the journal for their workers and so indirectly paid the expenses of the RLAB. In 1921 the DLV proposed that the RLB workers' groups should take part in negotiations of collective agreements, and that employers should be obliged not to grant any better conditions of work to workers organized in the League than to others. The RLB refused, and discussions were discontinued.

The Federal Minister of Labor, the National Economic Council,[8] the Federal Insurance Board, and the Reifa refused their recognition as a party to collective agreements—though many agreements were in fact concluded by such organizations without the legal effect of collective agreements proper, e.g. the principle of nondeviation was not valid for such agreements. In some districts the same agreement was concluded twice, once with the DLV and once with the RLAB. Only the former agreement could be extended to outsiders.

In order to achieve recognition, a sham law suit was begun by the Pomeranian employers' and workers' group of the RLB. When the courts rejected recognition because the union's statutes did not guarantee financial

[7] Walter Kwasnik (Bibl. #112m), Nos. 20, 27.
[8] Bibl. #155, 1920-1927, No. 352, and Bibl. #112m, No. 27, pp. 6off.

independence of the employer,[9] they changed the statutes in order to fulfill the requirements. On December 2, 1929, a district labor court recognized an agreement concluded by a union of the RLAB and on May 21, 1930,[10] a judgment of the Federal Labor Court recognized the Pomeranian union's ability to conclude collective agreements. The Federal Minister of Labor recognized it as late as November 1932,[11] in spite of the violent protests of the *bona fide* trade unions who saw in this move a threat to the labor movement and a decline of their political power. On February 16, 1933, shortly after Hitler came into power, the executive council of the Reifa granted recognition to the RLAB's Pomeranian union.[12]

The *bona fide* unions collaborated in concluding collective agreements. Of the agreements existing on January 1, 1931, those for 1,538,915 workers had been concluded with several unions and for only 176,933 with one.[13]

The first collective agreements included mere regulation of wages and hours but were gradually extended to other conditions of work such as holidays, subcontracts, etc. When labor suddenly acquired full bargaining right, it did not know how to apply its privileges. The agreements concluded in 1919 were badly constructed because of labor's lack of experience and the tendency to regulate wages in a too detailed way. Hours of negotiation were wasted in discussing trifles, while important issues escaped attention.[14] Neither side understood the real significance of a collective agreement. This difficulty was overcome after 1920.[15] During the inflation period new problems arose, especially in 1922 and 1923 when wages had to be adjusted to the rise in prices. Out of the experiences of this period, in which wages had to be negotiated without interruption, grew a separation of the wage tariff from other parts of the agreement. Since that time only a few collective agreements were made in one all-inclusive instrument (Volltarif). Most of

[9] On September 29, 1928, the Federal Labor Court had referred the complaint back to the lower court because it provided insufficient evidence that the RLAB was composed merely of employees and was independent of employers (Bibl. #115, IV, p. 294).

[10] *Ibid.*, IX, p. 487.

[11] Bibl. #119, December 17, 1932, p. 803. The same Minister of Labor, Schaeffer, had frequently denied recognition in his former office as President of the Federal Insurance Board.

[12] *Ibid.*, February 25, 1933, p. 120.   [13] *Sonderheft 58 zum RABl*, p. 20.

[14] Bibl. #112b, p. 53.

[15] Gradually the tenor and context of agreements improved. However, not all traditional dependencies could be easily overcome. The DLV in 1927 mentioned agreements in Pomerania which imposed penalties on the use of electric light after eight o'clock in the evening and others which prohibited affiliation with a political organization (Bibl. #150, September 29, 1927, pp. 988ff.).

them consisted of two parts, with wage rates (and sometimes hours) forming a separate part, and the covering agreement (Manteltarif) containing the more uniform matters applying to a wider territorial area, and concluded for a longer period. Wage agreements took into consideration district and local conditions. Thus a compromise could be achieved between uniformity and local variations. The majority of agreements covered counties, although the unions tended to enlarge the scope at least of the covering agreements to provinces. Only a few agreements were concluded with individual estates.[16]

Wage agreements were generally valid for one year and expired in the late autumn or on December 31, dates favorable for the deputatists with land who had to harvest their crops, but unfavorable for other workers. Many agreements defined a period within which new negotiations had to be opened or required new proposals to be submitted together with notice of termination.

Like all German collective agreements, the terms of agricultural agreements were of two types, normative and obligatory. The normative provisions, which had the character of a statute, regulated anything that could be included in an individual labor contract: wages, overtime pay, hours, holiday and vacation pay, subcontractors. The obligatory part regulated obligations and rights of the parties to an agreement, for instance the pledge to secure emergency work during strikes, and the use of agreed joint arbitration bodies. The duty to preserve peace for the duration of the agreement was inherent in every collective agreement without special clause. Only the norms of a collective agreement, not the obligations, could be extended to outsiders by the Minister of Labor. Some agreements obliged the worker not to demand better conditions, or the employer not to give privileges to unorganized workers; or employers' organizations privately constrained their members from granting more than the agreements provided. No union security or seniority clauses existed.

Enforcement of collective agreements could be supervised by works councils, and by joint bodies where they existed. Some help also was given by public employment offices which sometimes checked conditions of work when placing workers.

[16] Agreements in existence on January 1, 1929, covering workers in agriculture and forestry, according to bargaining unit:

Single estates	3,801 workers
One locality	3,478 "
One county	1,666,116 "

Source: Bibl. #139, Sonderheft 55, 1930, p. 3.

Although the Collective Agreement Statute had established the principle of nondeviation, it was not always possible to secure for farm workers wages laid down in agreements. In a study of Silesian farms made for the employers' organizations, Georg Feige found in 1926 great deviation from agreement standards, many districts paying less than standard, others more.[17] From 1925 to 1929 higher than agreed wages were frequently paid,[18] while in 1932 underpayment became more frequent.

There were general complaints of employers against breach of individual contracts. In some parts of the country dismissal testimonials were used to prevent infringements. Employers engaging workers without such testimonials from former employers were fined. The usefulness of these devices was doubtful. Trade unions were also opposed to breach of contract. The ZV pledged its members to faithfulness to contracts in its statutes because of possible damage by interruption of crop operations or care of livestock.

For foreign workers contracts were concluded in a different way. Each application for alien labor had to be accompanied by a standard contract signed by the employer. The text of this contract was drawn up by the agricultural committee of the Reifa; the model for it formed an appendix to the treaties. The contract regulated accommodations, the preparation of the common meals, and quantity of food to be supplied. Provision was also made for religious holidays and for attending divine service.

Subcontractors (Hofgänger)

A special problem concerned the Hofgänger (subcontractor). According to old traditional standards in some contracts the principal worker promised to perform part of the work himself and part with the help of a third person whom he had to provide. This obligation had originated in the old idea of allegiance to the estate owner and had been continued under free contractual relationships because of labor shortage in the sparsely populated parts of eastern Germany and the desire to make full use of service dwellings. The contract was concluded merely with the deputatist for the services of a third person: his wife, or one of his children, or an outsider for whom the

[17] 61 per cent of the districts paid lower wages to unmarried independent workers; 12 out of 25 paid them to married independent workers, while some groups working at piece rates earned more (Georg Feige, Bibl. #147, Table 10).

[18] The employers in the province of Saxony claimed in 1927-1928 that actual wages exceeded those collectively agreed upon by 23 per cent ("Entgegnungsschrift des Arbeitgeberverbandes auf die Denkschrift des DLV von 1928," quoted by Gustav Roeber, Bibl. #71, p. 35).

deputatist received "family wages"; or several simultaneous contracts were concluded which were connected with each other. In any case, the sub-contractor was under the domination of the owner who paid his cash wages and social insurance dues. Some collective agreements obliged the laborer's family to work only on the estate of the employer and forced the laborer's children over fourteen years of age who did not work on the estate to leave their father's dwelling;[19] otherwise the parents might be evicted.

The organized workers were opposed to the wife's obligation to be at the employer's disposal all the year round and to the restrictions on his children's mobility. Where the bona fide trade unions bargained, they frequently succeeded in abolishing the compulsion of wives and children to work. Even when the agreement did not explicitly require the laborer's wife to work on the estate, it was nevertheless expected of her.[20]

In a conference[21] called by the Minister of Labor in 1926 employers' and workers' organizations agreed that in view of the concentration of labor demand at certain times of the year, the work of workers' wives could not be dispensed with. This work, however, was to be restricted to such seasons. The Ministry was of the opinion that such labor should be obtained only on the basis of a separate voluntary contract and that any form of conscription of a wife to work by virtue of her husband's contract would defeat its own ends.

The obligation to subcontract workers who did not belong to the family, which was considered a relic of earlier feudal obligations, was especially resented. The laborer had to board and lodge the subcontractor and received correspondingly higher wages in kind for him whether a separate contract had been concluded or not. The Hofgänger himself received only very low

[19] Bibl. #150, October 6, 1927, pp. 988ff.

[20] An inquiry of the DLV in 1929-1930 gave the average hours worked by 107 wives of deputatists as follows:

Bavaria	2,885	Schleswig-Holstein	900
Silesia	1,858	Thuringia and Erfurt	881
Saxony	1,731	Mecklenburg Schwerin	768
Württemberg	1,690	East Prussia	534
Province Saxony,		Hanover	504
Anhalt, Brunswick	1,221	Pomerania	459
Brandenburg and			
Grenzmark	1,079		

Source: Bibl. #112o, p. 77. In a Brandenburg district a woman working as a subcontractor was allowed to stay at home at least one day a week for her household duties. Most of the employment of deputatist's wives was due to low wages of their husbands, not to contractual obligations.

[21] Zur Landarbeiterfrage (Bibl. #139, 1926, pp. 514ff).

money wages. Asmis reports wages of about 100 M. a year in the prewar period and frequently no wage at all for own children.[22] Workers strongly objected to subcontracts because lodging an extra adult stranger restricted the accommodations. It was difficult to get outside workers and sometimes young couples left rather than take a stranger into their home. In 1920 only the East Prussian agreement allowed contracts which obliged deputants to provide subcontractors. In Brandenburg and Schleswig-Holstein such obligation was ruled out. Other agreements did not mention subcontractors.[23] The East Prussian collective agreement tried to prevent breach of contracts by Hofgänger by making the laborer responsible for his subcontractor and by imposing a fine of 8-10 per cent of his cash wages. Other collective agreements frequently stated that breach of contract by the subcontractor was no reason for dismissal if the deputant was without guilt.

Public opinion was expressed in a judgment of the Federal Labor Court of May 8, 1929. Although the court did not consider the particular contract immoral as such, it expressed the opinion that widespread responsibility of the principal worker for the mistakes of another person "was opposed to general conceptions of fairness and decency prevailing in the last decade." The court declared that an appeal to tradition was no longer valid and that modern ideas had to serve as the standard in contracts of this nature.[24]

* * *

During the depression farmers, like other employers, complained about the lack of flexibility in collective agreements and demanded "relaxation" (Auflockerung), i.e. shorter duration, exceptions for indigent farmers, abolition of compulsory awards. From 1930 on, the government began to influence the wage policy by emergency decrees and pressure on arbitrators. It changed the content and duration of collective agreements in its Emergency Decree of December 8, 1931.[25] Although the labor press claimed that the principle of collective agreements had been unharmed,[26] interference with the freedom of negotiation had become so fundamental that the term agreement began to lose its meaning. The Emergency Decree of September 5, 1932,[27] in allow-

---

[22] Walter Asmis, "Zur Entwicklung der Landarbeiterlöhne in Preussen," Bibl. #130, Vol. 52, p. 593.

[23] Reichsverband der deutschen land- und forstwirtschaftlichen Arbeitgebervereinigungen. Zusammenstellung der wichtigsten Tarifbestimmungen aus den vom Reichsverband erfassten landwirtschaftlichen Tarifverträgen für das Jahr 1920. Berlin, 1921, pp. 40-41.

[24] Bibl. #115, Vol. VI, p. 20.   [26] Bibl. #122, 1931, p. 167.

[25] Bibl. #140, I, p. 699.   [27] Bibl. #140, I, p. 433.

ing reduction of wage rates below those agreed upon, partly abolished the principle of nondeviation.

The Settlement of Disputes and the Establishment of Collective Agreement by Award

Typical of the discrimination against agricultural labor in prewar times was the failure to establish a special court (as for industrial workers and commercial employees) to settle disputes concerning the labor contract in an easy, speedy, and inexpensive way. Chambers of agriculture frequently settled disputes. Some chambers had established tribunals with employers' and workers' assessors.[28] The German Workers' Central settled disputes of foreign workers.[29] During the war the Auxiliary Service Act of December 5, 1916, set up a system of conciliation committees composed of equal numbers of employers and workers (including those of agriculture) under a chairman appointed by the War Authority to deal with all kinds of individual and collective disputes.

Although the law was repealed in 1918, the conciliation committees were retained[30] and reorganized[31] for the settlement of collective labor disputes, including those in agriculture. In addition, they were entrusted with the decision of litigation arising out of the new labor law. The LAO provided that contested cases concerning the money value of wages in kind and the suitability of wages and work of disabled war veterans should be decided by the conciliation committees. The same was true for disputes arising out of the Works Councils Act and the War Pensions Act. For all other disputes farm workers had to apply to the ordinary courts.[32] The composition of the conciliation committees was unsatisfactory to trade unions because

[28] The tribunal of the Chamber of the Province of Brandenburg dealt with three disputes in 1911, and six in 1912; the Chamber received 78 and 60 complaints (Beschwerden) in those years which it tried to settle by conciliation. (Die Schlichtungstätigkeit der preussischen Landwirtschaftskammern und der Deutschen Arbeiterzentrale bei Streitigkeiten zwischen Arbeitgebern und Arbeitnehmern in der Landwirtschaft, Bibl. #139, July 28, 1914, pp. 580ff.).

[29] In 1912-1913 the Workers' Central received 1,115 complaints; 271 of employers, 646 of employees, 198 of consuls (*ibid.*, p. 583).

[30] Aufruf des Rates der Volksbeauftragten of November 12, 1918, Sect. 7 (Bibl. #140, p. 1,303).

[31] *Order of December 23, 1918 (Bibl. #140, p. 1,456).*

[32] In 1922 members of the DLV had 4,562 lawsuits (Bibl. #112f, p. 19), in 1927, 7,967, and in 1928, 9,430 (Bibl. #112l, p. 44). Of the 9,430 cases, 5,649 concerned wages, 1,275 dismissal, 939 housing, 935 social legislation, 207 dismissal of works councils, 425 miscellaneous.

the labor assessors frequently had not been nominated by trade unions but selected from among sick-fund assessors.[38] Moreover, the committees had no power of enforcement. The winner had to apply to an ordinary court for a writ of enforcement—an awkward and slow procedure.

When the arbitration system was reorganized[34] in 1923, jurisdiction over decisions in individual agricultural labor disputes was transferred from the conciliation committees to the industrial courts wherever they existed. Assessors (employers and workers) from agriculture were to supplement the assessors of the industrial courts. Where no industrial courts were available (for instance, in communities with less than 20,000 inhabitants), so-called labor-court chambers were set up, mostly in connection with conciliation committees. They were composed of an impartial chairman and one representative of employers and employees each. Collective disputes continued to be settled by the conciliation committees.

This regulation was still unsatisfactory because only disputes over the money value of wages in kind and dismissals could be brought to the industrial courts and chambers of labor. A worker with a grievance relating to other terms of his contract had to resort to an ordinary local court. Moreover, there was no appeal from decisions of industrial courts and chambers of labor.

With the enactment of the Labor Court Act of December 23, 1926,[35] all individual disputes concerning agricultural labor were referred to the labor courts. Thus from 1927 on, the same inexpensive, informal system worked in the interests of both industrial and agricultural workers. The law provided for a set of courts on three levels, all of them composed of professional and lay judges, the latter drawn from employers' organizations and trade unions. The possibility of establishing special chambers for specified occupations and industries, as for instance, agriculture, was provided.[36] Farmers and farm labor participated in two functions. Agricultural employers' organizations and trade unions cooperated in preparing lists for nominating assessors to the courts. Even for the Federal Labor Court the DLV provided one of

[38] Memorandum of the Gesellschaft für Soziale Reform (Bibl. #150, January 28, 1920, p. 402).

[34] Decree of October 30, 1923 (Bibl. #140, I, p. 1,034), and Administrative Orders of October 29, 1923 (Bibl. #140, 1924, I, p. 9).

[35] Bibl. #140, I, p. 507.

[36] Only Berlin and the southern states set up agricultural chambers with lay assessors of agricultural employers and workers in equal number. Disputes in agriculture were not numerous enough to justify specialization.

the assessors. Moreover, employers' associations and trade unions were entitled to represent their members as attorneys in the local and district labor courts.

The jurisdiction of the labor courts included employers, wage earners, salaried employees and apprentices of all income levels. Four types of disputes were covered: 1) between employers and employees arising out of the labor contract; 2) between fellow workers arising out of common employment; 3) between parties to a collective agreement; and 4) disputes arising out of the works council relation. The procedure was informal; complaints could be filed orally; parties usually appeared in person. First, the chairman attempted to bring about an amicable settlement. Failing this, the case proceeded as a lawsuit before the full court with two assessors.[37] Court fees were very modest: 1 Rm. for claims up to 20 Rm., 2 Rm. for claims from 20 to 60 Rm., and so forth. No fee was charged if the case was amicably settled. Appeal was possible in case the disputed sum exceeded 300 Rm., but could be admitted by the court because of the fundamental importance of the case, e.g. when the dispute was concerned with the interpretation of collective agreements.

The labor courts were popular both with workers and employers.[38] Decisions in everyday litigation, which represented more than nine-tenths of all cases, called for little criticism. The parties felt at ease in the courts and were helped by the chairman to formulate their idea of justice. The labor courts decided disputes on rights, i.e. those arising out of the interpretation of individual or collective contracts or of labor law. Disputes on interests, i.e. those arising out of the inability of the parties to conclude a collective agreement, were handled either by arbitration bodies, if they had been provided for in collective agreements, or, where none had been set up, by the public arbitration authorities.

When the conciliation committees had proved their inability to cope with postwar labor difficulties and the divergencies of opinion made a quick final reform impossible, a provisional regulation was enacted, based on the Reich President's emergency power. The Arbitration Decree of October 30, 1923, intended to be a temporary measure, was in fact maintained during the whole period of the Weimar Republic. It provided a network of arbitration bodies which were supposed to act in collective disputes. It was the aim of the German arbitration system to assist in establishing collective agreements.

[37] The procedure for works council cases was somewhat different.
[38] Frieda Wunderlich (Bibl. #92), pp. 107ff.

If no settlement could be reached in collective bargaining or by the agreed body, a decision was made by majority vote in the public arbitration body, which was composed of employer and employee assessors in equal numbers, with an impartial chairman appointed by the state authority. Assessors in all arbitration bodies were chosen from the lists of candidates submitted by the bona fide trade unions and employers' organizations.

The procedure was informal and aimed at freely consented agreements. If this failed, an award was rendered. The arbitration award had the full legal force of a collective agreement if accepted by the parties. If rejected, the award could be declared binding[39] provided it appeared just and reasonable, with due consideration for the interests of both parties and provided its application was desirable for economic and social reasons. The act of declaring the award binding replaced acceptance by the parties and endowed it with the force of a freely concluded collective agreement. Although the Minister of Labor from time to time emphasized that awards were to be declared binding only where "the impact of opposing forces threatened economic and social-political injury to the community,"[40] a strike in agriculture was considered such a threat to the public welfare that awards were declared binding whenever the parties rejected them. This policy met with disapproval from the employers. The power to declare awards binding made it possible for the government to help labor improve conditions of work and especially wages.[41] It made collective bargaining a combination of voluntary and compulsory procedure. The trade unions recognized too late that compulsory arbitration made them dependent on the government, whatever its character and policy, and that the rank and file lost interest in the unions because the state was determining their working conditions.

According to the statistics of the ADGB at the end of 1929,[42] wage agreements for 66.9 per cent of all farm workers covered were based on arbitration, and only 33.1 per cent had been concluded in free negotiations. Full agreements for 63.5 per cent of the workers included had been achieved by negotiation. Full agreement awards for 213,844 workers and wage agreements for 36,000 workers were declared binding.

Both labor courts and arbitration bodies could be replaced by similar institutions set up by collective agreement. Agreed-upon conciliation bodies,

---

[39] Compulsory arbitration had already been introduced by demobilization orders in 1919-1920.

[40] Circular of January 30 (Bibl. #139, 1924, i, p. 127).

[41] Wunderlich (Bibl. #93), pp. 17-18.   [42] Wladimir Woytinsky (Bibl. #91).

as well as free negotiations, however, became less important than arbitration by official bodies.[43]

Strikes

As we have mentioned earlier, many wildcat strikes occurred in the first revolutionary period after the war. The unions required some tranquility in order to bind the mass of new members to the organization, yet they were constantly being drawn into labor disputes by radical groups or inexperienced local officials. Most of the disputes were "disorderly" and the headquarters of the DLV was forced to place itself at the head of movements it had not initiated. Other strikes were political. The leadership warned the new members that strikes in agriculture were always considered dangerous by the public and that the deputatist in striking risked more than the industrial worker. Control could not be effectively carried through. "Socialism is work" was repeated time and again in government proclamations. President Schmidt of the DLV called the period after the revolution "one single strike movement in which one constantly played with the term 'strike' or even 'general strike.' "[44]

On November 27, 1918, Barth, the most radical of the People's Commissioners, said: "We understood how to make a revolution, but I must confess, we do not understand how to organize the army of workmen for carrying through the most necessary work to feed the people."[45] The Social Democratic newspaper "Vorwärts"[46] warned that workers "could easily die of their own victory . . . if they allowed themselves to be led by the militarists of the social struggle" instead of by trade unionists.

However, in spite of the protest against the exaggeration in striking, the DLV and ZV recognized the strike and applied it as a last resort, when employers refused collective bargaining. The unions protested when the military authority ruled in February 1920 for Berlin and Brandenburg that strikes and incitement to strikes in "vitally important undertakings" to which food production belonged were criminal offenses.[47]

[43] As early as 1921 Georg Schmidt, the President of the DLV, complained that "our members take it for granted that the government intervenes in each wage movement. I know of cases in which government agencies had been appealed to as soon as a dispute arose on a farm" (Bibl. #112, No. 12, p. 15).

[44] Bibl. #112, No. 12, p. 10.

[45] *Correspondenzblatt*, December 14, 1918, p. 459.

[46] Quoted in Bibl. #150, September 6, 1922, p. 965.

[47] Bibl. #112, No. 8, p. 149.

Gradually the flood of strikes ebbed. The November spirit did not last, and employers regained resistance. Bitter contests arose again in 1923 at the peak of the currency inflation, when wages could not keep pace with the constantly declining value of money. The biggest strike occurred in Silesia in 1923 and involved some 90,000 workers, according to the DLV. Employers estimated the number as 120,000. The strike lasted four weeks, and was terminated by an arbitration award. Trade unions complained that employers refused to pay wages in kind during strikes, that they excluded the worker's cow from the estate stable, barred the water supply, etc. Although employers would not ordinarily be expected to pay wages during a strike, withholding wages in kind might mean death of the worker's cattle and great hardship for his family.

During the revolutionary upheaval, voluntary groups and military engineer battalions had performed emergency work to maintain essential services during strikes. Early in 1919 the battalions were recognized as Emergency Corps (Technische Nothilfe), by the government to insure the maintenance of essential services in case of strikes. At first formed on a military basis, the service was transferred in November 1919 to a civilian basis under the Minister of the Interior. The corps which was composed of volunteers intervened in stoppages of work essential to public welfare (including agriculture) due to strike or public disaster. It did so only in case the trade unions had failed to respond to an official appeal to provide help for necessary work. During the revolutionary period, the free trade unions accepted the corps; but from 1920 on, they became hostile to it because of its being used as a strike-breaking instrument. In protesting against the Emergency Corps, the free trade unions pledged themselves to maintain during strikes such indispensable services as the care of livestock, feeding, and milking.[48] The Christian unions remained friendly for a long time, but in 1925 joined in a common protest of all federations.[49] From 1930 on, the use of the Corps became restricted to disasters such as large scale fires and floods.

After the stabilization of the currency (1924), trade unions made such watertight provisions in their statutes to regulate the calling of strikes that it became almost impossible to do so. The DLV ruled that every intended strike had to be announced to the executive committee four weeks in advance. All possibilities of negotiation had to be exhausted first. A three-

[48] Bibl. #138b, pp. 109, 110.
[49] Bibl. #122, 1925, pp. 130, 131.

quarter majority was required before a strike could be called.[50] Since most collective agreements and long term contracts expired with the calendar year, only on that date could a strike have begun without breach of contract, in other words strikes would have been of no practical use to the trade unions. 1923 and 1924 were the last years in which big strikes occurred. They disappeared to all intents and purposes. Although both bona fide trade unions stressed their recognition of the freedom to strike, the ZV became virtually nonmilitant. Not so the DLV, whose nonmilitancy was a matter of expediency.

STRIKES[51]

	Official Statistics[a]				DLV Statistics[b]	
	Number of Strikes[d]	Number of Undertakings	Number of Strikers[e]	Number of Days Lost[c]	Number of Undertakings	Number of Strikers
1919	163	932	22,253	115,951		
1920	366	3,220	53,606	227,168		
1921	302	1,876	36,770	353,809		
1922	331	2,853	56,228	468,207	5,332	48,111
1923	74	2,574	125,383	1,530,984	36,814	281,714
1924	19	598	14,557	139,922	2,227	24,319
1925	16	32	1,017	3,076	393	4,861
1926	6	19	264	2,500		341
1927	4	23	138	570		262
1928	2	2	26	20		
1929	4	24	339	1,694		
1930	3	13	322	1,484		
1931	15	21	484	2,870		

[50] They regulated the strike procedure by making the district or regional official the strike leader (depending on the magnitude of the dispute), and by demanding reports to the National Executive Committee as well as to the strikers themselves.

[51] Official figures of numbers of strikers, undertakings, and workers up to 1923 were inaccurate since the police authorities which collected the figures were not always given adequate information and because they omitted short stoppages.

[51a] Source: Bibl. #139, Nichtamtlicher Teil 1921-1922, p. 245; 1922, p. 188; 1923, p. 245; 1924, p. 365; 1926, pp. 232, 568; 1927, II, p. 267; 1930, II, p. 180; 1931, II, p. 180; 1932, II, p. 80; 1933, II, p. 226. Figures show slight differences in various issues of the *RABl*.

[51b] Source: Bibl. #112f., p. 15; Bibl. #112g, p. 27; Bibl. #112l, p. 24.

[51c] The figure is calculated by multiplying the duration of the strike by the maximum number of persons involved at the time.

[51d] In addition to three lockouts in 1920 (with 668 days lost), four in 1923; two in 1924.

[51e] The figures give the number of persons involved at one time, excluding those indirectly compelled not to work.

By 1926 the unrest of the postwar period had been overcome. The political power of trade unions was used to influence the arbitrator's attitude, not in individual cases, but as a general policy—a much easier way to improve conditions of work than by risky and unpopular strikes. However, unrest was revived during the depression of 1930 when Communists and Fascists used the plight of agriculture to incite the rural population to a few illegal strikes.

The figures of the Emergency Corps show the development of disputes.[52]

	Number of Emergency Helpers at Work in Agriculture	Number of Hours of Work
1919-1920	366	12,249
1920-1921	2,406	138,156
1921-1922	3,164	242,407
1922-1923	11,037	1,468,628
1923-1924	3,833	353,809
1924-1925	103	5,532
Total	20,909	2,220,781
		(Of a total of 6 million for all industries)

Works Councils (Betriebsräte) and Chambers of Agriculture

Works Councils[53] had to be elected for one year on farms which permanently (i.e. at least one year) employed twenty or more workers, or a works steward (Betriebsobmann) on farms with ten or more permanently employed workers. They were elected by direct secret ballot of employees (eighteen years of age and over), with proportional representation from lists usually set up by the trade unions. Foreign workers could vote but were not eligible for election. Members of the family were not counted as employees. Seasonal workers had the right to vote. If they more than doubled the number of workers or added at least fifteen they had the right to elect one member to the council or to vote for a steward. On farms with twenty to forty-nine workers the council consisted of three members. They were protected against dismissal. The councils were supposed to supplement, not

---

[52] Source: Hans Scholz (Bibl. #75), pp. 25, 33ff. About 22 per cent of the members of the Emergency Corps were farmers (ibid., p. 19).

[53] BRG, February 4, 1920 (Bibl. #140, I, p. 147, Section 4).

to usurp the functions of the trade unions, who had the right to be represented in council meetings. Their main duties were to agree on work rules with the employer (within the frame of the collective agreement), to help in the settlement of grievances, to foster accident prevention, to supervise the enforcement of collective agreements and arbitration awards, to appeal to the arbitration authorities in case of labor conflicts. They were expected to cooperate in the introduction of new methods of remuneration and in fixing of piece rates. Complaints of workers could be submitted to the works council during regular consultation hours. Dismissed employees could appeal to the council if there was suspicion of discrimination (sex, political, religious, or trade union), or if the dismissal seemed to be unjust or unduly harsh.

Work Councils[53] had to be elected for one year on farms which perma-industry. In 1927 they existed in only about 25 per cent of the farms in question,[54] more in the more densely populated center and south than on the remote estates of the east.[55] Trade unions blamed the employers whose autocratic attitude and disinclination to discuss technical and economic problems with their workers was considered responsible for the failure. Farm workers were shy, easily discouraged, and afraid of dismissal. Some even asked the employer whether he agreed to their acceptance of the office. They were not as able to express their demands as city workers were. They were isolated and lacked the numerical and moral support which workers had in mass industries. Employers claimed that workers were uninterested in the institution and that they refused to elect works councils. They emphasized the personal character of the relation between employer and employee in agriculture which made a representative institution superfluous. They criticized works councils as having created friction. Where only stewards existed the system seems to have worked satisfactorily. While employers strove to reduce the "collective" council to one-man representation, the DLV tried to strengthen the works councils by organizing them in districts and working out directives for their work and appointing county stewards (Kreisbetriebsobmänner) to help in elections. A handbook issued by the DLV for members active in the works council movement sold 5,000 copies in one year (1927).[56]

Chambers of Agriculture were semi-official bodies composed of farmers

[54] There were about 22,850 farms with more than 20 workers in the Reich in 1925 (Bibl. #153e, 1927, No. 19, p. 803).

[55] Bibl. #104b, pp. 11, 120ff., 183, 184.

[56] Bibl. #112l, p. 52.

on holdings providing an independent livelihood. They advised the government, subsidized agricultural associations, conducted schools, and provided information. Their work was centralized in the German Agricultural Council (Deutscher Landwirtschaftsrat), a body with great prestige.

Trade unions aimed at getting equal representation in the Chambers of Agriculture, in which agricultural workers were only weakly represented in some states. In Prussia they were not represented at all.[57] The Prussian chambers had been democratized by the law of December 16, 1920,[58] which from then on admitted to membership every farmer who delivered products to the market, whereas up to that time the requirement for membership was restricted to ownership of a farm of certain size or the payment of a minimum amount of land tax. "Out of a sense of inferiority which may have originated in the period of servitude, the peasants continued to elect big estate owners as their representatives."[59] A Prussian draft for reorganization of the chambers was introduced in 1927 but had not been accepted up to the time of the National Socialist revolution.

[57] In 1928 in the RWR an agreement was arrived at between representatives of the workers and of the employers, under the terms of which the workers agreed to accept one-third of the seats in each chamber instead of the equality they demanded. Representatives were to be chosen by direct and secret election (Bibl. #127, September 1, 1924). The Landarbeiter-Archiv of May 1928 (Bibl. #128, pp. 82ff.) gave the following survey:

Wage Earners in Chambers of Agriculture

Chambers	Per cent	Chambers	Per cent
Hamburg	33	Lippe	22
Braunschweig	29	Württemberg	19
Oldenburg	20-23	Baden	14
Mecklenburg-Schwerin	29		

Small representations cooperating with the Chambers existed in Bavaria, Saxony, Thuringia, and Mecklenburg-Strelitz

[58] Bibl. #137, 1921, p. 41.
[59] Otto Braun (Bibl. #11), p. 60.

CHAPTER VII. WAGES

Type of Compensation

I. WAGES IN KIND

WITH the increasing intensification of cultivation, the practice of sharing in grinding or threshing as part of the workers' wages had deteriorated. Only in some parts of the east did the worker continue to share in grain crops and to sell his share in the market. However, the distinction between workers on shares and deputatists was vague since it continued to be customary in large parts of the country to pay wages partly in kind and partly in cash. Workers in the north and east usually received a small cash remuneration, a dwelling with stable, a plot of land, pasture land, and supplies such as potatoes, milk, and fuel.[1] Thus deputatists frequently raised their own potatoes and other vegetables and cared for their cow or sheep. Up to the First World War the proportion of wages in kind had continuously decreased: in Brandenburg from 76.2 to 45.7 per cent within a period of 65 years; in Pomerania from 80.2 per cent in 1873 to 68.3 per cent before the war.[2] Payment in kind increased in the postwar period, due chiefly to the currency inflation during which wages in kind afforded protection against deterioration of income. In some parts of the Reich where payment in kind was previously unknown, particularly in the south on estates with vineyards and tobacco lands, it was introduced during the inflation, but disappeared after stabilization of the currency. It showed the following changes in 1928 as compared to the prewar and postinflation periods.

Percentage of Wages in Kind

District	Before the War[2]	1924[2]	1928[3]
East Prussia	82.5	84.9	83.0
Brandenburg	45.7	65.8	67.1
Pomerania	68.3	89.0	70.6
Silesia	17.7	74.2	74.3
Province Saxony	14.7	45.0	34.0
Schleswig-Holstein	48.2	64.8	69.8
State Saxony	7.6	44.6	35.4

[1] An East Prussian collective agreement provided 5 items of wages in kind: 1) dwelling, stable and garden; 2) cow or milk; 3) potato land; 4) furnace; 5) grain.

[2] Wolfgang Hucho (Bibl. #40), p. 71.   [3] Franz Hering (Bibl. #112k), p. 18.

Although the LAO prescribed that collective agreements determine the value of wages in kind many agreements failed to do so.[4] Other agreements attempted to overcome differences in evaluation of wages in kind by establishing standards. Thus, for instance, farm products were estimated according to prices prevailing in the produce exchange. However, employers disliked standardization because they were afraid that in many places a higher estimate of such compensation would result in higher taxes and social insurance dues, eventuating in demands for wage increases.[5] On the other hand, employers complained that workers underestimated wages in kind, especially since the treasury office assessed them at a very low rate.

On the whole employers preferred wages in kind because it was always extremely difficult to maintain sufficient cash resources. Wages in kind served to separate wages from market prices and fostered a community of interest between employers and employees. The attitude of trade unions toward wages in kind was divided, the Socialist unions aiming at its abolition. They argued that wages in kind were a cloak for low wages and created such a degree of dependence on the part of the worker as almost to cost him his freedom of contract and mobility. Strikes could be defeated by the refusal of the employer to provide forage for the cattle. Only with wages paid in cash did the free trade unions hope to place wages on an equality with those in industry. Wages in kind, they said, made it impossible for the agricultural worker to bargain at the most favorable time since to do so would endanger his home or his crop; evaluation was arbitrary, and work on deputat land extended the hours of work. Moreover, low cash wages interfered with paying trade union dues. The fight against wages in kind by the Socialist unions in no way represented the prevailing attitude of the rank and file who had come to realize too clearly during the inflation period that only wages in kind retained their value. Moreover, collective agreements frequently provided that wages in kind continue during periods of illness.[6] The Socialist trade unions, however, were determined to educate the agricultural worker to "advanced" ideas of abolishing the remnants of the feudal system.

[4] Hucho, "Die Naturallohnbewertung in der deutschen Landwirtschaft," Bibl. #139, 1926, Nichtamtlicher Teil, pp. 162-63.

[5] *Ibid.*, p. 164.

[6] Julius Schmitt (Bibl. #112d), p. 49. Some agreements provided that wages in cash and kind continue during periods of illness with deduction of sick cash benefits. Some allowed a short period of absenteeism for reasons beyond the worker's control without deduction.

The Christian unions and the RLAB argued that disadvantages were overcompensated by gains and that wages in kind were a valuable incentive to the worker to secure ultimate independence.[7] They stressed the economic security which wages in kind provided. Johannes Wolf, president of the RLAB, used the following reasoning to convince workers of the advantages of wages in kind: out of a hundred pounds of grain a worker gets a hundred pounds of bread and about ten pounds of bran for his cattle. If, on the other hand, he receives 10 Rm. as wages, he must buy his bread at the rate of 15 Rm. per hundred pounds; in other words, an additional 5 Rm. for the trade, and nothing for his cattle.[8]

2. EFFICIENCY WAGES

The increasing difficulties of agriculture in the period after stabilization of the currency and the necessity of restoring profitability of the estates by improving their efficiency led to the growing use of wages based on output or performance, although its spread was hampered in some parts of the country by the high percentage of wages in kind and by employment of foreign labor. Efficiency wages prevailed in hoe cultivation and harvesting. Silesian employers, especially, promoted them, others did not like to be burdened with calculations and were dissatisfied when faulty standards eventuated in losses.

Collective agreements for the most part fixed only minimum wages and stipulated that piece wages should provide about 25 to 30 per cent higher earnings. In gardening and cattle raising shares in profits were often granted. Premium wages were rare and where they existed, they were fixed by employers. Bonuses were provided for special work such as milking and strewing of fertilizers. In the employment of women, premiums sometimes were granted in order to shorten the hours of work. Women with households of their own were usually eager to finish their assignment in a shorter time.

Experience did not result in an easily applied formula. Time studies had to be made for each farm because of differences in soil, climate, and the efficiency of workers. Workers became suspicious because in some instances rates had been cut when earnings increased. Trade unions accepted piece wages provided minimum rates were guaranteed. Although they were

---

[7] Max Hofer (Bibl. #36), p. 19.
[8] Johannes Wolf-Stettin (Bibl. #87), p. 39.

inclined to get wage increases beyond agreed wages, they frequently opposed incentive wages out of fear of overstrain.[9]

Regional Differentiation

There was great regional differentiation of wages. In general, wages increased from east to west. A comparison based on the yearly earnings as calculated for the purposes of workmen's compensation disclosed that wages in 1905 were higher in regions of middle-sized holdings than in those of small and large farms; they were higher for the care of cattle and dairying than for tillage of the soil, higher in industrial areas than in rural. In some parts of the east the lowest class was preponderant.[10]

Development of Wages before the Depression (1929)

No uniform statistical data are available for farm workers' wages in the Reich up to 1924. Special regional investigations cannot be generalized because of the great regional differentiation of wages and because of different evaluation of wages in kind. There is no doubt that the rise of landless laborers following the Stein-Hardenberg reform kept wages at a low level. The pressure on wages was relieved by increasing industrialization, which transformed the surplus into a shortage of manpower. Although wages increased after the middle of the nineteenth century this increase could not keep pace with the general development of the wage level. Bierei, in investigating wages of deputatists in Posen, selected as typical for German workers, found that for the period from 1885 to 1906 no average increase could be calculated. Maximum increases only slightly exceeded 30 per cent, while wages of industrial workers had increased by 37-38 per cent. The variation[11] in the earnings of farm workers was considerable between different estates. The farmer had recovered the wage increase by price increases.

In the last decade before World War I wages of agricultural workers

[9] Bibl. #127, 1927, No. 8, p. 3.

[10] In Silesia 97 per cent of the population belonged to the lowest (5th) wage class (300-420 M. per year), in Posen 80 per cent. In Brandenburg and Pomerania, however, wages were higher than in the other parts of the east, and Mecklenburg had relatively high wages, i.e. prevailingly class 3 (540-660 M. per year). Baden on the whole had lower wages, i.e. class 4 (420-540 M. per year) than Württemberg where the majority of the wage earners fell into class 3, and the Palatinate was very low (2/3 in class 5). The northwest had very few in the lowest class (A. Saucke, "Der durchschnittliche Jahresarbeitsverdienst für land- und forstwirtschaftliche Arbeiter im Jahre 1905," Bibl. #125, 1906, Vol. 31, pp. 235ff.).

[11] Ernst Bierei, "Die Bewegung der Arbeitslöhne in der Landwirtschaft," Bibl. #130, 1911, Vol. 40, pp. 371, 379.

had increased. W. Asmis, whose figures, however, were contested by the trade unions, reported increases in some areas of the province of West Prussia (based on figures of the Chamber of Agriculture) of 28-44 per cent for deputant families from 1903 to 1913, for male servants from 22 to 68 per cent.[12]

In spite of the great shortage of labor, cash wages did not keep pace with prices during the First World War, although workers secured more copious payments in kind as food shortages increased. In the first period after the war, wage claims frequently exceeded the profitability of farms. Demands during the revolutionary period were almost unlimited in number and amount. Farmers, shocked by the revolution, easily gave in. Soon, however, the currency inflation began to endanger the worker's gains. By the spring of 1919 the expenses for married workers (including housing) had already risen to three or four times the peacetime expenditure.[13] While money wages increased by 146 per cent from 1914 to 1920, the price of pork increased by 183 per cent, butter 446 per cent, eggs 3025 per cent.[14] Wages fell during the following period of accelerated inflation. Although agricultural workers were much better protected than industrial workers against the effects of currency depreciation, the former felt the pinch in proportion to the percentage of cash wages in his income. According to the report of the DLV,[15] total hourly wages, estimated in gold, decreased from 1919 to the end of 1923 in East Prussia (a region with a large percentage of wages

[12] Walter Asmis (Bibl. #4), p. 487. He gives the income of a farm worker's family in Pomerania in 1907 as follows (pp. 507-508):

Yearly wages	920.70 M. (165.— M. cash,
	370.— M. food and lodging,
	385.70 M. wages in kind)
Wages of wife	172.00 M. (cash)
Christmas gift	20.00 M. (cash)
Total	1,112.70 M.

The income of an independent worker's family including subcontractor in three areas in Pomerania in 1910 was 1,393.50-1,645 M. (*ibid.*, p. 511); in Silesia the independent steady worker had an average of 507.86 M. (of which 100.12 were wages in kind); the whole family, 650-680 M. (*ibid.*, p. 529).

[13] Bibl. #102, No. 3, pp. 147-48.

[14] Friedrich Aereboe (Bibl. #2), p. 128. Aereboe gives the following example for the wages of a Lohngärtner in a Silesian district (*ibid.*, p. 136):

	1918-1919	1919-1920	1920-1921	1921
Relation of paper wage to prewar wage in per cent	80.60	200.80	698.00	1148.00
Index of the cost of living	195.37	429.78	831.05	1141.84

[15] Bibl. #112f, p. 17.

in kind) from 29 to 18 pfennigs, and in Bavaria and the State of Saxony, where cash wages prevailed, from 28 to 8, and 32 to 8 pfennigs, respectively. Long before the sliding wage scales automatically adjusted to the cost-of-living index were introduced for industrial workers, systems of automatic adjustment of money wages to currency depreciation had been adopted in agricultural agreements. Unions had been very reluctant to agree to this kind of adjustment,[16] fearing the loss of influence in the regulation of wages. For the most part the adjustment was made to the combined price of rye and potatoes. On September 1, 1923, the head federations of trade unions and employers' organizations agreed to a system of automatic adjustment of wages of all workers and to a sliding scale based on a computation according to the official index of prices.[17] It was an unsatisfactory regulation which deprived the unions of an independent wage policy and did not prevent delayed and insufficient adjustment of wages to the phenomenally increasing cost of living. After the stabilization of the currency the sliding scale was dropped.

Wages then picked up quickly; from 1926 they rose steadily and for many categories surpassed the prewar level.[18] Total wages of deputatists (unweighted) were on the average 24 per cent higher in the Reich in 1926 than before the war (varying from 5 to 58 per cent in various parts of the country), of domestic servants 29 per cent (male) and 35 per cent (female), of foreign workers up to 100 per cent. These figures do not include the parts of the wage applied to the worker's own economy.[19] Thus, in the sequence of increase, female servants were leading, followed by male servants, Freiarbeiter, and deputatists. However, in the following years increase in deputatists' wages took the lead. In comparing the wages of married depu-

---

[16] Ibid., p. 48.

[17] Korrespondenzblatt 1923, pp. 367-68, 370-71, 406ff. Each wage comprised a basic wage and a coefficient. The wage rate was determined by multiplying the basic wage by the coefficient and was computed weekly. The parties to a collective agreement determined the basic wage for a period of from four to eight weeks, while the coefficient was based on the cost of living index.

[18] The Statistische Reichsamt computed the weighted average value, in cash and in kind, of deputatists wages for 1926 in the Reich at 1,010.30 Rm. a year, for unmarried steady workers 797.05 Rm. in 2,900 working hours, or 34.8 pfennigs per hour (Bibl. #153e, 1925, No. 17, p. 581; 1926, No. 7, p. 222).

[19] Bibl. #104b, pp. 165-66. Family allowances, as an addition to cash wages, were provided only for 51,293 agricultural workers covered by collective agreements on January 1, 1931 (Tarifverträge für Arbeiter im Deutschen Reich, am 1. Januar 1931, p. 21). Wages in kind for deputatists generally varied according to the size of the family.

tatist as found by the Enquiry Committee[20] for 1910-1914 and 1926 with wages given in the annual report of the *Reichsverband ländlicher Arbeitnehmer*[21] (formerly *ZV*) for the year 1929, based on the same documentary evidence, the following increases of yearly wages are shown:

Yearly Wages of Married Deputatists

Territory	1910-1914	1926 (in Rm.)	1929	Increase in Per Cent,[22] 1914-1929
East Prussia	790	989	1088	38
Pomerania	807	1117	1283	59
Brandenburg	1013	1184	1259	24
Silesia	668	959	1093	64
Mecklenburg-Schwerin	1026	1076	1204	17
Schleswig-Holstein	892	1176	1430	60
Hanover	700	1107	1176	68
Kurhessen	1010	1062	1122	11
Saxony Province	999	1094	1240	24
Saxony State	831	1149	1255	51
Thuringia	830	993	1118	34
REICH AVERAGE (not weighted)	870	1082	1206	40

These wage rates of collective agreements include the worker's wages both in cash and in kind; the wife's wages are not included. Actual wages exceeded them.[23] An increase in wage rates in 1929 was estimated for Silesia to amount to 80 per cent of cash wages.[24] According to the Chamber of Agriculture of Stettin, deputatists' wages (including subcontractors) had increased in Pomerania by 50 per cent from 1912 to 1928. Wages of dairymen rose from 1,400-2,200 Rm. in 1926 to 1,700-2,500 Rm. in 1928.[25] Only the wages of managers of farms lagged, owing to the available supply of per-

[20] *op.cit.*, pp. 212. [21] Bibl. #144, 1929.

[22] Source: Gustav Roeber (Bibl. #71), p. 34.

[23] "Entgegnungsschrift des Arbeitgeberverbandes auf die Denkschrift des DLV von 1928," quoted by Roeber (Bibl. #71), p. 35. The Dairymen's Union in the September 15, 1930, issue of its journal, stated that in the state of Saxony total wages of deputatists amounted to from 1,547 to 1,722 Rm., exclusive of income from deputat land (Roeber, *ibid.*, p. 36).

[24] Dyrenfurth, "Wie wird sich die Lohnerhöhung des neuen landwirtschaftlichen Arbeiterlohntarifs für die Gesamtheit der schlesischen Landwirtschaft auswirken?" Bibl. #161, April 6, 1929, p. 457.

[25] Bibl. #112l, p. 36.

sonnel (many former army officers turned to this kind of work when the army was reduced in accordance with the Treaty of Versailles).

The differential between women's and men's wages (57:100) was larger than in nonagricultural occupations.[26] However, the deputat contained part of women's wages.

Relation of Agricultural Wages to Peasant Incomes and Industrial Wages

No statistics of real wages of farm workers are available. Official statistics include farm workers' wages since 1924 but report only total yearly money wages and the number of deputats.[27] Wages in kind, based on retail prices, were officially calculated only for 1924. The best measure for the farm workers' standard of living would be a comparison of their income with the farmers' and industrial workers' income. However, it is difficult to compare exactly the situation of the farm worker with that of an industrial worker or a member of a peasant family working on the family farm. No standard method of computation of payment in kind was generally recognized; it was difficult to calculate what part of the wage was used for the upkeep of the livestock, for instance, or how much the worker profited from higher selling prices if a portion was sold. All comparisons therefore have to be taken with a grain of salt. The income of the peasant was in many cases not higher than that of the worker. Münzinger, in assuming an interest payment of 5 per cent for the invested capital calculated the income of the Württemberg peasant and members of his family as lower than that of the farm servant.[28] According to von Dietze's calculation this was true for other parts of Germany as well.[29]

In spite of all the improvements achieved by 1930, the margin of difference between industrial and agricultural wages increased.[30] With 100 as the index of industrial wages for January 1925 and agricultural wages for December 1924, the Enquiry Committee[31] made the following analysis:

---

[26] Hucho (Bibl. #40), p. 44.

[27] The lack of real wage statistics is confirmed in a memorandum prepared by the Ministry of Agriculture for the Bizone on September 12, 1949.

[28] Adolf Münzinger (Bibl. #59), Vol. II, p. 873.

[29] C. von Dietze, "Die Lage der deutschen Landwirtschaft," Bibl. #125, 1929, Vol. 130, 3. Folge; Vol. 75, pp. 659-60.

[30] Relatively lower pay of farm workers has been a general European experience. According to a British government report the common ratio of real wages in agriculture to industrial wages of similar grade in England was about two to three in 1923 (Agricultural Tribunal of Investigation Final Report, London, 1924, p. 165).

[31] Bibl. #104b, p. 38. The calculation is based on figures provided by W&St and the DLV, both based on the same documentary evidence.

Extent of Difference between Industrial and Agricultural
Workers' Wages

(*January 1924 = 100*)

Workers	1924 January	July	1925 July	1926 January	July	1927 January	July	1928 January	July
Skilled industrial	75	92	114	119	119	120	128	130	134
Unskilled industrial	80	91	113	118	118	120	130	134	139
Agricultural (deputatist)	76	85	106	97	103	115	118	115	124

The farm worker had to rely heavily on the income of other members of the family.[32] When employers protested against mechanical wage increases by compulsory arbitration, the DLV published the following figures comparing the total wages of an agricultural worker (including those for his wife and an 18-year-old son) with the wages of a semiskilled worker in the building industry, in October 1927.[33]

	Agriculture	Building Industry
	(*pfennig per hour*)	
East Prussia	64.97	63
Silesia	77.32	71
Central Germany	92.08	80

Wages for young agricultural workers were particularly low in comparison with those paid in industry and commerce.

The official statistics of 1924, emphasizing the approximate value of their findings give the following comparison for industrial and farm workers' wages with perquisites calculation based on retail prices.

[32] A DLV inquiry among 145 typical families (87 of them deputatists averaging 5.11 persons per family) for July 1, 1929—June 30, 1930, disclosed 2.6 persons working per family. Out of 145 wives, 111 were wage earners (only four of whom were not in agriculture), or three out of every four. Of the children (including other relatives living in the family), 96 out of 123 over fourteen and 29 out of 328 under fourteen years of age were wage earners. The husband's earnings (cash and wages in kind) represented 54.1 per cent of the income, the wife's cash income 10 per cent, other members of the family 7.6 per cent; occasional earnings amounted to 4.8 per cent; the sale of produce of own land represented 13.7 per cent; 4.9 per cent were social insurance benefits and other assistance (Wilhelm Bernier, Bibl. #1120, pp. 35, 37-41, 48-49, 117-18).

[33] Bibl. #112 i, p. 7.

Comparison of Collectively Agreed Yearly Total Wages of Farm
Workers' and Unskilled Industrial Workers' Wages in the Lowest
Local Class in 1924[34]

Region	Farm Worker (Rm.)	Money Wages (Per Cent)	Printer (Rm.)	Textile Worker (Rm.)	Paper Worker (Rm.)	Lumber Worker (Rm.)
East Prussia	865	13.9	1104	816	—	852
Schleswig-Holstein	1139	31.9	1104	—	—	1152
Baden	1100		1104	984	1056	1200
Württemberg	1044	100	1104	960	1128	1224
Rhineland	1024	67.3	1104	1176	960	1008
Hanover	948	58.6	1104	1008	852	950
Upper Bavaria	830	73.5	1104	854	960	1128

Working hours of unskilled industrial workers were 2,400 a year, of farm
workers 2,900. Hourly wages of the latter were 20 per cent lower than those
of the former.[35]

In 1928 the DLV started the campaign "industrial workers' wages for
agricultural workers."[36] Falke calculated that the raising of the farm workers'
annual wages from 1,400 to 1,600 Rm.—i.e. by about 16 per cent—in order to
bring it up to the unskilled industrial workers' wage would have raised
the cost of production 8 per cent. Prices of agricultural products would
therefore have to be raised to make up for this increase.[37]

I. DEVELOPMENT DURING THE DEPRESSION

In 1930 the DLV was still able to obtain wage increases by negotiations for
65,687 workers; in 1931 no increases were possible,[38] and from the end of 1931
on wages began to decrease considerably. In order to carry out the deflation
policy of the government, arbitrators began to cut wages. On October 23,
1931, the East Prussian Land League informed the Reich President that it
would not be able to continue to pay the same wages and announced a
one-third cut.[39]

[34] Bibl. #153e, 1924, Vol. 4, No. 21, pp. 677-678.
[35] Memorandum of the agricultural administration of the Bizone, 1949.
[36] Bibl. #112j.
[37] Friedrich Falke (Bibl. #23), p. 41.
[38] Pressedienst des Deutschen Landarbeiterverbandes, May 27, 1932.
[39] Bibl. #112p, pp. 3-4.

The Fourth Emergency Decree of December 8, 1931,[40] allowed employers to reduce all wages on January 1, 1932, to the level obtaining on January 10, 1927. The cut was not to exceed 10 per cent, or if no cut had occurred since July 1, 1931, 15 per cent. This affected only wages in cash. The decree prohibited the termination of any agreement before April 30, 1932, and empowered the arbitration authority to prolong its validity until September 30, 1932. Employers' organizations and trade unions were to fix the new wage rates in an appendix to the collective agreement. If the parties were unable to agree, the rates were to be fixed by the arbitration officer, whose decision was final. The effect was that the wages of 791,288 men were reduced by a weekly average of 1.16 Rm.; of 498,698 women by 0.78 Rm., according to the DLV.[41] By the same decree, prices regulated by cartel and similar agreements and house rents were off 10 per cent. A commissioner for the supervision of prices was to see that the cuts were carried through and that they extended to the final consumer. Within a short time, the cost of living was falling and the wage cut was mitigated.

The Emergency Decree of September 5, 1932,[42] entitled employers in agriculture to cut cash wages in proportion to increased employment on the basis of the previous year. However, the decree was not applied in practice because it was much too complicated and employers and workers attacked it violently. It was repealed by the Decree of December 14, 1932.[43]

2. DISPOSABLE INCOME

In order to understand how much farm labor actually received in wages and was able to spend, it is necessary to deduct taxes and dues (in Germany, deducted at the source) and add services provided by social insurance and by the communities.[44] Deductions from gross wages included the wage, citizen,[45] and church taxes, and social insurance contributions.

[40] Bibl. #140, Vol. 1, p. 699. Emergency decrees were based on Article 48 of the Constitution, which empowered the Reich President to take all necessary measures for the restoration of public order and safety whenever these were seriously disturbed and endangered. This power was exercised at the height of the inflation in 1923 and in the depression 1930-1932. The right of the Reichstag to ask for repeal was not of much value because through fear of increasing the crisis, parliament usually did not dare to exercise its right. The application of emergency decrees during the depression was the first step toward changing the democratic government into a dictatorial one.

[41] *Pressedienst*, May 27, 1932.   [42] Bibl. #140, Vol. 1, pp. 433, 434.

[43] Bibl. #140, Vol. 1, p. 545.

[44] See Chapters on Social Insurance and Welfare Work in which these services are discussed.

[45] The citizen tax was introduced in 1930 as a community poll tax with a lower tax-free minimum than the wage tax—at low rates, however.

The wage tax amounted to 10 per cent of the income over a tax-free minimum which varied according to the size of the family. In 1926 the minimum including deductions for expenses amounted to 1,200 Rm. a year for the unmarried worker, increased by 120 Rm. each for the wife and the first child, by 240 for the second child, by 480 for the third. A worker with two children had a tax-free minimum of 1,680 Rm., with three children 2,160.[46] The wage tax was reduced in 1926 and 1928; the reduction for unmarried workers, however, was repealed on September 1, 1930. In 1931 an emergency tax (Krisensteuer) amounting to 1 per cent for the lowest income groups was introduced and in 1932 it was raised to from 1½ to 2½ per cent (Arbeitslosenabgabe). While most farm workers were exempt from the wage tax, they had to pay the emergency taxes. The tax burden for the farm worker was very light. The worker's share in social insurance contributions in 1928 amounted to about 9.5 per cent (for workers with annual incomes of 1,040 Rm.) to 8.27 per cent (1,560) to 9.92 per cent (1,300), and so forth.[47]

3. THE FAMILY BUDGET

According to the above-mentioned inquiry of the DLV[48] about 145 typical families earning a total average income of 2,417.76 M. expended it as follows:

	Expenditures (in Per Cent)
Food	29.1[a]
Clothing	13.0
Rent, interest, and repairs	0.9
Heat and light	2.6
Education	1.4
Amusements	3.0
Social insurance dues, membership fees, and taxes	9.0
Purchase and maintenance of stock	7.4
Repairs and furniture	4.6
Miscellaneous	5.5

[a] To which must be added 23.5 per cent of produce allowances consumed.

In view of their low standard of living, farm workers spent a larger proportion of their income on food than did industrial workers, less on housing

[46] Bibl. #153a, p. 126. These figures include unemployment insurance dues, not paid by all workers.
[47] Ibid., p. 159.
[48] Bernier (Bibl. #112 o), p. 49.

and miscellaneous items as shown in a study of the Reichsverband ländlicher Arbeitnehmer (formerly ZV)[49] for the year 1927:

	Per Cent of Total Expenditure	
	130 Agricultural Workers' Households (1927)	896 Urban Workers' Households (1927-1928)
Food	56.9	45.3
Clothing	15.3	12.7
Housing	13.9	17.5
Total	86.1	75.5
Other needs	13.9	24.5
Total	100.00	100.00

Hours of Work and Vacations

The LAO in conjunction with collective agreements shortened hours of work which, before the war, were from sunrise to sunset. The total number of working hours, restricted by the LAO to a maximum of about 2,900 a year, could be shortened by agreement. Only in a few parts of Germany (in the south and some districts in the east) did collective agreements fix a maximum of 2,900; some were fixed as low as 2,650. In general, 2,800-2,850 was the prevailing number. Compared with the prewar era, the total amount of working time probably decreased by 10 per cent on large farms, in other words, by 300-350 hours a year. The legal or contractual obligation to shorten hours was of greater importance in purely agricultural regions where hours had not been influenced by industrial working conditions before the war. In the first years after the war agreements shortened hours considerably. An additional cut came about by including in working hours the time required to reach the place of work. This may have involved a loss of 7 to 10 per cent according to the distance to be covered.[50] After the currency stabilization there was a slight increase in working time.[51]

Hours worked varied remarkably from district to district. In one Pomeranian district they were 2,950, and 2,850 in another bordering on it. On the whole, the total number of hours declined and the differences between the longest and shortest working day diminished from east to west and from south to north in view of the more industrialized character of the west and north.

[49] Max Hofer (Bibl. #37), quoted in Bibl. #121b, 3, p. 66.
[50] Bibl. #104b, pp. 42, 115, 168, 216ff.
[51] An inquiry of the DLV estimated the total average hours worked under collective agreements in the whole German agriculture at 2,900 for 1929.

Regulation of overtime, an innovation of the postwar period, varied regionally. A few collective agreements made it compulsory to work overtime if necessary. Since overtime and holiday work was paid at a higher rate, employers were careful not to make excessive use of it. The distribution of total hours over the months and days was regulated either by agreement or by the employer. Most agreements left it to the employer to determine the daily timetable. In many cases he had to consult his workers.

The working day of resident farm servants was seldom settled in the collective agreement. They had to work according to need. The Bavarian covering agreement provided a nightly rest period of certain length (eight to ten hours) which amounted to an indirect limitation of working time. Farm servants did not receive special rates for overtime.

The shortening of hours for agricultural workers was a more remarkable achievement in view of the fact that peasants usually had very long working hours,[52] longest in the peasant districts of the south, north, and east, shortest in the Rhenish wine country where agriculture was in contact with industrial centers.

The terms were most effectively carried out on large estates. On the small farm, division of labor was less developed; the work was less planned and more traditional. The worker had to perform many different operations without the technical equipment of the worker on the large farm. All these conditions tended to lengthen the work day, especially among workers who had to do field work as well as tend the cattle. Collective agreements applied in practice only to large farms. Enforcement of the provisions of the LAO on small farms depended on the class consciousness of the worker, his courage in demanding his rights, and his relations with the employer. The Enquiry Committee was of the opinion that the hours set in collective agreements were accepted throughout the country, even where employers and workers were not actually parties to the agreement. However, an inquiry of the Prussian Ministry of Agriculture into 130 farms of 6.5 to 5.5 ha. in 1929-1930 found that hours of family and wage workers averaged 250 a year above those of workers on large estates as regulated by collective agreements.[53] Some agreements (e.g. Brandenburg) excluded from the regulation

---

[52] Adolf Münzinger calculated hours of work on Württemberg peasant farms at an average of 12 for men and 13 for women, i.e. 3,554-3,933 a year, compared with 2,900 for agricultural workers (Bibl. #59, Vol. II, pp. 811-12).

[53] Fritz Klare, "Einsatz und Ausnutzung der menschlichen Arbeitskräfte in bäuerlichen Betrieben," Bibl. #130, 1932, Vol. 75, p. 127.

of hours farms where most of the workers lived as members of the farmer's household.

In certain collective agreements hours were not merely limited, but a minimum of working hours—e.g. eight a day—was guaranteed to workers with long contracts, in order to avoid irregular employment during the depression. In northern and eastern Germany payment in kind was given for the whole year, whatever the actual working hours. In the south and west, where payment in kind was less usual, wages were correspondingly reduced when there had been fewer hours of work than the agreement provided.

Evaluation of shorter hours was not uniform. In the first year after the war especially, employers with few exceptions complained of the lower output, resulting partly from shorter hours, which obliged them to employ more workers and machines. Workers denied that the shorter working day had any deleterious effect on production.

Practically all collective agreements provided annual vacations, the amount (usually not more than six days [though some agreements ranged up to twelve]) depending in many cases on the age of the worker. They shortened the yearly working time by thirty to forty hours. Some collective agreements excluded certain categories of workers (farm servants, Hofgänger) from the right to vacations, or provided shorter vacations for them. As a rule, workers were entitled to remuneration during vacations, payment for 8 to 9 hours being provided. Payments in kind were sometimes converted into cash. During this time work for other employers was not permitted.

CHAPTER VIII

SOCIAL PROVISIONS FOR LABOR

Social Insurance

O F THE SIX branches of the German social insurance system, four were applicable to the agricultural worker, sickness, accident, invalidity[1] (i.e. permanent disability, old age, survivors') and unemployment insurance.

I. SICKNESS INSURANCE

Agricultural workers were covered by accident and workers' invalidity insurance as early as the 1880's, but the sickness insurance law of 1883 did not include them. Legislators hesitated to introduce cash benefits for workers in parts of the country where compensation in kind prevailed and was continued in case of sickness.[2] The farm servant ordinances obliged the employer to provide initial care for his workers in case of sickness. A few states and communities used their right to extend sickness insurance by statute to the farm workers of their territory. When social insurance was codified in 1911,[3] the scope of insurance was extended to include farm workers by January 1, 1914. However, they were not accorded full rights of self-government. Special rural funds were set up in definite areas for agricultural, itinerant, home workers, and domestic servants, administered by appointees of the authorities rather than by those elected from the ranks of the insured and their employers. Moreover, employers had the right to claim exemption of domestic servants and agricultural workers, but they were nevertheless obliged to care for them in event of sickness. This right resulted in the exemption of about one-half of all workers.[4]

After the revolution of 1918 full equality was established, and rural funds were accorded the same right of self-government as other funds.[5] The right of employers to obtain exemption for agricultural workers and domestic servants was abolished.[6] Sickness insurance was governed by the following principles:

[1] A fifth, invalidity insurance for salaried employees including those in agriculture, was a separate branch.

[2] Bibl. #154, 6. Legislaturperiode, Second Session 1885-1886, Vol. IV, p. 400.

[3] Federal Social Insurance Code (Reichsversicherungsordnung, RVO) of July 19, 1911 (Bibl. #140, p. 509).

[4] Bibl. #3, Vol. I, p. 105.   [5] Decree of June 28, 1919 (Bibl. #140, p. 615).

[6] Decree of February 3, 1919 (Bibl. #140, p. 191).

a. Compulsory coverage

b. Legal claim to benefits

c. Financial self-support of the insurance carriers (sick funds) through employer-employee contributions.

d. Self-government of the sick funds (which are public bodies).

In 1931 there were 425 rural funds covering 1,846,000 insured.[7] To cover costs employees and their employers were assessed in the ratio of two to one, which entitled them to a proportional share in the self-government. Contributions[8] and cash benefits were graded according to wage groups. Contributions could be reduced and cash benefits cancelled in instances where yearly contracts in agriculture guaranteed a compensation to the sick employee equal at least to cash benefits. Medical benefits could not be cancelled.

Wage earners without income limits and salaried employees earning 3,600 Rm. or less a year were compulsorily insured. Insurance on a voluntary basis was available to farmers, who as a rule employed not more than two workers and who did not earn more than 3,600 Rm. a year, members of the farmer's family, and other persons who worked without remuneration. The funds could fix an age limit for admission of this group and could demand a health certificate. Persons who ceased to be subject to compulsory insurance were entitled to continue membership voluntarily under certain conditions. Voluntarily insured persons had to bear the whole amount of contributions.

Insurance entailed no special formalities for the workers; it began immediately upon employment. The insured were guaranteed medical treatment and, in case of incapacity to work, cash benefits. If sick, a worker could consult a physician of his own choice[9] and be turned over to a surgeon or other specialists if necessary. Besides medical treatment he was given medicines, dental care, minor appliances such as glasses or hernia bandages.

[7] Bibl. #153c, 1933, p. 388. Special rural funds were established only if both funds, rural and urban, had at least 1,000 members.

[8] The rates of contribution were defined by the bylaws of the individual fund within limits fixed by statute. The average rate was 6.43 per cent of earnings in 1929. Contributions were paid by employers who deducted the worker's share from his wages. Financing was under a pay-as-you-go scheme.

[9] The large majority of all licensed physicians served as insurance doctors with exception of some outstanding specialists. The associations of physicians and the funds bargained collectively and a special body, the National Committee for Physicians and Sickness Funds (Reichsausschuss für Ärzte und Krankenkassen) was empowered to determine broad policies concerning the relationship between the professions and funds.

Cash benefits of one-half of the basic wage[10] were paid from the fourth day of incapacity. Some funds adjusted cash benefits according to the number of dependents. Every fund could extend these minimum benefits within certain limits. Benefits could include hospitalization, home nursing, laboratory examination, X-ray and other electro- or physiotherapies and convalescent care. During hospitalization the patient's family received one-half of his regular cash benefits. The maximum period for all services was 26 weeks, unless extended by the fund. Death benefits were granted in lump sums.[11]

In the period of the Democratic government insurance coverage and the amount of benefits in kind were greatly extended. The most remarkable reforms were the improvement of maternity benefits and the inclusion of members of the family in medical and hospital treatment. After 1919 maternity benefits were granted not only for insured women but for members of the family of the insured person as well. After a qualifying period, the funds provided cash benefits, for ten weeks or longer, equal to the amount of sick benefits. Payment began four weeks before confinement and continued for six weeks after childbirth. If payment began earlier than four weeks prior to childbirth due to miscalculation of the date of confinement, it was nevertheless continued for six weeks after the birth of the child. Nursing mothers received an additional bonus of one-half the cash benefit for twelve weeks. Provisions were made for medical aid, midwife service, and a lump sum to defray the costs of confinement. Treatment in maternity homes could be substituted for cash benefits.

[10] According to the most usual calculation, the basic wage of each class was midway between the upper and lower limits of the class. Workers earning 0.40-0.80 Rm. an hour would have a basic wage of 0.60 Rm., irrespective of whether they earned 0.40, 0.50, or whatever wages within the limits of the class. In fact, benefits were more than 50 per cent since the worker did not pay taxes and insurance dues during his sickness.

[11] During the depression cuts in benefits were made with a view to restoring solvency of the funds, and because some liberal amendments had to be abolished when physicians complained that their time was taken up with trifling cases. The rights of the funds to dispense with the waiting period and cash pay on holidays were canceled, small fees for the first consultation and prescriptions introduced, not, however, without allowing for many exceptions (Decree of July 26, 1930, Bibl. #140, Vol. 1, p. 311; August 2, 1930, Bibl. #139, Vol. 1, p. 165; and circular of August 21, 1930, Bibl. #139, Vol. iv, p. 375). Grants of supplementary benefits were made contingent on the consent of the Federal Insurance Board. If the rate of dues exceeded 5 per cent of the basic wage, as was usually the case, consent had to be refused (Decree of December 8, 1931, Bibl. #140, Vol. 1, Part 5, p. 699). Many of these measures were imposed to steer the funds safely through the emergency, and former benefits were to be restored at its conclusion.

The importance of maternity aid may be gauged by the fact that two out of every three newborn infants benefited from social insurance. Infant centers were established all over the country. In rural districts equipment was provided locally and the physician traveled from one section to another. Every section had a public social worker, usually a trained nurse, who assisted the physician. Nursing benefits were paid only if the infant was brought to the center at regular intervals. Mothers received infant health education, and many unsanitary customs and superstitions could thus be overcome. In the schools children were given periodic examinations by circuit community physicians and nurses. In a similar manner, sick funds cooperated with public health administration and invalidity insurance in efforts to prevent disease and maintain standards of health.

Ignorance and indifference were systematically fought. The doctor's office, the dental clinic, the dispensary, the out-patient clinic were centers for a large scale educational program.

Although contributions and benefits were much lower in rural districts, owing to the lower cash wages of agricultural workers and the smaller risk of sickness,[12] the total benefits increased considerably as compared with the prewar period. Taking 100 as the index for 1913 the expenses of the rural funds per member had increased in 1928 to:

> 157.4 for money benefits
> 300.4 for medical treatment
> 193.7 for drugs and therapeutic appliances
> 210.6 for hospital care[13]

2. INVALIDITY, OLD AGE, AND SURVIVORS' INSURANCE

The law insuring workers in event of invalidity and old age, in force since 1889, included farm workers without designating an income limit. The RVO of 1911 added survivors' insurance to it.

Workers who had not yet paid one hundred weekly contributions could be exempt if they received no remuneration above free maintenance or if they worked only during the season for not more than twelve weeks at a

---

[12] In the country every third worker was incapacitated by sickness each year; in industry, every second worker (Ministerialdirektor A. Grieser, "Sozialversicherung und Landwirtschaft," in Bibl. #105, 50th Sonderheft, p. 150). Expenses of rural funds for the member were 36.62 Rm.; for other local funds, 65.16 Rm. in 1926 (*Statistik der Sozialversicherung 1926*, Beilage zu den amtlichen Nachrichten für Reichsversicherung, 1928, No. 2, *Sonderausgabe des RABl 1928*, p. 110).

[13] Grieser, *ibid.*, p. 151.

time and for a total of fifty days. Polish workers who were obliged to return to their country after the season were also exempt. Persons who ceased to be covered by insurance were entitled to continue the insurance on a voluntary basis. Farmers employing not more than two insured workers, and workers receiving no remuneration above free maintenance, or being only temporarily employed, were entitled to voluntary insurance up to the age of forty.

Contributions were paid in equal shares by employers and workers according to wage classes, with subsidies paid by the Treasury. Voluntarily insured persons paid the whole premium; for persons earning less than 6 Rm. a week and for apprentices the employer had to pay the entire premium. Employers had to pay their share of the contribution in respect of exempt foreign workers.

Pensions were payable in case of: 1) sickness lasting more than twenty-six weeks (thus dovetailing sickness insurance benefits); 2) permanent disability (i.e., when a person was no longer capable of earning one-third of the sum usually earned by a physically and mentally sound person in any employment to which he could reasonably be assigned on the basis of his strength, ability, training, and previous experience); 3) old age (i.e., a person was considered an invalid upon reaching sixty-five years of age); 4) to survivors in the event of the death of insured workers who had fulfilled the requirements for a pension.

To qualify for old age pension at the end of the democratic period manual workers had to have made 750 weekly contributions, for invalidity and survivors' benefits 250 compulsory or 500 voluntary weekly contributions. Periods of sickness were considered periods of contribution. To maintain the status of insured persons as a rule the payment of at least twenty weekly contributions every two years was required. Lost rights could be recovered under certain circumstances.

During the currency inflation, pensions had hopelessly deteriorated. However, after the stabilization of the currency, in changing from a capital to a pay-as-you-go system, the pensioners were protected against losses. In the middle twenties old age and disability pensions for manual workers comprised a fixed amount of 250 Rm. a year and a variable amount proportionate to the contributions paid (20 per cent). In addition, allowances were paid for each child under fifteen years of age (from 1928 on, 120 Rm. a year). Successive revisions of pensions were made: in the years following the currency stabilization (1924) they were raised; during the depression[14] they were reduced. In 1932 the average disability and old age pension in agriculture amounted to 28-30 Rm. a month,[15] but was reduced in the same year as an emergency measure. Institutional care could be substituted for the pension with the permission of the insured.

Widows who were incapacitated or were sixty-five years old (needy invalid widowers if the wife prior to her death had supported the family) received a pension until death or remarriage, and orphans up to the age of fifteen (a prolongation to twenty-one during a training period or indefinitely for incapacitated children was recalled in 1931). Illegitimate or adopted children, step-children, grandchildren—the last two if they were maintained by the insured—were included. Widows' pensions equalled six-tenths of the pension which would have been due to the deceased husband (reduced to five-tenths in 1932). Widows who remarried were entitled to a lump sum. Orphans received one-half of the pensions of the deceased (reduced to four-tenths in 1932). The total benefits payable to survivors could not exceed 80 per cent of the earnings for an able-bodied worker with the same occupational training as the insured person; by emergency decree survivors' pensions were restricted to the amount the deceased person would have received.

The institutions[16] were providing preventive and curative medical treatment at their discretion. Attempts to improve the health of the population were sponsored. Sanatoria gave treatment to insured tuberculars and their families and those afflicted with other serious diseases, and the insurance institutions contributed to the cost of medical treatment. The institutions financed housing schemes for the insured population. In cooperation with sick funds, community dispensaries were established to give medical aid to tuberculous persons, for those suffering from venereal diseases and cancer, for the physically handicapped, and others. Agreements secured coordination of the effort of the institutions and of sick funds, e.g. medical and dental

[14] Amendments were made, especially in the Emergency Decree of December 8, 1931 (Bibl. #140, Vol. i, p. 699) and June 14, 1932 (ibid., Vol. i, p. 273).

[15] Grieser, op.cit., p. 154. The conversion into American currency has to be made on the basis of 1 mark = 23.82 cents. However, the purchasing power of the mark was actually greater.

[16] Twenty-nine state institutions were insurance carriers, organized on a territorial basis. Carriers in prevailingly rural areas were subsidized by those in urban districts by partial pooling of resources. Workers were represented in the administrative bodies of the institutions.

treatment was provided by the sick funds, while invalidity insurance covered larger expenses, such as replacement of teeth.

3. WORKMEN'S COMPENSATION

Compulsory workmen's compensation, covering workers in agriculture and forestry (irrespective of income) from 1886 on,[17] included employers to a higher degree than did any other branch of insurance since there was little, if any, difference in the type of work small holders and workers did and not much distinction in their status.[18]

The interpretation of work accidents was liberalized by the democratic government. Covered were all accidents, by whatever cause, occurring while the worker was on the job, or while on the premises, including rest pauses. In 1925[19] the coverage was extended to all accidents on the way to and from the place of work.

Workmen's compensation was financed entirely by employers[20] who were grouped into compulsory mutual associations for various occupational fields or industries as, for instance, agriculture (decentralized in large areas, as for the provinces in Prussia). These associations—numbering 39 in 1932 with 524 sections[21]—were the exclusive insurance carriers. The Emergency Decree of December 8, 1931, provided for the participation of insured persons in measures for the prevention of accidents, thus meeting a long-standing claim of the trade unions.

Benefits were provided in case of disability and death. In the former, restoration of earning capacity had to be aimed at by all means. Benefits for injured persons comprised free medical attendance, vocational rehabilitation, and a pension (cash benefits) for the duration of incapacity. Medical and cash benefits were provided without delay during the first weeks by the sick funds as agents of the workmen's compensation associations for all persons covered by sickness insurance, but continued if necessary beyond the limits of these funds for an indefinite time and at higher rates. For those

---

[17] Law of May 5, 1886 (Bibl. #140, p. 132). The law came into force on April 1, 1888.

[18] In fact, all farmers were included. The official census of persons gainfully employed in agriculture was identical to the number of insured. Farm workers were only one fifth of the insured (Bibl. #153c, 1933, p. 394). 4.6 million enterprises were included.

[19] Law of July 14, 1925 (Bibl. #140, Vol. I, p. 97).

[20] The financial system was that of assessment according to risk and payroll at the end of each year.

[21] *Statistik der Sozialversicherung 1932*, Beilage zu den amtlichen Nachrichten für Reichsversicherung, 1933, No. 12 (Bibl. #139, Vol. IV, p. 487).

who were not included in sickness insurance the associations were obliged to pay cash benefits after thirteen weeks, but could voluntarily grant them earlier. They had to pay immediately in case of serious injuries. Medical attendance included treatment, hospitalization, medications and other therapeutic requisites, and equipment with artificial limbs and other appliances necessary to alleviate the results of the injury. In case of helplessness of the injured worker, nursing care or special attendance benefits were granted. If the injured was treated in a curative institution, cash benefits were paid to him and his family. Medical care as well as cash benefits had been liberalized during the period of democracy and vocational care[22] and compensation for occupational diseases were introduced.[23] Vocational rehabilitation, usually carried through by the offices for the assistance of the war-disabled, included vocational training with a view to the restoration or increase of working capacity and assistance in obtaining employment.

Workers who were fully disabled received two-thirds of the assessed wage loss from the day of stoppage of sick benefits or for the whole period of disability; in case of need of attendance, they received more. Partially incapacitated persons received the proportion of the full pension corresponding to the extent of the loss of working capacity.

Calculation of pensions for agricultural workers was not based on actual earnings as in the industrial branch of insurance, but on an average yearly wage. Formerly fixed by a superior insurance office, these wages were, from 1925 on assessed by a committee for each association, consisting of a chairman and at least four representatives of the employers and four of the insured. The assessment required the approval of the superior office. The average annual earnings were assessed by groups according to sex, age, and nature of employment. Wage rates fixed in collective agreements were to be given consideration, as were local wage differences. For persons under the age of twenty-one, pensions were calculated according to the prevailing wages, at age twenty-one, for similar work in the neighborhood.

If the pension was not less than 50 per cent of the full amount, a bonus of 10 per cent of the actual pension was payable for each dependent child under fifteen years of age. Pensions for incapacitated children and children in training beyond this age were ended by emergency decree in 1931. Illegitimate and other children were included, as in invalidity insurance. The total pension, including children's bonuses, was not to exceed the annual earnings of the injured person.

[22] Act of July 14, 1925 (Bibl. #140, Vol. 1, p. 97).
[23] Decree of May 12, 1925 (Bibl. #140, Vol. 1, p. 69).

The average pension for agricultural laborers was 148.84 Rm. a year in 1932 (compared with 440.94 for the industrial worker).[24] Workers complained that the assessed earnings were lower than actual earnings. In 1927 the DLV reported[25] that the assessed average wage was 600 m. in East Prussia while actual wages amounted to 904 m. The committees tried to avoid hardship, but the method of calculation could not be altered because of the difficulty of computing wages in kind.

The Emergency Decree of December 8, 1931, abolished small pensions for less than 20 per cent incapacity[26] (independent farmers 25 per cent). Such pensions had always been attacked as too low to be of any value to the standard of living, yet they were suspected of delaying the full rehabilitation of the injured worker. Restoration of the pension, in case the disability grew worse, was assured. The claim to medical attendance and vocational rehabilitation remained.

Pensions could be settled by a lump sum for purchasing land or paying off debts on a holding. On death by accident a funeral benefit was paid. The widow and children under fifteen years of age (or older in cases similar to those described under invalidity insurance) were entitled to pensions the total of which were not to exceed 80 per cent of the deceased worker's average annual earnings reduced to two-thirds by emergency decree in 1931. Usually the widow received 20 per cent and each of three dependents—child, parent, grandparent—20 per cent. If the three dependents were children of the deceased, nothing was left for other dependents. Incapacitated widowers were entitled to 40 per cent if they were in want and if the wife had supported them prior to her death. A lump sum was paid to the widow of a victim whose death was due to other causes and who was therefore not entitled to a pension.

The associations were obliged to issue safety rules and to supervise their enforcement. Violations were punishable. Inspectors were protected against dismissal. In 1926 there were only 83 technical officials (in 1932, 103) employed by insurance associations with supervision over 4.6 million undertakings;[27] in other words, one official to 55,481 (in 1932, 44,712) farms. In 1925 a center for prevention of accidents in agriculture was founded by

[24] *Statistik der Sozialversicherung 1932*, p. 500.
[25] Walter Kwasnik (Bibl. #112h, 2), p. 21.
[26] Bibl. #140, Vol. 1, p. 699. Pensions for accidents sustained from July 1, 1927 to December 31, 1931—the period of high wages—were cut 15 per cent, and for other accidents 7½ per cent by Emergency Decree of June 14, 1932 (*ibid.*, Vol. 1, p. 273). The cut by 7½ per cent was abolished for pensions concerning accidents after December 31, 1932 by Decree of October 19, 1932 (*ibid.*, Vol. 1, p. 499).
[27] Erwin Rawicz (Bibl. #68), p. 265.

all associations for pooling of experience, cooperation with the machine industry in safety devices, staging of exhibitions, and safety training.[28] The associations put pressure on machine repair shops to obey safety provisions.

In spite of strict safety rules accident frequency increased in agriculture. In industry the number of accidents compensated for the first time had been reduced from 7.14 per thousand insured persons in 1913 to 6.07 per thousand in 1928; in the same period the figures in agriculture increased from 3.35 per thousand to 6.08 per thousand.[29] Fatal accidents increased from 0.17 to 0.21 per thousand while they decreased in industry from 0.62 to 0.44 in the same period. The increase in accidents may be explained partly by improved reporting—sick funds insisted upon reporting of even minor injuries; partly by the liberalization of benefits which encouraged the raising of claims; and partly by the extension of coverage, for instance, to accidents on the way to and from work. The unfavorable business situation may, however, have led to neglect of safety measures. Inspection by the insurance association and training for safety had been improved, but the enforcement of safety rules encountered great difficulty in agriculture; tools and machinery were not always in good condition, and the poverty of farmers delayed repairs. Child labor, long hours, lack of knowledge of safety provisions, and growing mechanization increased the accident dangers.

It was greatly to the advantage of pensioners that they were entitled to preferential employment. Agricultural as well as all other employers employing more than twenty persons were obliged to fill a proportion (2 per cent) of their vacancies with men seriously injured by accident or military service whose earning capacity was reduced by not less than 50 per cent and who were entitled to a pension.[30] Employers could also fulfill their obligation to the injured person by providing holdings for settlement or lease from which adequate subsistence could be derived for himself and his family.

4. SUPERVISION AND SETTLEMENT OF DISPUTES

Special boards were set up which combined supervision of the institutions with the judicial settlement of disputes in sickness, invalidity, and accident

[28] "Die Unfallbelastung der deutschen Landwirtschaft," Bibl. #161, February 23, 1929, p. 251.

[29] Grieser, op.cit., p. 152.

[30] Gesetz über die Beschäftigung Schwerkriegsbeschädigter January 9, 1919 (Bibl. #140, p. 28), and of April 6, 1920 (ibid., p. 458) as formulated on January 12, 1923 (ibid., Vol. 1, p. 58) with frequent amendments. Enterprises with more than twenty and up to fifty employees had to employ at least one injured worker (Order of February 13, 1924, ibid., Vol. 1, p. 73).

insurance. They were established at three levels: local insurance board (Versicherungsamt), regional insurance board (Oberversicherungsamt), and Federal Insurance Board (Reichsversicherungsamt). The department entrusted with the settlement of disputes had considerable autonomy. So far as the adjudication of individual employees' claims was concerned, the tribunal was composed of employers' and workers' representatives under the chairmanship of a professional judge. The composition of the supervisory bodies was different.

5. UNEMPLOYMENT INSURANCE

Unemployment relief, introduced in 1918[31] for needy persons who were unemployed because of the war, included farm workers. The scheme frequently had to be modified because of currency inflation and decreasing financial resources of the government. From 1923 on, amendments brought it in closer alignment to insurance by placing it on a contributory basis. The insurance system which replaced it in 1927[32] covered farm workers. Farm servants were exempt (with the exception of those employed only temporarily), as were farm workers with contracts of at least one year's duration or carrying a six months' notice clause, and apprentices under indenture for not less than one year. All workers except farm servants, however, were to be included in time to get benefits whenever termination of employment was foreseen. Further, employed persons were exempt who at the same time were proprietors or tenants of holdings sufficiently large to provide subsistence and who worked for others, usually for less than half the year. The dependents of such owners were also exempt. Thus the line was drawn between being or not being exposed to the risk of unemployment. Migrant labor was included in order to prevent its drifting into other occupations. Exemptions were intended to induce employers to retain and enlarge their permanent staff. Out of a total of 2,600,000 workers 1,673,600 were exempt in November 1928.[33] Casual workers employed less than thirty hours a week and earning less than 45 M. per month were excluded.

[31] Decree of November 13, 1918 (Bibl. #140, p. 1305) and amendments.
[32] AVAVG (Bibl. #140, Vol. 1, p. 187).
[33] Exempt workers in September 1930 were:

Workers with own holdings	27,000
Workers with long-term contracts	552,000
Farm servants	1,014,000
Foreign workers	74,000
	1,667,000

Source: Grieser, op.cit., p. 154.

After two years, the government was to report to the Reichstag on insurance against unemployment in agriculture. Long before, however, complaints were heard concerning increase in the number of unemployed while scarcity of labor existed. Sons and daughters of land owners could live on their parents' holdings, receive benefits, and pick up odd jobs without reporting them, or peasants exchanged members of their families with neighbors and thus made them eligible for unemployment benefits. A special difficulty arose because benefits—calculated on wages of the previous three months—in the higher wage brackets exceeded the winter wages of agricultural workers so that workers preferred benefits during the winter to work in agriculture. By accepting low-paid winter work the benefits at the end of the work would have been lower. Deputatists tried to get short-term contracts with higher wages and insurance benefits during the slack season. Most of these problems were adjusted by the amendment of the law of October 12, 1929.[34] It based the amount of benefits upon the wages earned during the previous six months, not three months. A new definition of unemployment excluded from benefits persons engaged in agriculture and industry who could earn a livelihood jointly with wife, husband, parents, or offspring by cooperating in their work. This rule made it impossible for farmers' children to exchange work with one another on the holdings of their respective fathers for six months of the year and to claim benefits during the winter while living on their fathers' farms.

Unemployment insurance was administered by the Reifa. Committees composed of employers and employees controlled the work. Insurance was normally financed by contributions, one-half each from employers and workers, totalling 6½ per cent of basic wages (according to wage classes) in the depression years. Government loans covered the deficit until the fall of 1930 when the connections between the government budget and the Reifa were severed.

Financial distress made it necessary frequently to change the qualifying period, duration, waiting period, and amount of benefits. The last depended both upon the wage class and the number of dependents (after 1932, upon the locality, too). The unemployed person continued to be insured against sickness; contributions were paid by the Reifa.

As seasonal workers, agricultural workers were subject to restrictions.[35] During the winter of 1927-1928 their waiting period was lengthened.[36] In

---

[34] Bibl. #140, Vol. 1, p. 153.   [35] Wunderlich (Bibl. #94), pp. 52ff.
[36] Order of December 2, 1927 (Bibl. #139, 1927, Vol. 1, p. 548).

December 1928,[37] the period during which they received normal benefits in the off-season was reduced to six weeks; during the remaining weeks of the off-season they received smaller benefits and were subject to a means test. The length of the off-season was limited to a minimum of three, and a maximum of four, months within one year. After the period of seasonal employment the worker returned to insurance for the rest of his claim. This complicated and unsatisfactory system was abandoned in October 1929,[38] and the straight insurance principle restored. Benefits were reduced below those of other unemployed workers. In 1931[39] the period of benefits was limited to sixteen weeks and the equality of benefits with other unemployed workers restored.[40] However, farm workers were excluded from emergency benefits paid to other workers at the expiration of the insurance claim. In these circumstances, they received community welfare benefits, in case of need.

On June 14, 1932,[41] a needs test was introduced for all insured workers after six weeks, which practically meant discarding the insurance principle after this period. There were complaints that in small villages testing of need was too rigorous and partial.[42] Moreover, after 1931 insurance benefits were denied to married women as a legal right, even though they had fulfilled all requirements but were not in need, and persons under twenty-one years were excluded except insofar as they could not obtain the necessary support from members of their family.[43] Thus unemployment insurance had degenerated into a patchwork system of insurance and relief at the end of the period of democracy.[44]

6. SUMMARY

Whatever complaints there were against the other branches of social

[37] Act of December 24, 1928 (Bibl. #140, 1929, Vol. I, p. 1).

[38] Law of October 12, 1929 (Bibl. #139, Vol. I, p. 153).

[39] Emergency Decree of June 5, 1931 (Bibl. #140, Vol. I, p. 279).

[40] Wunderlich, *op.cit.*, p. 52ff.

[41] Bibl. #140, Vol. I, p. 273, and Order of June 16, 1932 (*ibid.*, Vol. I, p. 305).

[42] According to a special report by the Reifa, quoted by G. I. in *SP* (Bibl. #150), November 17, 1932, p. 1467.

[43] Emergency Decrees of June 26, 1930 (Bibl. #140, Vol. I, pp. 299, 319-20); December 1, 1930 (*ibid.*, Vol. I, pp. 517, 520); June 5, 1931 (*ibid.*, Vol. I, pp. 279, 319-20); October 6, 1931 (*ibid.*, Vol. I, pp. 537-41).

[44] Number of farm workers receiving unemployment insurance benefits:

	1927	1928	1929	1930	1931	1932
End of March		42.592	65.752	113.597	169.533	160.617
" " June		10.220	13.103	37.519	56.898	55.597
" " December	49.683	85.733	95.891	124.388	134.539	

Source: Statistische Beilagen zum Reichsarbeitsblatt 1928-1932.

insurance—on the part of the workers they were usually lodged against the insufficient amount of invalidity benefits—the system protected the worker's health and provided him with a minimum of subsistence. Labor considered social insurance one of its proudest achievements, an opinion which was shared generally.

Housing

The standards of housing provided for farm servants depended in general on the housing standards of the individual farmer and on the degree of patriarchal relationship. In some districts, however, even when the farmer had a nice home, the servants lived in a partitioned section of the stable or in the attic, spending the free hours of the day in the family rooms and enjoying their isolation at night. For deputatists rent-free quarters were part of the worker's employment contract.

In general, housing standards were modest; in the west better than in the east where the housing for hired laborers had been traditionally poor. Modern means of water supply, electric light, and gas were almost never found in their huts, whereas these services were available in city tenements. This can be attributed to a variety of causes: the primitive standards of former serfs, the financial stringencies of the estate owner, the absence of protective legislation, and the weakness of the bargaining power of the workers. On entailed estates conditions were worst because any expenditure for workers' dwellings would have deprived the younger children of their share of inheritance in favor of the entail heir. The law abolishing *fidei commissa* in Prussia applied only to the second heir in succession, and thus a possible improvement of dwellings was postponed. Housing on large estates, therefore, was inadequate in quantity and size, and often in need of repair and of certain essential comforts. Most of the migrating workers were housed in barracks.

The first years after the revolution brought increased difficulties. The general setback to building and the suspension of repair work during the war resulted in an acute housing shortage, which became intensified by the rapid rise in the number of marriages following the end of the war. Houses and barracks were overcrowded. Shorter hours of work increased the demand for labor. At the same time class feeling demanded higher standards, so that owners in Silesia, where housing conditions were especially bad, had to combine two one-room dwellings into one.

The housing shortage was aggravated by tenants' protective legislation

(Mieterschutz), which was intended to control rent, to restrict the right to give notice, and to ration the available housing supply. The great shortage of dwellings had already caused the Imperial government to provide in 1917 that tenants could appeal to the housing conciliation boards (Mieteinigungsämter) to decide on the validity of eviction notice and rent increases.[45] Notices were to be restricted to cases in which renewal of lease could not be expected. The Boards became empowered to fix rents, and to enforce compulsory leases if a voluntary lease between owner and tenant was unattainable. The prohibition against rent increases in a time of rapid currency inflation constituted a kind of expropriation of house owners whose revenue began to shrink more and more below the gold value of the rents.[46]

Beginning in 1924 the states were empowered to raise rents gradually to the prewar level. But the landlord was still deprived of the right to give notice. This meant separation of the work contract from the lease for those agricultural workers who were housed by their own employers. The worker could remain in his dwelling even after the termination of his work contract. Exceptions were provided only for cases in which dismissal without notice was legally justified or in which the worker terminated his contract without justification. At the same time, the Act stipulated that trade union activity and participation in a strike over conditions of work and wages did not justify termination of a lease. The old insecurity, associating dismissal with loss of dwelling, was thereby abolished. The workers' bargaining position thus was strengthened, especially in those districts in which other than agricultural work was available.

For the employer, however, the restriction meant a great handicap. Farmers complained bitterly that service dwellings were filled with workers not in their employ, making it difficult to employ another worker in need of a home. If they urgently needed the premise for another worker they were entitled to sue for an annulment and pay an equitable compensation, but

[45] Decree of July 26, 1917 (Bibl. #140, p. 659), and several ordinances, newly formulated September 23, 1918 (ibid., p. 1139). This decree gave much more protection to the tenant than the LAO.

[46] The situation did not change much after March 24, 1922, when by legislative act (Bibl. #140, p. 273) rents were to be fixed by the communities and by a later law, eviction notice was to be given by the local civil courts which, however, had to call in lay judges, half of them landlords, half tenants—Gesetz über Mieterschutz und Mieteinigungsämter of June 1, 1923 (ibid., Vol. 1, p. 353), reenacted on June 30, 1926 (ibid., Vol. 1, p. 347), amended by Law of February 17, 1928 (ibid., Vol. 1, p. 25), which gave more flexibility to the procedure for giving eviction notice and the Emergency Decree of December 1, 1930 (ibid., Vol. 1, p. 517).

could be obliged by the court to provide another dwelling for the evicted worker. Even if the courts decided in their favor, however, the police, obliged to care for the homeless, could compel the landlord to keep the tenant for as long as three months more.

The housing shortage was further aggravated by members of the worker's family refusing to work on the farm.[47] Employers complained that they paid interest, coal, and light for a whole family while only one of its members worked on the farm. In some parts of Germany the number of persons occupying service dwellings who were not employed on the estate had nearly doubled in 1925-1926 as compared with 1913-1914. The Enquiry Committee found that in parts of Saxony 17 per cent, in Silesia 12 per cent and in some instances 50 per cent of estate dwellings had tenants not employed on the estate.[48]

Lodging workers who had transferred to industry was a deterrent to the building of new homes. Many employers claimed they were unable to replace foreign by German workers because they could not accommodate the latter. Barracks which lacked comforts and sanitation prevented the replacement of foreign workers, because the natives usually refused to accept the low standard of living to which the Polish worker had been accustomed.

The question may be raised: why, in the face of such a large demand for dwellings, was building activity in the country not stimulated? Private business, in Germany as well as in other countries, was unable to build for two reasons: 1) the enormous increase in building costs; 2) prohibitive interest rates. From 1919 on, the impact of inflation became more and more obvious. What inflation meant in terms of building costs is best shown by the following table.[49]

Official German Index of Building Costs

Year	Building Cost Index	Price of Dollar
1913	1.00	4.20 M.
1918	2.28	8.00
End of 1921	18.08	184.00
1922 (July)	142.86	670.00
1923 (January)	2,798.00	17,970.00
1923 (October)	9 billion	25.26 billion
1923 (December)	1,488 billion	4,200 billion
Stabilization (Prices in gold)		
1924 (January)	1.42	4.20
1925 (January)	1.68	4.20

[47] Bibl. #104b, pp. 275ff. [48] Ibid., pp. 24, 132. [49] Bibl. #153d, Vol. 44, No. 4, p. 76.

After the stabilization of currency in 1924, the building-cost index remained rather high and inflexible; in 1929 it was 82 per cent above 1913; only when the depression reached its climax in 1931-1932, did the index decrease. Equally, the interest rate on mortgages remained as inflexible; in 1925 first mortgages required 10.5 per cent, in 1931 still 8.8 per cent. Under such conditions it was impossible for building activity to develop.

Public help became necessary. The authorities regarded building of farm workers' dwellings as a means of preventing the flight from the land, of reducing unemployment in cities by inducing former farm workers to return to the land, and of substituting German for foreign farm laborers. Beginning in 1918, therefore, considerable sums were appropriated by the Reich and the states to encourage the building of small dwellings. The first public subsidies provided after October 1918, however, did not aid the country because they obliged the communities to carry one-fourth of the contribution to the costs of building, and the rural communities were too poor to carry such a financial burden. Real help began in 1921 when money from the Productive Unemployment Relief was made available for agricultural workers' housing.[50] At first one-third of the building costs were paid by grants from unemployment relief funds. In 1923 the nonrepayable subsidies were replaced by loans, half of which were to be paid by the Reifa, half by the States. They covered up to 40 per cent of building costs, later up to 75 per cent. General instructions provided that the arrangement of buildings should permit the later acquisition of small holdings, "thus opening to the worker the opportunity of an economic step forward." Rural craftsmen were to rank with agricultural workers as possible beneficiaries. Loans for service or home dwellings were granted on condition that only German workers were to get them. Up to 1923 mainly service dwellings were built; from 1925-1926 on, privately owned houses increased in number because farmers lacked means to build and workers preferred to own their homes. From 1924 on, building activity was stimulated by subsidies defrayed by a special real estate tax (Hauszinssteuer).

Owned homes could be established as homesteads[51] which, according to

[50] Productive Unemployment Relief was created when an Order of October 27, 1919 (Bibl. #140, p. 1827) empowered the Reich Minister of Labor to encourage by means of loans and grants measures which were estimated to create opportunities for employment. A circular of January 7, 1921 (Bibl. #139, 1920-1921, p. 324) mentions as such measures building programs to enable city workers to return to the country. Beginning May 12, 1921 (*ibid.*, p. 628), such subsidies were granted.

[51] Homesteads consisted of a dwelling only or a dwelling plus sufficient land for a garden or small agricultural holding.

the Federal Homestead Act of May 10, 1920,[52] could not be divided or mort-gaged except with the consent of the designator, who in most instances was a public authority with the power of supervision. Restraint against home-steads on account of the personal debts of the holder were declared illegal. If the homestead was to be sold, the designator had a right to pre-emption at a price not to exceed that at which the homestead was originally sold, making allowance for any improvement.

On the ground of financial difficulties the federal government temporarily suspended subsidies for the construction of agricultural workers' service dwellings from productive unemployment relief funds,[53] and urged that workers be assisted in building their own homes. The Emergency Decrees of June 14, 1932,[54] empowered the Federal Minister of Labor, in agreement with the Federal Minister of Finance, to guarantee loans for repair work on old dwellings and farm houses.[55]

In spite of many difficulties, a certain amount of building was done,[56] but it was not sufficient to fulfill the large demand. The quality of housing was improved after financial assistance was made conditional upon the observance of certain requirements. Moreover, in many estates the existing dwellings were enlarged and improved. This was partly due to the rules of the LAO which demanded that accommodations be "unobjectionable as regards health and morals" (repeating a requirement previously laid down in the Civil Code). Some collective agreements repeated or emphasized the law, others did not venture to go so far because of the impossibility of changing dwell-ings in a short time, but they obliged employers to keep the dwelling in good repair. For unsatisfactory dwellings, agreements stipulated a lower charge, the balance being paid in cash to the worker. The stipulation in many agreements that only adults working on the estate were allowed to live in a service dwelling indirectly prevented overcrowding. However, such

[52] Reichsheimstättengesetz (Bibl. #140, p. 962).

[53] By Order of May 10, 1932 (Bibl. #139, Vol. I, p. 88).

[54] Bibl. #140, Vol. I, pp. 273, 284.

[55] The Decrees of September 4, 1932 (Bibl. #140, Vol. I, p. 425) and January 4, 1933 (Bibl. #139, Vol. I, p. 33) empowered the Federal Minister of Finance to spend up to 50 million Rm. each for repair work on dwelling structures (urban and rural).

[56] Agricultural workers' dwellings built with subsidies and loans out of the produc-tive unemployment relief fund in the Reich from 1921 to January 1, 1933 amounted to:

Service dwellings	25,629
Own homes	41,413
Total	67,042

(Bibl. #139, 1933, Vol. II, p. 79.)

clauses were resented as compulsion for adult children either to accept work on the estate or leave the family home.

The regime fully realized the importance of the housing question in the country, but general economic and financial conditions never permitted sufficient financial aid, so long as a deflationary course was followed. At that time, the fear of another inflation was so great that the eventual realization of the value of at least limited spending never could overcome it.

Social Welfare[57]

The rural worker or his family who became destitute during the period of the Weimar Republic enjoyed social services which had been deeply revolutionized after 1918. Before the World War poor relief benefits restricted to the "indispensable" minimum for the support of life deprived the worker of his political rights such as voting or public office. The measures taken by the public authorities bore the character of preventing the indigent from claiming relief. They were degrading and a deterrent. Moreover, the area covered by individual poor relief offices was too small, and therefore handicapped by lack of resources. Private charity was haphazard and patriarchal. A change occurred during the war when a dignified service, at first for dependents of soldiers, then for disabled soldiers and war widows and war orphans, was built up. After the war came a complete revolution in the conception of relief. Distress was attributed to economic conditions, not to personal circumstances. Welfare work was supposed to help adequately and permanently.

Changes in public services were achieved in two ways: by breaking up the poor law (removing unemployed, war invalids, survivors of war victims,[58] youth,[59] and other groups from the jurisdiction of the poor laws and caring for them under special systems), and by reforming the law itself. Disenfranchisement of poor relief recipients was abolished by the electoral law.[60] Public welfare was grouped in 3 branches; economic assistance, youth wel-

---

[57] The term Wohlfahrtspflege (welfare work) in Germany expresses about the same services as those implied in social work and public assistance in the United States.

[58] Gesetz über die Versorgung der Militärpersonen und ihrer Hinterbliebenen bei Dienstbeschädigung (Reichsversorgungsgesetz) of May 12, 1920 (Bibl. #140, p. 989); newly formulated June 30, 1923 (ibid., Vol. 1, p. 523); Gesetz über das Verfahren in Versorgungssachen of January 10, 1922 (Bibl. #140, p. 59) and frequent amendments to both. The statutes provided curative treatment, pensions, and other benefits.

[59] Reichsjugendwohlfahrtsgesetz (Federal Youth Welfare Law) of July 9, 1922 (Bibl. #140, Vol. 1, p. 633), and Decree of February 14, 1924 (ibid., Vol. 1, p. 110).

[60] Reichswahlgesetz of November 30, 1918 (Bibl. #140, p. 1345).

fare, and health welfare. The Federal Social Welfare Decree (Reichsfür-sorgepflichtverordnung)[61] aimed at helping all needy people and at fighting the causes of destitution. Small local authorities were replaced by larger district authorities,[62] poor law residence by usual residence. Public assistance guaranteed the necessities of life to the needy. The federal statutes established the principle that persons who could not provide minimum subsistence for themselves and their dependents, and who did not receive help from others, were entitled to proper maintenance including food, clothing, housing, medical aid in case of sickness, and the aid required in order to recover working capacity. The states or an authority empowered by them fixed relief rates according to the amount locally necessary for subsistence. They differentiated between the basic relief rate for the destitute in general and higher rates for certain groups such as inflation victims, war invalids and survivors, pensioners of social insurance (for the last two in addition to pensions). The rates were only directives, to be modified according to individual need. The needy person had the right to protest against the amount or type of relief granted or against rejection, and, in case of rejection of his protest, the right to lodge a complaint in an administrative court. Persons from the ranks of the needy or of their organizations or of private welfare agencies participated in the procedure.

A comprehensive organization for youth welfare provided assistance for indigent children. Foster children, i.e. children in care of other families than their own, were supervised, illegitimate children placed under public guardianship (Amtsvormundschaft), neglected or endangered or delinquent children put under protective supervision (Schutzaufsicht) or placed in reformatories (Fürsorgeerziehung).[68] Young people tried in the Court for Juvenile Delinquency were aided by the Youth Welfare Bureau. Besides care for indigent and problem youth social group work and recreational facilities were provided (Jugendpflege).

Maternity aid granted mothers whose income was below a certain mini-

---

[61] February 13, 1924 (Bibl. #140, Vol. I, p. 100) with the Reichsgrundsätze über Voraussetzung, Art und Mass der Fürsorge (Principles governing the conditions, nature, and scope of public welfare work) of December 24, 1924 (*ibid.*, Vol. I, p. 765). The decree was recodified by Act of June 8, 1926 (*ibid.*, Vol. I, p. 255) and August 1, 1931 (*ibid.*, Vol. I, p. 439).

[62] Larger regional authorities carried through expensive tasks, such as institutional care for the crippled and insane, and cared for persons without usual residence.

[68] Such measures were ordered by a court of orphans or a court of juvenile delinquency. Reichsjugendgerichtsgesetz of February 16, 1923 (Bibl. #140, Vol. I, p. 135).

mum, the same benefits as provided in the RVO, viz. medical attendance, payment of part of costs of confinement, benefits for several weeks preceding and following confinement. Cripples, blind, deaf and dumb received treatment and vocational education.

Health welfare was concerned with assistance to those not covered by health insurance or needing additional help. For medical treatment the county usually employed its own physician while specialists in addition treated the needy for a fee provided by the relief authorities. Infants of all mothers receiving maternity aid were checked and children in large schools supervised. Special health centers were provided for tuberculosis and venereal diseases.[64] Persons suffering from a venereal disease were obliged to secure treatment from a physician (those who were not insured and were needy were treated at public expense). Special provisions were made to protect the confidential character of such treatment. Institutional care was provided in hospitals, homes, asylums, and sanatoria.

With the extension and intensification of welfare work the old Elberfeld system which put the enforcement of the poor law in districts into the hands of the neighbors of the poor, citizens who served without pay, became insufficient. Although formally continued, it was more and more superseded by the work of professional social workers. Welfare, child, juvenile, and health departments were established by local and state authorities. In the rural districts all three usually united in one department, assisted by committees in which representatives of private welfare agencies and other persons experienced in welfare work participated. Since rural districts usually were not wealthy enough to build up specialized services like the cities, many of them employed a "family welfare worker," a case worker capable of specialized service who dealt with all the difficulties of the indigent family. Traveling all over the district, she assisted the doctor in the baby welfare center and in the physical examination of school children, dealt with educational and health problems, helped young offenders in the courts and made contacts with organizations that could help. Gemeindepflege, an old institution of the churches in their local parishes were centers providing a nurse who gave care in cases of emergency in the family. In rural areas these centers frequently had become welfare centers which cared for all types of need.

To be sure, public rural social welfare work could not be developed as completely as social work in the city. The rural population did not like to

---

[64] Reichsgesetz zur Bekämpfung der Geschlechtskrankheiten of February 18, 1927 (Bibl. #140, Vol. 1, p. 61).

be cared for. Transportation was bad: automobiles were too much a luxury to be general, and social workers almost always had to walk.[65]

Financial stress did not permit carrying out the complete health supervision the government was striving for or to grant benefits as generously as had been intended in enacting welfare legislation. When the number of unemployed no longer entitled to insurance benefits began to grow, public welfare became more and more relief for the very neediest. However, in some fields (care for crippled children, or for persons with tuberculosis or venereal diseases) a rather complete health supervision was achieved, thanks partly to the cooperation of the institutions of social insurance. Services for tubercular persons and young cripples improved from year to year. The guardianship did not overlook any illegitimate child. The Youth Bureau automatically became the legal guardian of every such child and began its service even before the birth.

Private organizations[66]—with the help of public grants—continued the work they had done in the prewar period in hospitals and homes for the old and disabled; in the educational field; and in assisting public relief authorities which could delegate services to them. There was mutual help and assistance of estate owners and their workers.[67]

[65] The depression meant the financial ruin of many rural communities. Health and youth service continued, though restricted, but economic aid deteriorated seriously. Since unemployment insurance provided benefits only for a limited period, more and more unemployed were shifted to communal help. Finances of the communities, however, deteriorated so much during the depression that they could not prevent destitution.

[66] Besides independent associations, there were seven nation-wide welfare organizations, three denominational, two workers' organizations, the Red Cross, and another with which most of the nonsectarian agencies and institutions were affiliated.

[67] The policy to improve rural conditions was sponsored by the German Association for Rural Welfare (Deutscher Verein für ländliche Wohlfahrtspflege), which promoted all measures to overcome shortcomings of rural life and carried on its own cultural activities in the country.

CHAPTER IX

SETTLEMENT OF AGRICULTURAL WORKERS

THERE was a strong desire on the part of the soldiers returning from the front after the First World War to sink roots and to own a home and a piece of land. The Constitution promised, therefore, that the distribution and the use of land would be supervised by the state in such a way as to prevent misuse.[1] There was, however, the fear of endangering the food supply by any revolutionary action. In 1919 Professor Max Sering, who for years had been a strong advocate of breaking up of large estates, was entrusted with drafting a settlement law.

The Federal Land Settlement Act of August 11, 1919[2] had as its main purpose the creation of new holdings of the size of small peasant farms, interspersed with smaller units for farm laborers and craftsmen and the enlargement of existing small peasant holdings to the size of a self-supporting farm by "adjacent settlement" (Anlieger-Siedlung).

The feeling that social justice demanded the restoration of the peasantry in the east resulted in the plan to convert one-third of the area of the large estates (21 million ha.) into peasant holdings since about the same proportion was assumed to have changed from peasant ownership to large estates during the preceding three centuries.[3] Moreover, the flight from the country

---

[1] Article 155.

[2] Bibl. #140, p. 1429 and Administrative Order of September 26, 1919 of the Federal Minister of Labor. The Order of January 29, 1919 had brought a preliminary regulation (Bibl. #140, Vol. 1, p. 115). Subsequent amendments and new formulations, June 7, 1923 (*ibid.*, Vol. 1, p. 364), August 18, 1923 (*ibid.*, Vol. 1, p. 805), July 8, 1926 (*ibid.*, Vol. 1, p. 398), and ordinances.

[3] No attack against the power of the landed nobility was planned, however. Professor Max Sering warned in 1934: "Compulsory elimination of the educated agriculturist would be an act of leveling (Gleichmacherei) which would prove dangerous for the community as a whole, not only because excellent enterprises would disappear, but most notably, because a social group would be destroyed in which great historical traditions have remained alive" (Bibl. #77, p. 87). Large estates would still own one-fourth of the eastern area instead of two-fifths as in 1919 (Sering, "Die Ziele des ländlichen Siedlungswerkes," *Deutsche Politik*, January 31, 1919, p. 7). It was, however, doubtful whether division of large estates would lead to an increase in output since the productivity of eastern estates was about one-quarter higher than those of peasant holdings, especially in mechanized grain production (Edgar Salin in Bibl. #7, 1932, Vol. 1, p. 719). Moreover, eastern holdings would have to be of larger size than those in the West and South, because of the differences in soil and climate.

was attributed chiefly to the landlessness of the eastern farm laborer and the poor working conditions on the large estates. The new settlement policy was designed to offer the worker the possibility of rising in the social scale as well as of overcoming his isolation in the region of the large estates. By settling workers it was hoped to end the rural exodus; the worker who had a small holding to fall back on would be ready to accept seasonal work on large farms without feeling disposed to migrate. Other reasons for settling workers were urban unemployment and the need of greater food production, which demanded more intensive cultivation of the soil.

The Federal Land Settlement Act outlined the principles of land acquisition and settlement but left it to the states to provide the machinery.[4] Insofar as they did not exist, the states set up settlement companies which became responsible for the organization of land settlement. The work thus was carried through by public or private nonprofit associations under state supervision.

They obtained the land in various ways. In addition to purchase in the open market it could be acquired by reclamation of marshy or waste land, by utilization of state domains, by pre-emption of farm land of 25 ha. and over, and if necessary by expropriation of large estate property in districts in which, according to the census of 1907, more than 10 per cent of the area cultivated formed part of estates of 100 ha. and over.[5] The duty to supply land and the right to expropriate was assigned not to officials but to land supply associations (Landlieferungsverbänden) whose members were the large landed proprietors in the settlement district. The associations considered their obligation to supply land fulfilled when one-third of the area classified as belonging to large land owners in 1907 had been parceled out or when the cultivated area of the large estate had been reduced to 10 per cent of the total area in the district. Suitable compensation, omitting increases in value due solely to the war, was appropriated in any case since no revolution was intended, but only a reform of the system of land tenure.

[4] After the World War the Ministry of Labor was put in charge of settlements in the Reich, from 1932 on the Ministry of Agriculture. In Prussia, where most of the settlement activities were centered, settlement was administered first by the Ministry of Finance, later by the Ministry of Agriculture. In the other states matters were handled by either the Ministry of the Interior, of Labor or of Finance.

[5] Expropriation was used mainly in 1921-1923 during the runaway inflation. Since 1924 land was bought in the market. Only 87 estates with 29,114 ha. of land were expropriated in Prussia in the first ten years (Bibl. #97, p. 236).

The associations had the right of repurchase if the settler did not live on the land or work it regularly.

In the early years following the passage of the Act many difficulties obstructed land settlement: costs and lack of construction materials for housing, shortage of farm inventory, opposition of estate owners and old officials who sabotaged the law, legal controversies concerning the interpretation of "suitable compensation," friction between Prussia and the Reich, absence of public sentiment with regard to settlement. Finally, inflation brought settlement to a standstill because funds were swept away before they could be invested. Since real estate was protected against the deterioration in value to which all liquid property was exposed, the owners were not willing to offer land for sale. With the stabilization of the currency in 1924, land was again offered but lack of funds was a great handicap until in June 1926 the federal government came in as a financing agent and stimulated the movement.

Settlement was also encouraged by the possibility of converting workmen's compensation and war disability annuities into a capital indemnification for settlement purposes.[6] Persons between twenty-one and fifty-five years of age were eligible for compensation if no considerable change in their conditions was expected and reasonable use was guaranteed. The compensations could be used for improving or enlarging existing holdings. The average sum granted by agricultural insurance associations was 1,380 marks. The law concerning compensation to severely injured war veterans[7] allowed farmers to commute their obligation to employ war invalids by leasing or selling land to such workers.

At first the Settlement Act gave little attention to agricultural workers as such since the latter had been rather disinclined toward becoming settlers. The Act merely provided the possibility of renting land up to 5 per cent of the arable area to workers. This, however, occurred between 1923 and 1928 in only about 3,509 cases,[8] predominantly forest workers. The Prussian Executive Order of December 15, 1919,[9] and amendments to the Federal Settlement[10] Act provided that when large estates were divided, their

---

[6] Second Gesetz über Änderungen in der Unfallversicherung, July 14, 1925 (Bibl. #140, Vol. I, p. 97) and second Verordnung über die Abfindung von Unfallrenten, February 10, 1928 (Bibl. #140, Vol. I, p. 22). Kapitalabfindungsgesetz of May 12, 1920 (*ibid.*, p. 989) and Law of August 4, 1921 (*ibid.*, p. 933) in the edition of September 19, 1925 (*ibid.*, Vol. I, p. 349).

[7] Law of April 6, 1920 (Bibl. #140, pp. 458, 459, Section 8).

[8] Bibl. #153d, 1933, No. 4, p. 24.   [9] Bibl. #137, 1920, p. 31.

[10] Law of June 7, 1923 (Bibl. #140, Vol. I, p. 364).

workers and salaried employees who lived on the estate and had been employed for more than two years, should as far as possible be established on the land as settlers or tenants. If this was not possible the settlement association was obliged to supply them with some other employment or pay at least three-quarters of their wages for half a year. In addition, they were allowed to remain in their dwellings for one year.[11] Lack of financial resources and easy placement on other estates hampered workers' settlements in the first years.

New financial stimulus was given to the settlement of agricultural workers during the depression. In case of lack of capital for small settlement, installation loans were to be granted and security guaranteed for the remainder of the purchase money. The guiding principles of November 10, 1931,[12] adopted by agreement between the Federal and the Prussian governments, provided that in addition to professional farmers preference in settlement should be given to unemployed agricultural workers and qualified veterans. The Principles also introduced important financial facilities for laborers' settlements.

In Prussia from 1923 to 1928, 1750 agricultural workers (17½ per cent of all settlers) were settled.[13] From 1925 to 1928 about one-fifth of all settled

---

[11] The fate of workers on divided estates has been recorded as follows by the East Prussian authorities for 1930:

Status of Workers after the Division of East Prussian
Estates on Which They Had Worked
(1930)

	Per cent		Per cent
Bought lots	17.5	Changed their occupation	1.3
Went to relatives' settlements	5.3	Migrated to the city	3.5
Became old age pensioners	7.2	Became unemployed	2.2
Remained farm workers	60.3	Did not continue occupation (death, marriage)	2.7

Source: Otto Albrecht, "Verbleib der Arbeitnehmer von besiedelten Gütern," *Schriften zur Förderung der inneren Kolonisation*, Berlin, 1933, p. 11, quoted by Fritz Rumpf (Bibl. #72), p. 94.

[12] Bibl. #139, Vol. I, p. 280.

[13] Bibl. #104c, pp. 101ff.

Occupational Status of 9,438 Settlers with New Holdings Placed in 1926-1928 before Settlement in the Reich:

	Per cent		Per cent
Independent farmers	48.4	Workers and salaried	
Peasants' sons	11.2	employees in industry	11.0
Agricultural workers and		Other branches of economic	
salaried employees	19.3	activity	5.4
Independent in industry			—
and commerce	4.7		[100.00]

Source: Bibl. #153d, 1929, No. 3, p. 65.

workers became independent peasants.[14] Weigmann[15] in examining the fate of farm workers who had been settled in Pomerania up to 1930 found that 67.2 per cent received 5-10 ha.; 5.3 per cent 2-5 ha.; i.e. were therefore expected to obtain part-time work on nearby farms or in the nearby village. In Mecklenburg the proportion of workers and salaried employees increased from 12.4 to 48.3 per cent from 1926-1930 and still more after that time.[16] In 1932 the settlers who had formerly been in dependent positions in agriculture amounted to 54 per cent.

The depression revived the settlement movement considerably. The Eastern Assistance Fund (Osthilfe) which provided subsidies to deeply indebted estates was to promote a new distribution of land in order partially to clear debts by the sale of land to settlement undertakings. However, the plan was more of a handicap than an aid to settlement. The owners of large estates succeeded in controlling the fund and using it for their own purposes, i.e. for enlarging their real estate holdings and for rehabilitating completely bankrupt estates. With authority vested in three agencies—the land at the disposal of the Eastern Assistance Fund, financial means provided by the Reich, and the administration by the state—settlement had become very difficult.

Yet, in spite of all the difficulties, the last years of the Weimar Republic saw an exodus from the towns, a back-to-the-country movement, due not merely to economic causes but to the longing for a simpler life, close to nature and to the soil. The government followed this new movement with great interest and attempted to smooth its way by various measures, especially by helping to settle the unemployed from the cities in the surrounding country.

Although settlement had been seriously handicapped by lack of means during the period of inflation and in the following few years, nevertheless 57,457 new and 96,147 adjacent settlements had been created from 1919 to 1932. These figures do not indicate a marked change in ownership structure. However, the success of settlement cannot be measured by numbers alone. Of greater value was the experience acquired, which laid the foundation for the greater success of settlements. In general the experience in the settlement of industrial workers had not been successful except when it

---

[14] Otto Albrecht, "Sesshaftmachung von Landarbeitern," Bibl. #63, p. 177.

[15] Hans Weigmann (Bibl. #105f), p. 76.

[16] Hans Jürgen Seraphim, *Der Mensch in der Siedlung*, Bibl. #125, 1933, Vol. 140, p. 702.

meant the return to the land of couples who had been raised on a farm and who had not long been estranged from country life. After years of experimentation with resettling of urban workers the settlement companies decided to give preference to applicants with agricultural background. Most of the large settlement undertakings generally considered the competent agricultural worker fit for settlement[17] because of his thorough knowledge of the soil and his habits of hard work and frugality. Lack of capital weakened his economic position, however, and he needed much professional advice in his first years. A system for advising settlers was developed, partly by using teachers of agricultural schools, partly by employing special experts. The settlers were advised on all questions relating to equipment, cultivation, care of livestock, marketing, and collaboration among themselves. Some criticism was directed in the first years at the division of land into too small holdings. Since the holdings assigned to agricultural workers were not self-supporting, their position, when they became unemployed in sparsely populated areas, was untenable. Moreover, confining the worker to one or two farms on which he had to accept work might have made him dependent. The tendency in the last years, therefore, was to increase the size of the workers' holdings up to the limit of independent peasant farms.[18]

Settlers frequently had a hard struggle, especially when they were hit by depression; however, the majority made good. Marie Philippi Jasny[19] found that the personal income of the settler including "food raised and consumed on the farm and the value of the residence, was only two-thirds to three-fourths of what the family could theoretically have earned by performing an equal amount of labor on the farms." The author is justified in emphasizing the fact that the settlers did not regard the farm as a capital investment, but as a means of achieving independent ownership and of "securing a home for the family through utilization of the family labor force."

It had been the policy at first to equip the individual holding completely, including spacious buildings, before offering it to settlers. Experience, however, showed that it was better not to burden the settler from the beginning with a full-sized and fully equipped peasant farm. "Advance settlement" which allowed for gradual expansion of area and buildings proved to be

[17] Bibl. #104, Vol. ii, 10, p. 110.
[18] Bibl. #153d, 1934, No. 3, p. 7.
[19] "Some Aspects of German Agricultural Settlement," *Political Science Quarterly*, 1937, Vol. 52, pp. 237-38.

the most favorable means of tying the settler as quickly as possible to his holding. Gradually a method was worked out to combine prospective settlers (if possible, natives of the area)[20] into groups and to encourage them to cooperate in the laying out and equipment of the settlement. Not all buildings were started in the beginning, and credits for further equipment were granted during the following twelve years. As a result, the scheme became much cheaper and a considerably larger number of workers could be settled; the settlers could slowly assume their new obligations, were less exacting, and more disposed to make the sacrifices which became necessary in the first years. Thus the technique of settlement was gradually developed.

Summary

In evaluating the attempts of the Weimar Republic to improve the conditions of farm labor, one must consider that during its existence the young Republic enjoyed only a few years—from 1924 to 1928—in which a peaceful development was at all possible. The postwar years were filled with turmoil—the revolution of 1918, followed by riots of Communists who tried to seize power whenever the Republic was endangered, the Putsch to restore the monarchy in 1920, the pressure of the Allies for reparations, the invasion of the Ruhr district by French troops. These crises brought the value of the currency down to zero, with hyperinflation ending in the last months of 1923. In 1929 the economic depression hit the nation most seriously. Growing unemployment, increasing political danger of National Socialism, prevented again a long-range policy.

Nevertheless, the years of the Weimar Republic brought about significant achievements in behalf of farm labor. Many discriminations against it that had existed in protective labor legislation were removed. For the first time (with the LAO) farm labor received its own protection, worked out by labor and employers themselves. Labor's right to combine was established: *bona fide* trade unions were recognized as representatives of labor; agriculture was covered by the law of collective agreements which established the norms of the agreements as minima and provided for the possibility of extending the agreement to those whom it had not included. Labor conflicts were decided by labor courts, whereas before the First World War, farm

---

[20] Disregard for this principle led to failure. For instance, the plans to transplant peasant sons from the fertile west to the barren regions and sandy soil of the eastern provinces along the Polian border were not successful. Religious and tribal relationship had to be considered.

workers had no court which decided their disputes in the same easy, speedy, and inexpensive way available to industrial workers and salaried employees. It took the revolution of 1918 to give farm workers the same right of self-government in social insurance as industrial workers enjoyed. Benefits in social insurance were extended and liberalized until the economic depression forced the government to impose drastic cuts. Only a few discriminations remained in workmen's compensation and unemployment insurance.

The economically underprivileged group of farm workers further gained by the new concept of need, which ascribed distress to economic causes, not to personal circumstances, and on this basis established a right to adequate help.

The remarkable progress in unionization, although slower than in industry, was another great gain. The powerful union movement helped the relatively weak farm workers' union to assert itself and to exercise political influence. The fact that some of the gains were lost in the period of National Socialism did not mean a permanent loss, as later developments disclosed.

The power of the landed aristocracy, however, remained unbroken and continued to be the main stumbling block to land reform which would have settled farm laborers on their own holdings. Moreover, the political influence of this group re-emerged in the later years of the Republic and counteracted labor's endeavor for social reforms, especially in the agricultural sector.

PART THREE

THE PERIOD OF NATIONAL SOCIALISM

CHAPTER I

THE AGRICULTURAL POLICY
OF THE THIRD REICH

Promises and Aims

To UNDERSTAND the attitude of the National Socialists toward farm labor, one has to understand the movement's agrarian aims and policy. National Socialism came into power with a well-defined agrarian program. The closely interrelated aims included de-urbanization; the preservation, increase, and immobilization of the peasant class; and the attainment of self-sufficiency in the production of foodstuffs. Excessive concentration of the population in urban and industrial areas and the resultant depopulation of rural districts were considered unfavorable to physical and mental health, the breeding of future generations, and the building of a large army—the last assumption based on the theory that peasants make better soldiers than do towns people. In a proclamation to the German nation issued on February 1, 1933, the "back-to-the-land" policy was termed one of the basic principles of the government program.[1] "German degeneration has been the consequence of concentration in big cities,"[2] said the chairman of the Reichsarbeitsgemeinschaft für Raumforschung in 1936. "The building site of the Third Reich is not the city but the country." Because an urbanized people can always be overrun by stronger nations, the peasants would have to renew the vitality of the nation: "The Third Reich will be a peasant Reich or it will not be at all."[3] *Ergo*, remigration to agriculture was to be the program.

The increase in the prestige of the peasant class and the creation of a new aristocracy of blood and soil were to be effected by "denomadization,"[4] by

[1] Norman H. Baynes (ed.), Bibl. #198, Vol. 1, p. 114.
[2] Konrad Meyer, "Raumforschung, eine Pflicht wissenschaftlicher Gemeinschaftsarbeit," Bibl. #296, Vol. 1, p. 734.
[3] Herbert Backe (Bibl. #167), p. 16.
[4] R. Walther Darré, the representative of these romantic ideas confronted the "creative" peasant with the "parasitic" and destructive "nomad." He stated that some qualities of the Nordic man may be attributed to his peasant status, and contended that laws of land inheritance had denordicized the German people (Bibl. #175, pp. 458ff.). His successor, Herbert Backe, said: "The National Socialist agrarian and food policy is based on two premises: 1) throughout history nations perished which lost their peasantry; 2) a people is free only if it can feed itself from its own soil even in times of emergency" in "Nationalsozialistische Agrar- und Ernährungspolitik," Bibl. #277b, p. 21.

stabilization instead of lability; rootedness (Verwurzelung) and perpetuity (Stetigkeit) instead of freedom of migration and busybody mobility; blood and soil instead of intellect and asphalt; folk and home instead of world-citizenship and pan-Europe.

Security of land tenure and social standing were to compensate the farmer for rearing large families and for carrying out government orders concerning agricultural production. By fostering their own life patterns and life values, the peasants would establish a new stronghold of German culture. In the National Socialist hierarchy of estates, peasants, together with soldiers and workmen, were to become the group with highest prestige. It was recognized that such a policy would require a substantial increase in small and medium-sized farm holdings. Hereditary farms and settlement policy were part of this program.

The third aim, self-sufficiency in food stuffs, stemmed from the experience of the city-starving war and the fear of another blockade. Self-sufficiency in food was a preparation for armed conflicts. Moreover, "an industrial and export economy is the symptom of a disease, and this kind of economy cannot in the long run provide a people with the means of subsistence. The products of the soil have to support the entire people, while the output of industry must find its markets in the national economy, principally in agriculture."[5] Self-sufficiency was to be realized by increased production, regardless of cost[6] and by conquest of foreign territory. No free play of the market would be allowed to disturb these objectives.

The New Organization and Its Operation

The Reich Food Estate (Reichnährstand, RN),[7] a compulsory organization of all producers, processors, and distributors of agricultural products, was responsible for the control of agriculture and was supposedly its representative. All agricultural organizations such as the farmers' cooperatives and the Chambers of Agriculture which were in operation prior to this date were

[5] Hitler in Hamburg in March 1928 (Bibl. #346, March 18, 1928).

[6] When W. Seedorf, an outstanding agricultural economist, said that efficiency is "not an output unconditionally as high as possible, but one which is proportionally high if compared with the input" ("Der Leistungsgedanke in der Erzeugungsschlacht," Bibl. #285, 1936, No. 28, p. 349), he was attacked by a young scholar because of having tried to oppose the German goal of liberty of food with "the most scanty arms of expenditure accounting" (Max Schönberg, Bibl. #296, September 1, 1936, Vol. 11).

[7] Gesetz über den vorläufigen Aufbau des Reichsnährstandes und Massnahmen zur Markt- und Preisregelung für landwirtschaftliche Erzeugnisse, September 13, 1933 (Bibl. #140, Vol. 1, p. 626) and additional decrees.

also incorporated into the RN, which regulated production, sale, and prices of agricultural products.

Territorially the RN in 1938 was divided into twenty state (or provincial) peasant corporations (Landesbauernschaften)[8] which in turn were subdivided into smaller units, the county (515 Kreisbauernschaften) and local (55,000 Ortsbauernschaften). The director of the RN, the Reich Peasant Leader, appointed by the Reich Chancellor, was at the same time Minister of Agriculture[9] and leader of the Party Office for Agrarian Policy. Each state, county, and local organization was presided over by sectional leaders. All leaders of state sections were appointed by the Reich Peasant Leader. They in turn appointed their subordinates.[10]

Although ostensibly self-governing, the supervision of the organization was in fact[11] exercised by the state, with the advantage of centralized leadership and the disadvantage of a huge and cumbersome bureaucracy which had 20,800 paid employees in 1938. It would be erroneous to assume that the officials of the new regime belonged to the aristocratic groups which ran the empire. Because the conservatives had stayed in office during the period of democracy as officials of the Chambers of Agriculture and other agencies, they were discredited. An entirely new group from the middle strata of rural society came to office.[12] Only the officials at the central and provincial headquarters were full-time, paid workers. The county and local peasant leaders worked on a voluntary or part-time basis. The leaders exercised important functions since National Socialist laws substituted con-

[8] Figures from Bernhard Mehrens, Bibl. #216, p. 8.

[9] On January 1, 1935, the Prussian Ministry for Agriculture joined the Reich Ministry of Agriculture under the title Reichs- und Preussisches Ministerium für Ernährung und Landwirtschaft. After the annexation of Austria, the name was changed to Reichsministerium für Ernährung und Landwirtschaft. At first Hugenberg, the leader of the German National People's Party, had been made Minister of Agriculture. On June 30, 1933, however, the pretense of coalition was abandoned and Hugenberg was displaced by R. Walther Darré, who in May 1942 was replaced by Herbert Backe.

[10] The Reich Peasant Leader directed the RN through two offices, the Stabsamt concerned with policy shaping, and the Verwaltungsamt, the office of administration with three divisions. To the first, Der Mensch, was assigned the care of the man, to the second the care of the farm, and increase of output by all means of rationalization. The third fulfilled the most important function, as the instrument of regimentation and control of prices, direction of agricultural production into the desired channels, displacing the market by planned organization.

[11] The pretense of self-administration of the RN was dropped shortly before the outbreak of World War II, when the RN was transformed into an executive agency of the Ministry. Only a few changes were necessary to put the administration on a war footing. Decree of August 27, 1939 (Bibl. #140, Vol. 1, p. 1495).

[12] Rudolph Heberle (Bibl. #34), p. 87.

sultation of the local or county peasant leader for democratic consent. Thus the local leader, the middleman between the organizations of the RN and the peasants in the village had to be consulted in all contracts concerning the purchase, lease, or surrender of farms, and in all cases of consolidation. He had to give his opinion on the fairness of the sale price of land, and supervise the deliveries to make sure that every employable person in his district was recruited for work.

Property Rights

The social revolution brought about by National Socialism is most apparent in the changes wrought in the conception of property, especially land. In Germany, because of her police-state tradition, ownership never had the attribute of a natural right. Nor was the conception of obligation connected with ownership completely abandoned. Some of the provisions of the Civil Code (which came into force in 1900) sound more liberal than they actually were. The Code declared that an owner was "free to dispose of his property at his own discretion," and that a proprietor had the right to use his property as he saw fit, to the exclusion of others, insofar as there were no limitations by law or rights of third persons (Section 903). Modifications of the private property conception were maintained, especially regarding property in land.[13] The general attitude of the democratic period was expressed by Article 153 of the Weimar Constitution, which not only guaranteed the right of private property, the nature and limits of which were to be defined by law, but proclaimed that "property rights imply property duties. Exercise thereof shall at the same time serve the general welfare." Expropriation was permitted only for the benefit of the community, and then only by process of law (auf gesetzlicher Grundlage). Adequate compensation was prescribed, and the right of appeal to the ordinary courts was granted.

The fact that National Socialism intended to effect a property revolution[14]—in spite of its proclamation favoring private ownership—is evident

[13] Not all common land was allotted to individuals. Extensive public ownership of forests was supplemented by state laws imposing controls, such as the requirement of permits for clearing and restrictions on the cutting of immature timber. Exploitation of the subsoil, canalizing, and the removal of water were put under public control. The Prussian Minister of War had in practice far-reaching veto rights concerning settlement and construction.

[14] Article 153 of the Weimar Constitution, with its guarantee of the right of private property, was suspended by the Decree for the Protection of Nation and State, Febru-

in the very character and philosophy of the movement; in its disgust for nineteenth century liberalism, its intention to replace Roman by "Germanic" law, its principle of leadership, its devotion to the soil, its resentment of existing wealth and privilege. Its emphasis on the insignificance of the individual, who was believed to derive his right to existence merely from his membership in a collective group, made it inevitable that the movement would eschew the idea of private ownership, a doctrine based on the natural rights of the individual. Behind the construction of the new system of ownership was a combination of three motives: the will to displace the group that had formerly held power, vindicated by an idealistic socialist theory; the will to justify changes as a return to Germanic ideas which had been lost through the introduction of Roman law; the will to power of a small group that intended to prepare the nation for war.

The peculiar fascination that the soil had for National Socialism made for a special treatment of land ownership. Four main methods were used for restricting property rights:

First, expropriation without compensation was practiced, which itself may be divided into two categories: *outright confiscation*, which was used against Jews, political enemies, and owners of strategic property in occupied countries, occasionally for the private gain of party leaders, and which was distinguished by its character of outright robbery; or *forfeiture of property* (Eigentumsverwirkung), because of dereliction of duty. The law of October 29, 1936,[15] which put the Four-Year Plan into execution, made possible the exclusion of unreliable persons from the professions or industry. And a decree of March 25, 1937,[16] provided that if the cultivation of land did not comply with the demands for adequate nutrition of the people and adequate maintenance of agricultural holdings, the court could either command the farmer to comply; establish supervision; order management by a trustee; lease the farm to an experienced farmer; or remove the owner from the farm (for a variety of reasons, including conflict with party principles). At first the latter measure was restricted to hereditary farmers but in 1943 it was made applicable to all farmers.

---

ary 28, 1933, issued by the Reich President, under his emergency power, based on Article 48 of the Constitution (Bibl. #140, Vol. 1, p. 83).

[15] Bibl. #140, Vol. 1, p. 927.

[16] Verordnung zur Sicherung der Landbewirtschaftung (Bibl. #140, Vol. 1, p. 422) and Ordinances of April 22, 1937 (Bibl. #140, Vol. 1, p. 535); August 31, 1938 (*ibid*, Vol. 1, p. 1174). At first restricted in its duration, the Decree of 1937 was prolonged indefinitely by Order of February 28, 1939 (*ibid.*, Vol. 1, p. 413).

A second major method of restricting property rights was condemnation with compensation, which became a common method of acquiring land for "community" purposes. In distinction from its former use as an action undertaken for specific technical purposes, this method came to be used as an instrument in preconceived plans, and its use increased tremendously. From March 24, 1933, to June 1, 1937, no less than ninety-seven new laws and decrees dealing with condemnation were passed.[17] Condemnation, formerly an "extraordinary event," became almost an "ordinary occurrence,"[18] an expression of the planning will of the Führer.[19] When it was provided, compensation was left to the discretion of the courts, which—according to official statements—attempted to balance the situation of the expropriated and the expropriator. Market value was only one factor to be considered; other factors were the individual owner and the common welfare, and even the "lack of space of the German people."[20] The right of appeal to the courts was permitted by some laws, but was excluded when expropriation "serves the eminent purpose of the Reich."

A third way in which the National Socialists restricted property rights was to subject to the consent of the authorities the sale or lease (including the forced sale) of agricultural or forest land amounting to more than 2 ha.[21]— thereby controlling the amount of purchase money or rent. Permission had to be obtained even for the removal of implements. The law was intended to prevent land from being sold to "unsuitable" elements, and from being used for purposes not in accord with National Socialist policy. In the typical manner of National Socialist legislation the law enumerated a series of

[17] Wolfgang Vogt (Bibl. #261), p. 32.

[18] Secretary of State Wilhelm Stuckart, "Die Enteignung in Vergangenheit und Gegenwart," Bibl. #165, 1937, pp. 99ff. This legislation provided for condemnation to serve the purpose of the army, the air force, national automobile roads, protection of "natural monuments," consolidation of small holdings, rural and city planning.

[19] Stuckart, op.cit., p. 111; also Theodor Maunz (Bibl. #215), p. 17.

[20] Preussisches Oberverwaltungsgericht, quoted in Bibl. #335, 1938, Vol. 59, p. 1096. A decision of the Preussische Oberverwaltungsgericht, the supreme administrative court of Prussia, pointed out that "as a rule compensation will be beneath the full or common value"—a situation that would certainly occur if the owner possessed several estates, or was not a farmer by profession and, in the case under consideration, because the owner was seventy years old, unmarried, and hard of hearing (Decision of January 25-26, 1938, ibid., pp. 382-83). In another case the same court reduced the amount of compensation because, among other reasons, the farmer had bought the property only four years before the expropriation (Decision of August 3, 1937, ibid., 1937, Vol. 58, pp. 1009-11).

[21] Law of January 26, 1937 and Ordinances (Bibl. #140, 1937, Vol. 1, pp. 32ff.) and Guiding Principles thereon issued February 8, 1937 (Bibl. #284, p. 218).

reasons for which consent could be refused, such as the violation of political and racial principles, and concluded by authorizing refusal on the grounds of "public interest," or, in plain language, for any or no reason at all. This law reflects the National Socialist obsession with the idea that the farming population must be "rooted in the soil." By setting prices very low, the authorities were easily able to prevent farmers from selling.[22] During the war all changes of ownership of agricultural land not absolutely necessary were prohibited.[23] The German press attributed this to the fact that land was being acquired for investment as a hedge against inflation, or in order to increase the food supply of the buyer.[24] In 1943 control was tightened because the traffic in small property had even increased: "The vagabonding capital is looking for investment opportunities."[25] No complete throttling was intended because that would have prevented badly managed farms from changing hands.

Finally, property rights were restricted, either by statute or by judicial decision, through making them contingent on certain obligations (Eigentumsbindung). These restrictions often limited the owner's power to dispose of his property, or stipulated the uses to which it was to be put. In these cases compensation was often expressly excluded, but sometimes it was permitted if the economic damage was severe. Many of these "property restrictions" would have been called expropriation during the time of the Weimar Republic.

The most striking interference with ownership was achieved through a rigid regimentation of all phases of production, distribution, and pricing, adopted for the sake of national self-sufficiency.[26] Although the land was

[22] Dellian in Bibl. #330, 1940, No. 24, p. 701. There were complaints about the legal insecurity resulting from such interference (Ministerialrat Heilmann, "Die privatrechtlichen Wirkungen des Preisstops im Grundstücksverkehr," Bibl. #139, 1941, Vol. v, p. 357).

[23] Decree of the Führer of July 28, 1942 (Bibl. #140, Vol. i, p. 481) and Order of March 17, 1943 (*ibid.*, Vol. i, p. 144); Decree of March 19, 1943 (Bibl. #139, Vol. i, p. 251); and June 15, 1943 (*ibid.*, Vol. i, pp. 350-51).

[24] Bibl. #320, August 6, 1942; Bibl. #321, August 7, 1942; Bibl. #331, August 16, 1942.

[25] "Das vagabundierende Kapital sucht Anlage," Bibl. #286, 3 Juniheft 1943, No. 18, p. 558.

[26] From 1936, records were kept of the production capacity of every farm; farm cards (Hofkarten) contained all pertinent data about the farm regarding the site, character of the soil, tillage plan, number of livestock, implements, members of the family with age, revenues, etc. (H. L. Fensch, "Arbeiten und Ziele des Reichsnährstandes auf dem Gebiete der bäuerlichen Betriebsforschung," Bibl. #296, 1938, Vol. v, p. 495). The farmer reported periodically any changes in crops, estimated yields,

not directly controlled, even before the war the status of the farmer was shifted in practice from that of an entrepreneur to that of an employee of the state, to whom existence on a low standard was guaranteed. The question of who held title became irrelevant when the farmer was required to follow official instructions exactly: the government determined the crops to be grown, where they were to be grown, and the prices at which specified quotas were to be marketed.

There is no doubt that by changing the conception of landed property National Socialism built up a new system of personal dependency. Justus Wilhelm Hedemann, one of the leading law scholars of the Third Reich, spoke of the farmer as an office-holder and vassal (Amtsträger und Lehnsmann).[27] He assumed that feudal "superior and subordinate ownership" would be reintroduced, even though the legal formulation was not yet precise.

The "Denomadization" of the Soil

The new conception of property found its most powerful expression in

---

quantities sold and utilized on the farm. A second card (Marktkarte), market card, contained the delivery obligations and actual deliveries (Bibl. #286, 2 Aprilheft 1944, p. 311). The RN employed inspectors (later replaced by commissions) whose chief work was to report monthly on crop conditions, sowings, prices, wages, stocks, etc. All reports were examined within two weeks after they were turned in so that the headquarters had a complete picture of current food production. The following examples of control in Bavaria were given: once a month cows were checked, for which the peasant had to pay 50 pfennigs; the cows were milked in the presence of a controller who then fixed the amount of milk to be delivered. Only a small amount could be retained by the peasant. The annual delivery quota of eggs per chicken was 65 (Bibl. #291, August 1937, A, pp. 75-76). When Bavarian farmers were unwilling to reduce hop cultivation in 1937 all areas were checked. Farmers who had raised more than in 1933 were ordered to plow under the excess. If they refused the labor service did it and the farmer was fined 10 pfennigs for every hop plant in excess. For some time farmers found a loophole in the rigid slaughtering regulations. They sent a light pig to the ration office and had its weight registered. Then they slaughtered a heavy one, keeping the difference. To stop this it was ordered that the ears of pigs weighed for slaughter had to be perforated.

During the war planning became still more comprehensive. Quotas were established as minimum for grain growers, for eggs and milk, based on averages over a period of several years. When the government wanted to increase crops (e.g. flax), the RN fixed the total additional quantity and assigned a share to each Landesbauernschaft which in turn divided the shares among the regions and individual farmers, who were advised how much they had to raise. Quotas were backed by bonuses, special foodstuff allotments, later war decorations for strict fulfilment, and penalties for delinquencies. The Supreme Court ruled that the farmer's wife too was responsible for delivery of obligations (Bibl. #283, October 1, 1944). However, few farmers were imprisoned or brought to concentration camps since their work was too much needed.

[27] J. W. Hedemann (Bibl. #191) II, Vol. 2, p. 355.

the Hereditary Farm Law (Reichserbhofgesetz, REG)[28] which was supposed to overcome whatever remnants there were of nomadization of the peasantry. It established the farm as the property of the blood-related families (Sippe) with the peasant, as trustee of the Sippe, not allowed to mortgage, subdivide, permanently lease, or alienate the farm from family possession without the sanction of special courts.[29] The law established inherited land tenure for farms up to 125 ha., large enough to support a family (Ackernahrung). The size of the smallest depended on the quality of the land and the nature of production. While only a few ha. might be sufficient in the fertile Rhine Valley, 10 ha. might be insufficient in the east where the soil is dry and sandy. The lower limit was an absolute requirement, the upper limit was more elastic. Larger holdings could be included by special permission, "for services to the welfare of the German people," e.g. the estates of Bismarck and Hindenburg.

The owner of a hereditary farm had the title of "Bauer" (peasant) which had a distinctly different meaning from "farmer." The title connoted a farmer whose family had held the same medium-sized farm through generations.[30] It was a title of honor—no one else was permitted to use it. It could be conferred only on German citizens or Germans of kindred stock or racial purity, viz., the mentally and technically competent, the impeccable or unimpeachable (ehrbar), those who could prove that there had been no Jewish or Negro blood in the family since 1800. The courts ruled that eligibility (Bauernfähigkeit)[31] would also depend on the degree of compliance with National Socialist policy relating to childbearing.

The order of inheritance was fixed by law and was characterized by blood

[28] September 29, 1933 (Bibl. #140, Vol. 1, p. 685) and Ordinances.
[29] Anerbengericht, with courts of appeal (the Erbhofgericht) and a supreme court (the Reichserbhofgericht). The local court consisted of a judge and two peasants; the higher and supreme court of three judges and two peasants each. In the autumn of 1944 it was decreed that the authorities had to postpone all hereditary farm cases not essential for the war effort (Bibl. #283, October 20 and 24, 1944).
[30] Darré defined the peasant as one "who has hereditary roots in the soil, tills his land and considers his work a duty toward his race" ("als eine Aufgabe an seinem Geschlecht"). "A farmer is without hereditary roots in the soil, tills his land and considers his work merely as a means of making money" (Darré, Bibl. #175, p. 107, No. 2).
[31] Bibl. #319, August 3, 1942. Those who were not farmers by profession were denied farm heritage; lack of will power, insufficient training, high age were other reasons for denying succession; likewise, persons suffering from a hereditary disease although their farming ability might be beyond doubt (Bibl. #293, November 30, 1938, Vol. VI, p. 67; March 23, 1937, Vol. IV, p. 281).

relationships and male preference. The order of succession was: (1) sons of the owner, their sons and grandsons (which of the sons was to get the farm was determined by local custom); (2) the father of the owner; (3) the brothers, their sons and grandsons; (4) daughters, their sons and grandsons; (5) sisters, their sons and grandsons; (6) other female descendants.[32]

This right of succession conflicted with custom in many parts of the country, and with tradition by discriminating against female succession. Peasants protested against the inferior position assigned their wives, and were not willing to disinherit their daughters in favor of nephews. The law therefore allowed the owner who had no sons or grandsons to give preference to his daughters, but stipulated that the legal line of succession should be restored in the next generation. In the intervening period the peasant was supposed to have come to understand that his blood maintains its purity better in the male line (sich nachhaltiger und ausgeprägter in der männlichen Linie vererbt).[33] Education in these ideas did not, however, proceed with great rapidity and in 1939 the possible preference of daughters had to be extended to the second succession.[34]

Co-heirs (descendants and parents of the testator) were not entitled to a cash settlement. The principal heir was obliged to support them on the farm only until they became age, or whenever, through no fault of their own, they lacked means of self-support (Heimatzuflucht). He was required to outfit them within reasonable limits when they left the farm.

[32] In districts in which the principle of closed inheritance had not been customary, the testator had some choice, limited, however, to his sons and grandsons. Other minor changes required the consent of the courts. If the original heir was already the owner of a hereditary farm, the farm then passed to the next heir but the first heir had the choice. If an heir refused or failed to qualify, the farm passed to the next heir. If no legal heir existed, the peasant selected the heir; if he failed to do so, the Reich Peasant Leader made the choice.

[33] Ministerialrat Vogels, "Weiterentwicklung im Erbhofrecht," Bibl. #284, 1939, p. 728.

[34] Decree of April 26, 1939 (Bibl. #140, Vol. 1, p. 843). The inferior position of women in the hereditary farm system is shown in the remark of a Württemberg judge: "In the public affairs of the village the peasant woman has no voice. . . . Among 600 hereditary farms owned jointly by husband and wife, the wife has never been a dominant force—one would do well to forego hearing her as a witness in Hereditary Court procedure" (Amtsgerichtsrat Setz, "Der bäuerliche Zeuge beim Anerbengericht," Bibl. #284, 1935, p. 173). A decree of the Minister of Justice of April 20, 1940, referred to discontent with regard to barriers to female succession (ibid., 1940, p. 480). In a book with preface of R. Walther Darré, a National Socialist writer defended depriving women of equal rights (Entrechtung), unaware of the insult to women with the argument that the legislation was in the interest of efficient farming (Gunter Martens, "Die Frau im Erbhofrecht," in Bibl. #207, p. 94). During the war when women's good will was urgently needed, the law was amended in their favor.

Attempts to evade legal disinheritance by supplementing a contract with secret promises of payment or by giving insurance premium, higher wages or gifts to co-heirs nullified the contract, if discovered.[35]

Disinheritance of co-heirs was a sharp break with German tradition. In the past, even where closed inheritance was customary, co-heirs were compensated by money payments, usually raised by mortgage, or by parts of the holding.[36] In some cases annuities were granted instead of capital shares. By tacit agreement the farm was undervalued for the benefit of the principal heir. Or he was granted about one-fifth or one-third of the value of the holding as extra inheritance prior to evaluating the assets of the legacy in order to protect the liquidity of the estate. Frequent over-indebtedness of farms due to the claims of co-heirs, or recall of mortgages on short notice, had long been regarded as harmful and was one of the reasons for the abrogation of equalitarian inheritance by the National Socialist government. However, many sons and daughters had remained on the farm for as long as ten or fifteen years, compensated only by maintenance and pocket money, producing the values which they received as compensation.[37] There had been conflicts in the past when farms were too small to maintain both the farmer's family and his parents. The National Socialists decided these conflicts in favor of the young. Subsistence for retired parents, so-called parents' portion (Altenteil), an old tradition on German farms, was greatly reduced. The compensation of the old folks became restricted to maintenance in kind, which during the war was limited by rationing prescriptions. Allowances, more and more restricted to a minimum by court order, were not secured by mortgage; an old farmer could not retain special tracts as his property.[38] Since old people received no cash they could no longer leave the farm if they were treated with harshness. Old farmers were therefore reluctant to retire. A farmer, having become too old, was considered incompetent by the courts and asked to retire. His heir could, if necessary, even

[35] In one instance, the Supreme Hereditary Farm Court rejected the claim of a community to have a peasant pay the asylum costs for an insane co-heir (Bibl. #293, May 11, 1938, Vol. v, p. 241).

[36] C. von Dietze (Bibl. #149d, pp. 148ff), Verhandlungen des Vereins für Sozialpolitik in Königsberg, September 1930. Peasants or peasants' wives became entitled to name their surviving spouse as heir to establish joint property with the same effect. The preference of brothers of the owner was changed in favor of daughters, unless the peasant made a divergent regulation (Erbhoffortbildungsverordnung September 30, 1943, Bibl. #286, 3 Oktoberheft 1943, No. 30, pp. 924-25).

[37] Sering (Bibl. #76) p. 847.

[38] Decision of the Reichserbhofgericht December 12, 1934 (Bibl. #126, 1935, p. 617).

succeed him by force. Entailed farmers frequently preferred to rent their farm to the son instead of transferring it to him, in order to avoid the scanty Altenteil, but the authorities were opposed to leases of this kind and prohibited them.[39]

An important feature of the law was the protection of the farm from foreclosure. The government prevented a further subdivision of farm property and overindebtedness, but the problem of supplying the hereditary farm with credit was not solved. The prohibition of mortgage loans hung a kind of credit embargo over the peasant, who could not even offer his crops as security. Improvements which would require investments—new machinery or buildings—were delayed. The difficulties encountered in the reduction of debts made the creation of new hereditary farms contingent upon the owner's indebtedness, not exceeding 70 per cent of the taxable value (Einheitswert) of the farm.[40] Short-term leases were not prohibited; if made for more than one year, however (three until 1936), they had to be approved by the courts. Permanent leasing was illegal.

The Hereditary Farm Law was based on the assumed racial superiority of peasant stock and attempted to establish the peasant as a new elite which was to become "the instrument of the racial regeneration of the German People."[41] "Once again 'Bauer' has become a title of honor. In fact, the peasants form a class, representing particular ethnic and national values, charged with special duties upon which the State has bestowed a distinctive position."[42] According to Darré,[43] "The home soil is no longer a commodity; it is not, as in the 'liberalistic' view, the private preserve of its present owner, but the concern of a higher unit, the clan in the sequence of generations." In the opinion of a high government official:[44] "The Hereditary Farm Act is opposed to the democratic principle." It did not recognize freedom and

[39] H. W. Spiegel, "The Altenteil: German Farmers' Old Age Security," Bibl. #336, June 1939, pp. 215-16.

[40] Erbhofrechtsverordnung, Section 1. Farms over 125 ha. could be considered even if indebted at a higher percentage.

[41] Darré (Bibl. #174), p. 42.

[42] Wilhelm Saure (Bibl. #240), p. 181 (semi-official guide to the law). It was forbidden to caricature the peasant in the movies or on the stage. His virtues were praised. He was glorified in novels. He had the elevated status of "renovator of blood," "carrier of the race," "feeder and breeder of the nation."

[43] "Reichserbhofgesetz und Agrarpolitik," Bibl. #284, 1934, p. 852.

[44] Ministerialdirektor Wilhelm Saure, "Demokratie als System der Vernichtung des Bauerntums," Bibl. #275, 1936, Vol. IV, p. 179. "Democracy is the arch enemy of the peasantry, a system to annihilate the peasantry," ibid., p. 168.

equality, but tied the estate to clan and folk. The peasant soil was not for the market.

The Hereditary Farm Law was not popular at the time of its enactment. To avoid unrest, an order issued simultaneously with the law prohibited oral or written discussion about the law without consent of the Reich Peasant Leader.[45] In spite of the widespread custom of closed inheritance, the compulsion of the law came as an extremely sudden innovation, especially to peasants in the south and west. Even in regions of closed inheritance the peasant had been free to dispose of his property during his lifetime or by will.[46]

Even those who at first believed themselves to be privileged under the Hereditary Farm Law became disappointed, since they felt too greatly hampered in their freedom of action. When in 1937 twenty holdings in a Bavarian community were to be declared hereditary farms, the owners divided their holdings among their children or sold lots in order to reduce the size below the legal requirement. When this "sabotage" was discovered, the National Socialist party (NSDAP) annulled the sales, and declared seven farms hereditary.[47]

[45] Bibl. #280, October 11, 1933.

[46] Efforts to secure provisions for closed inheritance in the 1900 Civil Code had failed, although only a proposal had been made to provide a legal scheme to which the farmer could have recourse if he intended to assign the farm to one heir (Friedrich Aereboe, Bibl. #1, p. 260). Even this moderate form was rejected; nobody thought of compulsion. Max Sering said: "I do not know of any living person who defends compulsory entails, who would want to fall back upon the medieval law of estates which made the peasant holdings closed units and which excluded free disposal by the owner and testator" (Bibl. #149b, p. 300). Aereboe said: "The reintroduction of a closed inheritance law on the ground that it is old German law is not permissible. Law has to conform and to change with need, not *vice versa*" (*op.cit.*, p. 261). He states that if the estate owners were to be asked whether they wished a closed inheritance law, 80-90 per cent would answer no. During the first World War, a peasant entail bill was drafted but it met with such opposition that it was withdrawn. Lujo Brentano (Bibl. #13, pp. 3, 8, 9) even denied that closed inheritance was an old German tradition, but considered it of Jewish and Roman origin. It sounds like prophecy when Brentano speaks of those "who fell in love with the whimsical scroll (Schnörkelwerk) of the decaying middle ages" (*ibid.*, p. 57). That the restriction on property rights was unpopular may be seen in the failure of the homestead, popularly called "the hereditary farm of the small settler." Here the owner could voluntarily undergo similar though less far-reaching restrictions toward protection. From 1919 to 1929, however, only 20,000 homesteads were established (G. J. Neumann, "Heimstättensiedlung und Kriegswirtschaft," Bibl. #111, February 19, 1937, p. 1916). Moreover, the homestead for habitation greatly exceeded the homestead for agricultural use.

[47] Bibl. #291, August 1937, A., p. 74.

The increase in the number of hereditary farms therefore was not as large as had been expected. The legislators had anticipated that there would be a million. From 634,752 farms, with 14,434 million ha. in the middle of 1936,[48] they increased to 685,000 (22 per cent of the total number of German farms), with 15,562 million ha. (37 per cent of the total agricultural and forested area) by the middle of 1938.[49]

Protests were frequently raised against the loss of the right to free disposal, the injustice to yielding heirs, the trustee character of the peasant, and the compulsion on which the institution rested.[50]

The large number of regulations necessary to interpret and supplement the law created confusion and aroused protests.[51] Frequent attempts to evade the law by illegal agreements which favored co-heirs reflected popular feeling. According to a National Socialist writer the large number of complaints readily led to the conclusion that "the entire legislation is a failure."[52] In 1935 10 per cent of all hereditary farms had to be exempted from the restrictions of the law.[53]

[48] Karl Hopp, "Erbhofrecht in Zahlen," Bibl. #284, 1936, p. 1566.

[49] Bibl. #153e, March 1939, pp. 166ff. Among them are 20,000 estates of less than 7.5 hectares, and more than 1,086 estates of more than 125 hectares. 180,000 farms, most of them ranging from 7.5 to 125 hectares, were not included, chiefly because the holdings could not support a family or because the owner was not eligible.

[50] In an historical study, one of the few forms in which criticism could be voiced in National Socialist Germany, Kuno Waltenmath shows how in ancient times the system resulted in the two- and even the one-child system, and in frequent intermarriages, how the peasant never acquiesced to his children becoming a landless proletariat. Waltenmath proves also that a similar law in Hanover caused flight from the land, prevented progress in intensification of agriculture, and led to annihilation of the peasantry, thus creating a caste which was neither peasant nor landowner. In 1873 the law had to be abrogated. This scholar adds, however, that the peasant under National Socialism faces three inexorable "beaters": the Reich Food Estate, the Party, and the labor service. "Die historischen Quellen des Erbhofgesetzes und seine Probleme," Bibl. #146, 1939, Vol. 63, pp. 547ff. With the prospect of leaving the yielding heirs "out in the cold," it could hardly be expected that peasants would be inclined to raise large families.

[51] Karl Blomeyer, "Neuerungen im Erbhofrecht," Bibl. #125, 1937, Vol. 146, pp. 452-53.

[52] Ibid., p. 469.

[53] 54,591 peasants received selling permits; 13,091 mortgage permits; 2,118 renting permits; and 5,769 permits to divide the farm. Karl Hopp (cited above, note 48), p. 1567. In March 1941 a National Socialist writer complained in the official periodical of the RN that too many hereditary farms were offered for sale. He emphasized that only important reasons entitled the peasant to sell and then only with permission of the courts. Relatives as possible heirs could protest against the change of clan (Sippenwechsel) (Eduard Dellian, "Das öffentliche Ausbieten von Erbhöfen," Bibl. #330, March 1941, No. 5, p. 113).

Against the security of tenure must be set the compulsory immobilization of the peasant's holdings and the restriction of his property rights. The peasants were rigidly bound to the soil; their activities and their standards of "honor" were supervised by the special courts. A peasant could be removed by the courts (Grosse Abmeierung) or a trusteeship arranged either for a certain period or permanently if the peasant lost his honorable character (for instance, by drunkenness, failure to pay his debts, loss of efficiency, coming into conflict with party principles). In fact not a few of them were dispossessed in favor of the next heir, in some cases for political reasons.[54]

As a result of the Hereditary Farm Law, inheritance, not achievement, became the principle of selection. Courts decided that the preservation of farms in the same family took precedence over considerations of proved ability.[55] The soil no longer fell necessarily into the hands of the most efficient cultivators: peasants who inherited a farm did not have to make strenuous efforts to meet interest and amortization obligations, and they were handicapped in getting credit for improvements. The fact that the farm could not come under the hammer promoted slackness. All of these factors did not help the government in its attempts to increase production. Whether the immobilization created by the REG would lend itself to adaptation to economic and technical changes was doubtful.

While peasants were tied to the soil, the ties binding large estates were being dissolved. In 1938,[56] with 910 fideicommissa still in existence, the government passed a law ordering their dissolution as of January 1, 1939. As of that date all fideicommissa and similar properties became free with certain temporary reservations. The step was the more remarkable since trafficking in land was held by National Socialism an outrageous characteristic of capitalism and liberalism. The apparent contradiction of dissolving large entails while creating new peasant entails showed the intention of the government to destroy strongholds of power which preserved the prestige of a small group of families.

No use was made of Section 4 of the REG providing for the division of large estates into hereditary farms. Far greater was the threat to the existence of small holdings which could be combined into larger estates.

---

[54] Bibl. #291, August 1937, A., p. 69.

[55] Bibl. #293, May 23, 1939, Vol. vi, p. 295; and January 30, 1940, Vol. vii, p. 256.

[56] 224 entails with 514,907 ha. were in the process of dissolution, so that only 686 entails with 922,318 ha. had not been affected by the process. Act of July 6, 1938 (Bibl. #140, Vol. i, p. 825) and Ordinances.

On the pretext of noncompliance with party orders, many small holders were proclaimed unfit. A few owners of farms below the size of self-supporting units were given the opportunity to increase their holdings to the size of a hereditary farm by acquiring adjacent land. A decree of June 14, 1940,[57] provided tax reduction in such cases. These were few. The custom of giving hereditary farms to some "meritorious" peasant or party boss as a reward for his services to the movement became widespread. Party leaders thus secured their relation to the soil.

The REG clearly shows the change in the German conception of property. With the elimination of the right to sell and to dispose at death, property rights were so restricted that it was doubtful whether the remaining rights should be called property rights at all. Peasant land was no longer a transferable good. With the change of land in the hands of the courts, it was the authorities who determined the adequate size of German estates and adapted them to a changing technique.

Moreover, abolition of the free disposal of lands deepened the gulf between the haves and the have-nots and destroyed the agricultural ladder. The progression of the landless to landownership, so urgently desired by a large portion of farm workers, became impossible as soon as land could be acquired only by inheritance. Yielding heirs who were denied claims to farm property, if restricted in their migration to cities, had to become workers on other farms. They were not willing, as was customary, to remain on the parental farm with no compensation after the father's death. They were the victims of a new system. They were to become a new proletariat.

Settlement Policy

I. SPACE PLANNING[58]

During the period of National Socialism, the settlement policy changed completely in character. It had to be coordinated with the war preparation policy of the government which was succinctly expressed in a speech of Hauptamtsleiter Dr. Ludovici.[59] Pointing to the fact that 70 per cent of the German population lived in cities exposed to air attacks, he said: "We must not only get more living space (Lebensraum) to grow, we must also see to it that the people are reasonably distributed." Protection against air

---

[57] Bibl. #284, 1940, p. 822, and Orders.

[58] Settlement planning had been started by the Democratic Government on a regional basis in the Ruhr and Elbe districts and Thuringia.

[59] Bibl. #264, p. 207.

attacks, decentralization of industries, de-urbanization of the population had to be planned.[60]

The intentions of space planning had already been indicated (September 22, 1933) in the Act to Lay Out Areas for Residential Settlements.[61] This law, intended to protect farm land by preventing cities from encroaching on it, authorized state and local authorities, in cooperation with the Minister of Labor, to set up regional and local plans for areas where residential settlements existed. Certain areas could, by ordinance, be reserved for small settlers, and others for residential, industrial, or commercial purposes. The ordinance had to stipulate how many people could be settled in the area, what types of buildings could be erected, and what services operated.

The full program was developed in 1935 when preparation for war had to be less concealed than in the beginning. To carry out planning, a couple of Reich agencies were created. The most important, the National Bureau of Spatial Organization (Reichsstelle für Raumordnung),[62] under the Reich Chancellor had to plan the adequate use of German space. It was made responsible for the organization and control of all national and regional planning authorities. It could resettle the population, determine the location of industries, and plan transportation, power supply, and soil improvements.[63]

[60] "Genuine space planning must take into account all modes and habits of life, folkways, customs (Lebensweise, Lebensform und Brauchtum), the degree of attachment to the home (Heimatgefühl), tribal consciousness, temperament and mental flexibility and, last but not least, the religious professions of the inhabitants of the individual settlement area as a means of judging the effect of cross-stratification (Ueberlagerung) under the newly arising order due to resettlement" (Hans Weigmann, Bibl. #265, p. 31). To this order belonged a "defense order" (Abwehrordnung) based on the principles of "defense geography," frequently called war space economy (*ibid.*, p. 28).

[61] Gesetz über die Aufschliessung von Wohnsiedlungsgebieten (Bibl. #140, Vol. 1, p. 659) and Ordinances. The task of settlement planning was assigned to a special commissioner under supervision first of the Minister of Economics and finally of the Minister of Labor. The Reich Minister for Food and Agriculture had jurisdiction for agricultural settlement, the Minister of Economics for small settlement.

[62] Act regulating the demand of the Public Authorities for Land of March 29, 1935 (Gesetz über die Regelung des Landbedarfs der öffentlichen Hand, Bibl. #140, Vol. 1, p. 468), and Decree of June 26, 1935 (*ibid.*, p. 793) and December 18, 1935 (*ibid.*, p. 1515). Aims of planning of the Reichsstelle, according to its first head, Hans Kerrl, former Minister of Justice in Prussia and Reich Minister of Education, were the following: (1) increase of the biological folkish strength (Volkskraft); (2) optimum use of the soil and its resources; (3) allocation of folk and landscape according to species; (4) intensification of the defense preparedness (Abwehrbereitschaft) of the German space (Bibl. #345, 1938, p. 543).

[63] The Decree of February 15, 1936 (Bibl. #140, Vol. 1, p. 104) divided the Reich into 23 planning regions (Planungsräume) in general coinciding with the provinces

The Reichsstelle established the Reichsarbeitsgemeinschaft für Raumforschung as a central body for directing research. The latter assigned special tasks to work groups (Arbeitskreise) which were organized all over the country. In universities, for instance, joint committees of students and faculty members[64] from various disciplines (geology, economics, transportation, population, anthropology) investigated problems in space planning and utilization of the territory. The first tasks assigned to such work groups concerned the flight from the land, for which eleven topics had to be worked out,[65] such as: facts concerning inner migration, culture and population movement, economic and occupational structure. In 1939 the central task was the east. Studies were made among others, about the absorptive capacity of the east, the consolidation of the German Volkstum in this area, the effects of eastern expansion on the old Reich.[66]

Characteristic of German space research was the so-called Hellmuth plan (named after the Gauleiter who conceived the idea of the plan) for the Rhön Mountains, carried out with the help of the University of Würzburg. In this area of scattered holdings and great poverty, the university started health examinations of the population, studies in hereditary biology, research in soil, climate, geology, water supply, and economic conditions. School children prepared pedigrees which were checked by the Church. Based on these studies, resettlement (Absiedlung) of dwarf peasants (of the smaller holdings) was to be started while the holdings of the remaining peasants were to be increased. Roads were built, marshes drained, partly with the help of the labor service. Similar investigations were started in other moun-

---

and states, with planning authorities and joint bodies (Landesplanungsgemeinschaften). See Bibl. #120e, March 23, 1938, p. 81. The joint bodies were formed by delegates of all public authorities of the army, transportation, agriculture, mining, labor, municipalities, the RN, the chambers of handicraft and industry. Each of the joint bodies was responsible for examining the conditions of its region and for constructing a plan. The authorities worked with 98 outside agencies (Aussenstellen) in 1942 which provided information about soil, climate, water supply, military grounds. The *Frankfurter Zeitung* (Bibl. #297) June 21, 1942, described how the Reichsstelle finds the place for industry by subtracting regions blocked up for military reasons, fertile soil, good forests, mineral resources, rivers, so called agglomeration centers, such as big cities and industrial centers. The remaining areas were recommended as construction regions (Aufbaugebiete) for industries. The Reichsstelle prepared in 1939 plans for the dismemberment of conquered Poland and drew the borders of the Government General. It had to populate the east with Germans.

[64] Bibl. #351, 1936, pp. 133, 216.
[65] Adolf Wagner, "Die Reichsplanung," Bibl. #288, 1936, Vol. 1, pp. 76-77.
[66] Friedrich Bülow, "Zum Forschungsprogramm der Reichsarbeitsgemeinschaft für Raumforschung," Bibl. #329, 1940, pp. 148ff.

tain regions.[67] The University of Berlin worked at the problem of moving the Siemens Works into rural surroundings.

Coordination of settlement and defense policies meant in the first place that military authorities' demands for land had priority. Loss of acreage to the armed forces was to be compensated by the reclamation of corresponding areas by the Reich Labor Service. The agricultural program had provided for extension of acreage by all means, but improved land was taken for training fields, air fields, fortifications and army roads. It was theoretically calculated that in the same period (1933-1936) in which, according to official figures, 650,000 ha. were claimed by the army, 536,000 had been won by reclamation.[68] However, this figure was reached by estimating improved crop yields expected to result from meliorations such as building of dikes and irrigation.[69] The statistics of arable land show a decrease from 20.471 million ha. in 1933 to 19.166 million in 1938—a loss of 1.3 million ha. in five years despite the reclamation work.[70]

The attainment of self-sufficiency of food supply meant preservation of large estates and enlargement of small agricultural holdings. The decision in favor of larger and middle-size holders was made after a bitter struggle within the party between the defenders of the party program, who advocated small farms, dense population, an aggressive policy against large estate owners, and the opposition, who demanded an increase of production of staple food by whatever means it could be achieved. No pressure was exerted for conversion of large estates into settlements because of the belief in the greater proficiency of large scale operations for providing food in the event of war. In the last years before the war, settlement in the sparsely occupied parts of the east had to be almost entirely abandoned. Thus the landless worker of the east remained without a farm.

[67] Bibl. #345, June 1938, p. 350, and Bibl. #297, April 3, 1939.

[68] Secretary of State Herbert Backe, "Der Stand der Erzeugungsschlacht," Bibl. #345, November 1938, p. 660.

[69] Werner Willikens, "Die Ergebnisse des Landeskulturwerkes in den Jahren 1937 und 1938," *ibid.*, December 5, 1939, p. 1326.

[70] Bibl. #308, 1934-1935, p. 22; 1938-1939, p. 23. The fact that only part of the shrinkage of land under cultivation was due to military use was explained in the letter of a large estate owner. In January 1938 he wrote: "The various fields are just put down on the statistical questionnaire as being a little smaller than they really are. Just work that out for the whole of Germany! The government can't measure it all, so there is always something left over for ourselves. The smaller farmers cannot, of course, manage so successfully, since they do not know as well as we do how to get about things." Bibl. #195, pp. 8, 9.

The true aims of settlement were revealed in Hitler's *Mein Kampf*:[71] it cannot be too strongly emphasized, says the author, that "German domestic colonization . . . can never suffice to secure the future of the nation without new land and soil." Conquest was the solution.

2. PEASANT SETTLEMENTS

The National Socialists in coming into power announced grandiose schemes for settling the population on the land. The party program of 1930 had already recognized settlement as a public task. "Settlement policy is one of the pillars of my program," Hitler declared on February 1, 1933. The goal of five million new settlements in the next decade was announced in the speaker's information material issued by the propaganda department of the NSDAP.[72] Kube, the governor of the Province of Brandenburg, promised the promulgation of a huge settlement plan "more important than the peasant emancipation of Baron von Stein."[73] But these schemes remained merely schemes; nothing came of them. In contrast to the constantly stressed aim of affording to yielding heirs and agricultural workers the possibility of becoming owners of land, settlement activities were reduced considerably.

The figures show a decrease of new settlements from 9,046 in 1932 to 846 in 1939. Between 1933 and 1939, 21,254 holdings with an area of 346,542 ha. were created, whereas 35,000 farmers were displaced after 1936 for the fulfillment of army requirements.[75] The Democratic government, in comparison, created 40,645 new holdings, totaling 455,300 ha., in the last seven years of its regime.

The reduction in the number of settlements was largely the result of the scarcity[76] and high price of land and the policy of diverting human and natural resources and building materials to military uses. Lack of land was due in part to military requirements, in part to the immobilization of land in hereditary farms, in part to the refusal of estate owners to sell—land was

---

[71] Adolf Hitler (Bibl. #196), p. 176.

[72] Bibl. #291, October 1937, B, pp. 3-4.

[73] Konrad Heiden (Bibl. #192), p. 310.

[75] Bibl. #150, July 15, 1940, p. 431. The figures up to 1936 still show settlement activities before 1933, since the settlement was counted only after the provisional credits had been converted into long term credits by the Siedlungsbank.

[76] German scholars busily confirmed "the oversettlement of the German space." According to E. Ostendorff, one half of all the farms in Germany had less acreage than the subsistence minimum required. He calculated that only 670,000 farms (of 5-30 ha., averaging 10.76 ha.) could be created if all estates over 50 ha. would be divided (Bibl. #328, pp. 32ff.).

Settlements during the Period 1918-1941[74]

Year	New Settlements	Total Area in 1,000 Hectares	Number of Persons Settled	Number of Holdings Enlarged	Total Area of Supplementary Lots in 1,000 Hectares
1912-22		75.5			36.2
1919-23	12,230			38,616	
1923		29.1			8.9
1924	2,797	26.4	72,539	4,838	6.6
1925	1,785	15.8		4,026	4.5
1926	1,906	25.5	8,681	3,552	4.5
1927	3,372	36.7	14,483	4,362	5.7
1928	4,253	50.6	17,568	5,552	6.8
1929	5,545	61.2	23,766	6,592	10.5
1930	7,441	79.8	31,733	7,378	15.9
1931	9,082	99.6	39,004	11,795	24.6
1932	9,046	101.9	40,286	9,436	17.8
Total	57,457	602.0	248,060	96,147	142.0
1933	4,914	60.3	20,719	8,480	17.0
1934	4,931	74.2	20,950	13,654	27.0
1935	3,905	68.3	17,020	13,156	23.1
1936	3,308	60.3	14,925	10,782	22.0
1937	1,894	37.6	8,429	10,793	21.4
1938	1,456	27.8	6,733	7,610	16.5
1939	846	17.9		6,828	12.0
1940	682			5,665	
1941	381	9.6		6,745	13.3

[74] Source: Bibl. #L53c, 1938, p. 90; Bibl. #153e, 1940, No. 11, pp. 170-71; Bibl. #153d, 1939, Vol. III, p. 7.

generally considered the safest form of investment—and, finally, to the government policy of maintaining large estates. In a country where few tracts of wild land were available for reclamation, the only real possibility of providing new settlements would have been the splitting up of large estates. The purchase of farms was rendered even more difficult because the former propertyless party leaders enjoyed preference in the market. The price increases that resulted from the scarcity of land are reflected in the fact that the average cost of land acquired for settlement in 1938 amounted to

1,457 Rm. per ha., as against 643 Rm. in 1932.[77] The price index rose in the east from 100 in 1933 to 120 in 1936, and in the west to 129.[78] Building costs increased comparably.

Because of the necessity of extracting maximum produce from the German soil, the government decided to devote most of its funds to small settlements instead of peasant settlements.[79] New peasant settlements would not reach the level of efficiency of older estates, whereas even the poorest soil could be allotted to small settlers with the certainty that they would utilize it to the fullest.[80]

Although the acreage offered was much smaller during the National Socialist regime, it became more and more difficult to secure paying applicants. This may have been due partly to a feeling of distrust on the part of peasants who had been dislodged for government purposes and who feared it could happen again, and to their disinclination to become bound to a new soil which was not the soil their fathers had tilled. Partly it was caused by the high cost of settlement, which prevented those without means, especially farm laborers, from competing. "Only young, financially strong people could be settled."[81] That people were willing to settle if means could be provided is revealed by the number of candidates examined for admission. In the period 1934-1939, when approximately 60 to 70 per cent of all applicants were rejected,[82] mostly because of poor health and the improbability of their raising large families, 44,500 were admitted and 17,000 provisionally accepted—a total of 61,500.[83] Only 21,206 were actually settled. In 1934, of

---

[77] Bibl. #153d, 1939, No. 3, p. 4.

[78] Bibl. #111, January 13, 1939, p. 714.

[79] Circular of the Federal Minister of Labor of June 30, 1936 (Bibl. #139, Vol. 1, pp. 222-23). Small settlements, formerly outskirt (unemployed) settlements, were prevailingly used for various purposes to provide house and garden to the industrial worker under the National Socialist regime. They had first to restore the industrial worker's "touch with the soil," to bring him close to nature, to dissolve the agglomeration of the population and to give the city dweller the opportunity to move away from cramped tenements. They had to bring the people out of cities where they could become targets of air attacks. They had to provide dwellings and land from which part of the family subsistence could be drawn and thereby enlarge the food supply of the nation and the supply of labor.

[80] Bibl. #286, 1936, No. 1, p. 27.

[81] Minister of Agriculture Darré at the Sixth Reich Peasant Day, Bibl. #275, 1938, Vol. v, p. 49.

[82] Franz Heinz, "Der Mensch und die Siedlungsbewegung," Doctoral dissertation, Heidelberg, 1937, pp. 53-54.

[83] Hartwich, Bibl. #139, 1941, Vol. v, p. 165.

15,948 applicants, 8,454 received certificates which entitled them to settle, and only 4,931 were settled.[84]

The settlement policy did not deviate in principle from the plans of the pre-Hitler period. It was carried out within the frame of the previous legislation, but was featured by strong administrative centralization; the tenets of the Democratic government were appropriated and proclaimed to be new National Socialist principles. The law of 1919 remained in force.[85] Jurisdiction in all matters concerning agricultural settlement was transferred from the states to the Reich.[86] The main points stressed in National Socialist planning of settlements were:

1) Holdings became larger in order to make it possible for them to use the most advanced methods of farming. The Democratic government had already enlarged the holdings from 1926 on. Prior to the advent of the National Socialist government, holdings of 7.5 ha. (which permit the utilization of one horse), and of 15 ha. (which permit the utilization of a two-horse team), were the standard. The average increased from 12.2 in 1933 to 19.8 ha. in 1937, but was reduced to 19.1 in 1938.[87] Since settlers were to become peasants,[88] holdings were laid out in sizes which allowed their evolving into hereditary farms. The average increase in size of adjacent settlements in part granted on a tenancy basis was from 1½ to 2 ha. in 1938.

2) In the first two years, land was mainly provided by reclamation of moor and wasteland because of the availability of cheap labor provided by the labor service. The self-sufficiency policy justified the heavy cost of reclamation. After 1935 the use of moor land declined, owing probably to economic recovery and to inroads made upon the cheap labor supply by the demands of military service. Unwillingness to divide estates shifted emphasis from the east to the west.[89]

[84] Bibl. #325, December 1942, p. 441.

[85] New regulations for its enforcement were contained in the Law for the New Formation of German Peasantry (Gesetz über Neubildung Deutschen Bauerntums) of July 14, 1933 (Bibl. #140, Vol. I, p. 517), the amendment to the Reich Settlement Act of January 4, 1935 (ibid., Vol. I, p. 1), and numerous decrees.

[86] The RN cooperated in all essential details. Provision of land, its division, assessment, etc., were regulated in cooperation with state, county, and local peasant leaders. A sharp reduction was made in the number of associations engaged in the work of settlement. Only about 40 of the original 200 settlement companies remained.

[87] Bibl. #153d, 1939, Vol. III, p. 6. Whereas 45.4 per cent of the new peasant holdings were 10 ha. and over from 1919 to 1932, holdings of this size amounted to 77.6 per cent of the total in 1938 (Bibl. #153e, 1939, No. 10, p. 415).

[88] Decree of April 15, 1937 (Bibl. #140, Vol. I, p. 546).

[89] While 61.7 per cent of all settlements had been located in five eastern provinces

3) Planning, which was already recognized as necessary in the last years of the Democratic government, was stressed under the slogan: Planned integration into the German living space (Planmässige Eingliederung in den deutschen Lebensraum).[90] It meant planning of the village (as to size of holdings, location of buildings, type of housing) according to the character of the area and the "clan habits" (Stammesgewohnheiten) of the settler group. In stressing the necessity of settling homogeneous groups from the same section of the country in compact village communities in environments similar to those they had left behind, the experience of the Democratic government was utilized. In National Socialist language, to individual German tribes (Stämme) certain reception areas were assigned which were akin to them in character of clan, mental attitude, and denomination (Stammesart, Geistesrichtung und Bekenntnis).[91] However, it is hard to understand why Bavarians had to go to Central and Upper Silesia, with a large Slav population, or Württembergers to Mecklenburg and Pomerania.[92]

4) The only revolutionary change concerned the selection of settlers, which had to be brought in line with the military and racial aims of the Third Reich. The whole family of the applicant, rather than the future peasant alone, was taken into consideration. This was done for racial-biological reasons as well as in consideration of the participation of the family in the work on the farm. "The settler was required to guarantee that his family (Geschlecht) would remain loyal to the soil (Scholle) for centuries and be willing and able to defend it against all attacks."[93] "Only racially highly qualified carriers of best blood heritage" (rassisch hochwertige Träger besten Erbguts) who on the basis of preparatory training and character could guarantee that they were willing to fit into the community of the new peasant village and to found in hard, expert, and purposeful work on the allotment a new peasant generation, valuable for the folk community (Volksganze),[94]

---

from 1919 to 1932, only 52.4 per cent were allotted to them in 1936 (Bibl. #153e, 1937, No. 18, pp. 745ff.). In 1934, 25 per cent of all new settlements were reserved for west-east settlers, i.e. peasants evacuated for military reasons from the west (Frank Glatzel, "Die Siedlung im Jahre 1933," Bibl. #338, March 1, 1934, p. 275). But only 17.4 per cent in 1934 and 15.4 per cent in 1935 came to the east from the west and south ("Deutsche Bauernsiedlung," Bibl. #338, April 30, 1937, p. 533).

[90] Karl Hopp, "Neubildung deutschen Bauerntums," Bibl. #284, 1935, p. 1617.
[91] Erich Molitor (Bibl. #223), p. 166.
[92] Hans Jürgen Seraphim, "Der Mensch in der Siedlung," Bibl. #125, 1934, Vol. 140, p. 710.
[93] H. Merkel and O. Wöhrmann (Bibl. #217), p. 43.
[94] Hopp, op.cit., p. 1618.

were settled. Warlike virtues and the desire to have children, as well as thrift and diligence, were primary considerations. A large number of children was not sufficient. The children had to meet the biological requirements. The family had to be familiar with the agricultural work they were expected to do. Farmers who gave up their holdings for public purposes, peasant sons, farm workers, and rural craftsmen were to be considered, with preference given to war veterans and trustworthy party men.

An elaborate procedure of examination was worked out. A special department of the office of the Reich Peasant Leader was in control. Applicants had to be 25 years of age, married or engaged. They had to provide certificates of their own good health, hereditary health, their desire for offspring, and the wife's fitness to endure repeated childbearing. The search of the pedigree usually went back to grandparents, and was applied to the wife as well as the husband. Applicants who fulfilled all requirements received a certificate of fitness, the so-called Neubauernschein. Only persons who had this certificate were to be settled. No new claims were given to boys and girls in the Labor Service.[95] Those who had savings and old claims were entitled to use the sums for small settlements, enlargements of gardens, building or enlargement of their own homes, and settlement training.[96]

Previous Employment of Settlers
(in Per Cent)[97]

	1934	1935	1936	1937	1938
Independent farmers	33.0	37.0	39.0	45.0	53.0
Sons of independent farmers	15.0	18.0	19.0	22.0	17.0
Farm workers	29.0	26.0	27.0	22.0	16.0
Farm salaried employees	12.0	10.0	7.0	6.0	5.0
Nonagricultural workers	11.1	9.1	8.0	5.0	9.0

3. THE DISPLACEMENT OF THE SMALL FARM

The inner contradiction of the rearmament program with that of return to the land forced the National Socialist government into plans for revolutionary changes in landholding. The pressure started with the plans for mechanization when German agriculture lost 1½ million of its population and labor-saving devices became an urgent necessity. Special emphasis was

[95] Decree of February 28, 1934 (Bibl. #140, Vol. i, p. 172).
[96] Decrees of August 8 and August 9, 1940 (Bibl. #140, Vol. i, p. 1097).
[97] Bibl. #153d, 1936, Vol. iii, pp. 30ff.; 1936, Vol. iv, pp. 25ff.; 1937, Vol. iv, pp. 18ff.; 1938, Vol. iii, pp. 22ff.; 1939, Vol. iii, pp. 3ff.

laid on the extended use of the small rubber-tired tractor. Since approximately a third of all labor in agriculture is transportation, it was estimated on small holdings the tractor would save 800 working hours a year and two horses.[98]

Mechanization, however, depended on the size of farm; for the tractor farm 20, or under particularly favorable conditions 10, ha. were needed;[99] smaller farms did not lend themselves to mechanization. The Institute for Business Research estimated roughly that about 50 per cent of the estates of 10 to 20 ha. and about 80 per cent[100] of those over 20 ha. could use the tractor. Wherever farms were divided into separate parcels, use of the tractor was impossible. Thus mechanization implied the need for drastic modifications in the structure of peasant farming.

At the end of 1938 articles in the press pointed to the impossibility of reorganizing small farms and advocated the abolition of holdings which could not be mechanized. In 1939 an announcement of the program for doubling the tractor output was the signal for field correction. Farmers with little property were to be doomed. On April 28, 1939, the DV reported:[101] "The agricultural leadership has virtually decided in favor of intensified use of tractors on properties qualified by the size of the area under cultivation. This forecasts a gradual elimination of the smaller farms and a fundamental structural change of the southwest farming properties." This change was compared to the change 120 years earlier when, in the northeast, peasants unable to support a team of horses were eliminated.[102] There were in the Reich, in 1937, 1,386,054 farms of 2 to 10 ha. and 388,983 farms of 10-20 ha.[103] many of which consisted of scattered strips. All of them were in the hands of individuals. The projected changes in German farming are still more striking if we consider that according to the census of 1925, 3,921,885 farms or 76.9

[98] Only 24,183 tractors were in use for all German agriculture in 1933; by 1939 the number had grown to 66,000 (Bibl. #153e, 1941, No. 3, pp. 54-55). According to official estimates 500,000 were needed (Bibl. #345, 1939, p. 577). In comparison, the U.S. had 1,626,000 tractors in use in 1939 (*Technology on the Farm*, U.S. Government Printing Office, August 1940, p. 3). However, such comparisons should take into consideration the extended use of locomobiles on larger estates in Germany.

[99] Bibl. #111, July 9, 1939, p. 1775.

[100] Bibl. #120e, 1939, No. 22, p. 142.

[101] P. 1458.

[102] Bibl. #111, August 25, 1939, p. 3212. That within the government the official policy did not find general approval is revealed in a remark of the Institute for Business Research, that combination of small farms into large units would reduce the rural population and endanger the already insufficient production of meat, butter, fat, cheese, and eggs (Bibl. #120b, 1939-1940, No. 1, p. 11).

[103] Bibl. #153e, 1940, Nos. 7-8, p. 117.

per cent of the total were smaller than 5 ha., and 4,878,040 or 95.7 per cent of the total contained less than 20 ha.[104] These small farm holders cultivated 53.4 per cent of the total agricultural area. Only 218,493 farmers or 4.3 per cent owned holdings with more than 20 ha. To mechanize such a farming system would have meant complete revolution.

The removal of small holders was to be achieved by various legal and political devices. The most conspicuous procedure was by consolidation of holdings into larger units. The regrouping effected by former governments had meant merely bringing together scattered patches and strips (without footpaths) into compact fields. Its aim was to abolish the waste of land and time and the compulsory succession of agricultural operations resulting from the involved position of the allotments (Gemengelage) whereby all the owners were forced to till the allotments and harvest the crops at the same time (Flurzwang). Majority consent had been needed to regroup the land of a village and in some fifty years no more than 2.9 million ha. had been consolidated.[105] In no case had this consolidation meant expropriation: it was instead an exchange of strips. The reform had been hampered by the conservatism of peasants, their attachment to their property, the complicated procedure, and the high costs of making the exchange, which were estimated at 500-800 M. per ha.[106] Under National Socialism costs could be somewhat reduced because the labor service provided cheap labor.

A law concerning regrouping of strip farms[107] which came into force January 1, 1938, superseding existing state laws, substituted compulsion for democratic consent. The simplified procedure was intended to speed the consolidation by disregarding the claims and wishes of the land owners. Consolidation was to be officially inaugurated by the authorities whenever they found it necessary for military purposes, agricultural efficiency, or other reasons. No majority vote of the owners was required. Only the local and state peasant leaders and party and community officials were to be consulted. "Collaboration of the RN supplanted the influence of the participants."[108] The Minister of Agriculture had the final decision.

In fact, regrouping was accelerated but not to the extent that the govern-

---

[104] Bibl. #104e, p. 2.

[105] Werner Henkelmann, "Grundstückszusammenlegung und Erbrechtsreform," Bibl. #7, pp. 604ff. and Ludwig W. Ries, "Arbeitsrationalisierung," *ibid.*, p. 623.

[106] Henkelmann, *op.cit.*, p. 606.

[107] Reichsumlegungsgesetz of June 26, 1936 (Bibl. #140, Vol. 1, p. 518) and Decrees of June 16, 1937 (*ibid.*, p. 629 and 654) and February 14, 1940 (*ibid.*, p. 366).

[108] Secretary of State Werner Willikens, Bibl. #330, 1939, No. 23, p. 876.

ment desired.[109] Thus in Thuringia, where more than 800 fields were declared in need of consolidation, only six were consolidated in 1937, eight in 1938, seven in 1939; in Baden some of the consolidations turned out to be mere regulations of ways.[110] The consolidated land as far as not needed for army purposes was used for meliorations, for compensation to farmers whose estates had been reduced by army requisitions, and for concentration of small holdings in the hands of a single holder as a hereditary farm. In 1938 only 5,200 ha. were used for new settlements.

The new consolidation would have meant uprooting of hundreds of thousands of small holders. Owners of insignificant (geringfügige) property were to be compensated in money only. To be sure, consolidation as such is a means of heightening agricultural efficiency, wherever plots are so scattered that draft and labor are wasted and orderly crop rotation is impeded. The regime undoubtedly intended to increase efficiency, to create a network of roads, and to regulate water conditions. The reform, however, was carried through without any consideration for the land owner and was used as a means of eliminating farmers who did not pass the eugenics test. It was supported by a policy of abolition of Allmends, common land which the peasant had the right to use and which often provided him with his only source of pasturage for livestock and wood for fuel. In Baden, where 21.9 per cent of all landholders, most of them small farmers, had the right to use the Allmend, representing 5.8 per cent of all arable land[111] in addition to forests, by laws of January 9, 1934,[112] and June 3, 1938,[113] the communities were required to withdraw the use of communal land from the peasants if the Minister of the Interior should declare another important use for it. In Hesse, by law of January 27, 1934,[114] the Minister of State was empowered to declare the use of Allmends abolished in the public interest.

During the Democratic period, the minimum size of soil needed for support of the family had been estimated to amount in Württemberg and

[109] Consolidation amounted annually to 95,000 ha. between 1933 to 1936; 105,000 in 1937; 125,331 in 1938 (Bibl. #153e, 1938, No. 19, pp. 793-94; 1939, No. 24, pp. 771ff.); for 1939 a consolidation of 150,000 was expected. The decrease of allotments by consolidation amounted to about 56 per cent. According to semi-official estimates, the total area needed for consolidation amounted to 8-9 million ha. (including Austria). With the then existing number of survey officials the accomplishment of such a program would have required twenty-five to thirty years (Bibl. #345, 1939, No. 23, pp. 1326-27).

[110] Bibl. #220, pp. 164, 251.

[111] Landwirtschaftsrat Kann, "Neuordnung des Allmendrechtes," Bibl. #330, 1940, No. 2, pp. 33ff.

[112] Bibl. #276, p. 13.

[113] Ibid., p. 47.   [114] Bibl. #299, 1934, Vol. 33, p. 7.

Baden to 1.75-2 ha. for the adult person (on the best soil, 1-1.25). A family composed of parents, a sixteen-year-old son and two school children would have needed 7-8 ha. on unfavorable, 4-5 ha. on favorable, soil.[115] Discussions of officials in the German press estimated that the future family farm equipped with the latest technical innovations, would be of an average size of 25-40 ha. or larger.

The drastic character of such measures, which would have forced hundreds of thousands to leave their land, can be understood only in the light of the traditional German relation to the soil. Farming in Germany means living in the same house, on the same soil, for generations. It means, for the villagers, a strong feeling of unity developed through their common tradition. The German farmer would never have moved to another part of the country because he believed conditions might be better there. The soil of his father was his fate. Dispossession for him meant indescribable anguish.

Under the new system of consolidation, agriculture would have taken on the color of large-scale industry. Small units would have disappeared. Centralization would not have stopped at holdings of 20 ha. because it would soon have been discovered that the more continuous use of machinery on large estates would mean ever greater savings in labor and production costs. The tractor is far more than a mere substitute for horses: it requires changes in the design and use of farm machines and in farm organization, and becomes, in time, the dominating force in determining the scale of farm operations. A process not unlike that which resulted from dissolution of enclosures in Great Britain could have been expected. The resettlements necessary for Baden were estimated to concern 60,000 farmers. About 98 per cent of the holdings in Württemberg were below 20 ha.[116] The resettlement plan for Württemberg would have meant a reduction in the number of farms (over 2 ha.) by 68,148 or 42.8 per cent. The type of peasant who combined industrial and farm work, so characteristic for this part of the country, would have disappeared.[117] In the Rhön District, 11,552 of the 13,735 farms were declared unable to survive.[118] The creation of the hereditary

---

[115] Adolf Münzinger, "Versuche zur Hebung der bäuerlichen Wirtschaft und zur Ausschaltung der bäuerlichen Arbeitsüberlastung," Bibl. #7, p. 698. While in the east minimum sizes would have been larger, they could be smaller in many other regions. Dr. Heinrich Niehaus gives the minimum size for a northwestern region as 5 ha., Dr. Ernst Marckmann for some Holstein region as 3-4 ha. (Bibl. #105b, pp. 130, 185-86).

[116] Bibl. #338, December 15, 1940, pp. 753-54, and Bibl. #286, August 19, 1940.

[117] Münzinger, "Die Württembergische Wirtschaft—Vorbild für den Osten," Bibl. #329, 1943, Nos. 5-6, p. 156.

[118] Bibl. #297, April 3, 1938 (Anton Betzner).

farm system showed that the government did not intend to introduce the Russian system of grain factories. The shortage of labor, however, and the desire to increase the output might eventually have compelled the government to sponsor large highly mechanized farms with few workers. Any system that increases the investment required makes it more difficult to acquire ownership. It seemed that the luxury of the peasant system was to be sacrificed to the increase in production of the nation's food supply. It was the opinion in influential National Socialist groups that the era of peasant farming would automatically end with the introduction of modern machinery and modern methods of farming, but the government was afraid of proclaiming officially any change in its attitude toward the peasants. When, after the conquest of eastern territory, the question of size was again discussed, several leading National Socialist agrarian experts stated bluntly that the family farm of 10 to 20 ha. had no longer a right to exist.[119] The Reich Commissioner for the Solidification of German Folkdom (Reichskommissar für die Festigung deutschen Volkstums) therefore in an Order of November 26, 1940,[120] fixed the size of the new settlement for medium soil conditions as 25-40 ha. The misgivings of those who predicted the loss of "rootedness" of "blood reserves," and the destruction of the "Landvolk" was met with the argument that such claustrophobia should not influence agrarian policy. "An overaged, petrified peasantry can give no racial or ideological support."[121] And the party district leader Schmidt demanded that peasant policy should have "the courage to get away from romanticism and tradition and to abolish the conservation of certain ideologies."[122]

In the Altreich, the war slowed up the "reform." According to a decree issued in the summer of 1940,[123] a new tractor could be obtained only when a farmer's old one was beyond repair, and then with the proviso that the old tractor be relinquished to the government for scrap metal.[124] When

---

[119] Arthur von Machui, "Zur Neuordnung der bäuerlichen Betriebe und ihrer Arbeitsverfassung," Bibl. #218, pp. 27, 216.

[120] Ibid., pp. 361ff.   [121] Ibid., p. 220.

[122] Ibid., p. 13.   [123] Bibl. #295, January 1, 1942, p. 21.

[124] The use of the tractor was allowed only for agricultural, not stationary work (Order of November 24, 1939, Bibl. #345, 1940, No. 1, p. 9). In 1942 the gasoline shortage limited the use of the small number of farm tractors to ten days a month. In December 1942 it was ordered that tractors should be converted to producer gas. The same applied to agricultural implements. For non-complying owners the fuel supply was stopped (Bibl #279, December 17, 1942). A special Reich Agency was established which worked out plans for transformation (Bibl. #286, September 18, 1942). Fuel production for tractors was halted July 1, 1942. However, shortage of petrol and Diesel oil rations prohibited the full use of tractors (The Economist, April 24, 1942, p. 530).

changes of ownership were barred in 1942, the situation was stabilized and the small owner was protected against loss of his holding for the duration of the war. In the spring of that year, an exchange of pieces of land (Landnutzungstausch) between farmers was inaugurated.[125] Although presumably the exchange was to be achieved by voluntary agreement, it was made clear that "those who resist can be forced."[126] Up to January 1944, two hundred such exchanges had been made.[127]

4. SETTLEMENT BY CONQUEST

The cessation of settlement in the Reich gains full significance only in the light of the aggressive expansion policy of the National Socialist government.[128] Settlement space was to be provided by conquest of new lands and displacement of their residents by Germans. More than 1.5 million Poles were expelled from Poland in the first two years of National Socialist occupation.[129] Similarly tens of thousands of Alsatians were expelled to France, Czechs were driven from their homeland, Slovenes deported to Serbia.

New settlers in the former Polish territories were to be peasants from the west but compulsory removal to the unfriendly east would have met so much resistance and stirred up so much unrest that the government did not dare to start it during the war.[130] Germanization, nevertheless, had to be achieved. "If we do not succeed in settling these territories with Germans," said the *Reichsarbeitsblatt*, "if we do not succeed in having the work of the German soldier carried on and completed by the German farmer and peasant, then

[125] In order to avoid surveying of land, only fields of similar quality and site were to be exchanged (Bibl. #314, February 27, 1943). Property rights were not to be changed, nor was the final postwar regulation to be prejudiced (Bibl. #346, July 29, 1944). Friedrich Siebold claims that property was frequently transferred and production increased by more than 20 per cent (Bibl. #321, February 23, 1945).

[126] Bibl. #286, 1. Maiheft 1943, No. 13, p. 414.

[127] *Ibid.*, 1 Januarheft 1944, p. 10.

[128] Hitler emphasized in innumerable speeches the necessity of conquering new territories "as a sacred right of acquiring that territory which alone will provide the daily bread for the increase in the population. To whom the Lord gives life, to whom He will also give territory if he will but take it" (Munich, November 21, 1927. Bibl. #346, November 23, 1927).

[129] Simon Segal (Bibl. #248), p. 56.

[130] To overcome the German resistance to migrating to the east, extensive tax exemptions, subsidies, priorities in the allotment of raw material and equipment, and lavish credits were offered. About fourteen such measures were taken (Bibl. #286, December 13, 1940, p. 41, and Bibl. #345, 1941, p. 425). That even those Germans who heeded the plea to settle in the east lacked the colonizing spirit was revealed in the bitter attacks of district leaders against those who intended to remain a few years, and return after having saved enough.

we shall not be able to keep the land that we have won with the sword. For history teaches us that every people that deserts the land, every people that leaves the tilling of its own soil to foreign races will sooner or later have to yield to a race of peasants, for only a race of peasants can outlast a foreign domination."[181]

It was easier, however, to evacuate the native population than to replace it with Germans. When the latter failed to pour into the emptied space "Folk Germans"[182] from the Government General were sent to the incorporated Polish areas. At the close of 1941 the Governor General could state that one million people had found new homes in Germany. After that, no further transfer was made. Another group designated to Germanize the conquered territories and to settle in Alsace-Lorraine, Luxembourg, Sudetenland, the Protectorate, Slovenia, and the Polish provinces were those "led back to the Reich" (Rückgeführte), later referred to as resettlers (Umsiedler).[183] They were "Folk Germans" who had lived in Tyrol, Estonia, Latvia, Lithuania, Volhynia, Eastern Galicia, Bessarabia, Bukovina, and Dobrudja. According to the treaties concluded with their respective governments they "returned" to the Reich. Officially the members of the German minority had the choice whether to stay or to return; however, there were more or less tangible pressures, such as skillful propaganda, which used the fear of bolshevization and promises of an idyllic future.[184] About 806,000 persons[185] were thus returned to the Reich until the end of 1942. The number of economically active members belonging to agriculture among these repatriated families varied according to the countries they were coming from. While Balts and Bukovinians were composed mainly of townspeople, a large number of other resettlers had been engaged in farming.[186]

The form of settlement in the east was to be the hereditary farm, larger, however, than in the Reich, because of poor soil (up to 250 ha. instead of 125). Settlers received more land than they had given up in their old home. Buildings were repaired and improved, and seeds, livestock, machinery, and

[181] Bibl. #139, 1941, Vol. v, p. 540.

[182] Folk Germans were defined as those non-German citizens who confess to be Germans confirmed by language, attitude, education, and conditions.

[183] Decree of October 19, 1940 (Bibl. #139, 1941, Vol. ii, pp. 36ff.).

[184] Joseph B. Schechtman (Bibl. #241), pp. 96ff., 182-83.

[185] Bibl. #286, April 1943, p. 344.

[186] Of 219,830 (with 117,974 gainfully employed) of the first set examined by the statistical office, 72,278 belonged to agriculture—20,282 as independent farmers and 16,398 as workers, besides the helping members of the family. Only 20 per cent of the Balts were engaged in agriculture (Bibl. #153e, 1941, No. 1, p. 1; No. 7, p. 151).

other inventory and implements were provided. Some of the settlers got three to four times as much as they had owned, e.g. 13 instead of 3 ha., 9.5 instead of 2. Houses were larger.[187] In some cases twelve to thirty small holdings were united to form one hereditary farm.[188] There were great difficulties of adjustment to these new farms of different size and soil, with different numbers and types of livestock in a hostile environment. Some settlers were shocked at the size of their property and asked, "How shall we get through with it?" German authorities supervised the work of the newcomers.

So far as not distributed, the holdings were administered by German trustees. "Like dams, German settlements are drawn across the land. A barrier was first laid along the frontier, then a strong folkish dam across the country. In time, the space between will be filled with German settlers. This procedure of nationalization creates strong German islands in the country."[189] All these settlers, however, were not sufficient to fill the gap created by the expulsion of Poles, and by those who would be expelled in the future. Moreover, the newcomers were not efficient because they had to adjust themselves to new soil and new conditions, and they were unfamiliar with the modern agricultural methods used in Germany.[140] Following the outbreak of the German-Soviet war, transportation difficulties increased. Colonization therefore had to be halted soon after it had begun. Eviction of Poles ceased. A people without living space were confronted by a space without people.[141]

Since Germanization proved too slow, the plan was conceived to transfer

[187] Hedwig Neumeister, "Von Hof zu Hof. Ein Stück der modernen Völkerwanderung im Osten," Bibl. #338, December 15, 1940, p. 756. Die Weltwoche (Bibl. #348), Zürich, November 28, 1941, claims that farmers from Latvia and Estonia who had together owned 86,000 ha. received 145,000 ha. of Polish land. For other examples, cf. Schechtman (Bibl. #241), pp. 296ff.

[188] Bibl. #297, January 26, 1941.

[189] Hedwig Neumeister, ibid.

[140] The resettlers, many of whom had come reluctantly, had to face more than economic difficulties. Farmers settled in small groups of countrymen frequently complained that Germans looked down on them as inferior. Many had lost knowledge of the German language. Dorfstuben, whose establishment was ordered in 1944 as community centers in villages, were supposed to overcome the difficulties of understanding. 150 such village rooms had been established in 1944; 250 more were to be constructed (Bibl. #346, June 28, 1944—signed J. G.).

[141] The DAZ (Bibl. #283) wrote on July 22, 1942: "The proportions between space and people have been reversed. The problem of how to feed a great people in a narrow space has changed into that of the best way of exploiting the conquered spaces with the limited number of people available" (quoted by Eugene M. Kulischer, Bibl. #305b, p. 27).

a large part of the Dutch population to a Netherland colony in the Wartheland.[142] This shrewd plan to wipe out the Netherlands as a nation and to establish it as a buffer belt against the Bolsheviks in the east, was answered with quiet resistance. The government was quick, therefore, to substitute for it another plan whereby young people of the conquered countries were sent as farm apprentices to eastern Europe[143] for colonization purposes and as assistants to German local commissioners.[144] Norwegian, Danish, and Dutch youth were called to work in the land service in western Poland and the Ukraine, with the promise that they might buy land at advantageous prices.[145]

The Condition of the Farmer

In the first two years of the regime market and price control were used to increase the farmers' share in the national income, largely at the expense of the processors and distributors of agricultural commodities. Farmers were exempted from unemployment insurance contributions[146]—a relief of 3,500,-000 Rm.; taxes and interest rates were reduced, indebtedness was gradually reduced, by adjustment[147] or redemption of debts, or by a transfer of land, or by a combination of these measures. Unpaid labor was provided, prices of fertilizers reduced. All these measures contributed toward an increase of the farmer's total returns. By 1936 prices had been raised by 30 per cent to the level of 1927.[148] Fixed prices gave the farmer security and relieved him from the risk involved in finding profitable outlets for his produce. After 1934, however, minimum prices were replaced by guaranteed prices which were kept as stable as possible. With the rise of prices of industrial products in 1936-1937, the price scissors, which had not been completely closed,

[142] Bibl. #314, November 10, 1941, quoted in *Netherland News*, November 1941, Vol. II, No. 2. The Nazi-dominated Netherland radio attempted to justify this scheme by referring to the Netherland population, which had trebled within a century, creating problems which could be solved only by colonizing the fertile soil of Russia.

[143] *Netherland News Digest*, January 15, 1943.

[144] *Deutsche Zeitung in den Niederlanden*, February 7, 1943.

[145] *New York Times*, April 5, 1942, and Bibl. #324, June 25, 1942.

[146] Law of September 22, 1933 (Bibl. #140, Vol. I, p. 656).

[147] Bibl. #297, September 2, 1943.

[148] The total interest burden was reduced from 730 billion Rm. in 1933-1934 to 560 in 1937-1938 (Bibl. #208, 1935, p. 9, and the same for 1937-1938, p. 9). The total amount of debts was reduced from 11.8 billion on July 1, 1933 to 11.1 billion on June 30, 1938. The total tax burden of 569 million Rm. (about 10 per cent of the agricultural income) in 1938-1939 was 50 million less than in 1928, although taxes had increased again since 1935 (Bibl. #341a, 2, pp. 28-29).

opened wider against the farmer. Increased expenses were due to government compulsion to buy fertilizers and machines, to standardize livestock products, *to the necessity of replacing migrating farmers' children by paid laborers, and to rising wages.* Hardly had the farmer been relieved of part of his debts, when he had to become indebted again.[149] Farmers were constantly urged to produce more, while shortage of labor, credit, and feed deprived them of help and tools. They were made dependent on state credit, which made it possible for the government to centralize control without concentration of holdings. The big estates could profit by breeding horses for the large demand of the army. The small farmer was especially hard hit by the rise in feeding costs for the small livestock he was accustomed to raise, while the embargo on the use of bread cereals raised on the farm for forage purposes forced the farmer to increase his purchases of forage.[150] Distillers were forbidden to use wheat and rye for distilling purposes.

From 1936-1937 on, the increase in expenditures was greater than the increase in receipts. Expenses amounted to 71 per cent of the proceeds of sales in that year as compared to 67 per cent in 1934-1935.[151] "We are approaching the point in the battle of production, or have reached it already, when increase in production does not strengthen but weakens the economic power of the farmer," said Secretary of Agriculture Backe.[152]

The share of agriculture in national income, which always had been unfavorable, remained smaller than the share of the work performed. Bauer and Dehen calculated that agriculture in 1937-1938 shared about 17 per cent in national income while the actual work performed was estimated to

---

[149] According to a 1938 study among estates whose debts had been adjusted, 81 per cent of those of hereditary farm size and 63 per cent of the large estates had contracted new debts (Leo Drescher, Bibl. #178). The figures include only two thirds of holdings of hereditary size.

[150] Decree of July 22, 1937, Bibl. #140, Vol. 1, p. 829. The prohibition of the fodder use of bread cereals was a severe blow to animal husbandry. "The disastrous feed shortage which literally deprives the small man of the basis of his existence is the most sinister feature in the whole picture. The government permits the keeping of livestock on each individual farm only within the limit of the farm's feed resources. In addition, feeding of rye and wheat has been labeled as treason to the nation. Thus the small farmer is confronted with the necessity of reducing his livestock or defying grain delivery regulations at the risk of being heavily fined or thrown into jail" (Marie Philippi Jasny in John B. Holt, "Recent Changes in German Rural Life," Bibl. #336, 1937, p. 283). In February 1943 the German press reported that a farmer who had sold seed for feeding purposes was sentenced to seven years of hard labor (Zuchthaus).

[151] Bibl. #120e, 1938, No. 2, p. 13.

[152] Bibl. #286, 1 Januarheft 1938.

Operating Expenditures of Agriculture[152a]

(in million Rm.)

Year	Total	New Machinery	New Buildings	Buildings Maintenance	Inventories	Fertilizers	Forage	Misc.	Cash Wages and Insurance Contributions	Taxes	Interest on Borrowed Capital
1924-1925	5703	272	231	265	617	631	763	437	1342	720	425
1927-1928	7992	303	405	366	704	690	1786	468	1755	730	785
1928-1929	8033	281	384	360	714	775	1515	471	1893	720	920
1929-1930	7881	242	366	351	678	768	1314	478	1994	740	950
1932-1933	5516	138	157	203	475	522	698	427	1486	560	850
1933-1934	5646	210	186	217	551	571	722	436	1513	510	730
1934-1935	5670	256	202	227	606	634	610	482	1563	440	650
1935-1936	6110	356	202	222	723	739	594	487	1707	450	630
1936-1937	6372	412	229	238	790	712	597	510	1824	480	580
1937-1938	6866	463	263	255	848	741	842	532	1852	510	560
1938-1939	7347	593	219	239	1026	810	845	564	1961	530	560

[152a] See Note, facing page.

Net Cash Returns in Agriculture[152a]
(in million Rm.)

	Total	Independent Farmers	Wage and Salary Earners
1928-1929	4200		
1932-1933	1632	300	1332
1933-1934	2744	1368	1376
1934-1935	3678	2235	1443
1935-1936	3735	2159	1576
1937-1938	4006	2268	1738

amount to about 24 per cent[153] of the total national work. A rise of 40 per cent would have been necessary in 1937-1938 to bring the cash income up to the level at which they would have covered the deficit. This would have necessitated a price increase of 30 per cent for all farm products. Since food amounted to about 50 per cent of total living costs in Germany, cost of total living would have to be raised 15 per cent.[154] Criticism was voiced on peasant meetings, blamed by the regime as lack of understanding for necessary measures.

With the outbreak of the war the situation improved insofar as the increase in the use of fertilizers and machinery had to be stopped, which made it possible to discharge some debts and thereby relieve the burden of interest. An exceptional financial liquidity developed among landowners owing partly to increased delivery duties, partly to a decrease in payrolls because

---

[152a] Bibl. #153d, 1936, No. 3, pp. 4ff.; Bibl. #153e, No. 22, p. 864; 1938, No. 21, pp. 850, 852; 1940, No. 1, p. 3. To farmers' cash incomes must be added the consumption of produce from the farm, the use of the dwelling house and increase in real capital from additions to buildings, machinery and working resources. The dues and donations which the farmer was required to make must be deducted. For the RN alone the sums to be paid amounted in 1936 to 70 millions for farmers (Bibl. #291, August 1936, B 24). Dues to the RN were raised from farmers as percentage of the land tax.

[153] Wilhelm Bauer and Peter Dehen, "Landwirtschaft und Volkseinkommen," Bibl. 120a, 1938-1939, Heft 4, Vol. 13, pp. 427-30. While this study showed a deficit of 4,300 million marks, an investigation of H. Reischle, the Chief of Staff to the RN, estimated the underpayment of agriculture at 4,558 million marks in the years 1937-1938 (Bibl. #333, op.cit., in the middle of the year 1939, p. 17). The rental value of houses owned by the farmers was not included.

[154] While the new price commissioner, Dr. Fischböck, explained that "just" prices could only be guaranteed to agriculture in the postwar period, Dr. Reischle demanded immediate price increases with shift to consumers in order to throttle surplus purchasing power (Bibl. #297, Reichsausgabe, April 13, 1942).

of the lower wages of alien labor, and to neglect of renewals and repairs. Farm debts could be reduced.

The tax on cattle slaughtering was abolished in May 1942 as a price subsidy to cattle breeders. Since costs of production increased and the price level had to be maintained, premiums were paid to farmers, at first for additional deliveries,[155] later for every product. The premiums were either borne by the state or financed by a system of levies. Premiums paid by the state were estimated at 1,000 million M. annually, or nearly 10 per cent of the total receipts of farm sales.[156]

In 1944 the food supply for the population could be provided only by forcing peasants to deliver beyond their quotas, which for them meant tightening their belts. In 1939 farmers were included in the rationing of food. The failure of the National Socialist regime to improve the economic situation of the farmer is clearly demonstrated by a high official of the RN, H. Reischle,[157] who in 1942 compared the fate of the owners of two equal estates in Silesia. One owner sold his estate to the State for 118.000 Rm. and the other maintained his as a hereditary farm. The latter was obliged to work harder than before that time, to pay higher wages because of man-power shortage, to pay higher prices for feed and tools. Even if not indebted, the estate would in six years bring only 3,020 Rm., i.e. an interest of 2.64 per cent and 2,000 Rm. for the labor of the family. The owner who sold his estate could, without working, count on a dividend income of 8,750 Rm. in the same time. The peasant, adds Reischle, is at a similar disadvantage if compared with the industrial producer.

Rearmament, in depriving the peasant of his workers and in keeping farm prices and wages down, sacrificed the interests of the peasant and farm worker to the superior aim of warfare. Reckless collection of taxes and dues, credit difficulties, the impossibility of acquiring land, delivery obligations, and compulsion to raise special crops were the high price to be paid for protection against the risk of the market. The small improvement in revenue and security had to be paid for by increasing regimentation, supervision, bureaucracy, red tape, friction, and impairment of freedom. The hazards of a free economy were replaced by the hazards of a change of government policy.

The reaction of many peasants was that of hatred for the regime. "The

[155] Bibl. #324, July 24, 1942.
[156] *The Economist*, October 31, 1942, p. 545.
[157] Bibl. #349, May 25, 1942, Nos. 9-10, Vol. VII, pp. 207ff.

coming resistance of the farmer," wrote a large estate owner in 1938, "springs from the almost religious association of the genuine farmer with his possessions, his property, his fields, which he wants to tend and look after himself, where he wants to be master." All this was still hidden below the surface of events.[158] The peasant not only resented the economic pressure, but he also felt disturbed by the impious attitude against venerable tradition, the defamation of religion, the shattering of family life and breaking of paternal authority by the Hitler youth.

Self-Sufficiency

When the two first romantic points of the National Socialist program were abandoned after a very short time, only the third, self-sufficiency, remained. It had to maintain itself against resistance of farmers on the one hand, and the competition of industrial autarky on the other. When the National Socialists came into power, Germany was practically self-sufficient in bread grains, sugar, and potatoes, but covered not quite half her requirements of fats, and much less of textile raw materials. Since the supply of untilled land was practically exhausted, the regime had to rely, for any increase in her agricultural output, on land reclamation, drainage, and irrigation. This program was largely carried out by the members of the Labor Service, but had to be stopped during the war and even prior to it. The autarky program included, in addition, cuts of imports; intensification of production, especially by mechanization; agricultural training; shift of consumption from deficit to surplus products; and large-scale storing.

Modernization of agriculture in the form of improvement of farming methods had been from the beginning part of the battle of production. Of the innumerable propagandized measures—from using standardized seeds to plowing up of pastures—increased use of fertilizers was considered of special importance, and was achieved by a reduction in prices, credits for their purchase, and reduced railway rates for their transports. From 1932 to 1939 the use of fertilizers per ha. doubled.[159] Mechanization was encouraged by subsidies and tax exemption of machinery. Funds were allotted for cooperative use of machinery and extended lending of machinery.[160] The

---

[158] Bibl. #195, p. 12.

[159] Compared to 1931-1932 the consumption of nitrogen fertilizers had risen by 120 per cent in 1938-1939, phosphoric fertilizers by 80 per cent, potash by 110 per cent (Bibl. #153e, 1940, No. 1, p. 4). However, consumption of fertilizers in 1931-1932 had been considerably below that in 1928-1929.

[160] The overburdened machine industry was instructed to concentrate on labor-saving

idea of an increased food supply was hammered into the farmer's mind by campaigns, mass meetings, radio, films, literature, and all other means of publicity.[161]

The government relied on suburban settlements[162] and allotment gardens[163] which were to be equipped so as to enable the settler to produce vegetables and fruits and raise small livestock.[164] Hours of work in such gardens were additional to those worked in business. It was officially claimed that even after ten hours' work, the worker in heavy industry considered it relaxation to occupy himself on his land.[165] Wives' and children's help was another important addition. Even the poorest soil could be used. Contracts provided compulsory training.[166] The settler or gardener had to plant according to

agricultural machinery. Since plants were occupied with armament work and supplies of metal were restricted, designs had to be changed in order to save material. Machines were standardized on a larger scale. Costly or inefficient types were eliminated.

[161] At a farm congress, held each year under blazing lights with spotlights crossing the sky, loudspeakers bearing the echo of rolling voices, enthusiasm was generated for the battle of production.

[162] Cf. footnote 79 above.

[163] Subsidies for establishing such gardens were extended to fully employed workers and were enlarged.

[164] At first the holders of settlements and gardens were compelled to keep livestock. Stables had to be built according to prescribed types. From 1944 on, however, keeping small animals such as rabbits or poultry was criticized as strain on the fodder supply, and restricted to those who provided the necessary fodder themselves and produced their total consumption of vegetables and potatoes. Anyone keeping more than the legal number had to deliver the animals, or risked having confiscation and punishment (Bibl. #283, July 19, 1944). Later it was ruled that rabbits exceeding the number of persons in the household had to be wiped out. Keeping of geese, ducks, and turkeys was prohibited beginning April 1, 1945 (Decree of February 28, 1945, Bibl. #113, No. 32, March 3, 1945).

[165] Ministerialrat Wilhelm Gisbertz, "Bedroht die Kleinsiedlung die deutsche Ernährungslage?" (Bibl. #139, 1939, Vol. II, p. 174). Gertrud Laupheimer and Marie Högel-Wertenson calculated for Brandenburg, Posen, and Westprussia in 1931-1932 that one fourth to two fifths of an acre of garden land, depending on the quality of the soil, provided half self-sufficiency, i.e. production of the total requirements of vegetables, potatoes, dry legumes, fruits, meat, milk, and eggs for a low-income family with two or three children (Bibl. #210, pp. 33ff., 40ff.). Since low-income families spend about 50 per cent of their income on food, half self-sufficiency meant that raising foodstuffs corresponded to a fourth. According to the Minister of Labor the gardeners, small settlers, and houseowners produced in 1939 about one third of the total vegetable crop (Franz Seldte, "Apell an Kleingärtner," Bibl. #139, 1942, Vol. V, p. 167).

[166] As another device to increase efficiency, professional contests were staged every year by the DAF and the Hitler Youth for boys and girls from fourteen to eighteen years of age. The participants had to answer practical and theoretical questions about their work (e.g., when to plant potatoes, how to clean a cow), and girls about household work also. Tests in political views included questions about the German character of the Sudeten and Volga Germans, differences between folk and race, why not to

the views of experts and was not allowed to grow plants without permission. In case of contravention, the settler could be ousted. By 1943 the German Advisory Services, intended originally to be built up by the RN to train farmers for the increase in output, soon degenerated into control. The Settlers League, which had been established by the DAF to train settlers, announced that settlers were not allowed to buy vegetables.[167]

Another help came from the Food Assistance Work (Ernährungshilfswerk) of the NS Volkswohlfahrt from November 1936 on.[168] Households had to save all refuse, which was collected by the Ernährungshilfswerk (in cars provided by the communities) and used to fatten pigs.

Since it proved impossible to achieve self-sufficiency by increasing production, a policy of building up foodstuff reserves was inaugurated with the beginning of the Four-Year Plan.[169] At the end of 1938 a quantity of grain,

---

buy in department stores, and why to hate Jews (Günter Kaufmann, Bibl. #303c, pp. 39-40). A third test was given in sports. Victors in local contests took a district test and district victors a Reich test. Reich victors were introduced to Hitler and were rewarded by promotions, scholarships, participation in festive performances.

Participation of RN members in professional contests

	Total	Boys	Girls
1934	33,000		
1937	250,000	150,000	100,000
1938	282,137	167,499	114,638
1939	420,809	247,077	173,732

Of 100 participants in 1937, 9.9 per cent were apprentices, 22.4 per cent farm workers without training, 44.4 per cent peasant sons, 23.3 per cent others (Reinhold Seume, "Berufswettkampf in der landwirtschaftlichen Ausbildungsordnung," Bibl. #312, 1938, No. 7, p. 336). The contests (discontinued during the war) stimulated ambitions and rivalry but did not improve efficiency—as the complaints about their outcome prove. Nor did the appointment of ten thousands of volunteer Vocational Youth Stewards in 1944 exercise any effect (Bibl. #346, August 7, 1944).

[167] Bibl. #317, March 11, 1943. Although tenants of small gardens were protected against notice except in case of non-payment of rent, or if the land was needed for defense purposes, notice was required in case the tenant neglected his duties as a good gardener. If the lessee did not give notice in such cases the local association of small gardeners was obliged to take over. If this organization failed to do its duty it could be dissolved. When bombing resulted in evacuation the Minister of Agriculture suggested that small gardens be provided to the evacuees. 100-200 qm. of land was to be attached to each emergency shelter. The Association of Small Garden Owners was to provide tools and fertilizers, and neighbors were to help (Bibl. #283, July 19, 1944; Bibl. #286, 1 Januarheft 1944, p. 13). Garden owners or tenants had to allow people bombed out of their dwellings to live in the shacks, and were obliged to have their garden cultivated by others in case they were removed to other places by military or labor conscription (Bibl. #301, January 2, 1945).

[168] Bibl. #345, April 20, 1939, pp. 573-74.

[169] By Decree of August 11, 1938 (ibid., 1938, p. 660), the Reich agency for grain was entitled to requisition large rooms including gyms, dancing halls, etc. for storage

sufficient to satisfy a full year's needs of the population, was stored. Until the middle of 1939,[170] however, because of shortage of building material and labor, silo capacity for food storage could be provided for only about one-tenth of the holdings larger than 2 ha.

In spite of some improvement in yield, the elaborate production battle did not reach its goal.[171] The deficiency in fats could not be overcome, even though soaps were deprived of edible fats and some increase was achieved by whale fishing, which provided, in 1938, 7.5 per cent of the home-produced fats. The large gap in fodder supply was only partly closed, and imports could not be substantially reduced. Output in root crops, sugar beets, milk, and pigs fell in 1938, owing to shortage of labor.[172] Industrial and agricultural self-sufficiency were conflicting objectives: increase in flax, hemp, and rapeseed could be achieved only at the expense of foodstuff production. A substantial proportion of the potato and sugar-beet harvest was diverted to industrial purposes and lost to human and animal consumption. The needs of warfare—armament production—slowed down considerably the progress in agricultural production which had started during the democratic regime.[173]

The degree of self-sufficiency achieved in peace time could not be maintained during the war. The whaling fleet was not able to continue, sugar beets produced alcohol for motor fuel, nitrogen was applied to the manufacture of explosives. The fertilizer supply was drastically reduced, and frequently arrived too late because of transport difficulties.[174] Manure was lost owing to slaughter of livestock; many draught animals were mobilized;

---

purposes. In addition, a program for accelerated construction of granaries was announced. To provide the necessary means, a Decree of October 17, 1938 allowed forward delivery contracts with advancing of money for bread grain (Bibl. #140, Vol. 1, p. 1442).

[170] Hermann Hildebrandt, "Futteraufbewahrung und Gärfutterbereitung in der deutschen Landwirtschaft," Bibl. #345, June 5, 1939, p. 718.

[171] The government's claim that the degree of self-sufficiency in foodstuffs, i.e. the share of domestic production in total consumption, was raised from 75 per cent in 1932 to 82 per cent in 1937 (Bibl. 120f, November 2, 1938, Nos. 43-44, p. 90) is unreal, as calculations were based on rather doubtful indices and estimates.

[172] According to the Ministry of Agriculture, shortages of fruits and vegetables became permanent since 1938 (Herbert Backe, Bibl. #168, p. 19). Supply of meat and eggs was disturbed (*ibid.*, p. 19). In meeting requirements of edible fats and oils domestic production accounted for only 45 per cent of total consumption in 1939.

[173] The new industrial plants deprived the farms not only of manpower but frequently also of their water supply. Reich auto roads deprived the farmer of land and in cutting his property compelled him to make detours since he was not allowed to cross them with his vehicles.

[174] Bibl. #346, September 21, 1944.

manpower, seeds and fodder were lacking. By 1938-1939 less machinery was supplied to agriculture because preference was given to war machinery. In 1942 the construction of new machinery was made dependent on government consent.[175] Subsidies were granted for repairs, but even these were finally made dependent on consent of the authorities. The quotas for iron and steel for farm machinery were cut. Substitutes had to be found for tin and copper.

Since increase of production failed, two measures were taken to secure the food supply: direction of consumption (Verbrauchslenkung), and conquest in order to achieve self-sufficiency on a wider territorial basis. The government used its propaganda to change the eating habits of the consumer. He was instructed to increase fish consumption, and to shift to potatoes, which, together with bread grain, covered two-thirds of the caloric content of the daily food ration and produced more calories from the same land area. Rationing was introduced in September 1939. The Winter Help was utilized to support the food and raw material policy of the government[176] by distributing abundant foodstuffs and to introduce saltwater fish consumption in those parts of the country where it had been in short supply.

During part of the war the army of occupation was fed in foreign countries. In conquered countries, stores of foodstuffs were seized, and this booty improved the food supply of the German people. A planned food economy was established in all conquered countries, more or less centrally controlled by Berlin. Attempts were made to integrate agriculture into the greater German Wirtschaftsraum. The ideal of Germany's autarky was widened to that of Continental Europe.[177] However, from December 1942 on, the Grossraum began to shrink. In his harvest thanksgiving appeal to the rural

[175] Bibl. #297, August 28, 1942; Bibl. #271, October 3, 1942. However, machines were exported to the Ukraine and Southeastern Europe. In the beginning of 1943 a new type of steward (Kreisfachwart Technik in der Landwirtschaft) was nominated for each county peasant association. They had to care for the common use of machines in villages, for expert treatment of machinery, repair and quick help in case of damage by bombardment (Bibl. #321, January 26, 1945).

[176] Bibl. #345, March 23, 1939, pp. 482-83.

[177] With the call for the battle of production, said Backe on a visit to Holland, "the first valid attempt was made to break the chains of the world division of labor and to create the presupposition for a European community" (Bibl. #319, June 30, 1944). "To speak figuratively, in the mosaic of economic dispersion and Eigenbröteln of our continent a kind of land consolidation is necessary" ("Grossraumwirtschaft eine Realität," Bibl. #286, 1 Märzheft 1944, p. 186). However, in 1940-1941 the Yearbook of the DAF wrote that the Grossraum has not achieved more autarky than had the old Reich before the conquests (Bibl. #310, 1940-1941, Vol. I, p. 565).

people in 1944, Backe had to admit, "From the point of view of our food supplies, the beginning of the sixth year of war sees us in a situation similar to that at the beginning of the Great War. We must again rely on ourselves, on our strength, and almost solely on the possibilities of our soil."[178] In 1945 the impact of military operations resulted in losses of supplies and disruption of transportation and distribution.

Although agriculture in 1939 was better prepared to meet the impact of wartime shortages than it had been in 1914, self-sufficiency was certainly a failure. In order to be autarkic during a war, Germany would have needed an agricultural production at least 40 per cent superior to its average needs, according to her own experts,[179] since a decline in production and a great demand for the forces were to be expected. Her peacetime 20 per cent inferiority, according to optimistic estimates, shows the tremendous gap in supplies.

In December 1940, a postwar Ten-Year plan was announced by Darré under the slogan "mechanical rearmament of the village" (Aufrüstung des Dorfes). The realization of the plan would have amounted to approximately 40 billion M. for building improvement, modernizing of machine inventory and workers' dwellings. Not included in this amount were costs for the improvement of livestock.[180]

[178] Bibl. #301, September 30, 1944.
[179] Major Beutler, "Gesichtspunkte für die Beurteilung der wehrwirtschaftlichen Kraft," Bibl. #193, p. 22.
[180] Bibl. #120e, 1941, No. 1, January 14, pp. 1ff. Other sums would be required for the development of agriculture in the incorporated eastern area and the Alsace. Approximately 13 billion marks would be needed for replanning of villages and the same amount for the improvement of fields, roads, bridges, and forests.

CHAPTER II

THE EMPLOYER-EMPLOYEE RELATION

THE REGIME had not been able to fulfil the promises to the small farmer, who together with his family provided the main labor force. How did hired labor fare? It was clear that National Socialism could not recognize any power but that of the party. Groups which were powerful during the Weimar Republic, therefore, had to be destroyed: this settled the fate of trade unionism.

Trade Union Substitutes

Trade unionism, which had already suffered a severe blow from the Bruening emergency decrees which cut wages without union consultation, received a setback under the government of von Papen, "the government of barons" (June-November 1932) with its protest against the "welfare state." All trade-union federations, under the impression that a new era of political reaction had started, declared their determination to struggle for the safeguarding of labor's rights. "There is no power that can extinguish the free trade unions of Germany," wrote Leipart, President of the ADGB, in a personal letter to union members. However, the movement had lost its *élan*. Weakened by unemployment in the depression, accustomed to rely on state help, the unions passively allowed National Socialism to spread. There was no general strike when von Papen, who had been appointed Commissioner of Prussia by the Reich President, dismissed the Prussian cabinet ministers, a coup d'état which greatly helped the enemies of democracy. The appeal of the ministers to the Supreme Court received a favorable decision which, rendered in October, came too late to be significant. A para-military Iron Front, formed in 1931 by the SPD, Reichsbanner, the unions, and other democrats, was called to action only to protect democratic speakers in the election campaigns.

In spite of distrust, the union leaders showed some willingness to confer with the successor of von Papen, General von Schleicher, during his two months' government. Neither did the unions strike when Hitler was appointed Reich Chancellor on January 30, 1933. The desire to prevent bloodshed, to avoid a civil war—with the Iron Front on the one side, and millions of stormtroopers, the steel-helmet organization of former soldiers on the other, and the army uncertain—was too strong. They did not believe that Hitler would stay long in power; they hoped to survive his reign as they had survived Bismarck's antisocialist law. There were rumors that the free trade unions would discontinue collaboration with the SPD, that unofficial relations had been established between the unions and the NSDAP. The unions of the three movements were willing to amalgamate and to compromise with the government. But the government had other plans.

The first months after Hitler's coming to power were full of intimidation. Local offices were repeatedly raided, periodicals prohibited, leaders arrested. Former trade unionists were dismissed from public office and publicity was given to invented stories about embezzlement by union leaders. But the trade-union leadership refused to resort to direct action. They believed that by severing their political ties they would be able to continue as partners in collective agreements, labor representatives in joint bodies, and advisers to the government in labor legislation.

The National Socialists before coming into power had not succeeded in conquering the German working class. Their chief means of political propaganda among workers were workshop cells (*Betriebszellen*), formed on the Russian model. Party members in a plant were united in these cells under a cell steward. The function of the cells was to fill the plant with National Socialist spirit and fight Marxism, trade unionism, and internationalism. All cells were united in the National Socialist Plant Cell Organization (*Nationalsozialistische Betriebszellenorganisation*, NSBO). These cells were pitifully weak before the National Socialist rise to power. At the end of 1932 they had only 294,042 members[1] as compared with more than 6,600,000 members of the trade unions. Only after January 1933 did workers, under compulsion, flock into them. After the National Socialist terror broke out in full force many workers sought protection in the NSBO so that in May 1933 membership was closed in order to keep the party organization free from revolution profiteers and from disguised enemies of the regime, and to preserve it as a shock troop. After the seizure of power, the cell steward, who very often had shifted from Communism to National Socialism, exercised a power which made him frequently the dictator in the enterprise. This was less true for agriculture where the patriarchal relationship had been preserved in many parts of the country.

After Hitler had come into office, works councillors by terror and intimidation, were forced to resign, since the regime particularly resented the workers'

---

[1] *Der Betrieb*, Führer- und Informationsorgan der NSBO, Berlin, August 1, 1933, p. 2.

opposition to the party which was revealed in the 1933 spring elections. Those who refused were arrested and kept in custody until they had signed their resignation. Some indeed never signed. A law of April 4, 1933,[2] empowered the authorities to refrain from elections and to replace those stewards who were hostile to the regime by others. The law was followed by wholesale removal of works councillors and replacement by cell members. The act abolished the protection of workers against dismissals for political beliefs, provided in the BRG. Such dismissals were to be justified if based on an unpatriotic attitude of a worker, viz. disagreement with National Socialist philosophy. In 1934, the BRG was repealed.

On April 6, 1933,[3] Franz Seldte, the Minister of Labor, a former industrialist and leader of the Steel Helmet war veteran organization, published in a circular a demand that the trade union monopoly be broken up. On April 18, he proclaimed the recognition of the nonmilitant unions, including the RLAB.[4] This was a sop for the German National People's party, which participated in the coalition government and whose members, the big estate owners, demanded recognition of the RLB unions. The recognition was merely a gesture. The National Socialists did not intend to recognize any of the existing organizations. Trade unionism, the bulwark of labor power, had to be shattered.

In the beginning of April 1933, Hitler ordered the party chief of staff (Reichsorganisationsleiter) Dr. Robert Ley,[5] a veteran of the National Socialist movement and Hitler's personal friend, to form a committee of action for the protection of German labor. The committee, which was composed of seven NSBO members with the help of the SA and SS, the storm troops and elite guards of the NSDAP, raided the offices of the ADGB and Afa League on May 2. Funds were confiscated, leaders arrested, and the NSBO took over the administration and the press. The powerful trade union movement ceased to exist. Reinhold Muchow, leader of the NSBO, stated, "Workers, we pledge to protect all the rights you have so bitterly gained in many hard struggles."[6] Since a sudden destruction of the trade unions would

[2] Gesetz über Betriebsvertretungen und wirtschaftliche Vereinigungen of April 4, 1933 (Bibl. #140, Vol. 1, p. 161).

[3] Bibl. #139, Vol. 1, p. 107.

[4] *Ibid.*, p. 111. The right to represent labor in labor courts was given to the NSBO and the Steel Helmet Organization.

[5] Dr. Douglas M. Kelley, the psychiatrist to the Nuremberg jail found that Ley had a deteriorated brain, possibly accelerated by alcohol (Bibl. #206, pp. 152ff.).

[6] Bibl. #272, May 15, 1933, p. 8.

have been too great a risk "in a revolutionary and dangerous period,"[7] and might have driven them underground, Ley published a manifesto in which he said: "We do not intend to destroy the trade unions. No, workers, your institutions are sacred and inviolable to us National Socialists." "German workers, I swear, we will not only keep intact everything that already exists but we shall also extend still further the protection and the rights of the German worker."[8] This was not the only oath to be broken.

All unions of workers and salaried employees were united in the German Labor Front (Deutsche Arbeitsfront, DAF), which in a solemn conference presented itself on May 10 as the true successor of the trade unions[9] under the guardianship of Adolf Hitler. Persons commissioned by the NSBO were put in charge of the unions. The DAF was introduced as a reformed trade union organization, because it was considered dangerous to the state to make men homeless, deprive them of the protection of an organization, and exclude them from the activities of the state.[10] The twenty-eight unions of the ADGB were amalgamated into fourteen, and the members of the Christian, Hirsch Dunckers, and other manual workers' unions were assigned to them. An Association of German Farm Workers, composed of eight former unions, formed one unit. A second unit of nine salaried employees' unions was formed out of the DGB, the Afa League, and GDA members.

In spite of the threat to give employment to DAF members only, membership in the associations at first increased slowly, showing the widespread hostility of the working class toward the new leaders. That the construction of the DAF on a trade union basis had been only a fake became evident in November 1933 when the associations of the DAF were dissolved. The old employers associations dissolved themselves. An appeal issued on November 29, 1933,[11] jointly by the leader of the DAF, the Reich Minister of Economics, the Reich Minister of Labor, and the representative on economic questions in the Führer's office stated, "The DAF is the organization of all persons engaged in production without distinction as to economic and social position. In it the worker and the employer stand side by side instead of being separated by organizations for the defense of particular economic and social interests." On the same day the office staffs of the NSBO and the DAF were

[7] Bibl. #253, pp. 7-8 (an official explanation issued by the Minister of Labor).
[8] Bibl. #304, May 6, 1933.
[9] Bibl. #338, May 18, 1933, pp. 609ff.
[10] Robert Ley (Bibl. #211), p. 16.
[11] Bibl. #338, December 7, 1933, p. 1418.

amalgamated. The NSBO gradually disappeared within the DAF. Employers disliked the alleged successors of the trade unions not less than labor itself. In fact, their suspicion and unwillingness to accept office in the organization was even harder to overcome since the DAF, although intended to represent a "community of interest," at first did not lose its identification with the worker. Its name did not merely show the National Socialist inclination to use military terms for its activities, it conveyed the idea of union *against* someone.

While 1933 had been the year of destruction and liquidation, the year 1934 saw the building up of the National Socialist labor constitution. The DAF received its final shape, and the National Socialist Labor Law provided the basis for the new structure. During 1934[12] the DAF was built up on a new basis which abolished distinction between employers' and employees' organizations and disrupted the old trade union loyalties. It was composed of eighteen (later twenty) Enterprise Communities (Reichsbetriebsgemein-schaften); i.e. groups of establishments classified under occupational sections, one of them the community of agriculture.[13]

The territorial organization of the DAF followed that of the party. It was divided into districts (Gaue),[14] counties, locals, cells, and blocks. Besides workers, salaried employees and employers as individual members, there were corporate members, such as the National Socialist Culture Chamber, and others. Membership remained legally free but became practically com-pulsory. No rival organization was allowed to exist. Even associations of workers of various denominations which were not trade unions had to dissolve. Dr. Ley, the head of the DAF, was appointed by Hitler and he appointed or discharged the other leaders of the DAF who were primarily chosen from party organizations. The finances of the DAF were controlled by the party treasurer. The original property of the DAF consisted of the trade union property which had been seized and sequestered.[15]

---

[12] It received its formal constitution by Decree of the Führer and Chancellor of October 24, 1934 (Bibl. #346, No. 298); newly formulated on November 11, 1934 (Bibl. #338, November 1, 1934, pp. 1308ff.).

[13] The communities since 1938 were called more correctly trade offices, Fachämter, since they were merely administrative departments. According to information of the International Transport Workers' Federation, the trade offices were dissolved in the spring of 1943, which showed clearly the character of the DAF as an amorphous mass (Bibl. #307, April 16, 1943).

[14] The National Socialists had formed special districts (Gaue) as a basis for the elaborate structure of party organization. The Gau was the highest in a descending order of areas.

[15] According to the view of the DAF, which was confirmed by the Federal Labor Court, the DAF was created by a revolutionary act and was not the legal successor of

The DAF was not supposed to represent labor's interests. It was not concerned with the usual union business. Its main functions were the securing of labor peace, "education" to National Socialism, and increasing the efficiency of labor. It had to reconcile the German working class with the National Socialist regime, and many of its activities served this purpose. As an association of the NSDAP it had to serve party interests first. It derived its functions from authority granted by the State and the party, whose policy it carried out.

In its desire to win the workers, to control them in their leisure time, and to exclude other influences, the DAF quickly developed its leisure-time organization, "Strength through Joy" (Kraft durch Freude) in which farm workers participated. Its Sports Office provided for all kinds of athletics. In 1937 it employed 150,000 sports stewards. "Strength through Joy" provided recreation and vacation trips. Holiday boats, later used for troop transportation, were chartered to take several thousand workers a year for cruises in the Baltic and Mediterranean. The worker's prestige was enhanced by participating in the Reich Peasant Day, the RN Fair, and other celebrations. Many more participated in weekend trips and hiking tours. Groups were taken to party conventions and to Olympic games. Plays and movies went on tour to remote villages. Village community evenings (Dorfgemeinschafts-abende) brought entertainment. However, increasing overburdening of farmers and laborers made it impossible for them to use recreational possibilities. "There is no sense in establishing a reading room," wrote two scholars, "if it is certain that the villagers will have neither time nor strength to use it. No leisure (Feierabend) activity can be thought of before leisure time has been restored."[16] During the war, trips had to be discontinued owing to lack of transportation. Activities were at first replaced by recreation for soldiers in hospitals. On January 26, 1942, Ley ordered discontinuation of all activities not essential to the war,[17] and by 1944, all nonwar activities were completely discontinued.

---

the trade unions. It therefore did not have to take over their liabilities. Thus former trade union officials who were dismissed forfeited their rights to pensions, although considerable special contributions had been paid to the old age insurance funds of the unions (Judgment of February 28, 1934, Bibl. #274, Vol. xx, p. 102, and other decisions).

[16] Bibl. #220, Karl Seiler and Walter Hildebrandt, Franken, p. 211.

[17] Bibl. #286, 1942, No. 26, p. 843; No. 31, p. 1003. Still stricter orders were issued at the beginning of 1943 (Bibl. #271, March 5, 1943). Housing of evacuees from bombed cities became the main concern.

The Department of KdF "Beauty of Work" which tended to improve the amenities of work, had a section "Beauty of the Village,"[18] which promoted orderliness and cleanliness. Swimming pools were established and stadiums and shooting galleries were built. The village inn was to assume a cheerful appearance. School buildings, railway stations, and Hitler Youth homes were to become models of beauty. Fences had to be repaired, billboards removed, and dung heaps transferred. The village lime tree and the soldier's monument were surrounded with beautiful fencing. Signposts were designed by "artists." Village life was made more attractive by the revival of old customs such as peasant dances, spinning evenings, harvest festivals. The Village Book was supposed to record everything of value to village life: folklore, customs, family and tribe origin, building styles, early history of the village, songs, folk wisdom, dialect, schools, health, and administration.[19] The war put an end to this work.[20]

The Reich Works Community of Agriculture[21] was territorially divided into 14 district and 225 regional communities, and employed 1,000 officials. The works community continued the publication of the former free trade-union periodical, *Der Landarbeiter*, which became an instrument of National Socialist propaganda. By free distribution it increased its circulation to 750,000, a figure which, however, considerably decreased in the following year. On August 1, 1934, the title was changed to *Das schaffende Landvolk* (*The Creative Landfolk*). For branches of agriculture, special periodicals were continued.

The continuous rivalry between the RN and the DAF was settled by an agreement of October 6, 1935. According to it the RN became a corporate member of the DAF and superseded the Enterprise Community Agriculture.[22] Membership was no longer legally voluntary but regulated compulsorily according to the Reich Food Estate Law.[23] After that time the RN

[18] At the party convention in 1936 Dr. Ley claimed that 143 model villages and 3 estates had been beautified (Bibl. #272, October 1, 1936, p. 17). More than 5,000 villages were included, said *Arbeitertum* (Bibl. #272) on March 15, 1938, p. 4.

[19] *Ibid.*, March 1, 1938, p. 5.

[20] The DAF gradually developed from an instrument of labor protection to a government department of labor control. During the war it was used more and more in the interest of increased efficiency, supervision of foreign labor, and of disciplining labor, especially by fighting absenteeism (Werner Scheunemann, "Sozialpolitik der Härte," Bibl. #286, 3 Augustheft 1944, pp. 694-95).

[21] Bibl. #281, March 15, 1935, pp. 42ff.

[22] Wolfgang Siebert (Bibl. #252) A, p. 18; Orders of November 4, 1935, *ibid.*, A, p. 19; June 19, 1936, *ibid.*, A, p. 20.

[23] Act of September 13, 1933 (Bibl. #140, Vol. 1, p. 626).

took over part of the functions of the DAF for agriculture, such as the professional education of the worker and settlement of disputes. Other functions, such as legal advice, leisure time activities, and beauty of work, were left to the DAF. A Reich Labor Steward (Reichsgefolgschaftswart) was appointed and labor stewards added to the state, county, and local offices of the RN.[24]

It was especially the department "Care of Man" (Der Mensch) which was to take over the DAF functions. It was supposed to educate the farmer politically, to spread National Socialist philosophy, and to arouse his pride in farm work and peasant culture. It was not an organization of the farm population for the purpose of communicating with the government, but an instrument of the government through which it spoke to the farmer and the farm worker. The department did not attain any significance. The fact that labor protective policy was no function of the RN was recognized when Backe, shortly after he superseded Darré as Reich Peasant Leader and Minister of Agriculture in June 1942, dissolved the department "Care of Man" with the argument that guidance of man (Menschenführung) was the task of the NSDAP.[25] Neither DAF nor RN protected the interests of the worker.

National Socialist Labor Law

I. THE "WORKS COMMUNITY" AND THE REICH TRUSTEES OF LABOR

The new employer-employee relationship (as regulated in the Labor Act, Gesetz zur Ordnung der nationalen Arbeit, AOG)[26] was to be based on a works community (Betriebsgemeinschaft) with the employer as the leader of the enterprise and the employees as his followers.[27] The laborer was to identify himself loyally with the interests of the farmer, who in turn was obliged to care for the welfare of his followers. Both had to further the aim of the enterprise and the well-being of the nation. The regime claimed that the former law was based on the assumption of a fundamental antagonism

---

[24] There were 19 state and 191 regional stewards in 1935 and 559 county stewards in 1938, to whom 441 assistants had to be added; 1,008 paid officials and 53,739 voluntary workers were active in that year (Methling, Bibl. #275, Vol. 3, p. 191; Mathias Haidn, *ibid.*, Vol. 5, p. 122).

[25] Bibl. #297, June 26, 1942.

[26] January 20, 1934 (Bibl. #140, Vol. 1, p. 45) and Orders.

[27] The term "followers" (Gefolgschaft) remained so unusual that a semi-official periodical pleaded in 1941 for the reintroduction of the word "worker" (Bibl. #338, November 15, 1941, pp. 865ff.). During the war, the term "followers" was replaced frequently by the term "squad" or Mannschaft (Scheunemann, *op.cit.*, p. 695).

between employer and employee which could be moderated, not abolished, while the new law was based on fellowship. Employer and worker were considered as members of a team and no separate organization, no class interest was allowed to exist. The relationship was to be "based upon loyalty, honor, and accomplishment."[28]

Most of the functions of the former trade unions and employers' associations were assigned to labor trustees (Treuhänder der Arbeit, called Reichstreuhänder der Arbeit, RTA, after 1937).[29] They were introduced by the Act of May 19, 1933,[30] which entrusted them with three tasks: to regulate conditions of work, to maintain labor peace, and to prepare the new social order. The AOG superseded this provisional arrangement and placed the institution on a permanent basis.[31] According to the AOG, the trustees were to be government officials, appointed for large economic areas, of which fifteen (plus those in the invaded countries) were subsequently fixed, until these areas were made identical to the forty-two party districts in 1943.[32] Trustees could be appointed for special industries and groups of workers (e.g. for the fish industry, for Germans abroad, for foreign workers). They made decisions on their own responsibility but were subject to the supervision of the Federal Minister of Labor, after 1942, to the Commissioner General of Manpower.

In order to achieve the main tasks, maintenance of industrial peace and determination of wages and conditions of work, they were granted certain powers: They could issue collective rules (Tarifordnungen) for groups of enterprises (after 1939, for individual enterprises as well) in place of former collective agreements, and draw up guiding principles for shop rules (Betriebsordnungen) which the employer set up for his undertaking. They supervised the formation and operation of the confidential councils and decided disputes where they occurred. They decided appeals of confidential councils against decisions of the leader. They acted as prosecutor in the Social Honor Courts. They had the task of providing information about employer-employee relations. However, their functions gradually concentrated on the issuance of collective rules, especially on wage regulations. Their powers were considerably extended by the Wage Stop Order of 1938.

[28] Siebert, op.cit., p. 5.
[29] Law of March 19, 1937 (Bibl. #140, Vol. 1, p. 342) and Order of April 9, 1937 (Bibl. #139, Vol. 1, p. 89).
[30] Bibl. #140, Vol. 1, p. 285. Order of June 13, 1933 (ibid., Vol. 1, p. 368).
[31] Section 18ff.
[32] See below, p. 302, section on Employment Offices.

Shop rules were obligatory for undertakings with more than twenty employees. No special regulations were made for seasonal businesses. Investigations had to be made, therefore, to determine whether during most of the year at least twenty laborers and salaried employees had been employed. If this was not the case the undertaking did not receive shop rules for the season.[33]

Collective rules were to be issued whenever the establishment of minimum conditions for the regulation of employment in groups of undertakings was urgently needed. They were registered with the Federal Ministry of Labor and published in the *RABl.* Both collective rules as well as shop rules were binding and had the character of legal regulations.

In enterprises of more than twenty employees a confidential council (Vertrauensrat) was to be formed. The law provided that lists of confidential men were to be drawn up by the leader of the establishment in agreement with the shop cell steward (or where there was no steward, with the shop steward of the DAF). The workers were required to vote for the list or reject it. Together with the employer, the confidential men formed the confidential council.

Since elections revealed opposition, they were postponed by law from March 31, 1936 on. After that time the RTA nominated new confidential men.[34] Meetings were to be called whenever the employer thought it necessary, or upon the demand of one-half of the council.[35] The confidential council cannot be compared with the former works council. It was not freely elected, did not have to be consulted in cases in which the works council had to be, and could not complain against dismissals. Moreover, inclination to consult the confidential men was not strong on the large farms. In fact,

[33] Shop rules had to include starting and finishing time of work and of rest periods, principles for calculating piece-work wages, frequency of the payment of remuneration, grounds for the termination of employment without notice and the imposition of fines, and use of wages forfeited by unlawful termination of employment. They could also include provisions regarding wages and other conditions of work.

[34] In the incorporated Polish districts, confidential men were to be appointed by the RTA from lists provided by the employer in agreement with the shop stewards (Decree of April 26, 1941, Bibl. #140, Vol. 1, p. 237). Since Poles were not to be counted in considering the number of workers, hardly any farm will have formed a confidential council.

[35] The confidential council could appeal to the RTA against decisions of the leader which did not appear warranted by the social and economic conditions of the plant. Confidential men were protected against dismissals. Unsuitable men could be recalled by the RTA. The confidential men had to advise the employer on all measures concerning improvement of efficiency, conditions of work, safety, and so forth, and had to attempt to settle grievances.

they remained only a "paper council." In 1939 the RTA of Pomerania warned the estate owners to call the councils regularly every three to four weeks.[36] Similar advice was given by the RTA for southwest Germany in 1941.[37]

The National Socialist claim that class antagonism had been overcome had no meaning for agriculture where there never had been a class war comparable to that in industry. Ley,[38] Göring, and several RTA trustees admitted, however, that the AOG was premature and that the principle of community of interest could not be fully realized. The exodus of farm labor to the cities did not indicate much community spirit, and the party discovered that where no community spirit already existed, none could be artificially created. In fact, the RN, the DAF, and the RTA were instruments of state regulation and party control. There was no self-determination left, neither for the employer nor for the worker, nor for the so-called community of both.

2. CHANGES IN LABOR LAW

The laws and decrees regulating collective agreements, works councils, and arbitration, and the articles of the Weimar Constitution granting freedom of coalition were rescinded with the enactment of the AOG. The protective laws which were not "collective" were upheld, amended, or at least interpreted in the National Socialist spirit. The Provisional Agricultural Labor Act of 1919 remained unchanged. So did the Civil Code which supplemented the LAO.

SETTLEMENT OF LABOR DISPUTES. The Decree of the Reich President concerning Treason against the German People (February 28, 1933),[39] prohibited incitement to strike. To disturb orderly work maliciously in vital enterprises with at least ten workers became a criminal offense, punishable by imprisonment. Still higher punishment was provided if the planned stoppage or disturbance concerned war work or work essential for the needs of the people. Passive resistance could be prosecuted, too.[40]

After the abolition of the arbitration bodies, other means had to be found

---

[36] Bibl. #338, 1939, p. 80.   [37] Bibl. #139, Vol. v, p. 170.

[38] Bibl. #297, October 19, 1934. Employer and employee often relapse into their old habits, said the RTA of Saxony (Bibl. #297, October 26, 1934).

[39] Bibl. #140, Vol. I, p. 85, Section 6.

[40] In spite of the prohibition of strikes, the Technische Nothilfe which had been created to provide emergency work was maintained and put under the leadership of the Reichsführer of the SS "as a police formation for important technical services" (including work on farms). By the Law of March 29, 1939, it was destined to help in war emergencies (Bibl. #319, September 28, 1944).

to settle conflicts. The task to maintain peace was entrusted to various institutions. Officially the confidential council, the DAF, the RN,[41] the RTA had this task, and their principle was to decide conflicts within the shop, with the help of the local labor steward. The employer, as chairman of the council, in conflicts of general importance could appeal to the RTA. This was done in only a few cases: since the procedure was complicated, and frivolous complaints could be punished, appeals were discouraged. Workers could not appeal directly to the RTA but only through the council which the employer had to convene.

Individual conflicts continued to be handled by the labor courts, which were maintained after fundamental changes in composition, jurisdiction, and procedure.[42] Jurisdiction of the courts in collective law ceased with the abolition of trade unions, works councils, and collective agreements. The only conflicts to be dealt with remained those between individual employers and employees or between fellow workers. The DAF had the monopoly of appointing assessors; at the outbreak of the war, the latter were abolished in the lower courts of first instance. Legal advisory bodies, set up by the DAF separately for employers and employees, advised members of the DAF, including farmers and farm workers, in all questions of labor law and social insurance. The offices tried at first to settle the case, and only if they failed to do so could the complaint be made in the labor court. The right of representation was fundamentally changed. The DAF offices provided representation in the first instance of labor and social insurance courts. They granted representation only if the case had a chance of succeeding and was in accordance with National Socialist principles. This made the worker dependent on the National Socialist party and considerably reduced the number of cases brought into the courts. Lawyers could be permitted in special cases by the DAF or the Federal Ministry of Labor. In the district labor courts and the Federal Labor Court they were obligatory.

Employers had to pay fees for advice and representation and the court expenses. Workers had to pay only if they went to court without consent of the office. The office could withdraw assistance at any time if it considered the case hopeless or the contending party had made false statements. The

---

[41] At the third Reich Peasant Day, Reich Sub-Department Leader Methling said that the RN had succeeded in settling many disputes outside of the courts (Bibl. #275, Vol. 3, p. 191).

[42] Act of April 10, 1934 (Bibl. #140, Vol. 1, p. 319), amended March 20, 1935 (*ibid.*, p. 386), and September 1, 1939 (*ibid.*, p. 1658). See Frieda Wunderlich, Bibl. #92, pp. 151ff.

party involved then had to refund expenses to the DAF. After the worker or employer had appealed to the office he was not allowed to compromise, withdraw the complaint, or make any other move without the consent of the office. Needless to say that judges were purged and brought in line. The establishment of agricultural chambers in numerous courts (separated for manual workers and salaried employees) pointed to a relatively large activity for agricultural workers, although in general activities of the courts considerably decreased.

The right to exclude jurisdiction of the Federal Labor Court system and to establish special tribunals which formerly could be exercised by collective agreement was put in the hands of the trustees of labor. The collective rules for Thuringia[43] provided labor tribunals of two instances, with final decision in the second.[44] In most of the other districts the existing agreed tribunals were abolished.

Reduction of litigation in the courts may be partly explained by the distrust in adjudication. Impartiality no longer existed. Party members received preferential treatment. So-called enemies of the state were deprived of legal protection. Refusal to allow children to join the Hitler Youth or to give the Hitler salute, failure to contribute to the Winter Help, listening to a foreign radio, were all recognized as reasons for dismissal. Frequently employer or worker used the shorter way of party influence to realize their claim.

In 1944[45] litigation was curtailed in the course of the combing-out process inaugurated by Goebbels as plenipotentiary for the total war effort. Only litigation essential for the war effort was permitted. Moreover, the district labor courts were abolished, and appeal for review to the Federal Labor

[43] September 21, 1934 (Bibl. #139, Vol. vi, p. 387), and March 21, 1936 (*ibid.*, pp. 614-15).

[44] Collective rules for Oldenburg in 1934 contained the clause that disputes about the rules were to be decided by the courts. Complaint to the court had to be preceded by arbitration in which the Reichsbetriebsgemeinschaft Agriculture and the county peasant leader cooperated (Collective rules of August 18, 1934, Section 12, Bibl. #139, Vol. vi, p. 296). Another trustee provided in three collective rules for the following steps: first, attempt of the confidential council, then consultation of the county peasant leader. In case of failure a tribunal was to be formed composed of one employer and one worker under the chairmanship of the county peasant leader. In important cases appeal could go to a tribunal under the chairmanship of the state peasant leader with two employer and two employee assessors (Collective rules for Mecklenburg-Lübeck of May 17, 1934, Section 15, *ibid.*, p. 48; and rules for Schleswig-Holstein of June 15, 1934, Section 15, *ibid.*, p. 81; and July 26, 1934, Section 9, *ibid.*, p. 198).

[45] Decree of September 27, 1944, Bibl. #140, Vol. i, p. 229. Similar simplifications in social insurance litigation procedure were carried through beginning February 1945 (Bibl. #301, February 19, 1945).

Court admitted only if expressly granted in the Labor Court decision because of the importance of the case. At that time Labor Courts had already become insignificant because of the delegation of litigation to other agencies,[46] such as DAF, trustees of labor, and others. The jurisdiction of the employment offices in questions of quits and dismissals especially narrowed the task of the Labor Court. In Social Insurance Courts, representatives of the insured persons and of employers were almost entirely eliminated (except in the Federal Board). Appeals were restricted.

A new set of courts, Social Honor Courts[47] (Soziale Ehrengerichte) were supposed to protect the honor of the worker as well as of the employer. They punished offenses such as: (1) misuse of authority and malicious exploitation of the workers or offences against their honor by employers or managers; (2) wilful and malicious agitation among workers so as to endanger industrial peace, illegal interference by the confidential men with the leadership of the establishment, and disturbance of the community spirit; (3) repeated frivolous and unfounded complaint to the RTA or obstinate opposition to his written orders by members of the works community; (4) unauthorized publication by confidential men of business secrets which had become known to them in performance of their tasks.[48]

Notices of offenses against social honor were to be given in writing to the RTA who investigated the cases, especially heard the accused and then decided whether to turn the case over to the court. If he did so, the chairman could dismiss the case as unfounded or decide in a preliminary hearing, even sentence the accused to a minor penalty or bring the case to the full court. In event of dismissal of the case, the RTA, and in some cases of punishment the defendant, could request a full trial in the court. The Social Honor Court decided at its discretion on the basis of evidence; the RTA could attend the proceedings and the accused could be represented at the trial by counsel.

Penalties which could be imposed were: (1) warning, (2) reprimand,

---

[46] Wunderlich, op.cit., pp. 172ff. Professor Heinz Rohde claimed in December 1944 that the government had refrained from uniting ordinary and labor courts, which would have been a consistent step, because the latter would have been considered as reactionary ("Die Arbeitsgerichtsbarkeit," Bibl. #315, 1944, No. 8, p. 117).

[47] AOG, Section 35ff., and Order of March 28, 1934 (Bibl. #140, Vol. I, p. 255).

[48] Courts were established for each district of the RTA with a Federal Social Honor Court as court of appeal in Berlin. The lower courts were composed of a professional judge as chairman, one employer and one confidential man as assessor, both chosen from a list prepared by the DAF. The court of appeal consisted of two judges named by the Minister of Justice in agreement with the Minister of Labor, one employer and one worker.

(3) disciplinary fines up to 10,000 M., (4) disqualification for the position of a leader of an establishment or for functioning as confidential man, and (5) removal from the job. Disqualification as leader did not mean dispossession. An appeal against the decision of the court could be made by the RTA in all cases, by the defendant only when the fine exceeded 100 M. or inflicted the fourth or fifth penalty. The Federal Social Honor Court fully reviewed the decision, could alter it at its own discretion, and could even impose a heavier penalty. If the sentence provided for disqualification as leader or as confidential man or for removal from a job, the RTA supervised the enforcement. The Minister of Labor in agreement with the Minister of Justice had the right to pardon.

The Social Honor Courts were not supposed to compete with the Labor Courts, but to supplement them in cases of malicious intention. Only a small number of cases was brought before the courts (the total between 200 and 340 a year), most of them against employers and supervisors (165 to 300). Of 204 cases brought into the courts in 1935, 45 concerned farms.[49] This proportion was relatively high because the trustees of labor were advised to use these courts for forcing employers to improve housing conditions and employees not to break contracts. In 1939, of the 120 employers who were tried, 32 were farmers;[50] in 1940, 24 out of 59 (18 of whom were punished);[51] in 1942, 4 out of 22 (2 punished).[52]

The courts set up as revolutionary tribunals especially punished abuses of authority (such as beating of workers, immoral advances toward female employees), and malicious exploitation of labor (e.g. inadequate housing and persistent refusal to undertake improvements).[53] An owner was punished if, in spite of the demands of the RTA, he did not make the necessary housing repair, although it was recognized that the peasant was social-minded and heavily burdened with debts.[54] Courts punished employers who provided rat-infested quarters or other unsatisfactory housing conditions.[55] Provision of insufficient or unsuitable food was considered a wilful breach of social duties.[56]

[49] Bibl. #139, 1936, Vol. II, p. 67.   [50] Ibid., 1940, Vol. V, p. 347.
[51] Ibid., 1941, Vol. V, p. 311.   [52] Ibid., 1943, Vol. V, pp. 471-72.
[53] November 14, 1934 (Bibl. #274, Vol. XXII, p. 128).
[54] Decision of March 22, 1937 (Bibl. #274, Vol. XXX, p. 110).
[55] January 8, 1935 (ibid., Vol. XXII, p. 216); February 5, 1935 (ibid., Vol. XXIII, p. 74).
[56] November 29, 1934 (ibid., Vol. XXIII, p. 124); February 1, 1935 (ibid., Vol. XXIII, p. 127); June 6, 1935 (ibid., Vol. XXV, p. 182).

On the worker's side, breaches of contract were punished,[57] until the Decree of December 22, 1936, entitled the employer to retain the work book in such case.

The Social Honor Courts were not of numerical importance, but may have worked as a deterrent. They could intervene in cases not punishable in other courts, as, for instance, in the frequently mentioned case in which a farmer refused transportation for driving the seriously ill children of his worker to the hospital.[58] However, the regime had quicker and cheaper means of exerting pressure.

TENANT PROTECTION.[59] Tenant protection, as introduced under the Weimar Republic, was continued under the National Socialists. The RN worked out model lease contracts[60] which provided as a rule for an eighteen-year duration for farms and nine years for single parcels, in order to make possible expenditures yielding long-term returns. According to these contracts compensation would be granted to the tenant for improvements which increased the value beyond expiration of the lease (e.g. establishment of silos). The landlord had to agree to the improvements in advance. In case of contention, final decision was made by a referee appointed by the county peasant leader. Principles for the computing of rent were laid down in detail. The model contracts provided that authorities could change them at will. Thus protection was transformed into regimentation. Like farmers, tenants could be dispossessed if they did not fulfill the orders of the authorities.[61]

PROTECTION AGAINST DISMISSAL. Protection against unjustified dismissal had to be newly regulated after cancellation of the Works Council Law. According to the AOG a worker employed in an undertaking with at least ten employed persons was entitled, after an employment of one year, to

[57] Bibl. #139, 1936, Vol. II, p. 418. There were 75 such cases in 1936, six in 1937 (Bibl. #284, 1938, p. 240).

[58] March 11, 1935 (Bibl. #274, Vol. XXIII, p. 239).

[59] An amendment of 1937 gave the owner the right to give notice if he wanted to till the land himself, and thereby diminished the protection of the tenant (Act of September 30, 1937, Bibl. #140, Vol. I, p. 105). The regulations were newly promulgated on July 30, 1940, without change in principle (Bibl. #140, Vol. I, p. 1065). The intention, however, was not, as in the legislation of 1920, to compromise between landlord and tenant, but to safeguard the national food supply.

[60] They are described by Henry William Spiegel (Bibl. #255, pp. 128ff.).

[61] Decree of April 23, 1937 (Bibl. #140, Vol. I, p. 535). There were two other rent controls in addition to that of the courts. The Price Commissioner held down prices in the frame of the general price policy and official permit had to be given to all lease contracts of more than 2 ha. and of land belonging to hereditary farms.

complain to the Labor Courts against his dismissal if in his opinion the notice was unduly hard and not justified by the condition of the undertaking.[62] If a confidential council existed it had to certify that the questions of continuance of employment had been unsuccessfully raised in the council. If the court ordered the employer to cancel the dismissal, the employer could displace the repeal of dismissal by paying a compensation calculated by the court according to the duration of employment, the economic situation of the dismissed person, and the solvency of the establishment. The worker could refuse to resume employment if he had found another job. He could claim compensation only up to the date of his entry into the new employment. The maximum compensation was six twelfths[63] of the last annual earning. If, however, the notice of dismissal was manifestly arbitrary or given on frivolous grounds by an employer abusing his authority, the court could assess the compensation at an amount not exceeding the last annual earning. No appeal to the Federal Labor Court was possible in dismissal complaints. Workers in small enterprises lacked the dismissal protection. The complaints for recall of dismissal decreased when employment opportunities improved. The protection became unimportant when in 1939 all separations were bound to the consent of the employment office. The employment office had to decide according to the interests of the allocation of labor. If employer and employee did not get along at all, it was in the interest of war production to give the consent for separation (especially in case of living-in workers). There was no appeal against decisions of the employment offices which were entitled to recall decisions only if the latter had been based on fraud or error. Consent to dismissal could be given retroactively.[64]

MATERNITY PROTECTION. Like the Imperial government during the First World War, the National Socialist government improved maternity protection during the Second. A law[65] covering farm workers, but not wives of peasants and helping members of the family, provided that expectant mothers

---

[62] AOG, Section 56ff., amended by Act of November 30, 1934 (Bibl. #140, Vol. 1, p. 1193).

[63] The AOG had at first provided a compensation of one third of annual earnings only. As high officials in the Ministry of Labor pointed out the confidence in employers had been too great and more severe measures had to be taken.

[64] Circular of December 12, 1939 (Bibl. #139, Vol. 1, p. 594) and April 24, 1940 (*ibid.*, Vol. 1, pp. 251-52).

[65] Law of May 17, 1942 (Bibl. #140, Vol. 1, p. 321) and Order of May 17, 1942 (*ibid.*, Vol. 1, p. 324). The scope of the Act was extended during the war to include Germans and Folk Germans in the eastern occupied territories. The benefits were further conferred upon women nationals from several foreign countries (Bibl. #305a, p. 235).

who were Folk Germans or of German citizenship (except Jews) were not to be employed if, according to a doctor's view, the life of mother and child would be endangered. They were not allowed to do heavy work or deal with unhealthful materials nor to do work which required continuous standing. They, as well as nursing mothers, were not allowed to work more than nine hours a day, overtime, on holidays, on Sundays, or on night shifts. The factory inspection could permit exception in special cases.[66] Women were not to be dismissed against their will because of their pregnancy. During this time, and until four months after the birth of the child, it was illegal to give notice for any reason if the employer knew the pregnancy or confinement or was informed about it immediately. However, the woman could give her consent. Exceptions could be admitted by the RTA. Women could be freed from work in the last six weeks before childbirth. Employment was prohibited for six weeks after childbirth, for nursing mothers eight weeks, after a premature birth, twelve weeks.[67]

Women who could not do the normal work in the first months after childbirth were to be occupied only according to their strength. Time used for nursing was to be paid, not to be made up or deducted from pauses. The Minister of Labor could extend the prohibition to work overtime, at night, holidays, and Sundays to mothers of children below the age of fourteen. He could order that women had to get a free half day during the week.

Contraventions were punishable. Enforcement of the law in agriculture was supervised by factory inspectors in agreement with the RN. That is, the factory inspector had to hear the regional peasant leader before prohibiting a heavy occupation or giving orders concerning working time, nursing intermissions, etc. If he decided against the opinion of the peasant leader, the

[66] Non-German pregnant women, as far as not included, were obligated to inform the employer of the pregnancy and the probable day of confinement. They were not to be employed in dangerous work and could refuse work if confinement was to be expected within two weeks. For six weeks after the confinement employment was prohibited.

[67] Pregnant women were exempt from conscription in the first years of the war. Those who became pregnant during their compulsory service, could request release with the consent of the employment office if they could not be persuaded to continue until the beginning of the legal maternity leave (Order of March 7, 1941, Bibl. #139, Vol. I, p. 166). The woman insisting on leaving before that time lost her rights to supplementary benefits ("The Effects of General Mobilization on the Employment of Women in Germany," Bibl. #121a, September 1944, p. 346). If a pregnant woman lived far from her place of work and had to use transportation that might induce miscarriage, the employment office, on advice of a physician, had to arrange for her transfer to an undertaking near her home without loss of wages (Order of June 20, 1943, Bibl. #139, Vol. II, p. 243).

latter could appeal to the higher administrative authority, which decided finally in agreement with the state peasant leader.

The law marked a great progress for women farm workers since no prohibitions of work or protection against heavy work had so far existed in agriculture. However, enforcement could not but meet great difficulties since the factory inspectors hardly had time for adequate supervision. Moreover, they were advised (Circular of the Minister of Labor, May 17, 1942) to grant exemptions from protection in the interest of the armament industry and the food supply during a transitional period.[68]

Enterprise Contests and Social Policy of the Farm

Among the means of stimulating improvement of working conditions were the contests of German enterprises in which farms participated. The participants had to show economic and social achievements and National Socialist spirit. The DAF, which staged the contest, had worked out requirements,[69] among them quality of goods, honest calculation, efficiency wages, provision of job security, old age assistance, leisure time activities, enforcement of protective laws, care for the families of workers, good housing conditions. Peaceful labor relations were credited. Those who fulfilled best the idea of a works community received badges and were celebrated as victors. Special badges were granted for model training, care for health, housing, and promotion of KdF.[70]

Of thirty enterprises which received the title Musterbetrieb (model enterprise) in 1937, two were farms.[71] They all had very good housing conditions, gave additional wages in kind, cared for workers' families with many children, provided warm meals for the family when a child was born. The title "model enterprise" committed the owner to redouble efforts lest he lose his title in the next contest.[72]

---

[68] *Faschismus*, August 26, 1942, p. 133.   [69] Bibl. #338, April 23, 1937, p. 483.

[70] Karl Arnhold, *Der Deutsche Betrieb*, Leipzig, 1939, p. 59.

[71] Bibl. #272, May 15, 1937, p. 7. In 1938 six farms (among 103 victors) received the title, three of them tenant farms (Bibl. #315, April 30, 1938, p. 206). In 1940 of 119 model enterprises five belonged to agriculture (Deutsche *Bergwerkszeitung*, May 1, 1941).

[72] In the last year before the war increase of efficiency was emphasized more and more. Saving of labor, replacement of men by women became important criteria (G. Oeltze von Lobenthal, "Wer wird nationalsozialistischer Musterbetrieb?" Bibl. #111, April 21, 1939, pp. 1412ff.). In 1940 the Commissioner of Efficiency Contest declared that all improvements likely to increase the purchasing power of workers had to be prevented. Activities formerly encouraged were now to be restricted. Increase of output was to be the only yardstick during the war period. The name model enterprise was changed to "war model enterprise."

CHAPTER III

CONDITIONS OF WORK AND WAGES

Collective Rules—General Development

IN ORDER TO AVOID A SUDDEN CHANGE which might have endangered economic stability and the standard of living of the worker, the Minister of Labor provided in the beginning of the regime that collective agreements carry over—amended if necessary—until the enactment of the AOG, after which they would be promulgated in the form of collective rules.[1] Those not promulgated were invalidated on June 30, 1937.[2] This meant practically a prolongation of existing working conditions.

In distinction from the collective agreement which had been concluded by trade unions and employer organizations, the collective rules were state law, not autonomous law, and covered all employers and workers concerned. The AOG seemed to intend to displace collective agreements by shop rules, to consider the social structure of the country as being centered around the establishment as the social and economic unit. Collective rules were to be subsidiary, necessary in a transitional period in order to prevent disorder and underselling and because employers could not yet be trusted to take care of their workers without state interference. However, in accordance with the democratic legislation, whenever the provisions of collective rules differed from those of shop rules, the former were to have priority if they were more favorable than the latter. Collective rules were supposed to be flexible; they could be immediately canceled, if unsatisfactory. Too rigid wage agreements were to be loosened, not only in the interest of individual establishments,[3] but in order to decentralize industry and break the predominance of urban interests, which, according to rural employers' complaints, had so far governed collective agreements.

In the beginning the government believed that the trustees of labor would gradually be able to release from the collective rules any undertaking which

---

[1] Order of March 28, 1934 (Bibl. #139, Vol. I, p. 85). For farm workers there existed 132 district and 35 undertaking full and covering agreements on January 1, 1934, plus 97 district, 2 local, and 13 undertaking wage agreements and 2 district hour agreements (Bibl. #139, 1936, Vol. II, pp. 320, 322). Collective agreements concluded for one undertaking were invalidated as of September 30, 1934 (*ibid.*, Vol. I, p. 146).

[2] Order of June 28, 1937 (Bibl. #139, Vol. I, p. 164).

[3] There was only one collective rule valid in each establishment. A Decree of October 15, 1935 (Bibl. #140, Vol. I, p. 1240) provided that individual establishments could be exempted if special conditions made it impossible to fulfill the collective rules.

had adopted adequate shop rules until finally no collective rules would be necessary, and the severance from the previous scheme would be fully achieved. The actual development took another course. Exemptions for individual enterprises were hardly granted. It became more and more necessary to rely on state guidance. The collective rule became the predominant method of regulating conditions of work. Guiding principles for shop rules became unimportant. This was especially so in agriculture where shop rules could be applied only on large farms.

In the first years the trustees who had only very small staffs were largely assisted by the DAF or the RN in drawing up the rules. At the Third Reich Peasant Day in 1935 a high official of the RN said that the latter had been able "to have the trustees of labor set up a large number of collective rules for various professional groups and regions."[4] However, in the course of time the government influence became dominant.

Although decentralization had been intended, regulations became much more centralized than during the Democratic period. Collective rules covered larger territories (province or small states), frequently replacing many local agreements. Thus the collective rule for agricultural workers in the two provinces of Brandenburg and Grenzmark which came into force on January 1, 1937, replaced twenty-seven local and district collective agreements which had been concluded during the years 1931-1932;[5] the rules for Mittelelbe in 1940 replaced fourteen;[6] in East Prussia thirty-seven different regional scales were replaced by three wage groups, and in Pomerania twenty-six were replaced by three.[7]

The distinction between covering and wage agreements was maintained. The collective rule was arranged in such a way that the covering rules preceded the wage scale and that the latter frequently was divided into district scales. Special collective rules were frequently issued for migratory workers, milkers, and shepherds. The separation of rules for manual workers and salaried employees was maintained, although the regime intended to equalize conditions of work of manual and nonmanual workers.

Collective Rules—Special Terms

The regime stressed the idea that progress had been made, especially in the introduction of periods of notice, granting of holidays, the payment of

[4] Methling, Bibl. #275, 1935, Vol. III, pp. 192-93.
[5] Bibl. #139, 1936, Vol. VI, p. 1273.
[6] August 1, 1940 (Bibl. #139, Vol. IV, pp. 947ff.).
[7] Methling, *op.cit.*, p. 197.

short periods of absenteeism, and the transformation of subcontractors into independent contractors.

I. PERIODS OF NOTICE

Introduction of long periods of notice, in contrast to the former practice of dismissing the worker with short notice or without any at all, may have represented progress for industrial workers in the period of depression. It never was an advantage for farm workers, who had enough jobs available. In the boom they were eager to make use of all opportunities and long periods of notice merely prevented them from doing so. In fact, this privilege gradually developed into an undesirable tie.[8]

There was a great diversity in the periods of notice: the rules ranged from one week to half a year, to one year, and were frequently differentiated for deputatists and workers not living on the farm. Some rules mentioned that, if possible, yearly contracts should be promoted. Some rules merely stated that the laws had to be applied (Civil Code and LAO). Others provided longer terms of notice after a probationary period. The Brandenburg rules provided that a regular worker who had been employed on a farm for more than one year could be dismissed only with three months' notice, to run either to December 31 or March 31, according to custom.

2. VACATIONS

A real achievement was the generalization of the claim to paid vacations which were to be granted after employment of six to twelve months, as a rule. The regime recognized that workers had to be compensated for losses resulting from wage stabilization on the depression level and that increased speeding up and prolongation of hours might become detrimental to the workers' health if not compensated by vacations. "Strength through Joy" would not have been feasible without free time for the worker. In fixing the scale, account was taken of length of service and age. The average duration was 4.4-9.9 days in 1937. Injured persons and those injured in the struggle for National Socialism were allowed extended leaves, to which were added days of sickness which occurred during the vacation.[9] Up to the war no

---

[8] The RTA of Saxony reported that in 1938 of 5,488 notices 4,659 had been given by employees and 829 by employers (Bibl. #111, January 20, 1939, p. 758).

[9] In addition to regular vacations the worker became entitled by law of February 15, 1935, to demand a leave for participation in an approved course of physical education. During each course of military sports the worker and his family were maintained by the government (Bibl. #140, Vol. i, p. 197; and March 19, 1935, Vol. i, p. 382).

indemnity in the form of money payment was allowed. Young workers were given longer vacations, on an average from 8.6-11.4 days,[10] later raised according to the Youth Protection Law. Vacations for young workers were to be given in the slack season, so as to enable them to spend their time in a Hitler Youth camp. Workers boarded by the farmer received compensation for the board which, according to some rules, was canceled if the worker accepted other employment during this time.

At the outbreak of the war,[11] all rules concerning vacations were suspended. Two months later they were restored,[12] as of January 15, 1940. Vacations not granted during the blacked-out period were to be granted later. Since a four-and-a-half-month interruption had increased the vacation time accumulated, money indemnity payment was allowed in many cases, even for young workers[13] if required by war needs. However, money redemption was to remain an exception.[14]

Soldiers on leave for work were to be granted a six-day vacation after three months of work. Wives of soldiers and conscripted workers separated from the family were entitled to paid vacations during a leave from service of their husbands (from twelve to eighteen days)[15] from which vacations had to be deducted. In some cases mothers who had lived with their sons could be released part time from work so as to be able to look after their sons on leave. In October 1943 women having a household of their own

[10] Helmut Egloff, "Gestaltung des Arbeitsverhältnisses," Bibl. #202, München, 1937, p. 75 and Bibl. #338, June 27, 1935, p. 774. By Order of June 14, 1939 (Bibl. #140, Vol. I, p. 1029) the legal regulations concerning leaves for children and young people in industry based on the Youth Protection Law (Jugendschutzgesetz of April 30, 1938, Bibl. #140, Vol. I, p. 437) were extended to young people in agriculture, horticulture, vinage, forestry, and so on. This meant annual vacations with pay for fifteen days for juveniles under sixteen years of age, and twelve days for those beyond that age, after three months' service in both cases. The length of the period was raised to eighteen days for juveniles in a camp or on a trip arranged by the Hitler Youth. Young people participating in "defense" or "efficiency exercises" of the Hitler Youth received three weeks (Circular of April 22, 1942, Bibl. #139, Vol. I, p. 238). Vacations frequently had to be spent in participation in National Socialist celebrations.

[11] Order of September 4, 1939 (Bibl. #140, Vol. I, p. 1609).

[12] Order of November 17, 1939 (Bibl. #139, Vol. I, p. 545); and Orders and Circulars of February 16, 1940 (Bibl. #139, Vol. I, p. 78); May 27, 1940 (ibid., p. 256); March 9, 1940 (ibid., p. 123); December 11, 1940 (ibid., p. 623); June 13, 1941 (ibid., p. 357).

[13] Circulars of May 27, 1940 (Bibl. #139, Vol. I, p. 286), and June 13, 1940 (ibid., p. 357).

[14] Bibl. #139, 1941, Vol. v, p. 170.

[15] Circular of February 26, 1940 (Bibl. #139, Vol. I, p. 87); March 7, 1941 (ibid., p. 150); June 25, 1943 (ibid., p. 359).

became entitled to a four hours'[16] unpaid leave per week and one day per month.

In 1943 and 1944 vacations for adults were restricted to a maximum of fourteen days.[17] Beginning on Saturdays or Mondays was prohibited.[18] All vacations were suspended by Order of August 11, 1944,[19] with exceptions granted for men over sixty-five and women over fifty years of age, wives during leaves of their soldier husbands, holidays for cures provided by the DAF or social insurance institutions, for members of the Hitler Youth participating in courses for premilitary training or educational courses, veterans dismissed from the forces, persons damaged by air attacks, inducted men for the regulation of their private affairs. Suspended vacations were to be compensated for in cash.[20]

3. PAYMENT FOR ABSENCES

An innovation in collective rules was the provision that absences on account of serious illness or death in the family, birth of a child, moving, or civic duties, up to a maximum of about five days in a year were to be paid and not to be deducted from annual vacations.[21] In case of illness of the worker himself, payment of wages in kind was usually continued up to four, six and even ten weeks, as had been traditional in many parts of the country. In districts with only cash wages, some rules provided for payment of the difference between sick benefits and 90 per cent of the wages according to length of service. Alien workers continued to receive lodging and food, but had to pay for it.[22] Some rules provided that employers had to supply a car in urgent cases (e.g. for midwife, doctor, etc.).

Not all changes were improvements. While collective rules issued for East Prussia in 1934[23] secured for the highest deputatist fourteen days of full cash wages a year during sickness and for subcontractors one-half of the cash wages, the rules of 1939[24] stated that no obligation to pay cash wages during periods of sickness existed.

[16] Order of October 22, 1943 (Bibl. #140, Vol. III, p. 325).
[17] For young and handicapped persons they could be extended.
[18] Orders of April 14, 1943 (Bibl. #139, Vol. I, p. 267); December 8, 1943 (Bibl. #113, December 15, 1943); May 3, 1944 (Bibl. #139, Vol. I, p. 185).
[19] Orders of September 1, 1944, October 25, 1944 (Bibl. #139, Vol. I, pp. 313, 338).
[20] Bibl. #301, February 9, 1945.
[21] Section 616 of the Civil Code allowed compensation for short time absenteeism. However, the rule could be waived in the labor contract.
[22] Collective rules of January 8, 1940, Section 9 (Bibl. #139, Vol. IV, pp. 38-39).
[23] October 26, 1934 (Bibl. #139, Vol. VI, p. 496).
[24] February 21, 1939 (*ibid.*, p. 189).

In case of interruptions due to *force majeure*, frequently one-half of the wages had to be paid.

4. OLD AGE AND SURVIVORS' PROVISIONS

A return to more patriarchal conditions was indicated in the provision of the Brandenburg rules that a deputatist who retired after thirty years of service because of age or invalidity should receive if possible a free lodging for himself and his wife to the end of their lives as well as certain allowances in kind. Persons receiving this help were to do light work on the farm; if they were occasionally employed on other agricultural work, they were to be paid appropriate cash wages.

Some collective rules provided payment of wages to survivors for a short period after the death of the worker.[25]

5. SUBCONTRACTORS

Collective rules were intended to reform the institution of subcontractor (Hofgänger), especially to end the automatic obligation of the wife to work on the farm. Some (Pomerania, Brandenburg) prohibited in contracts concluded with deputat workers any clause obliging the workers to bring wives and children or third persons to work on the farm. Separate labor contracts had to be made with such persons. The deputatist was not liable for any damage caused by them. The rules stated, however, that the wives of workers were expected to give their services when necessary. The usual clause was that they should not withdraw (sich entziehen) from milking, washing, slaughtering, harvest work, without urgent reasons.

Rules for East Prussia[26] in 1934 repudiated failure to provide subcontractors as a reason for dismissal for the deputatist. The obligations of the wife were restricted to milking and washing and their hours had to be two less than those of men.[27] Wage rates for subcontractors were included in the rules. In 1939[28] contracts covering subcontractors were abolished in East Prussia and the employer became obliged to conclude separate contracts.

Rules for Pomerania[29] replaced the term "Hofgänger" by "young workers"

---

[25] In Westphalia wages were paid for six days for workers who had been one year on the farm, twelve days for those who had been two years, eighteen for three years. In Kassel wages for fourteen weeks had to be paid to all survivors (Bibl. #310, 1938, Vol. I, pp. 402-03).

[26] Bibl. #139, Vol. VI, p. 496 and Bibl. #310, 1938, Vol. I, p. 406.

[27] In some contracts wives had to get one free hour before meals.

[28] *Ibid.*, Vol. VI, p. 189.

[29] April 2, 1935, Bibl. #139, 1935, Vol. VI, p. 580. On December 8, 1934, the RTA

and provided two separate contracts: one with the deputat worker who provided shelter and food for the young worker, and one with the employer who provided money wages and deputat. The duration of the contracts was the same as that of the deputat worker.

That subcontracting of wives was not abolished was revealed in a Federal Labor Court judgment of May 21, 1940. The court decided that a loyalty bonus increasing at the end of each year had to be denied to a wife who, according to her husband's contract, was obliged to work on the farm.[30] Interesting is the argument of the court that "the own resolution of the wife of an agricultural worker is in general not of decisive importance for belonging to the estate" (nicht von ausschlaggebender Bedeutung für die Zugehörigkeit zum Betrieb) since she is by law obliged to share her husband's residence.

While the collective rules of Silesia[31] provided for separate contracts, a special study showed a slight increase in the work of farm workers' wives in 1935 as compared to 1912, due to the military and labor services of young men[32]—a phenomenon experienced all over the country.

6. CHILD LABOR

Only three collective rules in 1938 contained restrictions on child labor. In East Prussia, according to the collective rules of 1934, contracts with children below the age of ten were invalid; above this age, if the child was obliged to attend school, contracts could be made only with the parents' consent. They were to be occupied with only light work and to be paid .50-1 Rm. a day.[33] These restrictions were discarded in the collective rules of 1939.[34] In Brandenburg young people below the age of eighteen years were not to be occupied with heavy work.[35] In Saxony, the work had to be selected according to the physical capacity of the child.[36]

The Federation of Workmen's Compensation Associations, in collaboration with the RN, drew up a list of agricultural operations forbidden for persons

---

had already ruled that notice could not be given to deputat workers who, without fault of their own, were unable to provide subcontractors (Bibl. #139, Vol. VI, p. 612).

[30] Bibl. #290, August 24, 1940, A, p. 1392.

[31] Collective rules of March 20, 1935 (Bibl. #139, Vol. VI, p. 193), replaced by the collective rules of February 12, 1936 (*ibid.*, Vol. VI, p. 131).

[32] Toni Walter, *Die Frauen in der schlesischen Landwirtschaft*, Berlin, quoted by Else Lüders, "Die Frauenarbeit in der schlesischen Landwirtschaft," Bibl. #338, January 15, 1937, p. 82.

[33] Bibl. #139, 1934, Vol. VI, p. 496.

[34] *Ibid.*, p. 189.

[35] December 10, 1936, Section 8 (Bibl. #139, 1936, Vol. VI, p. 1273).

[36] Collective rules of June 30, 1936, Section 4 (Bibl. #139, Vol. VI, p. 708).

under a certain age. Children under twelve years of age, for instance, could not take cattle, horses, mules, and donkeys to water. Children under fourteen were not allowed to drive vehicles, to work on threshing floors or on machinery, etc.

7. HOURS OF WORK

No essential change in regulation of hours of work was effected. The great shortage of labor extended hours of the farmers themselves and of their wives. Münzinger found that the hours of men farmers (which in 1929 had averaged 3,554) had increased to 4,539; of the peasant wife from 3,933 to 4,797, i.e. the working day amounted to more than fifteen hours for the man, and 16 for the woman.[37] For the period of May 1, 1941, to November 1, 1941, the University of Göttingen investigated hours of peasants and found the peasant himself worked on an average of 80.5 hours a week, the peasant wife worked 81.9 hours, and helping members of the family worked 76.3 hours. Some peasants worked up to 90, during the harvest 100, hours; women worked up to 96.4 hours, besides household work. Children worked up to thirty hours or more.[38]

In comparing hours actually worked in 1929-1930 according to an enquiry of the DLV[39] with hours worked in the same districts according to the collective rules in force in 1938, the DAF found that hours were in the second period up to 240 a year longer (Württemberg 240, Brandenburg 199, Schleswig-Holstein 192, East Prussia 81½).[40]

Overtime was as a rule admitted without restriction. Overtime rates mostly amounted to 50 per cent of the cash wage on weekdays and 100 per cent on Sundays and holidays and wages in kind were increased in the same proportion. The rules of the Saarpfalz[41] provided that no overtime was paid for urgent harvest work necessitated by weather conditions. In some collective rules shortening of pay during short hours in winter was admitted. From 1938 on, the power of the RTA was used increasingly to lengthen hours of work or to admit overtime, even without overtime pay. Thus collective rules for Düsseldorf in 1937[42] contained the following clause: "Regu-

---

[37] Adolf Münzinger, "Die Arbeitsbelastung der Bauernfamilie. Ein Beitrag zur Landfluchtfrage in Württemberg," Bibl. #329, 1940, No. 10, p. 390.

[38] Bibl. #297, May 8, 1942 and May 9, 1942.

[39] Wilhelm Bernier, Bibl. #112 0, p. 56.

[40] Bibl. #310, 1938, Vol. i, p. 389.

[41] Collective rules of March 24, 1937 (Bibl. #139, Vol. vi, p. 496).

[42] September 6, 1937 (Bibl. #139, Vol. vi, p. 941).

larly recurring overtime which the employee has assumed as a basic part of his job is not paid for especially. In case the county peasant leader reports urgent necessity, the worker's claim for overtime pay becomes invalid. Such emergency cases are to be reported by the peasant leader to the trustee." During the war working hours were increased, and the harvest Sunday rest was abolished.[48]

Wages

I. GOVERNMENT WAGE POLICY: PRINCIPLES

Wages during the period of National Socialism were dominated by the state, and had to serve the aims of the general policy of the regime. These aims were: attachment of the worker to the soil, high efficiency of work, and inclusion of wages in the general price-freeze policy. Several principles were established to serve these aims.

INCREASE OF WORK LEASES. The government declared an increase of work leases to be desirable. The worker was to be held to the soil and to be transformed if possible into a Heuerling, i.e. a tenant worker with a small holding who leases land and pays rent in the form of labor. This system which existed only in some parts of Germany was to be spread because the National Socialists concluded that it gave the worker the feeling of being a peasant himself. Of course, the worker, becoming thus attached to the soil had to be racially pure. The RTA in Silesia, therefore, made the conclusion of Heuerlings' contracts dependent on his consent.

However, no progress was made in spreading the system. The number of Heuerlings, which amounted to only about 30,000, seemed to decrease. Land and labor shortages did not allow for increasing the land leased to workers and restricting the days they worked on the landlord's farm. There was no intention to reduce large estates and the worker would have needed means to buy implements. Short growing seasons in the east did not warrant scattering labor over small areas. Reports about the main areas in which the Heuerling system existed agreed that there were tendencies on the one hand to commute the obligation to work on the estate into a money payment so as to transform the Heuerling contract into a lease contract. On the other hand the Heuerling was inclined to accept a job in industry and to have only his wife and children work on the estate and his leased plot.[44]

---

[48] Decree of September 15, 1939, of the Minister of the Interior (Bibl. #334, 1939, A, p. 1937).

[44] Bibl. #220 (Artur Schürmann, *Niedersachsen*, pp. 47-48, Walter Seifert, *Weser-Ems-Land*, pp. 71-72).

In Westphalia, where the intensity of work on the estate hardly left the Heuerling any time to care for the leased plot, the number of Heuerlings decreased from 7,612 in 1927 to 5,188 in 1937, i.e. by 31.8 per cent.[45] In the last period of the regime the Heuerling system was criticized as "antiquated" by National Socialists.[46]

INCREASE OF WAGES IN KIND TO WAGES IN CASH. When no expansion of the Heuerling system could be accomplished, at least one step was to be taken in this direction: an increase in wages in kind in proportion to wages in cash. The worker was, if possible, to be assigned some land which he could till in his spare time and thus supplement his cash wages. Three purposes would be reached thereby: the worker could be attached to the soil, he would work longer hours than the LAO allowed, and a community of interest would be developed between the worker and the farmer for whose crops the worker would feel responsible. Class feeling, which easily seized the landless worker, would thus be overcome. "The pure cash wage is Jewish Marxist, dissolves all ties, and is fit for Soviet Judäa," said a high official in the RN.[47] Following government orders the trustees of labor therefore, aimed to enlarge the deputat proportionately. A special program was launched in East Prussia which provided 2,600 cows for married workers.[48] According to the Yearbook of the Labor Research Institute of the DAF the relation of wages in kind to wages in cash for married deputatists in 1938[49] did not change during the National Socialist period. As frequently happened, two principles of the regime were contradictory: in this case wages in kind and efficiency wage. The less important, wages in kind, had to yield.

During the war, deputats had to be restricted wherever they surpassed the rations granted to so-called Selbstversorger.[50] Collective rules, therefore, had

---

[45] *Loc.cit.*, Friedrich Hoffmann, *Westfalen*, pp. 6, 13.

[46] Von Machui, *op.cit.*, pp. 226ff.

[47] Matthias Haidn, Reichshauptabteilungsleiter, *4. Reichsbauerntag*, Bibl. #275, 1936, Vol. IV, p. 115.

[48] Peasant Erich Spickschen, *ibid.*, p. 244.

[49] Wages in kind amounted to 79 per cent in East Prussia, Pomerania 85.2 per cent, Mecklenburg 77.5 per cent, Schleswig-Holstein 65.2 per cent, Brandenburg 61.3 per cent, Silesia 73.8 per cent, Saxony 43.4 per cent, Thuringia 36.6 per cent, and Wiesbaden-Hesse 26.2 per cent. In the Rhineland, Baden and Württemberg, in accordance with former custom, wages in kind were not generally paid. Workers who did not live on the farms received wages in kind in some districts only and in a much smaller proportion than the deputatists; the highest proportion was 21.4 per cent in Saxony (Bibl. #310, 1938, Vol. I, pp. 391-92).

[50] Orders of August 27, 1939 (Bibl. #140, Vol. I, p. 1521, Section 13); July 29, 1940 (*ibid.*, Vol. I, p. 1045).

to be amended to provide that in cases of large proportions of wages in kind (for instance in Mecklenburg 70 per cent of the total)[51] part of it had to be compensated in money. In spite of these restrictions the Reich Labor Steward in 1944 demanded that farm workers develop a model deputat farm including all branches of garden, field, livestock, and meadows which should make him independent of the market. The state labor steward was to give the owner of such a model deputat farm a revocable document[52] of honor.

LONG-TERM CONTRACTS AND LOYALTY BONUSES. When in the course of time efficiency was more frequently stressed, other means of holding the worker to the soil had to be sought. Long-term contracts and loyalty bonuses belonged in this category. Loyalty bonuses were paid to workers remaining on one job for at least a year. In general bonuses increased with the length of the period the worker stayed. According to most rules, they amounted to 10 Rm. for each year up to a maximum of 30 Rm. Schleswig-Holstein provided 25 Rm. at the end of the first year for married workers and 5 Rm. more each following up to 75 Rm.[53] Harvest loyalty bonuses, usually in the form of grain, were paid if the worker was still on his job on October 31.

In the beginning collective rules attempted to tie the worker by allowing the employer to withhold a large part of his wage until the end of the contract. The worker who broke his contract forfeited the withheld amount. However, in 1937,[54] the Federal Labor Court declared illegal all detentions beyond those provided in the LAO, i.e. restrictions up to one-fourth of the due wage. In the same decision the court recommended setting a low cash wage level and granting high fidelity bonuses in order to reach the same aim legally. This opinion was attacked[55] as a proposal to circumvent the law. It reveals that loyalty bonuses may have been nothing but postponed wage payments.

[51] Amendment of September 28, 1942 (Bibl. #139, Vol. IV, p. 1140) and many similar changes.
[52] Bibl. #286, 1 Maiheft 1944, p. 366.
[53] Collective rules of September 16, 1936, Section 13 (Bibl. #139, Vol. VI, p. 1119). In Mittelelbe 5 Rm. were paid for the second and third year, 10 for the fourth and fifth, and 15 for the following. Rules of August 1, 1940 (Bibl. #139, Vol. IV, pp. 947ff.).
[54] Decision of February 24, 1937 (Bibl. #274, Vol. XXIX, p. 169).
[55] Bibl. #338, June 1, 1938, pp. 665-66. Bibl. #315, 1938, p. 214; *ibid.*, supplement *Der Vertrauensrat* 1937, p. 142.

EFFICIENCY WAGES. During all periods of changing wage policy one fundamental principle remained. Increased efficiency was to be stimulated by wage incentives. The additional production achieved by piece wages ranged between 15 and 33 per cent, most frequently being about 25 to 30 per cent.[56] Piece wages were paid to deputatists and harvest workers but not to farm servants. Some rules provided bonuses for especially good work (care of cattle), for increased output, dirty work (fertilizing), and harvest work. Sheep breeders were given wool bonuses.

The negative counterpart was a clause contained in most rules which permitted lower wage rates for workers who were partly incapacitated because of physical or mental deficiency. This clause had been introduced because persons with mental defects or those who could not accomplish the necessary speed in industry were usually shifted to farm work. Some rules required the consent of the RTA before the clause could be put into effect;[57] for the most part, however, only the consent of the confidential council or the county office of the RN was necessary. Such clauses opened the door to evasion of minimum wages during the depression but became unimportant during the boom.

In 1941, the Institute of Scientific Management of the DAF (Arbeitswissenschaftliches Institut) began preliminary studies for a Reichslohnordnung, a plan to replace "the liberalistic system of wage chaos by a scientific wage system,"[58] which would provide equal wages for equal efficiency. While the former principle of wage payment was based on skill, the DAF sought to prove that specialized workers could contribute more than all-round skilled workers.[59] Revision of the wage structure was started during the war with the intention of mobilizing hidden output reserves. Thousands of occupations were examined as to their requirements. A first attempt to reclassify workers in the metal and building industries supplanted the three customary

---

[56] The trustees followed a varying policy after the wage stop had been ordered. Frequently a certain percentage of workers was prescribed, entitled to receive an efficiency bonus. According to some rules the consent of the RTA for the bonus was required (Arthur Nikisch, "Die Entwicklung des Kriegsarbeitsrechts seit Beginn des Jahres 1940," Bibl. #290, A, November 2, 1940, p. 1857).

[57] In a judgment of October 6, 1937, the Hanover district labor court stressed that inefficiency, the basis for wage reductions, could be due only to physical or mental deficiency, not to such circumstances as lack of training or skill, nor to laziness (Bibl. #338, October 15, 1938, p. 1227).

[58] Bibl. #286, Januarheft 1942, p. 32; Bibl. #310, 1940-1941, pp. 169ff.

[59] Bibl. #283, July 30, 1942.

categories of skilled, semiskilled, and unskilled by the value of the type of work done.[60] "The distinction between skilled, semiskilled and unskilled labor reflects the class structure of the bourgeois society. . . . Socialistic is the simple question what a person can do and what he performs," said a leading National Socialist.[61] The trustees of some eastern districts, Warthegau, Lower Silesia, and others, ordered a new wage scale for agricultural and viticultural workers. The new scale was adjusted for six groups, ranked according to knowledge and performance. The first group covered simple performances which could be carried out by workers who lacked knowledge and experience—e.g. evacuees and workers transferring from other occupations. Group 2 included all general kinds of agricultural workers and trained farm workers; group 3, trained farm workers and foremen able to handle machines; group 4, workers doing difficult and responsible work; group 5, workers with master performances; and group 6, machinists, estate gardeners, etc. In addition to the basic wages, performance bonuses were provided without application for exemption from the wage stop. Within the group workers were to be graded according to efficiency. At the end of 1944 the new grouping had been carried out for farm workers in fifteen districts.[62]

REGIONAL AND SEASONAL DIFFERENTIATION. The attempt to maintain the wage level, as will be described below, meant the maintenance of the great regional and seasonal diversity and inequality. "'What nature has shaped so unbelievably diversified and unequal as agricultural returns in Germany cannot be equalized by organizations and decrees."[63] Thus the old principles of regional and seasonal differentiation were maintained, although some equalization was effected by wage raises in lower paid districts. Pomerania had three wage regions, Thuringia four, Saxony five, and Brandenburg six to

---

[60] In the steel, metal, and lumber industries, for example, workers were graded in eight classes, and a piece-rate list for 1,965 jobs was set up. In percentage of the ordinary skilled workers, the average time rates were as follows: (1) simplest, 75 per cent; (2) simple, 80 per cent; (3) semi-skilled, 87½ per cent; (4) intermediate, 92½ per cent; (5) ordinary skilled, 100 per cent; (6) difficult skilled, 110 per cent; (7) highly skilled, 120 per cent; (8) most highly skilled, 133 per cent. This spread of 70-80 per cent was much larger than former differentials. Women got 75 per cent of men's time rates and could rise only to class 5 (Wilhelm Jäzosch, "Leistung und Lohn," Bibl. #286, 1 Januarheft 1944, pp. 19ff.).
[61] Nonnenbruch in Bibl. #346, September 23, 1944.
[62] Bibl. #286, 2 Dezemberheft 1944, p. 966.
[63] Matthias Haidn, Bibl. #275, 1936, Vol. IV, p. 114.

seven.[64] In East Prussia, for instance, the deputatist in 1938 received a monthly wage which was graded differently in summer and winter according to the three wage regions; cash wages varied from 222 to 240 Rm. for 2,950 hours of work a year. In Pomerania cash wages were between 195.65 and 279.50 for 2,795 hours a year. Mecklenburg 282.39 for 2,800 hours, Silesia 294 for 2,800, Brandenburg 358 to 580 for 2,900 hours.[65] Women's wages were somewhat lower.[66] The differential between men's and women's wages did not increase. Women's wages in the highest group were 63.9 per cent of men's wages in Westphalia in 1938, 84.8 per cent in the Rhineland. Supervisors, gardeners, craftsmen, received higher rates.[67]

In a decision of April 16, 1943, the Federal Labor Court ruled[68] that in interpreting collective rules the conditions of war had to be considered. It should be the task of the judiciary to adapt the rules to the changed conditions.

2. POLICY CONCERNING THE AMOUNT OF WAGES, 1933-1938

The policy concerning the amount of wages followed the general price policy of the National Socialists who had intended to maintain the equilibrium of wages and prices as it existed at the beginning of the regime, i.e. to stabilize wages at the depression level. Consumption was to be kept down in order not to impair the increased supply of armaments. The decline in wage rates in the first period had ceased some months before the beginning of the regime but no new upward movement had started. The official slogan in the first period was that wages were not to be raised before the last unem-

---

[64] An official inquiry found the following regional differentiation in 1937 (Bibl. #153e, 1941, No. 21, p. 405):

Yearly Total Wages (Cash and Kind)
(in Rm.)

	Married Deputatists	Male Servants	Female Servants
East Prussia	1,313	807	688
Silesia	1,233	815	735
Thuringia	1,333	979	802
Schleswig-Holstein	1,573	1,140	846
Rhineland	1,423	957	793
Württemberg	1,236	1,043	848

Wages increased up to the age of thirty-five to forty-five, then decreased.

[65] Bibl. #150, November 1, 1938, pp. 1317ff.

[66] Bibl. #310, 1938, Vol. II, pp. 597-98.

[67] Compensation of apprentices and learners (Anlernlinge) was regulated by special Order of the Commissioner General of Manpower, February 25, 1943 (Bibl. #139, Vol. I, p. 164). Collective rules in 1944 contained educational grants of 15 Rm. in the first year, 20 Rm. in the second (e.g. Warthegau, Bibl. #139, Vol. IV, p. 196).

[68] Bibl. #139, 1943, Vol. V, p. 342.

ployed had found work. The trustees, therefore, were advised not to interfere with the wage level as developed in collective agreements,[69] except for the lowest paid groups or in certain branches or localities where wages had been obviously too low. Agricultural wages in some local districts belonged in this category. Thus the RTA for East Prussia restored cash wages as they had been in December 1931, abolishing thereby cuts made in the last years of the depression.[70] Frequently trustees had to interfere in the first years in order to prevent wage reductions contrary to collective rules. In some collective rules wages were reduced.[71] In a few cases some additional privileges were lost. Collective rules for Silesia in 1936[72] empowered the trustee to reduce cash wages by 5 per cent and reduce or cut harvest bonuses in emergency districts. To judge all changes is impossible, since the trustees were entitled to exempt individual enterprises from collective rules without publication in the *RABl.*

When unemployment began to disappear, the regime proclaimed that the wage level of 1933 was not to be upset by adaptation to the business cycle. However, since minimum wage rates were provided in collective rules, the trustees were powerless when the increasing labor shortage caused employers in their search for manpower to offer inducement wages and thereby to

[69] Circular of October 17, 1933 (Bibl. #139, Vol. 1, p. 271).

[70] Bibl. #150, August 10, 1933, pp. 953-54. This meant practically an increase of the wages of deputatists during the summer months from 20.50 Rm. to 23.70 a month. Other wages were not affected by this rule.

[71] They were reduced for gardeners and steady male workers, partly for dairymen in Hesse (June 22, 1934, Bibl. #139, Vol. vi, p. 126; July 26, 1934, *ibid.*, Vol. vi, p. 191; August 18, 1934, *ibid.*, Vol. vi, p. 491; November 28, 1934, *ibid.*, Vol. vi, p. 620), for unmarried workers in Silesia in 1935 (March 20, 1935, *ibid.*, Vol. vi, p. 193), for deputatists, married, seasonal, and young workers in Pomerania (April 2, 1935, *ibid.*, Vol. vi, p. 580).

Farm Servants Yearly Minimum Cash Wages in Württemberg
(in addition to full board and shelter)

	(in Rm.) January 1932	May 1932	From September 1, 1934
Wage class 1:			
Men over 20 years of age	624	468	416
Women " " " " "	416	336	300
Wage class 2:			
Men	442	364	338
Women	364	288	264

Frequently higher wages were paid.
Source: Adolf Münzinger, "Die Arbeitsbelastung der Bauernfamilie," Bibl. #329, 1940, No. 10, p. 395.

[72] February 12, 1936 (Bibl. #139, Vol. vi, p. 131).

stimulate labor turnover. Restrictions imposed on the mobility of labor—introduced in 1934, abolished in 1936, and reintroduced in 1939—reduced the pressure of demand for labor, but could not completely prevent wages from being influenced by the rule of the market; this trend, however, was much stronger in industry than in agriculture. The official statistics (shown in table following) give the average yearly wages of agricultural workers in 1937.

Average Yearly Wages of Agricultural Workers
With 300 Days of Work and More in 1937[73]

(In Rm.)

	Gross Cash Wages	Perquisites	Total Gross Wages	Deductions	Total Net Wages
Married workers with deputat	698	715	1,413	75.92	1,337
Married workers without deputat	1,227	58	1,285	91.66	1,193
Unmarried workers	672	263	935	67.64	867
Farm workers' wives	535	168	703	47.17	656
Unmarried women	471	221	692	45.95	646
Men servants	486	490	975	64.66	911
Women servants	371	431	803	51.72	751
Farm work masters	942	719	1,662	102.04	1,560
Milk, cattle, and swine masters	1,545	1,065	2,610	149.45	2,460
Milk, cattle, and swine assistants	806	656	1,462	84.76	1,377
Estate craftsmen	939	713	1,652	100.99	1,551
Machinists, tractor drivers, and so forth	1,062	582	1,644	102.55	1,541

During the years 1936-1938, metal and building workers succeeded in earning wages up to 100 Rm. or more a week, while the average pay of all workers was not more than 27 Rm. Wages of coal hewers had increased by 46 per cent from January 1933 to January 1939 (with consideration of all supplements such as reduction of social insurance dues).[74] The farm worker

[73] Source: *Statistisches Handbuch von Deutschland* 1928-1944, ed. Länderrat des Amerikanischen Besatzungsgebiets, München, 1949, p. 473.

[74] Bibl. #111, June 2, 1939, p. 1716.

could not keep pace. Official statements tried to show the insignificance of the differential[75] but their comparisons did not provide the right picture. Wage rates fixed in collective rules for industry did not correspond closely to reality because they did not take into account overtime, Sunday pay, and other payments above the rate. The industrial worker raised his income considerably by working longer hours and by such devices as upgrading and social grants from his employer.

The farm worker could not increase his hours to any extent as they had never been as short as those in industry. Nor could he expect his employer, who frequently was a little man with a small income himself, to increase his income by allowances and bonuses to the same degree as the industrial entrepreneur could. The difference between wages of industrial and farm workers widened. Flight from the land was greatly stimulated by this discrepancy.

1938-1939

Indirectly the government had tried to stabilize wages by establishing the rule that expenditure representing payment of wages above standard

[75] Helmut Reinke (Reichsbauerntag 1936, Bibl. #275, Vol. 4, p. 263), comparing the wage of a Hamburg dock worker (1,560 Rm.) with the Pomeranian farm worker (1,078.43 Rm.) claimed that the difference of 422 Rm. was overcompensated by higher expenses in urban living, the rent amounting to 380 Rm. in the first, 84 Rm. in the latter case. The DAF made a calculation according to three types of prices for wages in kind: (1) producer price (price of farm); (2) retail price in the country; (3) retail price in Berlin. The wages in kind of an agricultural worker in Mecklenburg could then have amounted in 1938, according to the first measure, to 830 Rm. a year, the second 1,248 Rm., and the third 1,935 Rm. If cash wages were added, the farm worker would have been equal in standard to the semi-skilled metal worker. The last two calculations which the DAF calls material living space are fictitious, since the worker in the city does not live in the same way (Bibl. #310, 1938, Vol. 1, pp. 342ff.). The differential became clear where wages of nondeputatists (Freiarbeiter) were compared with industrial wages. The DAF in its 1939 yearbook (Vol. 1, pp. 406ff.) gave the following hourly wages comparison between the two groups:

Hourly Wages of Nondeputatists and Semiskilled
Building Workers in the Reich in 1937
(*in pfennigs*)

	Semi-skilled Building Worker	*Semi-skilled Agricultural Worker*
Westphalia	50-72	36-40
Württemberg	50-74	33-36
Silesia	50-70	34
Saxony	55-73	35
Nordmark- Schleswig-Holstein	57-91	40-43
Hesse	53-75	35-49.5

was not to enter computation of labor cost. This meant that standard wages, not actual wages, were the upper limit of permissible labor costs. In spite of this pressure in 1938, a year and a half after the inauguration of the Four-Year Plan and the price-freeze order, the government found its price policy threatened by constant wage increases in war industries. Manufacturers were trying to entice workers from their competitors and from farms by offering them advantages which in fact were wage increases. This threatened to upset the price and wage system as well as the government's policy of allocation of labor. The actual wage regulation had slipped from the authorities. Wage-policy tactics therefore were reversed and a new slogan of "just wages" was launched, since the old slogan about abolishing unemployment had lost its appeal.

The Order of June 25, 1938,[76] entitled the trustees of labor to take all measures necessary to ensure that the wage movement should not operate to the detriment of defense and the fulfillment of the Four-Year Plan. For this purpose they were authorized to set not only minimum, but also maximum wages in industries specified by the Minister of Labor,[77] if necessary by the amendment of contracts of employment and shop rules.

Not all wage increases were supposed to be suppressed by the trustees. Improvements for wage earners, such as farm hands, who had traditionally very low wages were officially recognized. Moreover, wage increases due to increases in efficiency were not to be prohibited. The entrepreneur was allowed to promote workers to higher age and professional brackets. Consent, however, was not to be given either to raises due merely to the scarcity of labor (so-called Konjunkturlöhne, boom wages), or to raises which would have necessitated a rise in prices, or to increases intended to lure labor away from other work.

The power of the trustees to make individual decisions, and their attempts

---

[76] Verordnung über die Lohngestaltung (Bibl. #140, Vol. 1, p. 691).

[77] Building and metal industries were specified for wage ceilings. Very little use, however, was made of this right before the outbreak of the war. Of greater importance was the second provision, which emphasized the power of the trustees to make the validity of new work regulations depend conditionally on their approval. Employers were forced to apply for a permit before changing the existing rates. If they applied for an increase, permission was refused. Thus the trustees were entitled to set wages for any individual undertaking. Contraventions were punishable by unlimited fines or imprisonment. With the Decree of June 1938, a new period of wage policy was started. It ended the first period during which the slogans "fight against the schematism of collective agreements" and "adjustment to what the enterprise can bear" prevailed. After June 1938, the prevention of inducement wages became the most important aim of the wage policy.

to prevent circumvention of the Wage Order resulted in a great variety of measures which led to inequality,[78] enhanced by the social policy of the enterprise. In industry men were promoted to higher wage brackets, received Christmas and other bonuses. Employers paid the social insurance contributions of the workers, provided beverages, warm meals, buses to the place of work, uniforms, marriage and sickness benefits, potatoes and coal, scholarships for children, even compensation for the wage tax.[79] Again, agriculture could not keep up the pace. Münzinger, in investigating flight from agriculture in Württemberg, compared wages of industrial and farm workers in the same village in which living expenses were alike. The male farm servant on two farms earned (including board and shelter calculated in cash) 1,011 and 1,068 Rm. a year respectively, working 85.4 and 86.2 hours a week, while the skilled industrial worker earned 1,637 Rm., the unskilled 1,469 Rm., both in a forty-eight-hour week. The hourly wages of the farm workers were 23.2 and 24.2 pfennigs; of the skilled industrial workers, 68 pfennigs; the unskilled, 61 pfennigs.[80] In Hesse the unmarried farm worker earned before the outbreak of the war about 40 per cent less than the industrial worker.[81] While wage increases in agriculture or within each industry could be prevented within certain limits, there would have remained the incentive of changing from low-paid to higher paying work, especially from agriculture to industry. The wage policy, therefore, was backed by the policy controlling engagement and dismissals which will be described in the following chapters.

THE WAR PERIOD

With the increasing shortage of labor, temptation to pay higher wages made wage control during the war even more urgent than before. According to National Socialist philosophy, workers as soldiers of the home front were not to enjoy better conditions than soldiers at the military front. Prior to the outbreak of the war, prominent National Socialists demanded a reduction of wages to the level of soldiers' pay, with feeding of the population in canteens. "We must have no profiteers among the workers any more than

---

[78] Ministerialdirektor W. Mansfeld, "Zur Verordnung über die Lohngestaltung," Bibl. #350, 1939, p. 43.

[79] An article in the *Monatshefte für NS Sozialpolitik* (Bibl. #315), 1937, p. 542, enumerated nineteen types of social benefits.

[80] Adolf Münzinger, *op.cit.*, 1940, pp. 395-96. In the Völkischer Beobachter (Bibl. #346) of September 6, 1944, D. Preuschen (Breslau) reported on the great human tensions created by moving factories into the country and thereby demonstrating to the farmers and farm workers the differences in working hours and income.

[81] Bibl. #220, Eduard Willeke, *Kurhessen und Hessen-Nassau*, p. 144.

among the employers."[82] This proposal was not accepted because reduction of wages would have resulted in reduction of output.

The trustees were ordered "to adjust earnings to war conditions in conformity with detailed instructions of the Minister of Labor and to lay down binding maximum wages and other conditions of work" by collective rules, regardless of existing determinations.[83] Thus the trustees' power to establish wage ceilings which had existed so far for the metal and building industry only was generalized. The Minister of Labor, who until this time had been entitled only to suggest guiding principles for the wage policy of the trustees, was now empowered to make provisions differing from the existing wage and hour rules and protective legislation. For workers transferred to other jobs the wage rates of the new job applied. Contraventions were punishable by fines without limit, imprisonment, or penal servitude. An appeal could be lodged with the Minister of Labor.

Orders of October 12, 1939,[84] provided a complete wage freeze on the level of October 16, 1939. The RTA were entitled to permit exceptions and to demand reduction of any enticement wages or raises provided after October 16 which had not been based on an increase of efficiency. Piece rates and bonuses were not to be altered except by authorization of the RTA; reductions were also prohibited. The Order of September 4 had already allowed additional social services only insofar as they were not wage increases.[85]

---

[82] Otto Sperlich (Bibl. #254) 1938, pp. 58-59.

[83] Orders of September 1, 1939 (Bibl. #140, Vol. 1, p. 1863); September 4, 1939 (*ibid.*, p. 1609); and the Ordinances of September 16, 1939 (*ibid.*, p. 1689). Since the two-fold powers of the Orders of June 1938 and September 1939 created confusion, an Order of April 23, 1941 repeated the power of the RTA to fix wages and entitled the Minister of Labor to act when wages beyond a RTA district were involved. So far, a special RTA had been appointed for such cases (Bibl. #140, 1941, Vol. 1, p. 222). The Commissioner General of Manpower became entitled by Decree of January 11, 1944 (Bibl. #139, Vol. 1, p. 40) to issue collective rules as well as guiding principles for shop rules and individual contracts, the scope of which surpassed the territory of a Trustee of Labor.

[84] Bibl. #140, Vol. 1, p. 2028 and Orders of November 7, 1939 (Bibl. #139, Vol. 1, p. 527); December 12, 1939 (Bibl. #140, Vol. 1, p. 2370); February 23, 1940 (Bibl. #139, Vol. 1, p. 85); March 26, 1940 (*ibid.*, Vol. 1, p. 126); June 14, 1940 (*ibid.*, Vol. 1, p. 302); April 11, 1940 (*ibid.*, p. 187); July 20, 1940 (*ibid.*, p. 402); November 16, 1939 (*ibid.*, p. 544); December 15, 1939 (*ibid.*, p. 595).

[85] As before, excesses were discouraged by the rule that expenditures for social services were not to be taken into account in the calculation of prices, except insofar as they were customary and not contrary to the principle of sound economic management (Decree of September 4, Section 23, No. 3, Bibl. #140, Vol. 1, p. 1609). Calculation of prices was to be based only on stop wages or collective rules' wages, not on efficiency bonuses, even allowed in collective rules (Bibl. #286, December 6, 1940, p. 372).

Increasing recurrent allowances (family allowances, profit sharing, Christmas bonuses, and so forth) and granting new nonrecurrent allowances or abolishing them where they existed were declared illegal. Improvement in old age security, whether as grants or contribution to own pension funds, supplements to social insurance dues, premiums to group insurance were allowed only if granted to all workers and if the enterprise was able to grant them permanently without price increase. Increases due to higher efficiency, promotion to higher brackets if in line with the usual policy and procedure,[86] and such grants which did not increase the income of the worker, were permitted.

At first the government intended not only to freeze wages, but also to cut them. The Decree of September 4 canceled supplementary pay for overtime, Sunday, holiday, and night work.[87] Surprisingly enough, on November 16, 1939,[88] most of the sacrifices were revoked. Additional pay for work at night or on Sundays and holidays was restored as of November 27, 1939. An Order of March 29, 1940,[89] reintroduced overtime pay for agriculture and forestry. Why this change of policy? The government's argument that night work produced a greater strain and holiday work higher expenses would have been valid on September 4. The earlier argument that the worker should not claim extra pay while the soldier had to do his duty without consideration of time[90] had not lost its validity. The true reason was the intense discontent of the workers, who answered the September regulation with soldiering and increased absenteeism. Workers were trying to obtain

[86] November 7, 1939 (Bibl. #139, Vol. 1, p. 527). The trustees were ordered to agree if employers paid the difference between maternity benefits and wages. They were allowed to pay wage differentials to expectant and nursing mothers who were prevented from doing overtime and heavy work (Bibl. #139, 1940, Vol. v, p. 528). Similarly earnings of disabled soldiers could be made up to the average previous level. Bonuses for useful suggestions could be granted up to a maximum per cent of the saving achieved by it. Free vitamins could be granted. In 1943 employers were empowered to take over additional workmen's compensation up to 6.50 Rm. a month (Circular of February 11, 1943, Bibl. #139, Vol. 1, p. 166).

[87] In proportion to savings made thereby prices should be decreased. This use of the savings was soon given up, probably because the government did not intend to raise real wages and stimulate consumption and because the money was needed for war purposes. On October 11, 1939 (Bibl. #140, Vol. 1, p. 2053), it was ruled that the employer had to deliver the saved sums to the Treasury. Employers in agriculture and forestry were exempt from this obligation (Decree of October 25, 1939, *Reichssteuerblatt*, Berlin, 1939, p. 1087).

[88] Bibl. #140, Vol. 1, p. 2254.

[89] Bibl. #140, Vol. 1, p. 570. For industry it was reintroduced on September 3, 1940 (*ibid.*, p. 1205).

[90] Bibl. #345, September 20, 1939, p. 1058.

doctor's certificates to save them from overtime work. Production began to show a serious decline.

Thus in 1940 the wage situation was about the same as before the war, except that the wage stop had become quite general, and complete ceilings could be provided. In the following years the measures taken by the government especially concerned three problems: prohibiting evasion of the wage freeze by tightening up loopholes without lessening the intensity of effort, dealing with the unrest of conscripted workers who had to live separated from their families, and settlement of such new problems arising out of warfare as time lost in air raids. Moreover, regulations of wages of alien workers had to be added. All interferences show the readiness of employers to pay higher wages. To the first point belong the repeated orders forbidding employers to pay all or part of the taxes of their workers,[91] forbidding them to add premiums to the interest paid to workers on their savings accounts.[92] Some orders dealt with abuses in the promotion of workers.[93] Unless expressly provided for by law, collective or shop rules, including the regulations in new shop rules, had to be approved by the RTA.[94] "Regular attendance" or "good health" bonuses were made dependent on the consent of the trustees, since regular attendance is a duty and need not be rewarded.[95] Farmers were threatened who gave children digging potatoes more food than customary and who paid them at piece rates.[96] An exact definition of "change of work" which justified higher wages was decreed. Change meant that the new work had to be of a totally different nature.[97]

Maximum wages were to be lowered if the performance of the worker slackened. Controllers of sickness insurance were ordered to find illegal wage increases and report offenders. The trustees complained about the far too numerous applications for exemption from the wage freeze.[98]

Special regulations became necessary for conscripted workers who were

[91] Circulars of April 12, 1940 (Bibl. #139, Vol. I, p. 199); August 8, 1940 (*ibid.*, Vol. I, p. 147); November 29, 1940 (*ibid.*, Vol. I, p. 625, and Vol. v, p. 444).

[92] Limits in the workers' Christmas bonuses to the last weekly wage were ordered in 1940 (Circular of November 9, 1940, Bibl. #139, Vol. I, p. 551) and in 1941 they were not allowed to exceed that of the preceding year.

[93] December 16, 1939 (Bibl. #139, Vol. I, p. 7).

[94] Order of April 25, 1941 (Bibl. #139, Vol. I, p. 212, and Vol. v, p. 239).

[95] Bibl. #139, 1942, Vol. I, p. 7.

[96] H. W. Singer (Bibl. #292) April 1942, p. 25.

[97] Bibl. #297, *Reichsausgabe*, July 20, 1942.

[98] The RTA in East Prussia ruled in the beginning of 1943 that such applications should be decided only on April 1 and October 1, except in special cases. Collective applications for workers had to be made at least six weeks before these dates.

obliged to work so far from their homes that they could not go back after the day's work. A flood of regulations was issued providing different allowances for these workers and for nonconscripted workers who were doing work important for the state and were not allowed to change their working place (so-called Gleichgestellte).[99] After the spring of 1944, this provision included those who had to change jobs because of air-raid destruction, and, after the autumn of 1944, business owners and employees of closed shops who had taken new work.[100] In 1943 these allowances were consolidated into three kinds:[101] (1) the separation allowance (Trennungszuschlag) which could amount to a maximum of 22.40 Rm. a week for men separated from their dependents (for women losing the benefit of a common household 10.50 Rm.); (2) the special allowance (Sonderunterstützung) to be paid if necessary to secure the economic situation of the worker (as compensation for formerly higher wages or the fulfillment of previously undertaken obligations). This allowance was a full income differential to be paid if wages (below 48 Rm. a week for men; 39 Rm. for women; in 1944, uniformly raised to 60 Rm.)[102] were reduced to 90 per cent for married, 85 per cent for unmarried workers. An allowance for rent or mortgage interest could be added to the benefit. (3) An additional bonus (Sonderzuwendung) could be given for uninterrupted service of conscripted workers who could not be freed from conscription and had lived away from their dependents for at least twelve months (others, eighteen months). This bonus amounted to a maximum of 1 Rm. per work day. The first two allowances were extended to disabled war veterans in 1944.

A new problem had to be solved during the war when workers were prevented from working during air-raid alarms and due to air-raid damage. Wages lost during alerts were to be paid up to 100 per cent (at first 50 per cent, then 90) with employers being compensated from the unemployment

[99] Circular of November 8, 1939 (Bibl. #139, Vol. I, p. 512); Decree of November 14, 1940 (ibid., p. 560). An Order of November 25, 1943, provided that no "Gleichstellungen" should be made in the future (ibid., Vol. I, p. 513).

[100] Decrees of January 3, 1944 (Bibl. #139, Vol. I, p. 193) and October 19, 1944 (ibid., p. 394); and Ministerialrat Kalkbrenner, "Erweiterung des Personenkreises und der Leistungen der Dienstpflichtunterstützung," ibid., 1944, Vol. v, p. 199. In March 1942 the number of conscripted workers with separation allowances was given at 7.8 per cent, September 8.5 per cent of all workers (ibid., 1943, Vol. v, p. 248).

[101] Circulars of February 8, 1943 (Bibl. #139, Vol. I, p. 112), amended February 10, 1944 (ibid., Vol. I, p. 92); May 30, 1944 (ibid., Vol. I, p. 228); June 12, 1944 (ibid., Vol. I, p. 246); July 30, 1944 (ibid., Vol. I, p. 276).

[102] Bibl. #346, August 14, 1944 and September 14, 1944; Bibl. #283, August 9, 1944; Danziger Vorposten, August 15, 1944.

insurance fund.[103] As much of the lost time as possible was to be made up before damage could be claimed.[104]

Workers conscripted into the Volkssturm received six weeks' wages, from the seventh week on, at the level of soldiers' pay, with family benefits. The employer was refunded for paying these sums.[105] Farmers inducted into the Volkssturm received compensation of 0.50-2.50 Rm. an hour according to former income.[106]

3. WAGES OF ALIEN WORKERS

In the treatment of foreign workers the desire for maximum efficiency and the policy of degrading undesirable nationalities frequently conflicted. Discriminations were made between workers of the subjugated countries according to the alleged racial qualities of the nationality of the worker and the role the nations would have to play in the New Order. The blood of Jews was considered so pernicious that they were to be annihilated. Poles[107] ranged low in the blood hierarchy, Soviet workers and Croats followed. Frenchmen and Belgians were treated with some respect, the Scandinavians and Dutch were considered closely related to the master race. However, the hierarchy was changed according to the behavior of the suppressed and to political exigencies. Conditions were complicated by the differentiation between citizens, Folk Germans, citizens on recall, aliens and workers of mixed status. Czechs living in the area incorporated in the Reich became German citizens. Of Czechs living in the Protectorate, those confessing themselves members of the German Folk who spoke German were declared citizens, the other 96.5 per cent "Protectorate nationals," were neither Germans nor

[103] Decrees of June 19, 1940 (Bibl. #139, Vol. 1, p. 339); Order of July 6, 1940 (*ibid.*, pp. 355, 424, 472, 504, 511, 533; Vol. v, pp. 335, 339, 582; *ibid.*, 1941, Vol. 1, pp. 218, 374). The employer received in addition 90 per cent of the social insurances dues he had to pay. Decree, November 20, 1940 (Bibl. #139, Vol. 1, p. 569); and April 21, 1941 (*ibid.*, Vol. 1, p. 210); 1942 (*ibid.*, Vol. v, p. 521); Orders of July 9, 1943 (*ibid.*, Vol. 1, p. 352); July 16 and 21, 1943 (*ibid.*, Vol. 1, pp. 399, 400); January 25, 1944 (*ibid.*, Vol. 1, p. 66); September 14, 1944 (*ibid.*, Vol. 1, p. 329); December 6, 1944 (*ibid.*, Vol. 1, p. 436). Farmers were obliged to repair damages themselves. Only if this was beyond the farm's capacity was community help to be provided (Bibl. #301, October 11, 1944).

[104] Time spent in air defense was not to be made up or to be compensated for as overtime. If workers' dwellings were damaged by bombing, up to two weeks of work compensation could be paid.

[105] Bibl. #301, January 26, 1945.　　　　[106] Bibl. #346, January 28, 1945.

[107] In the first period the definition of Poles was drawn on a racial basis. Under an Order of February 25, 1942 (Bibl. #139, Vol. 1, p. 93) this principle was abandoned and the territorial adopted.

aliens.[108] In labor law they were treated like Germans, in vacations and trips home like aliens.[109] Germans born in Silesia and Alsatians and Lothringians[110] were on parole and were closely watched to make sure whether they were true Germans. Resettlers were to be treated as prospective citizens (eindeutschungsfähig).[111] Owing to the lack of Germans to fill the empty eastern space, almost anyone willing to confess being a German could be included in the master race by certificate. Such ease of certification did not simplify the chaos of differentiation.

Of workers whose wages were not regulated by foreign treaties, different groups were formed:[112] (1) Polish, (2) eastern workers, (3) other alien workers;[113] Jews and gypsies. All but the third group were outside the scope of labor legislation and collective rules for German workers and their conditions of work were governed by special provisions.

a.) The "other alien" group was, as a matter of principle, entitled to receive the same wages as German workers—provided their output reached the standard of the German worker—but not higher wages.[114] However, discriminations were made. The special and loyalty allowances were paid to Germans and Folk Germans only.[115] Children's allowances were in some cases granted only if the children received a German education.[116] Everyone but Jews could receive air-raid compensation. In 1944 alien workers who were occupied at lower wages than agreed upon could receive, for a period up to thirteen weeks, a special compensation not exceeding 90 per cent of

[108] Decree of March 29, 1939 (Bibl. #334, p. 783) and Order of April 20, 1939 (Bibl. #140, Vol. I, p. 815). Gerhard Jacoby (Bibl. #201) pp. 80-81.

[109] Circular of July 21, 1943 (Bibl. #139, Vol. I, p. 407).

[110] Circular of July 9, 1943 (Bibl. #139, Vol. I, p. 409).

[111] Circular of July 26, 1943 (Bibl. #139, Vol. I, p. 414).

[112] There were originally six groups: (1) eastern workers, (2) Poles, (3) Jews and Gypsies, (4) workers from the Government General, (5) workers from the Eastland, and (6) other aliens. Workers from the Reich Commissary Eastland (Latvia, Lithuania, Estonia) were treated like foreign workers from the west, but paid a special tax which, however, was abolished in December 1942 (Order of December 28, 1942, Bibl. #139, 1943, Vol. I, p. 33). Workers from the Government General and Bialystok (until the same date) were treated like Poles. Regierungsrat Knolle, "Die Einsatzbedingungen der Arbeitskräfte aus den besetzten Ostgebieten" (Bibl. #139, 1942, Vol. v, pp. 127ff.).

[113] French, Belgians, Dutch, Danes, Norwegians.

[114] Decree of August 2, 1940 (Bibl. #139, Vol. I, p. 424); Circular of January 23, 1941 (ibid., Vol. I, p. 100 and Vol. v, p. 134). Frequent repetitions of the warning not to pay higher wages to alien than to comparable German workers proved that employers were inclined to attract alien workers by higher wages.

[115] Decrees of February 8, 1943 (Bibl. #139, Vol. I, p. 112); July 20, 1943 (ibid., p. 401); February 10, 1944 (ibid., p. 92).

[116] Bibl. #305a, p. 115.

the differential. The employer was refunded by the employment office.[117]

Foreign workers were ordered to bring clothes and footwear with them. In cases where this was impossible, or when clothes had to be replaced, they were to be supplied with the minimum necessary to protect their health against the hazards of weather.

According to the collective rules of August 27, 1941, married workers were to receive home leave after every six months of uninterrupted service in Germany (unmarried, widowed, and divorced workers, after twelve months).[118] However, practical difficulties (transport, provision of documents, obstacles created because of unwillingness to lose the worker) made fulfillment of these promises more and more impossible.

Foreign workers paid the same taxes and contributions for social insurance as Germans and were entitled—so long as they stayed in Germany—to receive in principle the same benefits. However, since they were to be removed after the war many of their rights were illusory. Until 1941 foreign workers (including those injured by accident) whose recovery was not to be expected within two weeks (after 1941, three) were not to receive medical treatment in Germany but to be sent back to their country. Hospitalization was restricted to extraordinary cases. Workmen's compensation was as a rule paid until the return of the worker to his country. Then, according to agreements with the respective countries, the institution of the country took over the care, refunded by the German insurance system.[119] In invalidity and old age insurance "the German authorities endeavored to induce the old age and invalidity insurance funds of the foreign countries to credit the accounts of their respective nationals as if the amounts received by the German funds had been received by those non-German funds."[120]

b.) Special collective rules were issued for Polish agricultural workers[121]

---

[117] Order of August 11, 1944 (Bibl. #139, Vol. 1, p. 287; Bibl. #301, September 11, 1944).

[118] A circular of March 4, 1941 (Bibl. #139, Vol. 1, p. 143) set out the following reasons for a foreigner's return to his country: (1) family furlough, (2) home furlough, (3) furlough for special emergencies (death, and so on), (4) short leaves, e.g. for collecting winter clothes for fellow workers, (5) sick leave.

[119] Bibl. #305a, p. 226.

[120] *Ibid.*, p. 228.

[121] Bibl. #139, 1940, Vol. IV, pp. 38-39. The title was changed from rules for alien workers (except those included in State treaties, which practically meant Poles only) into Reich collective rules for Polish agricultural workers when difficulties arose with workers of the Government General (June 25, 1940, *ibid.*, Vol. IV, p. 727). Practically the scope remained the same. In 1943 the Trustees began to fix maximum wage rates for Polish workers in their districts and the rules of January 8 were discarded (Order

on January 8, 1940. These rules covered the Reich but did not include the incorporated eastern territory. The Reich was divided into four wage areas. Wage rates were 10 to 20 per cent lower than those for German workers, because the German worker was accustomed to a higher standard of living than the Polish worker, according to official comment. Monthly money wages of married farm hands in some East Prussian districts amounted to:

	German[122]	Non-German[123]
Winter	15 Rm.	6-8 Rm.
Summer	22 Rm.	9-12 Rm.

Wages in kind were similarly differentiated. Hours of work were similar to those in rules for German workers. In the incorporated former Polish areas, too, wages for Poles were lower than for Germans. In the Danzig, West Prussian district[124] unmarried Germans over twenty-one years of age received, besides free board and dwelling, monthly wages between 25.50 to 27.50 Rm. in winter; 37 Rm. to 39 Rm. in summer (those with apprenticeship 10 per cent more) plus 70 to 96 Rm. a year; non-Germans over twenty-one years received 21 to 23.50 Rm. during both summer and winter. In the Wartheland wages of Polish farm workers at the end of 1941 amounted to 80 per cent of those of German workers for a normal working week of sixty hours. From the sixty-first hour on, overtime pay of 10 per cent could be paid.[125] Collective rules, issued in 1944 for German as well as Polish workers show that discrimination continued until the end of the war.

As an example, there was the differential in monthly wages and maximum bonuses for workers over twenty one years of age, as established according to the collective rules for the Warthegau. The maximum wage for a highly skilled German worker amounted to 87 Rm. per month, and for the corresponding Polish worker, to 61 Rm.; and while the maximum monthly bonus for the German was fixed at 27 Rm., that for the Pole was set at 10 Rm.[126]

---

of March 1, 1943, *ibid.*, Vol. IV, p. 212). Workers receiving hourly wages had contracts for unlimited time, according to an amendment to the rules of November 2, 1940 (*ibid.*, 1938-1939, No. 32, Vol. IV). Their dismissal was allowed only with the consent of the employment office. During the first ten weeks one mark a week was withheld. This sum was paid only in case of orderly leaving of work.

[122] Collective agreement of February 21, 1939 (Bibl. #139, Vol. VI, p. 189), amended May 16, 1940 (*ibid.*, Vol. IV, p. 585).

[123] May 17, 1940 (*ibid.*, Vol. IV, p. 582).

[124] Collective rules, May 25, 1940 (Bibl. #139, Vol. IV, pp. 618ff.).

[125] Bibl. #294, May 18, 1942, p. 74.

[126] Collective rules of August 12, 1944 (Bibl. #139, 1944, Vol. IV, pp. 196ff., 204ff.).

There were other discriminations. The collective rules in the Danzig, West Prussia, and other districts obliged the Polish workers' wives to work and asked German workers' wives to work only if possible. Any individual regulations concerning hours of work or payment of wages in case of sickness and other emergencies were illegal if they surpassed those fixed in the Reich collective rules.

Poles in the Reich and in the incorporated areas were entitled to remuneration only in return for work actually performed. Employers were prohibited under threat of severe penalties from allowing a number of privileges of Germans, such as wages on public holidays, during illness, old-age pension, maternity benefits, family and children allowances,[127] Christmas and other bonuses to their Polish workers. "Such measures were instituted to encourage the growth of the German population and for the protection of German mothers, and it would not be compatible with sound racial sentiment to allow such benefits to be paid to Polish employees," said an official comment.[128] In case Poles were sent away from the Reich, separation allowances were paid, but at a rate only two-thirds that paid to German workers.[129] Polish workers were covered by social insurance (as described above). Juveniles were to receive only the same leaves as adults, not the extra vacations to which German youths were entitled. They as well as adults were to be granted only minimum rights in respect to vacations. In home traveling all workers were treated as unmarried, i.e. received only one vacation a year instead of two, if indeed they received any vacation at all. From 1941 on, vacations were suspended but could be granted on a voluntary basis,[130] e.g. in case of death in the family. In the autumn of 1942, in order to counteract absenteeism, it was planned to grant vacation trips to trustworthy Poles.[131] However, such trips had to be stopped in February 1943,[132] and although permitted again as of December 1943, they were not carried through[133] in practice.

---

[127] If justified by efficiency and behavior, married Poles with a family of at least five could receive an extra wage of three marks a week.

[128] Oberregierungsrat H. Küppers, "Die Stellung der Polen im Arbeitsleben," Bibl. #139, 1941, Vol. v, p. 532.

[129] Circular of June 23, 1943 (Bibl. #139, Vol. i, p. 382).

[130] Decrees of March 31, 1941 (Bibl. #139, Vol. i, p. 195); February 28, 1942 (*ibid.*, p. 124); March 24, 1943 (*ibid.*, p. 212).

[131] Order of September 29, 1942 (Bibl. #139, Vol. i, p. 430).

[132] Orders of February 18, 1943 (Bibl. #139, Vol. i, p. 167) and April 24, 1943 (*ibid.*, Vol. v, p. 188).

[133] Bibl. #139, 1944, Vol. v, p. 79.

Polish workers were to be treated as outcasts.[134] They were not allowed to eat at the same table with German farmers. They were to be lodged and fed in special barracks. In some places they were forbidden to use public conveyances and to enter restaurants, and were restricted in their mobility to a small area. They were excluded from places of entertainment and allowed to see only German propaganda newsreels. The population was warned by placards and leaflets not to fraternize with the inferior Poles.[135] In commenting on the discrimination, a high official in the Ministry of Labor explained that "the profound hostility of the Polish race towards the German race . . . made it impossible for Poles to be treated on a footing of equality with Germans. On the contrary, it was necessary for every effort to be made to ensure that the Pole should be clearly placed in a situation of inferiority as compared with members of the German race. . . ."[136] However, the frantic appeals to German racial pride, threats, and severe punishment for making contact with foreign workers failed. Repetition of threats and the constant sentences passed on Germans for the crime of fraternization show that in spite of the party's policy, there were friendship and good will between German farmers and farm workers and the foreign workers.

c.) While the attitude toward Poles changed little, concessions were

[134] The Decree Concerning the Organization of Criminal Jurisdiction Against Poles and Jews in the Incorporated Eastern Territories of December 4, 1941 (Bibl. #140, Vol. I, p. 759) provided that death sentences should be imposed even if not prescribed by law and even upon juveniles "if the offence points to particularly objectionable motives or is particularly grave for other reasons." Death sentences were imposed on Polish workers who assaulted their employer.

[135] The *Wochenblatt der Landesbauernschaft Sachsens* wrote on October 25, 1941: "It must be repeatedly stated that in agricultural work contact exists between alien workers and Germans which easily results in insolence on the part of the aliens. Even if the laborers work satisfactorily, there is no reason to allow them particular favors. This applies above all to Poles and Serbs. . . . Therefore, always remember, keep your distance from all alien workers and prisoners of war and remember that you are a German." Germans who treated foreign workers as members of the family were warned that "the heaviest punishment will be inflicted on them" (*Westfälische Zeitung*, May 11, 1942). "No means are sharp enough to combat those Germans who cannot regard Poles as necessary evils which it is not yet possible to remove," wrote Eugen Petrull in the *Ostdeutscher Beobachter* on January 1, 1941. In order to prevent the Pole from insinuating himself unnoticed among the German people and to enable every German to know whether or not he was dealing with a Pole, a police order of March 8, 1940 decreed that Polish workers employed in the Reich should wear a purple "P" on a yellow background on his clothing (Decree of March 8, 1940, Bibl. #140, Vol. I, p. 555). "It was thus ensured that work even occasionally carried on jointly with members of the German race should not result in narrowing the distance to be maintained against every individual Pole."

[136] Küppers, cited above, note 128, 1941, Vol. v, p. 532.

gradually made to another group of underprivileged, the "Eastern Workers" (Ostarbeiter).[187] These workers were outside of German labor legislation (except for safety and hours of work provisions). They worked not under labor contracts but in a special employment relationship.[188] As a consequence, prevailing wages and other labor standards were not applicable to them unless specifically ruled. They were supposed to live in special barracks under strict discipline, and to receive wages reduced by the amount which the National Socialists considered the Russian standard of living to be below the German standard. Their wages were computed at a percentage paid to German workers for equal performance. The difference did not accrue to the employer but was paid by him as a special tax (Ostarbeiterabgabe).[189] Forty-nine marks a month were deducted for board and lodging, so that the remaining money income was very small.

Difference of German and Eastern Workers' Wages
(in Rm. per week)

German Workers	Eastern Workers	Deductions Tax, Board, Lodging		Eastern Workers Received[140]
11.90-12.60	12.04	......	10.50	1.54
14.00-15.05	12.95	1.40	10.50	2.45
20.30-21.35	15.05	5.60	10.50	4.55

[187] They were defined in the Order of June 30, 1942 (Bibl. #140, Vol. 1, p. 419), and Circular of July 29, 1942 (Bibl. #139, Vol. 1, p. 434), as "those non-Germans recruited in [since 1944, coming from] the Reich Commissariat of the Ukraine, in the General Commissariat of White Russia, or in those sections east of those districts, and bordering the former republics of Latvia and Estonia and who, after the occupation of these territories by the German army, were transferred as labor forces into the Reich and into Bohemia and Moravia." The change in the attitude toward non-Polish workers from the East was manifested in the change of their badges. Their first "Ost" was a discrimination. Later their badges showed a wreath of sunflowers, including for Ukrainians a trident, for White Russians an ear of grain and a cogwheel, for other Russians the cross of St. Andrew in the colors of their country. Those who had belonged to German associations received arm badges which entitled them to special privileges (Bibl. #301, August 28, 1944). Finns were exempt from wearing badges.

[188] Their work relations were at first defined in the Orders of January 20, 1942 (Bibl. #140, Vol. 1, p. 41); February 9, 1942 (Bibl. #139, Vol. 1, p. 75); February 27, 1942 (ibid., Vol. 1, p. 93); June 30, 1942 (Bibl. #140, Vol. 1, p. 419); August 1, 1942 (Bibl. #139, Vol. 11, p. 453); March 1943 (ibid., Vol. 11, p. 149); July 23, 1943 (ibid., Vol. 1, p. 406); November 16, 1943 (ibid., Vol. 1, p. 567); April 22, 1944 (ibid., Vol. 1, p. 248); June 13, 1944 (ibid., Vol. 1, p. 248); January 8, 1944 (ibid., Vol. 1, pp. 22-23).

[189] Employers in agriculture paid only half of the tax. Foreign workers were considered privileged because they did not have to pay dues to the NSDAP and other organizations and did not have to do military and labor service. J. Oermann (Bibl. #228), p. 16. They paid dues to the RN.

[140] Bibl. #139, 1942, Vol. 1, p. 324.

Since the system failed to provide sufficient incentives, the cash earnings of the lower groups were increased in May 1943 from 17 to 20 per cent and the deductions for board decreased so as to guarantee that a minimum of 2.80 Rm. a week could be paid out.[141] They could also be put on piece rates.[142] In 1944 a new regulation differentiated wages according to districts, age, and sex.[143] Overtime bonuses were to be paid after sixty-six hours of work.

Separation allowances could be granted up to two-thirds of the amount for the German worker. The rule that piece wages had to guarantee time wages did not apply. Higher wages than provided by orders required the consent of the trustees; lower wages to be reported to the trustees were allowed only if justified by attitude and performance, wages were paid only for work actually done. Bonuses for output or for difficult and unpleasant work could be granted. In case of bad weather the worker received board and lodging, but no cash wages. No family allowances, marriage or death bonuses, or premiums for night and Sunday work were paid. Children below the age of fourteen years were to receive 40-90 per cent of the wages of adult workers. In the second year, Eastern workers received one week's paid vacations in a special camp in Germany; in the third and fourth year, two weeks' paid vacation, which could be spent at home. However, home trips had to be canceled when the war in the east took an unfavorable turn. Eastern workers were at first excluded from social insurance.[144] From April 1, 1944 on, Eastern workers had to pay the regular social security contributions and were included in the general German social insurance system.[145]

Foreign workers were to send a large part of their wages to their families at home in order to keep down their consumption in Germany. The amount varied according to the country of origin and the nature of the individual's work. They were not allowed to take savings with them when they went home except through the official clearing transfer.

In order to keep the foreign workers in Germany, it was necessary to provide some care for their families in case of sickness and childbirth. Arrangements were made with social insurance institutions of the Pro-

[141] Decree of April 5, 1943 (Bibl. #140, Vol. I, p. 181); Circular of April 14, 1943 (Bibl. #139, Vol. I, p. 270).

[142] Bibl. #139, 1942, Vol. v, pp. 509, 510.

[143] Bibl. #140, Vol. I, p. 69; Order of June 29, 1944 (Bibl. #139, Vol. I, p. 239).

[144] Decree of August 19, 1942 (Bibl. #139, Vol. II, p. 466). In case of sickness, confinement or accident they were entitled to free board, lodging and medical, dental and hospital services.

[145] Orders of March 25, 1944 (Bibl. #140, Vol. I, p. 68), and Circular of April 22, 1944 (Bibl. #139, Vol. I, p. 428).

tectorate, Croatia, Slovakia, Denmark, Italy, Norway, Hungary, Roumania, Bulgaria, and France to provide medical help for the families of foreign workers. Help was granted in general by the foreign country under German supervision.[146]

For prisoners of war the employer provided housing, clothing, tools, guards, and paid to the authorities of the camp 60 per cent of the wages provided in collective rules for German workers, or of locally prevailing wages; for piece work, an additional 30 per cent. At melioration work the entrepreneur had to pay maintenance and 20.80 Rm. a month to the authorities. No bonuses (overtime, Sunday work, etc.) were paid.

In 1943[147] it was ruled that prisoners had to receive besides shelter and board 0.70 Rm. a day (Poles, 0.50 Rm.; Soviet Russians, 0.35, the difference to be paid to the camp). In addition, especially industrious and efficient non-Russian prisoners could receive up to 20 per cent of prevailing wages, Russians 0.30 Rm. per work day. Piece wages were paid according to collective rules or prevailing wages; 10 per cent to the camp, 40 per cent to the prisoner (Russians 20 and 30 per cent to the camp). Inefficient prisoners were to receive less in agreement with the trustee. Prisoners were paid in camp currency, the use of which was restricted to certain shops.

Hours of work were to be at least as long as for German workers.[148] Prisoners received benefits, if injured, for the duration of their imprisonment.[149] In case of illness they were treated in camps or in special hospitals.

4. THE MOVEMENT OF MONEY WAGE RATES

The only figures available to judge the movement of money wage rates are those of collective agreements in the pre-National Socialist time and of rates of collective rules. From figures published in the Official Statistical Yearbook we have selected three districts in East Prussia (Gumbinnen, Königsberg, Rastenburg) which had separate rates in collective agreements

[146] See the discussion in *The Exploitation of Foreign Labor in Germany* (Bibl. #305a), p. 216.

[147] Order of September 8, 1943 (Bibl. #139, Vol. 1, p. 477).

[148] Decree of July 31, 1941 (Bibl. #139, Vol. 1, p. 368). Farmers were not allowed to have prisoners eat at their table. However, the rule that they had to work separate from German workers could not be carried through.

[149] Act of September 3, 1940 (Bibl. #140, Vol. 1, p. 1201); and Decree of October 28, 1940 (Bibl. #139, Vol. 11, p. 392); August 14, 1941 (*ibid.*, p. 394). In 1944 (Order of September 12, 1944, *ibid.*, Vol. 1, p. 340) wages were graded. For wages up to 2 Rm. of a German worker the non-Soviet prisoner received 0.50 Rm., the Soviet prisoner 0.25 Rm.; for 2-4 Rm. of the German worker 1 Rm. and 0.50 Rm. respectively.

Yearly Wages of Married Deputatists[150]

District	Year	Wages (in Rm.)	Hours	Housing and Stable	Fuel (50 Kg.)	Land are[e]	Potatoes zentner[f]	Milk liter[g]	Live-stock	Grain, Legumes (50 Kg.)	Other Wages in Kind
Gumbinnen	1929	223.35	2,897.5	1	52	24.1		1,460		32	Small livestock
	1932	192.81	2,913.0	1	52	23.4		1,464		20	" " } & sheep
	1937	231.00	2,899.0	1	56	29.8		1,278		35	" "
Königsberg	1929	233.40	2,897.5	1	52	28.4		1,095		32	Small livestock
	1932	201.48	2,913.0	1	52	27.7		1,098		32	" " } & sheep
	1937	231.00	2,899.0	1	56	29.8		1,278		35	" "
Rastenburg	1929	213.45	2,897.5	1	59	28.4		1,460		32	Small livestock
	1932	184.86	2,913.0	1	59	27.7		1,464		20	" " } & sheep
	1937	231.00	2,899.0	1	56	29.8		1,278		35	" "
Thuringia	1929	671.77	2,800.0	1		25.6		—		16	2 teams (of 2 horses each)
	1932	559.55	2,800.0	1		25.6		—		16	5 zentner straw
	1937	572.30	2,800.0	1		25.6		365		16	375 kg. "
Vogtland	1929	751.13[a]	2,775.0	1		—	36	182.5		15	2 teams of 2 horses each
	1932	648.40	2,800.0	1		—	36	183		12	" " " " " "
	1937	592.68	2,725.0	1		20		365		15	500 kg. straw, 39 kilowatt electric light
Schleswig	1929	485.69[b]	2,825.0	1	30	19.9		1,095	1	30	Small livestock, 10 zentner straw
	1932	397.80	2,841.5	1	30	19.9		1,098	1	30	Small livestock, 5 zentner hay
	1937	448.88	2,832.5	1	35	25		1,095	1	30	Goats
Rhineland Köln	1929	1,063.51[c]	2,851.0				22	365		7.8	12 zentner straw
	1932	862.25	2,823.0				26.8	366		9.4	
	1937	1,188.00[d]	2,917.0					—		—	
Baden	1929	1,429.78	2,900.0								
	1932	1,201.75	2,928.0								
	1937	1,080.40	2,920.0								
Württemberg	1929	1,329.82	2,900.0								
	1932	no collective agreement									
	1937	1,013.96	2,939.0								

a Besides money for tools.
b Besides loyalty bonus of 10-30 Rm.
c Besides loyalty bonus of 26-35 Rm.
d Besides share wages.
e 0.02471 acres.
f About 110 lbs.
g About 2 pints.

150 Source: Bibl. #153c, 1930, p. 309; 1933, p. 285; 1938, p. 350.

		Unmarried, Steady, Independent Workers[151]				Servants		Young People				
						Wages in Rm.		Wages in Rm.				
District	Year	Wages (in Rm.)	Grain (50 kg.)	Potatoes (50 kg.)	Other Wages in Kind	Men	Women	Men	Women	Grain (50 kg.)	Potatoes (50 kg.)	Other Wages in Kind
Gumbinnen	1929	879.54	14	—	—	333.74	283.79	560.8	531.84	14	—	—
	1932	757.39	14	—	—	293.09	249.23	466.08	451.52	14	—	—
	1937	753.74	16	—	—	330.00	222.00	463.84	405.86	16	—	—
Königsberg	1929	885.77	14	—	—	316.94	200.10	567.04	538.07	14	—	—
	1932	742.82	14	—	—	271.60	171.42	466.08	451.52	14	—	—
	1937	753.74	16	—	—	330.00	222.00	463.84	405.86	16	—	—
Rastenburg	1929	885.77	14	—	—	316.94	199.80	576.04	538.07	14	—	—
	1932	771.95	14	—	—	271.60	171.17	495.21	466.08	14	—	—
	1937	753.74	16	—	—	330.00	222.00	463.84	405.86	16	—	—
Thuringia	1929	756.96	8	21.8	—	505.25	382.90	314.45	304.50	4.7	12.4	—
	1932	641.83	8	21.8	—	418.59	325.49	264.38	265.72	4.7	12.4	—
	1937	709.50	8	21.8	—	432.22	328.22	275.45	275.45	4.7	12.4	—
Vogtland	1929	751.13	6.1	24.4	152.5 liter milk	596.35	596.35	342.64	360.34	6.1	24.4	like steady
	1932	468.40	6.1	24.6c	50 kg. straw	458.12	444.16	265.24	287.32	6.1	24.6	independent
	1937	607.42	9.2	24.5c	—	396.00	372.00	248.61	276.10	6.1	18.4	workers
Schleswig	1929	239.45	—	—	—	522.50	425.50	310.00	260.00	—	—	—
	1932	1,079.77	—	—	—	371.00	314.00	230.00	182.00	—	—	—
	1937	1,157.00	—	—	—	400.00	420.00	240.00	220.00	—	—	—
Rhineland	1929	1,104.17	7.8	12	—	714.55	—	395.78	—	4.2	12	—
	1932	914.70	7.8	12	—	584.25	—	325.72	—	4.2	12	—
	1937	1,283.48b	—	—	—	528.00b	420 00b	168.00a	162.00a	—	—	—
Baden	1929	1,222.34	—	—	—	681.06	476.20	631.00	446.81	—	—	—
	1932	985.18	—	—	—	547.10	381.80	492.96	336.68	—	—	—
	1937	992.80	—	—	—	478.33	338.74	476.84	311.56	—	—	—
Württemberg	1929	1,124.25	—	—	—	658.50	476.50	664.92	469.16	—	—	—
	1932d	—	—	—	—	—	—d					
	1937	1,013.96	—	—	—	577.00	282.00	individual contracts		—		—

a Besides board and room.
b Besides loyalty bonus.

c The same as 1929, but 513.5 l. milk.
d No collective agreement (since May 1, 1932).

151 Source: Bibl. #153c, 1930, p. 309; 1935, p. 286; 1938, p. 351.

but formed one wage district in collective rules, two central German districts (Thuringia and Vogtland, the latter in the State of Saxony), one northwestern (Schleswig-Holstein, later part of the wage district Nordmark), one western (Rhineland Köln), two southern (Württemberg, Baden). The three last are more easily comparable since they do not have wages in kind, the computation of which makes comparisons so difficult. Wages are presented for married deputatists, so-called independent workers, male and female farm servants, and young persons.

The year of highest wages of the Democratic period was 1929. In 1932, the wages were at the depression low. In 1938, collective rules had reshaped and displaced the old agreements.

Wages of farm servants who usually received free board show a decline from 1929 to 1937 with the exception of two East Prussian districts. As compared to 1932, improvements occurred in East Prussia, Schleswig, and Thuringia. Young people, too, had lower wages in 1937 than in 1929 or, in some districts, lower even than in 1932. Wages of unmarried independent workers whose income in kind changed only in the Vogtland improved only in the industrial Rhineland in comparison to 1929 and improved in Königsberg, Thuringia, Baden, Schleswig, and Rhineland compared with 1932.

The picture for deputatists is more confusing because we cannot judge what the larger piece of land in East Prussia and Schleswig may have meant in cash value. We can see that cash wages in East Prussia were raised in comparison to both years (Königsberg only to 1932). In Thuringia milk and straw will not have compensated for the loss of 99 Rm. from 1929. Wages increased in the Rhineland, but decreased in Baden, Württemberg, Vogtland, Schleswig in comparison to 1929.

In general we cannot read a considerable improvement as to 1929 out of these figures, but rather a leveling down. However they do not give a realistic picture. That earnings must have increased without reaching the 1929-1930 peak (of 1,994 Rm.) can be seen from the increase in payrolls in agriculture from 1,486 Rm. in 1932-1933 to 1,852 in 1937-1938, while in the same period the number of agricultural workers fell by 20 per cent.[152]

In general, the main objective of wage policy to maintain wage rates was

---

[152] It meant for farm workers an increase in cash wages but not in wages in kind when, by Order of December 3, 1937, payment for twelve legal holidays was prescribed (Bibl. #139, Vol. 1, p. 320); Act of February 27, 1934 (Bibl. #140, Vol. 1, p. 129). Payment on May 1 had already been ordered by Law of April 26, 1934 (*ibid.*, p. 337). The express reason given for the payment of holidays was that the Four-Year Plan put an extra strain upon the workers.

not achieved in spite of wage control and the complete control of mobility of labor. It was necessary constantly to take new measures to prevent wages from increasing. Complaints in semiofficial comments show the difficulties of preventing wages from following the natural tendency to rise, while maintaining responsibility and efficiency in labor.[153]

5. FUTURE PLANS

There can be no doubt that the government did not intend to abandon wage control in the postwar period.[154] Since the old wage structure was dissolved by a variety of disguised wage increases and a not-less-large multitude of trustee regulations the question of the "economically right wage" (volkswirtschaftlich richtiger Lohn) was discussed ever since the Order of June 1938 made it clear that the government intended to reserve to itself all control of wages. In May 1939, Dr. Mansfeld[155] thought the time had come to establish a completely new wage structure. Whereas differences in income and wages due to soil quality and distance from markets had heretofore presented an insoluble problem, he argued, now everything was open to political management. Fixing of price zones, commodity quotas, and transport policy could be supplemented by fixing of wages. Price fixing had already abolished many regional differences in the cost of living. It now would be necessary to find a just wage according to type of work, training, effort, economic possibility, location, cost of living.

In introducing a trustee of labor in Austria in 1940, the Federal Ministry of Labor explained that a new differentiation of wages was to be built up. Miners would be at the top, followed by building and metal workers.[156] When, in April 1942, the administration of wages was taken from the Ministry of Labor and put in the hands of the Commissioner General of

[153] The *Frankfurter Zeitung* (Bibl. #297), December 30, 1942, quoting from an article of Packenius, threw doubt on the agricultural wages stop, claiming that wages had gone up in an extraordinary degree. "Whoever wants to keep capable workers pays more than collective rules prescribe." "It is not possible to get anyone to work in the fields if he must reckon that as deputat worker he can expect no more than 70 per cent of a mason's wage or 66 per cent of those of a carpenter."

[154] "In an economy directed by the state it would be an anachronism to withdraw wages from the influence of the state and the so-called free development would direct tempo and amount of wage formation," Mansfeld, Bibl. #111, August 25, 1939, pp. 2313ff.

[155] "Leistungssteigerung und Sozialpolitik," Bibl. #345, 1939, pp. 656ff.

[156] Bibl. #139, 1940, Vol. v, pp. 501-02.

Manpower, it became evident that wage policy would be subordinated to labor allocation policy.[157]

Concerning farm workers' wages it was strongly felt that their low standard as compared to industrial workers' wages was one of the main reasons for the flight from agriculture and that the average hourly wage of 40 to 50 pfennigs (average yearly 1,200 Rm.) did not provide a fair minimum of subsistence. In its discussion of the valuation of farm labor the DAF[158] claimed that wages would have to be raised at least 50 per cent to guarantee a cash wage of 60 pfennigs. Since it was assumed that agriculture could not carry such a raise of its production cost and since neither price increases nor subsidies were desirable the solution was postponed until the European Gross Reich would have been definitely established. As an immediate measure the Labor Institute of the DAF proposed an increase of the loyalty bonus from 200 Rm. in five years to 100 Rm. a year, which would have meant a wage increase of 5 per cent. They furthermore wanted to free the farm worker (not the employer) from the payment of social insurance dues. No solution was suggested to the problem of how to finance sickness, invalidity, old age, or survivors' insurance without such contributions. None of these proposals materialized.

6. DISPOSABLE INCOME

In considering the worker's disposable income we have to add services and benefits he received and to subtract compulsory and voluntary deductions.

ADDITIONS TO WAGES. To the additions belong benefits of social insurance and welfare services, both of which will be described in following chapters, paid vacations, recreation, and entertainment provided by "Strength through Joy." These amenities were provided in a very able way and certainly helped to make low wages tolerable before the war.

Other benefits introduced during the National Socialist period were marriage loans, furniture loans and grants, and children allowances. Marriage loans to healthy young people were granted at first under the condition that women[159] had been employed for a certain length of time before their

---

[157] "The Commissioner General of Manpower regulates wages according to the requirements of labor allocation." Decrees of March 27 and April 24, 1942 (Bibl. #139, Vol. I, pp. 207, 257).

[158] Bibl. #310, 1940-1941, pp. 359ff.

[159] Act for the reduction of unemployment of June 1, 1933 and the following decrees (Bibl. #140, Vol. I, p. 323).

marriage and that they would give up paid employment for whatever period the husband earned more than the bare minimum of subsistence.[160] The loans were given in the form of bonuses to be used for the purchase of furniture and other household goods; no interest was to be paid but every month 1 per cent had to be paid into a sinking fund. If a child was born, one-fourth of the loan was canceled and payment into the sinking fund could be deferred for one year. Marriage loans were granted at an average of 660 Rm. per couple.

Three special privileges were provided for the agricultural population: (1) marriage loans could be converted into a gift if the bridegroom or bride had been employed continuously in agriculture, forestry, or rural handicraft for at least five years before the marriage, and if the one or the other continued to do so for ten years without interruption. If before the expiration of the ten-year period neither husband nor wife was working in the prescribed occupations, the marriage loan became repayable. But amortization was postponed without interest as long as one of them worked in agriculture.

(2) The same law provided for loans to farm persons married after June 30, 1938, if husband and wife were willing to serve the Reich loyally. They were paid in cash, instead of vouchers and could be spent on a wider range of goods, including cattle, machinery, and tools. The sum amounted to 400 Rm. if one party had worked five years continuously in agriculture or in a rural occupation, 800 Rm. if both had worked five years. If both continued to work in a rural occupation for another ten years the debt was reduced by 500 Rm. and a further 100 Rm. for each additional year, so that the loan expired after thirteen years. The cancellations were halved if only one partner fulfilled the conditions. But if the continuity was broken, the remainder of the loan had to be repaid.

(3) Grants for agricultural wage earners, salaried employees, and rural craftsmen (married after December 31, 1933) were direct gifts, paid in cash, which could be repeated every five years. They were obtainable on the same terms as loans, and amounted to 400 Rm., if both husband and wife had worked continuously in an agricultural occupation for the previous five years, to 200 Rm. if only one partner had fulfilled this condition. In either case the applicant had to declare that he intended to continue the same type of work. A young couple could thus receive:

[160] These conditions were subsequently changed, as will be discussed in the next chapter.

At the marriage	about	600 Rm.
Furnishing loan		800
Furnishing subsidy		400
Total		1,800 Rm. and 400 Rm. every five years.[161]

Another increase which the agricultural population shared with other low-income groups gave consideration to large families. Lump-sum subsidies for families with four or more children under sixteen years of age (einmalige Kinderbeihilfen), which could be given only once, were provided by an Order of September 15, 1935.[162] These were at first, like marriage loans, in the form of vouchers for the purchase of furniture, linen, and household appliances[163] up to 100 Rm. for each child below sixteen, with a maximum of 1,000 Rm. for the family. The families had to be German citizens or Folk Germans, racially pure, bodily fit, loyal to the regime; they had to guarantee by their reputation that the subsidies would be used for improvement of their economic condition. The subsidies were granted only upon request.

From July 1936 on, current cash allowances for children (laufende Kinderbeihilfen) were granted to all those insured against invalidity or sickness or to unemployed persons, if their income did not exceed 185 Rm. a month. Subsequent orders extended the grants to families with three and more children. The grants finally amounted to 10 Rm. per month for the third and fourth child and 20 Rm. for each additional. After December 1940, allowances were made available for the entire population, no matter what their income or property was. However, the administrative authority, in agreement with the NSDAP and health authority, could protest if the grant of the allowance "appeared incompatible with the purpose of the decree," i.e. in case

[161] In May 1941 the furnishing loans were extended to those who had married after December 31, 1928, and had been agricultural workers or rural craftsmen for at least five years (Bibl. #286, May 23, 1941, p. 1211).

[162] Bibl. #140, Vol. I, p. 1160; Orders of September 26, 1935 (*ibid.*, p. 1206); March 24, 1936 (*ibid.*, p. 252); June 10, 1936 (*ibid.*, p. 504); August 20, 1936 (*ibid.*, p. 649); August 31, 1937 (*ibid.*, p. 989); March 13, 1938 (*ibid.*, p. 241); December 20, 1938 (*ibid.*, p. 1931); December 9, 1940 (*ibid.*, p. 1571); January 30, 1941 (Reichssteuerblatt 1941, No. 14, pp. 105ff.).

[163] From 1937 on, the grants could be used for the acquisition or improvement of settlements. By Decree of December 20, 1938 (Bibl. #140, Vol. I, p. 1931), it was decided that families which did not produce their fourth child until after January 1, 1939, should be given the grants only if these were used in connection with the acquisition or improvement of settlements. This also applied to families which received part of their grants by the specified date.

purity of blood and political irreproachability were not assured. For single women (if the father of the children was known), and for children who were completely orphans, all current and additional subsidies could be granted from the first child on. To heads of households more than 85 per cent incapacitated or receiving sick benefits, subsidies could be granted for the first and second child, too. After 1938, training subsidies (Ausbildungsbeihilfen) and scholarships in schools could be granted additionally for eugenically healthy children (of families with four or more living children) who were inclined toward sports (sportlich entwicklungsfähig) and "whose promotion appeared particularly welcome from the point of view of National Socialism." If the father died in the war, subsidies had to be paid from the first child on. In December 1940 it was ruled that the main subsidy of 10 Rm. a month should be granted for every third child and those following under twenty-one years of age. The allowance of 20 Rm. previously granted from the fifth child on was reduced to 10 Rm. but lump sums paid as compensation for the loss. All children's subsidies were paid by the Reifa. Appeal from rejections was finally decided either by the district leader of the party, if the regional leader was responsible for the refusal, or, in other cases, by the civil authorities. Allowances for children meant a considerable improvement for the standard of living of large families, and farm workers had large families.[164] A worker's family with six children received an allowance of 60 Rm. (from 1940 on, 40 Rm.) a month in addition to the lump sum they had received prior to 1938.

To wives of servicemen (the Armed Forces, Labor Service, Armed SS) financial assistance could be granted for the continuation of the farm. Farm workers' families received support, the wife 40 per cent of the husband's net income before he was in service in addition to children's benefits, rent, maternity assistance. Family support was only to supplement income from other sources; however, two-thirds of the income from work was exempted from consideration of total income. Special regulations secured the income

[164] In 1933 there were four and more children born in the existing marriages of 40.3 per hundred families of farmers; 34.4 per hundred families of farm workers; 24.8 per hundred families in the average population (Friedrich Burgdörfer, Bibl. #340, p. 65). A study of the birthrate in peasant and industrial workers' families in the Black Forest showed that in the period 1919 to 1923 the former had 4.28 children per family, the latter 2.53; in the industrious Rhine Valley, the difference was smaller, 2.75 to 2.52. In the Black Forest the most prosperous peasants had more children, in the Rhine Valley, they had fewer (Hermann Schubnell, Bibl. #245, pp. 60, 65, 114, 117).

of the deputatist's family. Maximum limit for the total income of a family on benefit was the preservice income.[165]

DEDUCTIONS FROM WAGES. Compulsory deductions were wages and citizen taxes, social insurance contributions, RN dues and Winter Help contributions.

Under the National Socialist regime the tax burden increased for unmarried persons but was relieved for fathers of large families. In 1936 the tax of single persons was 60 per cent higher than those of married people without children.

Wage Tax of Workers with an Income of 1,880 Rm. a Year[166]

(Per Cent of Income)

	Unmarried (Rm.)	Married with One Child (Rm.)	Married with Three and More Children
1928	2.75	1.65	—
1932	5.08	3.25	—
1935 on	6.07	1.21	—
1936 (Wages and Citizen Tax)[167]	7.74	2.88	—

During the war taxes for unmarried persons and those who after five years of marriage had remained childless were increased by 40 per cent.[168] The exemption of most of the wage earners from the war tax on income and the complete wage-tax exemption of extra pay for overtime was somewhat offset by the considerable increase in tobacco, beer, and alcohol taxes.

Social insurance contributions did change insofar as the farm worker had no longer to pay unemployment insurance dues. Thus about one-half of all farm workers were relieved. The others had been exempt. Sickness insurance dues were slightly decreased.[169]

[165] Decrees of June 26, 1940 (Bibl. #140, Vol. I, pp. 911, 912); Circulars of October 2, 1939 (Bibl. #334, p. 2079); October 21, 1939 (ibid., p. 2183).

[166] Bibl. #153e, 1938, No. 4, p. 160.

[167] Bibl. #153a, 1937, No. 35, p. 146.

[168] Richard Bargel (Bibl. #169), p. 70.

[169] The Act of July 5, 1934 (Bibl. #140, Vol. I, p. 577) provided that contributions hitherto borne one third by employers and two thirds by workers had to be borne by both parties equally. The enforcement of this rule was to be ordered at a later date but it was never put into force. Average contributions in rural funds were 4.35 per cent for workers in 1928 and 3.69 in 1935 (Bibl. #153a, p. 148).

Contributions of Workers in Percentage of Income[170]

INCOME PER YEAR	Invalidity 1928	Insurance 1936	Sickness[171] 1928	Insurance 1936	Unemployment 1928	Insurance 1936	Total 1928	Total 1936
1040	3.00	3.00	4.90	3.85	1.60	—	9.50	6.85
1300	3.00	3.00	5.24	4.12	1.68	—	9.92	7.12
1560	2.50	2.50	4.37	3.43	1.40	—	8.27	5.93
1820	2.57	2.57	4.66	3.69	1.51	—	8.74	6.26

[170] Bibl. #153a, p. 159. According to official estimates taxes and social insurance contributions increased for the average industrial worker from 11.5 per cent in 1928 to 13.5 per cent in 1937 (Bibl. #153e, 1938, No. 4, p. 160), which would still mean a reduction to about 10.25 for those workers who before 1933 paid unemployment insurance dues.

Average Compulsory Deductions from Gross Wages
(wage tax, citizen tax, social insurance contributions)
in Per Cent of Income of
an Average Industrial Worker in 1936

Income per year	Unmarried	Married no children	1 child married	2 children	3 children and more
1040	13.20	12.30	10.30	10.30	
1300	17.36	15.20	12.36	10.76	
1560	15.86	13.26	10.29	9.39	8.96
1820	17.83	14.74	13.03	9.89	9.52

Source: Bibl. #153a, p. 162.

[171] Based on sick fund contributions of 4.66 per cent of the basic wage in 1928 and 3.66 in 1936 in Berlin. Average contributions in rural funds were 4.35 per cent for workers in 1928 and 3.69 in 1935 (*ibid.*, p. 148). Due to low evaluation of wages in kind farm workers frequently paid lower percentages. An official inquiry of the Federal Statistical Office and the RN found in 1937:

Earnings and Deductions of Farm Workers:

	Gross Wages (Rm.)	Deductions, taxes, social ins., RN dues (Rm.)	Per Cent of gross	Net Wages (Rm.)
Married deputatists	1,413	76	5.4	1,337
Married farm workers	1,285	92	7.2	1,193
Unmarried farm workers	935	68		867
Women " "	703	47		655
Girl " "	692	46		646
Male farm servants	975	65	6.7	913
Female farm servants	803	52	6.5	751
Milker foreman	2,610	150		2,460
Farm work foreman	1,662	102		1,560

Source: Bibl. #153e, 1941, No. 21, pp. 403-04.

To compulsory deductions and dues have to be added "voluntary" contributions which frequently were no less compulsory. Thus the worker had to contribute to the Air Defense League, the Association of Germans Abroad, Sport Associations, the Thanksgiving Sacrifice of the Nation (Dankopfer der Nation). He was also supposed to subscribe to party publications, to support party celebrations, to buy Hitler portraits and memorial tablets, to contribute to the construction of a new Zeppelin and youth shelters; to pay installments toward the "people's car" three years before the car was due to be delivered. A complete enumeration of donations and sacrifices would be impossible.[172] Membership dues for party organizations were another obligation. Storm troopers paid 1.40 Rm. a month (if a member of the party, 1.80 Rm.); Hitler Youth 0.50 Rm. a month.[173]

According to official statistics, the industrial worker with an income of 2,400 Rm. and two children dedicated in 1936 about 16.8 per cent of his income to compulsory and voluntary contributions; if some indirect taxes are included, 22 per cent.[174] The worker without children with the same income would have to pay 6.63 per cent taxes, 9.95 per cent social insurance contributions and 4.01 per cent "voluntary" contributions, plus 5.41 per cent indirect taxes, i.e. a total of 26 per cent.

[172] Bibl. #291, December 1935, A, pp. 46ff.; May 1936, A, pp. 87ff.; August 1936, B, pp. 17ff.; May 1937, A, pp. 28ff.; November 1937, A, pp. 57ff., 72ff.; 1938, No. 1, A, pp. 56ff.

[173] *Ibid.*, August 1936, B, p. 35.

[174] Bibl. #153a, p. 177. Taxes and Contributions in 1936.

	Per Cent	
Wage tax	2.08	} total 3.44
Citizen tax	1.16	
Church tax	0.20	
Tariff duty	0.62	} total 5.20
Excise tax	1.98	
Turnover tax	2.60	
Sickness insurance dues	3.90	
Unemployment " "	3.45	(not paid by farm workers)
Invalidity " "	2.60	
Voluntary contribution	3.41	
Total	22.00	

Composition of Voluntary Contributions	Per Cent
DAF	1.40 (farm worker RN)
NSDAP	0.97
NSV	0.25
Gifts	0.36
Air Protection League	0.10
Association of Germans Abroad	0.08
Miscellaneous	0.25
Total	3.41

In addition workers had to pay 0.30-1.20 Rm. a month to the RN[175] and 10 per cent of the wage tax during seven, later six, winter months to the Winter Help;[176] those who were exempt paid 25 pfennigs a month.

Dr. Charlotte Lorenz[177] calculated in 1938 from an income of 2,400 Rm. the following deductions amounting to 624 Rm. for the childless family of the industrial worker and 528 for the family with two children, i.e. 26 and 25.1 per cent of the income.[178]

[175] Workers earning up to 70 Rm. a month in cash and kind paid 0.30 Rm.; from 70-120 Rm., 0.60; from 120-150 Rm., 0.90; with more than 150 Rm., 1.20 Rm. Employees with three and more children paid the dues of the lowest class. Penalties and supervision secured enforcement. Exempt from payment were workers who received only wages in kind, those who worked only avocationally in agriculture, wives of dues paying members and other members of the family who were not eligible for social insurance (*Beitragsordnung des Reichsnährstandes für die bäuerlichen und landwirtschaftlichen Betriebe* of April 24, 1936, Bibl. #113, July 8, 1936, No. 156).

[176] On June 15, 1938, the Federal Labor Court delivered the following verdict in a typical case: "The dismissal was justified. It is indeed true that the contribution [to the Winter Help] is and must be, according to the will of the Führer, absolutely voluntary. By his refusal to pay the contribution, however, the employee in question has so placed himself outside the community of the people that the employer and the personnel cannot be expected to tolerate his continued employment" (Bibl. #274, No. 36, Vol. 34, pp. 205ff.).

[177] "Verbrauchshaushalt und öffentlicher Haushalt," Bibl. #338, October 1, 1938, pp. 1201-02.

[178] The sums have been computed for the agricultural workers by omitting 3.5 per cent unemployment insurance due and replacing 1.6 and 1.3 per cent KdF by 0.6 per cent RN. Computed deductions from a Farm Worker's Income of 2,400 Rm.:

	Family without children (Per Cent)		Family with 2 children (Per Cent)	
Direct taxes				
Income tax	4.4		2	
Citizen tax	1.8		1.2	
Church tax	0.4		0.2	
Total direct taxes		6.6		3.4
Excise tax	2.3		2.0	
Customs	0.7		0.6	
Sales tax	2.4		2.6	
		5.4		5.2
Sickness insurance	3.9		3.9	
Invalidity insurance	2.6		2.6	
		6.5		6.5
NSDAP	1.0		1.0	
NSV	0.3		0.3	
Air Protection League	0.1		0.1	
Association of Germans Abroad	0.1		0.1	
Gifts	0.6		0.3	
Miscellaneous	0.3		0.3	
RN	0.6		0.6	
		3.0		2.7
		21.5		17.8

The burden of donation and dues for the total population was roughly estimated in 1936 to amount to about 2.3 billion Rm.,[179] corresponding to an increase of the tax burden by 15 to 20 per cent.

The variety of deductions (five legal and two semiofficial) and the complicated methods of calculation became so burdensome when not enough clerks were available to make the calculations that in 1941-1942 the wage tax and insurance system were simplified.[180] At first the range of the various wage classes was reduced and wage tax and war additions were unified. Then the citizen tax was abolished and the wage tax correspondingly increased. Since the tax exemption was lower for the citizen tax, the exemption limits were lowered for the income tax. To farm workers, however, an additional exemption was granted[181] of 13 Rm. a month for unmarried persons and married persons with not more than two children; for others 26 Rm. a month. In invalidity insurance the contribution was calculated on the same basic wage as in sickness insurance, so that the employer had to apply only one method of assessing the basic wage.[182] In invalidity insurance all dues were unified to 5.6 per cent of the wages or salary. All dues were to be collected as a single sum by the sick fund which retained its part and distributed the other to the different branches. The stamp system used in invalidity and old age insurance was abolished.[183] Other simplifications in 1944 freed from taxation and social insurance contributions deputat or other grants of the employer for the sick worker, Christmas, and other nonrecurrent bonuses.

7. PURCHASING POWER

Real wages of farm workers were less affected than those of industrial workers by price increases and shortages because they were secure in their food supply in spite of severe delivery obligations. Concerning other expenses, they were in the same situation as industrial workers who had to be satisfied with goods of lower quality for which they paid the same or slightly increased

---

[179] Bibl. #291, August 1936, B, pp. 39-40.

[180] Decree of February 20, 1941 (Bibl. #139, 1941, Vol. v, pp. 168, 281); July 1, 1941 (Bibl. #140, Vol. i, p. 362); July 12, 1944 (*ibid.*, p. 166); September 10, 1944 (Bibl. #139, Vol. ii, p. 281).

[181] Order of April 24, 1942 (Bibl. #140, Vol. i, p. 252).

[182] Order of June 15, 1942 (Bibl. #140, Vol. i, p. 403; Bibl. #139, 1942, Vol. ii, p. 290).

[183] Bibl. #297, *Reichsausgabe*, April 25, 1942; Orders of September 10, 1944 (Bibl. #139, Vol. ii, p. 28).

prices of the former better qualities. Although the government was interested in keeping the population content and in supplying them with as many consumer goods as the war preparation allowed, the requirements for rearmament limited the goods available for civil consumption. Shortage of clothing, shoes, household goods were expressed in rising prices. The index of the cost of living had increased up to 1939 by 7 per cent, up to 1944 (June) by another 10.7 per cent.[184]

After the outbreak of the war, shortages of labor and materials led to considerable price increases, especially in clothing. From August 1939 to August 1942 clothing prices increased by 30 per cent.[185] Rent and fares remained practically unchanged. Prices for furniture were 21 per cent higher in 1942 than in 1936.[186] The index figures are misleading in that they do not reveal deterioration in quality, unavailability of low-priced articles of consumption and enforced substitutions, black markets, and rationing. The Institute for Business Research stated in 1939[187] that the index underestimated the actual price movement and an article in the *Wirtschaftskurve* claimed an increase of 10 to 15 per cent living expenses in Frankfurt am Main instead of the 7 per cent recorded by the official index. There were complaints that price reductions granted as compensation for increase of other goods were ineffective because they concerned goods which were not in the market.[188]

Even before the war, food imports and storage of foods for the army caused shortages in butter, eggs, some fruits and vegetables. As early as 1937 some articles disappeared from the market; substitute materials were used in

---

[184] Bibl. #153e, June 1944, p. 89.

Index of the Cost of Living (1913-1914 = 100)

1933	118.0	April 1942	136.6 (= 8.2 per cent more than 1939)
1939	126.2	July 1942	138.9
1940	130.1	September 1944	141.2

(Bibl. #153e, 1941, No. 14; 1944, No. 7, p. 111).

[185] Clothing Index

	1933	106.7	
	1937	125.7	
December 1941		166.4	
March 1942		170.8	(Bibl. #153e, May 1942, p. 141)
March 1944		181.7	(*Ibid.*, April 1944, p. 64)
September 1944		185.1	(*Ibid.*, 1944, No. 7, p. 111)

[186] Bibl. #297, February 9, 1943.

[187] Bibl. #120a, 1939-1940, Vol. 14, No. 1, pp. 14-15. In 1939 the Statistical Office put its index calculation on a new basis.

[188] *Die Wirtschaftskurve*, Frankfurt a.M., 1938, pp. 301ff.

the production of others. In the summer of 1939 the authorities issued orders forbidding shopkeepers to close their shops early. Housewives bought in the morning to make sure they would get the goods, and shopkeepers who had nothing left to sell closed down in the afternoon. Because of the bad impression closed shops made, early closing had to be prohibited. After the outbreak of the war, in part even before, rationing was introduced for food-stuffs, clothing, soap, coal, and some household articles.[189] The longer the war lasted, the more rationing was tightened and extended to additional commodities and services. The clothing ration reduced the purchases of a worker's family to about 40 to 50 per cent of the peacetime level in 1940.[190] In October 1941 the clothing ration was reduced by 40 per cent[191] and extended to articles formerly unrationed. Permission to purchase an overcoat (unless the person had a large number of points from previous cards), was given only if the applicant could prove that he had no wearable overcoat.[192] Many articles of common use formerly obtainable on the clothing card were in 1941 classified as "nonessentials," purchasable only with a special permit on application. Shoes, the supplies of which had become more and more difficult, were obtainable only by special permits if the applicant proved urgent need. Shoes granted for work were not allowed to be worn on the way to and from work. The worst difficulty in clothing were poor quality, due to the use of substitute materials, and the trouble people had to go through to utilize their points. In August 1943 all ration points for clothing were can-celed and sales stopped for the duration, except for air-raid victims and children.[193] The clothing and textile industries became obliged to take over

[189] An investigation of the Association for Consumption Research (Gesellschaft für Konsumforschung) covering about 10,000 consumers in 1941 found that the most urgent demand was for clothing, followed by furniture and tobacco, chocolate, and so forth (Genusswaren), Bibl. #286, January 5, 1943, p. 424.

[190] Harry A. Franklin, "Wartime Agricultural and Food Control in Germany," Bibl. #295, April 1940.

[191] *Economist*, November 8, 1941, p. 566. 120 points were granted for sixteen months. How large this ration was may be judged by the fact that a suit required 80 points, two-thirds of the total. The clothing card issued in December 1942 extended duration to eighteen months and reduced the points to 100, and extended it again to formerly unrationed articles. Bibl. #314, November 11, 1942. A man's suit required 60 coupons, a shirt 20, a blouse 15 (*Business Week*, December 16, 1941).

[192] Bibl. #346, October 10, 1941.

[193] Bibl. #331, August 8, 1943. Moreover, from 1941 on, households were put under strong pressure in winter to contribute all the heavy woolens the people possessed for the benefit of soldiers at the eastern front. Collections were continued after the retreat and used for the Volkssturm and the evacuees from the east.

repairs, material for which was to be taken from the old clothing itself.[194] However, the clothing of the population must have deteriorated below standards of health protection, so that in the autumn of 1944 production was regulated and certain types prescribed which industry was allowed to sell.[195] In shoe exchanges, two worn pairs of shoes in good condition could be exchanged for a new pair.

New heavy reductions in nearly all articles of consumption were ordered in 1942 (coal, drugs, books, tobacco). Soap was not only rationed but reduced to poor quality. Even furniture was sold only on cards and became practically unobtainable. In 1943 pots, pans, and other household articles were put on the list of rationed goods available, however, to the bombed-out portion of the population.

Since goods could not be purchased—even rations were not always available—barter exchange gradually developed from the most primitive form of fixing posters on trees and garden fences or on blackboards of agencies, to advertisements in the local press, which in some papers filled several pages. Exchange organizations were formed, called Tauschringe, Tauschstellen, Tauschzentralen, and Tauschvermittlungsstellen.[196] The Ministry of Economics, by Decree of December 15, 1944, defined which barter transactions were lawful and tried to simplify the barter trade by authorizing the Wirtschaftsgruppe Einzelhandel, the official representation of the retail trade, to take it over and by issuing model statutes for the exchange rings and centers. Rates of estimates were to be approved by the Reich price commissioner.[197] Barter of food was illegal.

As an incentive for farm workers to stay on the land, supplementary rations were granted and unrationed goods preferentially allocated to them in 1942.[198]

---

[194] Fritz Kluge, Bibl. #283, September 30, 1944. One enterprise employed 2,500 workers for fixing old clothing only (Bibl. #286, 2 Februarheft 1945, p. 101).

[195] Bibl. #301, November 30, 1944.

[196] Tauschringe were formed by several retail shops which accepted used goods and gave them away. Tauschstellen were independent institutes, e.g. for the exchange of shoes, established by the NSDAP or official economic offices. Tauschzentralen were established in large and middle-sized cities by public authorities of the retail trade. They were small department stores. Tauschvermittlungsstellen, sometimes established by municipal authorities, gave surveys of demanded goods and supply offers by lists and posters.

[197] Bibl. #286, 2 Februarheft 1945, pp. 101-02.

[198] Rationing was to be used to discriminate according to the consumers' functions in the war economy and also according to their racial and political acceptability. Soldiers

Finally efforts were made to restrict the spending of income. When in the autumn of 1941 the problems arising from excessive purchasing power became pressing, German workers were appealed to to save regularly a fixed part of their wages and to freeze these savings until a year after the end of the war.[199] In order to make the "iron savings" scheme popular, it was exempt from wage tax and social insurance contributions by the worker—the employer paid 2 per cent of the saved sum. In addition insurance benefits were based on the full wage, including savings. The amount saved was deducted at the source. Considering the loss of public revenue connected with these investments their extent was subject to limitations. The maximum amount which could be saved tax free was 26 Rm., in case of overtime work 39 Rm. a month. Bonuses could be saved *in toto*.[200] Bonuses were made subject to the wage tax in order to encourage their being saved. A temporary suspension of payments was allowed in certain circumstances, such as sickness. In cases of emergency (death, marriage of a woman, or birth of a child), withdrawals were admitted in an amount needed for the extra expense. The deposits bore the same rate of interest as other long-term savings deposits. The response to iron saving remained small.

Due to full employment, family cash income rose. There was more money to spend—especially in large families—in spite of large deductions; there were, however, fewer things to spend the money on. No precise conclusions can be drawn concerning the standard of living. Real income and consumption figures seem to prove that in spite of diversion of a large part of the national income to rearmament and of civilian consumption control the standard of living of the masses before the war improved in comparison to 1932.[201] The war deprived the worker of the compensations of "Strength

and Gestapo were to receive the highest rations, followed by skilled and essential workers. Unskilled workers and unemployables followed. At the bottom were the undesirables, such as Jews and inmates of concentration camps whose extirpation by lack of food seemed desirable to the regime. Karl Brandt shows how food was made a political instrument "Food as Political Instrument in Europe," (*Foreign Affairs*, April 1941, pp. 1ff.). "Food could establish equality or set up distinctions," it could "liquidate" inferior individuals and groups (p. 4).

[199] Orders of October 30, 1941, November 10 and December 13, 1941 (Bibl. #139, 1941, Vol. I, p. 538); 1942 (*ibid.*, Vol. v, pp. 19, 108, 133); December 10, 1942 (*ibid.*, 1943, Vol. II, p. 2); February 12, 1943 (*ibid.*, Vol. I, p. 145).

[200] A Circular of February 12, 1943 empowered the trustees to make the consent to bonuses dependent on their being saved (Bibl. #286, March 13, 1943, No. 24).

[201] See the thorough study of Otto Nathan (Bibl. #224), p. 363.

through Joy" and imposed sacrifices the amount of which cannot be measured in money alone.

Social Insurance and Other Care for the
Health of the Nation

The first social insurance amendments tended toward centralization: replacement of public control and of self-administration by the leader principle.[202] The right of decision was placed in the hands of party men.[203] These changes meant a severe blow to the working class, which—with a two-third majority in administration—always had felt sickness insurance to be their own business and which had had a considerable influence in invalidity, old age, and survivors' insurance. Now they were completely deprived of control and inside information. The advisory committees through which employers and workers participated in administration of all insurance carriers, had very little right of codetermination. The members were appointed.

I. SICKNESS INSURANCE

Up to the outbreak of the war, the worker in sickness insurance was personally affected by the following reforms: All "non-Aryan" and "Communist" doctors and dentists were removed.[204] The great gap following this purge and the wish to favor party men led to a reduction of the qualifying period of practicing before admission to sick fund practice from two years to one for SA, SS, and ex-service men.[205] This meant some deterioration in the quality of medical services. Medical control of the fund doctors was tightened.[206] The relation of the patient to the physician changed, owing to the doctor's obligation to report mental disorders or hereditary sickness.

[202] Act of May 18, 1933 (Bibl. #140, Vol. 1, p. 277); and Order of May 19, 1933 (*ibid.*, Vol. 1, p. 283).

[203] The Act of July 5, 1934 (Bibl. #140, Vol. 1, p. 577); and Orders of December 21, 1934 (*ibid.*, Vol. 1, p. 1274); May 25, 1935 (*ibid.*, Vol. 1, p. 694).

[204] Orders of April 22, 1933 (Bibl. #140, Vol. 1, p. 222); June 2, 1933 (*ibid.*, Vol. 1, p. 350). Jewish war veterans who were at first exempt from the removal followed later. The relation of doctors and dentists to the funds was also changed.

[205] Order of May 9, 1933 (Bibl. #140, Vol. 1, p. 260) and May 17, 1934 (*ibid.*, Vol. 1, p. 399); newly formulated September 8, 1937 (*ibid.*, Vol. 1, p. 977); September 28, 1933 (*ibid.*, Vol. 1, p. 696); May 9, 1935 (*ibid.*, Vol. 1, p. 594); January 12, 1938 (*ibid.*, Vol. 1, p. 29).

[206] Decrees of March 30, 1936 (Bibl. #139, Vol. IV, p. 107); July 15, 1936 (*ibid.*, Vol. IV, p. 230). The supervision of doctors and curative and preventive functions were shifted to the invalidity insurance institutions in 1934.

Many who were afraid to spoil their children's chances if suspected not to be of good stock preferred not to see a physician at all.

Sick funds were included in the price freeze and not allowed to raise contributions or benefits without permit of the price commissioner.[207] Thus cash benefits were frozen at the depression level. In order to improve benefits for large families (i.e. with four or more eugenically healthy children of German blood) funds became entitled to pay higher additional benefits to them without additional dues and to reduce benefits for childless families or families with correspondingly few children.[208] Large families were freed from paying the fees for the physician and certificates.[209] Considerable extensions in personal scope and services were introduced during the war, safeguarding the insurance rights of mobilized men and their families.[210] They were to retain rights as they existed at the moment of their mobilization, although dues were suspended for both the employer and the insured person. Maintenance of rights entitled them to free medical aid for their families. Soldiers themselves received treatment from the military medical service. In 1941 the qualifying period of three months for family benefits was abolished. In case of death of a mobilized man the family received the death benefit.

Sickness insurance benefits in kind were extended to survivors of war victims, of victims of the Labor Service, and like services of the SS, civilians injured by war activities, and their families, dues of these groups to be paid after 1941 by the Federal government.[211] The supervision of doctors and curative and preventive functions were shifted to the invalidity insurance institutions in 1934. Social insurance pensioners[212] were included

---

[207] Bibl. #111, October 1, 1937, p. 8. However, in 1944 cash allowances, paid to families of persons in hospitals, was increased (Bibl. #139, 1944, Vol. v, p. 115). Contribution policy was also liberalized. In 1937 the average rate of rural funds was 5.61 per cent.

[208] Circular of February 20, 1937 (Bibl. #139, Vol. iv, p. 47); and Circular of May 3, 1937 (ibid., p. 230); Decision of September 8, 1937 (ibid., p. 351).

[209] Decree of May 4, 1938 (Bibl. #139, Vol. iv, p. 191).

[210] Decrees of June 13, 1938 (Bibl. #139, Vol. iv, p. 240); and September 4, 1939 (ibid., p. 452); Oberregierungsrat Grünewald, "Die Krankenversicherung im Kriege" (Bibl. #139, 1939, Vol. iv, pp. 508ff.).

[211] Decree of April 20, 1939 (Bibl. #140, Vol. i, p. 791); and Reichsabkommen of May 5, 1939 (Bibl. #139, Vol. v, p. 53); Orders of August 18, 1941 (Bibl. #139, Vol. ii, p. 348); March 10, 1943 (ibid., p. 129).

[212] July 24, 1941 (Bibl. #140, Vol. i, p. 443); November 4, 1941 (ibid., p. 689); November 9, 1943 (Bibl. #139, Vol. ii, p. 421).

in 1941, dues to be paid by the insurance institutions and the insured, from whose pensions 1 Rm. a month was deducted for this purpose. In consideration of citizens and "Folk Germans" "returning" to the Reich, the age limit for voluntary insurance was raised to fifty-five until one year after the war.[213]

Danger of deterioration of health caused extension of medical services in scope and duration. A great improvement was the abolition of time limits for medical assistance, comprising care by general practitioners and specialists—at first only for persons suffering from venereal disease—so long as the insured person and the member of his family needed it.[214] Hospital treatment and cash benefits were restricted as a rule to twenty-six weeks (with possible extension by rules of the fund). Medical aid could be continued beyond this time to insured persons who "according to competent medical opinion would probably become able to work within a reasonable time." For persons suffering from venereal disease, hospitalization could be granted without time limit. Pharmaceutical help for members of the family was free of charge only for venereal diseases. In the case of other diseases the funds had to pay one-half the cost of medicines but the rules of the funds could provide for payment up to 80 per cent. In April 1943 compulsory dental treatment of young people was ordered.[215] The restrictions imposed on funds by Emergency Decree not to grant more than the legally prescribed benefits were removed by law of January 15, 1941. However, the Minister of Labor was entitled to order restrictions.[216] Fees on medical certificates were removed in March 1945.

Improvements in maternity benefits were introduced in the spring of 1943. Funds were entitled to raise maternity and nursing benefits for wives and daughters of insured persons and to extend nursing benefits for these groups and the insured themselves to six months.[217] The improvements were extended to eugenically healthy needy women who were not entitled to insur-

---

[213] Sickness insurance was extended to all German employers in the occupied territories, if they employed workers in the interest of the Reich (Decree of October 26, 1939, Bibl. #140, Vol. 1, p. 2175).

[214] Erste Verordnung zur Durchführung des Gesetzes zur Bekämpfung der Geschlechtskrankheiten of November 16, 1940 (Bibl. #140, Vol. 1, p. 1514); Act of January 15, 1941 (Bibl. #140, Vol. 1, p. 34 and Bibl. #139, Vol. 11, p. 73, Grünewald); Decree of March 12, 1941 (Bibl. #140, Vol. 1, p. 128); Circular of May 20, 1941 (Bibl. #139, Vol. 11, p. 197); codified as of November 2, 1943 (Bibl. #139, Vol. 11, p. 485).

[215] Bibl. #314, April 28, 1943.

[216] Circular of February 1, 1941 (Bibl. #139, Vol. 11, p. 85).

[217] Order of February 10, 1943 (Bibl. #139, Vol. 11, p. 75).

ance benefits if they earned less than 3,600 Rm. a year (or with husband 4,200, and for every dependent, 300 more).[218] The right of insured persons and their families to obtain treatment against sterility at the expense of the fund was secured.

While on the one hand the group of persons entitled to benefits and time limits for benefits in kind were extended, control concerning the claim for benefits was tightened. Out-patient clinics, which had provided remedial and preventive care were closed. Convalescent institutions and the carrying out of preventive health measures were taken from the funds and concentrated in invalidity insurance institutions which could be more readily controlled. In spite of the pre-war boom, the average duration of sickness did not increase[219]—a fact that in itself indicated stricter control of the capacity to work. Before a patient could be declared "incapacitated" and receive sick benefits he had to be re-examined by the "confidential physician" of the fund. Oral reports confirmed the suspicion that controlling physicians were ordered to send people back to work as quickly as possible. In 1937 the Reich physicians' leader announced that in the future insured persons would have to keep for one year the physician they had chosen.[220] The Association of Insurance Practitioners wrote to its members in 1939: "It is more than ever the duty of the insurance practitioner to note immediately when a patient recovers his earning capacity and not leave the matter to be detected by the controlling physician." By law of January 15, 1941,[221] medical control examinations were decreed especially important for preventing misuse of benefits. Grants of small remedies were restricted; drugging was to be sharply controlled, and the physician bound to maximum limits. Since hospitals were to be reserved if possible for army requirements during the war, hospital treatment was granted less generously.

Since the expulsion of non-Aryans and the absorption of many doctors by the army had reduced the number of those available for the civilian popula-

[218] Decree of June 5, 1943 (Bibl. #139, Vol. v, p. 307). In 1942 a general assistance for tuberculous persons with an income below 7,200 Rm. (married 8,400, for each dependent 600 Rm. more) was introduced. All uninsured persons and their families could receive without obligation of refunding medical, hospital and curative treatment and financial assistance (Order of September 8, 1942, Bibl. #140, Vol. I, p. 549).

[219] It was 29.1 days per incapacitated person in 1932 and 21.1 in 1939 (Bibl. #153e, June 1943, p. 153). However, the percentage of sick workers increased from 30 in 1932 to 49 in 1939 without reaching the figure of 1929—58.

[220] Bibl. #111, September 24, 1939, p. 2524.

[221] Bibl. #140, Vol. I, p. 34.

tion, physicians were overwhelmed with work.[222] Lack of physicians, dentists, drugs, and medical supplies made it impossible to maintain the standards of medical services during the war. The free choice of doctors had to be restricted. The chief health office in Bremen in August 1942 urged the population of rural areas to consult a community nurse before consulting a doctor, because the latter were overburdened.[223]

The *Schwarze Korps*, the organ of the SS, published on August 17, 1944, an appeal to physicians not to certify too many vacations. "The physician can no longer creep into the snail-shell of his profession." The article demanded to have 10,000 or even half a million persons suffer to protect the life of 90 millions. Dentists were ordered in July 1944 to give only treatment vital to health, and rather to extract teeth which would require too much treatment. A decree of Goebbels (October 1944) admitted the difficulties in providing medical care for the population. He ordered military hospitals to extend their consultation services to the civilian population.[224] The National Socialist attitude against the insurance idea was expressed in a statement of Professor Bockhacker, head of the DAF's Central Office for Health and Protection of the People:[225] "The antiselection process practiced by doctors, which neglects natural selection and elimination, has had an even worse effect than equalization. A considerable percentage of people—asocial and loafers—use the extensive medical care customary for all comrades without deserving it. Consequently the insurance ideal in social insurance must be replaced by the idea of maintenance, that is everyone who has done his duty toward the people's community will be provided for. The extent of aid is not to be determined by some scheme of equalization but by the extent of the person's achievements."

2. INVALIDITY, OLD AGE AND SURVIVORS' INSURANCE

There was less extension of invalidity, old age, and survivors' than of sickness insurance. Voluntary insurance was made possible for all citizens up to the fortieth year. However, little use was made of it. The first reforms brought reduction of benefits in contradiction to promises made by the

---

[222] One writer claims that the controlling physicians had to examine up to 150 persons a day (Bibl. #195, p. 59).
[223] *Bremer Nachrichten*, August 18, 1942.
[224] Bibl. #283, October 7, 1944.
[225] Bibl. #271, May 7, 1944.

regime that old age provisions would be considerably raised. All future pensions were reduced by an average 7 per cent by law of December 7, 1933.[226] A member in the fourth wage class, to which many male farm workers belonged, received a pension of 151.20 Rm. a year (formerly 216 Rm.), after 250 weeks. Widows' pensions which continued to be five-tenths and orphans four-tenths of the pension to which the deceased was or would have been entitled in case of invalidity were reduced in the same proportion.[227]

Pensions could be suspended if the beneficiary had engaged in any activities hostile to the state after January 30, 1933.[228]

The Act of December 1937 brought some improvements which intended to promote marriages, to favor large families and to prevent losses to persons serving in the forces or the labor service. Women wage earners became entitled—as hitherto only salaried employees had been—to claim repayment of one-half of their contributions in case of marriage. Widows of wage earners, even if not invalid, became entitled to widows' pensions if they had to care for more than three children. Orphans of manual workers could receive pensions until their eighteenth year.[229] Allowances for children of invalidity and old age pensioners and pensioners of workmen's compensation could be extended similarly. For large families children's allowances were increased. Even after the improvements, benefits at the outbreak of the war were still below the 1932 level.

During the war it was ruled that time spent in military and labor service was to be counted without obligation to pay dues, pensions were calculated as if the average contributions for the three months preceding mobilization had been paid during their military service in war time. For farm workers it was favorable that insured persons who were not paid in cash or were

---

[226] Bibl. #140, Vol. I, p. 1039; and Order of May 17, 1934 (ibid., Vol. I, p. 419).

[227] Bibl. #139, 1933, No. 36, Vol. IV, Appendix, p. 11. Moreover, the financial reorganization, drawn up in 1933 and carried out in 1937—with unemployment insurance subsidizing invalidity insurance—extended the qualifying period from 750 to 780 weeks in case of old age; from 250 to 260 for invalidity insurance; from 500 to 520 for voluntarily insured, with a minimum contribution of twenty-six weeks a year (Act of December 21, 1937, Bibl. #140, Vol. I, p. 1393).

[228] Act of December 23, 1936 (Bibl. #140, Vol. I, p. 1128, Section 8). A clause in the law of December 7, 1933 hinted to a stricter definition of invalidity in physical examinations. The Order of May 17, 1934 provided that a pensioner, who without cause refused to undergo a subsequent examination or observation, could be deprived temporarily of his pension, provided he had been warned of this consequence.

[229] Act of April 19, 1939 (Bibl. #140, Vol. I, p. 793). Further improvements concerned persons entitled to two kinds of benefits at once, such as workmen's compensation and invalidity benefits.

earning only very low wages or who were at the beginning of their working life were deemed to have paid their contribution in the second, not in the lower wage class.[230] No claims were forfeited during the war, owing to lack of payment of dues. Invalidity benefits were no longer discontinued when the recipient became gainfully active.

In the case of insured persons who died as soldiers during the war or became disabled by a war injury in the forces, the qualifying period was deemed to have been completed.

Pensions were increased in 1941[231] and 1942.[232] The increase in 1941 amounted to 7 Rm. a month for invalidity and old age pensions, 5 for widow(er)s, and 4 Rm. for orphans. After the increase pensioners received about the same amounts as in 1932 with considerably lower purchasing power. Those whose benefits had been fixed after January 1, 1934, continued to get the lower amounts.

In 1942 children's allowances of invalidity, old age insurance, and workmen's compensation were raised to the rate already in force for the third child and the following (120 Rm.). However, the increase was to be granted only for future pensions, not retroactively. Another slight improvement entitled a woman worker or a worker's widow to receive a pension at the time of the death of her husband if she was maintaining four or more children, or two under the age of six years, who were entitled to orphan pensions; or at the age of fifty-five, if she had borne four living children. Divorced wives could receive a survivor's pension with the permit of the Ministry of Labor, if the deceased husband had been obliged to pay alimony. It goes without saying that racial and hereditary soundness became principles of selection for curative treatment.

In order to counteract the mental depression which seized the people when they realized that the war would not be over in a short time, universal old age pensions were promised for the postwar period. According to an announcement of the government, old age insurance was to be replaced after the war by a scheme for general old age assistance. The existing contributory scheme was attacked by Dr. Ley in articles in *Angriff* on the ground that "under it pensions are paid according to the number of contributions and not with welfare as the criterion" and that "the single person gets

---

[230] Decree of October 13, 1939 (Bibl. #140, Vol. I, p. 2030); Act of January 15, 1941 (*ibid.*, p. 34); and Order of October 8, 1941 (Bibl. #139, Vol. II, p. 413).

[231] Act of July 24, 1941 (Bibl. #140, Vol. I, p. 443).

[232] Act of June 19, 1942 (Bibl. #140, Vol. I, p. 407); Order of June 22, 1942 (*ibid.*, p. 411).

the same pension for a given number of contributions as the father of a family who has greater responsibilities." Contributions, he urged, should be abolished. In the new scheme everyone who had done his duty to the community would be guaranteed a pension at the age of sixty-five. The amount was to suffice to secure a standard of living "natural for a German," but would not make saving unnecessary. There would be no differentiation according to former occupation or income. The pensions were to be financed out of general taxation and, as a grant of the state, "the only way of realizing a socialistic folk community." It was supposed to absorb about 10 per cent of the national income. A special honor bonus would be paid to war invalids and accident-injured persons.[233]

A similar assistance was to be paid to people incapacitated at a younger age by accident or other reasons, or who were prevented from working (mothers, for instance), and for widows and orphans.[234]

Such a scheme would have swept away all independent rights to a pension. It would have been a reward for National Socialist behavior. "Enemies of the state are excluded from the plan," wrote Ley. "The plan does not apply to the unsocial minority." The realization of the plan was promised "after victory and after the destruction of the moloch of capitalism."

3. WORKMEN'S COMPENSATION

In Workmen's Compensation, reforms concerned mainly extension to new groups. By Act of February 17, 1939,[235] coverage was extended to all categories of employed persons, including employees in agriculture, the labor service,[236] the Land Year,[237] the RN. Accidents caused by the war were covered if the connection with occupation, work place, or traveling between home and working place was given. Pensions were slightly raised and employers entitled to take over additional payments to pensions of insured workers and survivors.[238] The cuts of the Emergency Decree of June 1932 (by $7\frac{1}{2}$ and 15 per cent) were abolished from January 1942 on. Pensions for widows with more than two children were increased by raising the maximum of total survivors' pensions from two-thirds to four-fifths of the

---

[233] Bibl. #324, November 25, 1940.
[234] Bibl. #346, February 13, 1942.
[235] Bibl. #140, Vol. 1, p. 267; and Act of March 9, 1942 (*ibid.*, p. 107); Act of March 9, 1942 (*ibid.*, p. 107). Sixteen million pensions were covered in 1939.
[236] Bibl. #139, 1942, Vol. v, p. 336.
[237] Act of March 9, 1942 (Bibl. #140, Vol. 1, p. 107).
[238] Circular of February 11, 1943 (Bibl. #139, Vol. 1, p. 66).

yearly income of the deceased. Annual earnings were to be assessed (for all accidents occurring after December 31, 1942),[239] by appointed committees, composed of employers and insured persons, for groups according to occupation, sex, and marital state for the whole Reich simultaneously for the duration of four years.[240] Collective rules were to be taken into account. The average annual compensation in 1938 amounted to 155 Rm. for injured persons and 198 for survivors.[241] For war invalids the possibility of inclusion in workmen's compensation was improved in order to induce them to return to work. They could be insured even if more than 60 per cent incapacitated.[242] It may be mentioned as a curiosity that the Federal Insurance Board decided that pensions were not to be suspended during a stay of the pensioner in a concentration camp. It shows the dual character of the National Socialist state—on the one hand an institution which intended to eliminate persons through torture, on the other hand the old bureaucracy dealing with such cases on the basis of legality.

A general People's Accident Insurance (Volksunfallversicherung) was announced in 1943,[243] to be carried through by private associations as "community enterprise" (Gemeinschaftswerk) as soon as the war situation permitted. The new insurance was to have only two premiums, one for family insurance, the other for individual insurance, without gradation according to occupational danger.

4. SUMMARY

A deterioration of social insurance in the beginning was followed by improvements, especially after the outbreak of the war. Up to that time, the predepression level of benefits had not been reached. When during the

---

[239] Order of November 13, 1942 (Bibl. #140, Vol. I, p. 657).

[240] Circular of July 21, 1943 (Bibl. #139, Vol. II, p. 355).

[241] "60 Jahre reichsgesetzliche Unfallversicherung" (Bibl. #153e, 1944, No. 6, p. 108).

[242] In the course of the orders of the plenipotentiary for the total war effect, workmen's compensation was simplified by Order of November 9, 1944 (Bibl. #140, Vol. I, p. 324). Only accidents causing more than seven days' (heretofore three) incapacity to work had to be reported. Fatal accidents were to be reported to the police if either the employer or the family of the injured worker so desired. Appeals were limited to cases where the decision might affect the war effort (Order of November 9, 1944, Bibl. #140, Vol. I, p. 324).

[243] Bibl. #324, December 2, 1942. A monthly contribution of 1 Rm. (family, 1.50) was to guarantee lump sums of 1,000 Rm. in case of death, 5,000 Rm. of full invalidity and in case of partial invalidity a proportional sum. 3,000 Rm. were to be paid in case of invalidity or death of the wife, 1,000 Rm. in case of death and 1,000 Rm. of invalidity of a child. No daily benefits were to be paid. It was to cover traveling, motor car, and other trips.

war the health of the population became a matter of deep concern, measures were taken which tended to efface the distinction between insurance and assistance, and to bring groups of the noninsured population under similar care as the insured. Medical care was extended so as to cover a large part of the population for longer periods. Accident insurance was made general, and a scheme announced to make private insurance available to the common man. "Social insurance has been freed from its business character," said the Minister of Labor.[244] The pension system announced for the old was to cover the whole population, abandoning the insurance principle.

However, while the system broadened in scope and in duration, controls were tightened. Necessities of the labor market influenced the decisions of physicians concerning capacity to work. The great deprivation of labor remained the loss of the right of self-government. Dissatisfaction of the population with the increasing red tape and bureaucracy caused the government repeatedly to admonish the administration not to forget the insured himself in the mass of legal regulations. "Merely formal considerations of law (Rechtsbedenken) should by no means result in cutting off or curtailing justified claims of the insured."[245] "It is not feasible to refuse a claim for formal legal reasons if the law in understanding interpretation could admit a favorable solution. . . . The first question to be examined is whether the claim of the insured could not be fulfilled according to National Socialist principles in the frame of the law."[246] A report of the DAF mentioned criticism of the controlling physicians which according to the DAF could be due to the difficulties of their task, as the Minister of Labor claimed, or to lack of fit physicians.[247]

Some of the measures, as the loss of a fortnight's right under health insurance[248] in case of absenteeism and the announcement of the old age

[244] Bibl. #278, July 30, 1944.

[245] Circular of the Federal Insurance Board of July 30, 1941 (Bibl. #139, Vol. 11, p. 311).

[246] Circular of May 16, 1942 (Bibl. #139, Vol. 11, p. 313).

[247] Bibl. #176, January 1, 1938 to December 31, 1938, p. 218. The attitude of the administration was of great importance since by Order of October 26, 1943 (Bibl. #140, Vol. 1, p. 581), preceded by Order of October 28, 1939 (ibid., p. 2110), appeals against decisions of the insurance boards became possible only if the latter admitted them because of the importance or doubtfulness of the case. The insured was allowed to present only one medical certificate while authorities could present several. The abolition of hearings made the insured dependent on the written briefs of the local advisory bodies of the DAF.

[248] Bibl. #346, February 13, 1942.

pension scheme show that the government intended to abandon the insurance character, i.e. the legal claim of the worker in favor of an assistance scheme.

Housing

In the first year of the regime construction of farm workers' dwellings was neglected because building for rearmament and construction of party buildings was considered to be of greater importance. Just as during the depression, money was allocated in 1933 for repairs, extensions, conversion of houses into smaller dwellings,[249] and the construction of own homes. When the government realized that lack of housing induced young workers who intended to marry either to migrate to cities or refrain from marrying, the Reifa became empowered to provide subsidies from unemployment insurance funds.[250] A subsidy of 300 Rm. for six years each, a total of 1,800 Rm., could be given to build houses for additionally employed[251] married workers with one-year contracts or for retiring workers whose former dwelling was freed for active workers. These sums proved too small. Construction costs of a dwelling amounted to about 3,600 Rm. and farmers could not afford to provide the lacking 1,800 Rm. although they were entitled to deduct from income tax returns any sums spent on the construction of agricultural workers' dwellings.

All methods proved inadequate. The shortage of dwellings for agricultural workers at the end of 1937 according to the RN amounted to 350,000.[252] In July 1937 the RN complained that due to lack of housing only 30 per cent of farm workers in marriageable age were married.[253] Hence, the Commissioner of the Four-Year Plan, in order to stimulate housing and relieve the finances of the Reich, took a new line. By Decree of March 10, 1937,[254] the Prussian

---

[249] Law for the reduction of unemployment of June 1, 1933 (Bibl. #140, Vol. 1, p. 323) newly formulated on January 24, 1935 (*ibid.*, p. 471); and September 11 (Bibl. #139, Vol. 1, p. 232). Law of September 21, 1933 (Bibl. #140, Vol. 1, p. 651). Decree of March 9, 1940 (Bibl. #139, Vol. 1, p. 139); reformulated June 25, 1941 (*ibid.*, Vol. 1, p. 303); March 27, 1940 (*ibid.*, Vol. 1, p. 170); September 8, 1941 (*ibid.*, Vol. 1, p. 388).

[250] Orders of August 10, 1934 (Bibl. #140, Vol. 1, p. 786); August 28, 1934 (Bibl. #139, Vol. 1, p. 202); January 2, 1935 (*ibid.*, Vol. 1, p. 15); April 28, 1935 (*ibid.*, Vol. 1, p. 144); and March 18, 1937 (*ibid.*, Vol. 1, p. 84).

[251] The condition "additionally employed" was dropped in 1937, Order of December 6 (Bibl. #139, Vol. 1, p. 328).

[252] Klaus Thiede, "Landflucht und Arbeitsordnung auf dem Lande," Bibl. #329, 1939, Vol. 3, p. 8. 15,800 new homes were built, 7,600 rebuilt up to the spring of 1938 (Franz Seldte, Bibl. #249, p. 187; and Bibl. #310, 1938, Vol. 1, p. 349).

[253] Bibl. #291, October 1937, B, p. 13.

[254] Bibl. #140, Vol. 1, p. 292 and many ordinances, especially August 4, 1937 (Bibl. #139, Vol. 1, p. 289). The total monthly expenses for work dwellings amounted to 12-16 Rm., for own homes 20-23 Rm. (Werner Mansfeld, "Der Wohnungsbau für

State Agricultural Mortgage Bank (Landesrentenbank) was empowered to grant special long-term loans for the construction and equipment of rental dwellings and own houses for Heuerlings, farm laborers, and rural craftsmen "of good hereditary health and political reliability."[255] Alienation, sale, borrowing on mortgages and division of own homes erected with such government means was subject to approval of the authority.

On April 1, 1939, the periodical of the DAF wrote that housing for farm workers had been a failure since the owners for the most part were unable to provide the sums they had to contribute.[256] Dwellings constructed did not even suffice to cover the current need and did not compensate for the great deficit piled up in the past. Moreover, workers who migrated to industry frequently remained in the dwelling, although the Ministry of Interior in 1938 provided that the local authorities could compel persons to quit who used dwellings on farm premises without being connected with the undertaking.[257] However, the courts fixed long evacuation terms.[258] Families of soldiers called up for war service could stay in the dwelling if they needed it. Many collective rules contained clauses restricting lodging to minor children and other persons the worker was obliged to support.

When, by Order of August 4, 1939, a housing construction freeze was ordered for all buildings over 5,000 Rm., exceptions in the interest of agri-

---

Landarbeiter," Bibl. #345, April 1937, p. 211). Taxes were reduced. A worker's dwelling amounting to 7,500 Rm. without land (1941, 9,000 Rm.) was financed as follows:

	1939	1941
Bank loan (85 per cent of 7,000 Rm.)	5,900 Rm.	5,800 Rm.
Subsidy of the Reich	600	2,500
Own Capital	1,000	700
Total	7,500	9,000

Source: Bibl. #139, 1939, Vol. 1, p. 275 and 1941, Vol. 1, p. 285.

[255] The Reich Homestead Law was amended to guarantee that homesteads would be given only to citizens, with preference to fighters for National Socialism and families with many children (Law of November 24 and 25, Bibl. #140, 1937, Vol. 1, pp. 1289, 1291).

[256] Bibl. #272, p. 17. From October 1937 to October 1, 1938, 3,000 dwellings had been built with those loans; 7,346 were under construction. Permits had been granted for a total number of 13,383 up to that date (Seldte, Bibl. #249, p. 186). The Kölnische Zeitung (Bibl. #314) of February 20, 1943 gave the figures of 27,308 approvals as to October 1, 1942. When bombing began, all housing plans had to be dropped in favor of the construction of emergency bungalows for bombed out people. These bungalows were small wooden huts without sanitation, gas, or electricity.

[257] Circular of April 23, 1938 (Bibl. #139, Vol. 1, p. 264). It was estimated that 10,000 to 12,000 dwellings could be freed in this way (Staatssekretär Backe in Der Vierjahresplan, Bibl. #345, January 1939, p. 115).

[258] Otto Betz, "Die Frage der Räumungsfristen bei Landarbeiterwerkwohnungen," Bibl. #290, October 7, 1939, p. 1780.

cultural production were to be permitted[259] if only a little iron and wood were to be used. Later permits and loans were given to repair and rebuild houses damaged by air-raid bombardments.[260] Subsidies granted for repair of farm workers' dwellings were restricted to families with at least three children in 1943.[261]

It was not only that housing facilities were badly lacking: a large number of workers' dwellings should have been demolished, others needed repair. The trustees of labor used pressure in inserting in collective rules the clause that housing had to fulfill all requirements of health and decency and in threatening to take action against farmers who did not comply.[262] Reform became still more necessary in the incorporated former Polish provinces in which the standards had been lower than in Germany proper. Thus the collective rules for the Wartheland[263] prescribed that a dwelling had to have at least one room and kitchen, doors, unbroken window panes, and a roof which did not leak. Further stipulations were that planks of the well should not be rotten; manure had to be at least twenty metres away from the house.[264] When conditions remained desperate, the government in 1940 promised a great housing program, to be started after the war. A Decree of the Führer of November 15, 1940,[265] announced the principles of the program. Social housing was to be a matter of the Reich, promoted by government subsidies whenever private funds were not sufficient. Rents were to be brought down to a bearable level.[266] Farm workers' dwellings were to receive special attention in the program. Dwellings were to be provided for biologically valuable,

[259] Circulars of February 16, 1940 (Bibl. #139, Vol. I, pp. 109, 110); Circular, December 22, 1939 (ibid., p. 48); Circular of August 29, 1940, gave direction for rural construction (ibid., p. 477).

[260] Decrees of Minister of Labor of July 10, August 7, 1942 (Bibl. #297, July 31, 1942).

[261] Order of March 8, 1943 (Bibl. #286, 1 Juniheft 1943, No. 16, p. 517).

[262] Bibl. #338, July 9, 1937, pp. 283ff.; November 1, 1938, pp. 1317ff.; and Bibl. #310, 1938, Vol. I, pp. 398ff. Social Honor Courts were supposed to help in the improvement of housing conditions by punishing farmers who offered unhealthy, unsatisfactory dwellings. A few judgments imposed fines and severer punishments for such reasons (May 27, 1935, Bibl. #274, XXIV, p. 113; March 22, 1937, ibid., XXX, p. 110, and many more). On January 9, 1935 the Deputy of the Führer decreed "the Reich Peasant Leader is willing after examination of the economic situation to deprive unsocial peasants who in spite of economic capacity have their workers live in undignified dwellings of their capacity to be peasant" (Bibl. #310, 1938, p. 399).

[263] Bibl. #139, 1940, No. 3, Vol. IV, p. 82.

[264] Special grants were given for the improvement and repair of housing in the frontier and newly conquered districts.

[265] Bibl. #140, Vol. I, p. 1495.

[266] Circular of the Minister of Interior of January 16, 1941 (Bibl. #334, Vol. IV, p. 96). Ley was appointed Commissioner of the future housing program and the district leaders commissioners for their respective districts.

politically dependable families with many children or procreative faculties. This postwar program, in fact, was the realization that not enough had been done and that to bolster morale something more had to be promised. The discrepancy between National Socialist promises and achievements proved that even a totalitarian regime was unable to solve a problem which the Weimar Republic, hampered by inflation, deflation, financial dependency, and economic depression, could not handle efficiently.

Welfare Work

Welfare work changed its character completely according to the Hitler word: "If you want to live, you must fight for it; and if you refuse to do so in this world of ceaseless fighting, you do not deserve to live."[267] Distress was no longer attributed to economic circumstances; therefore, the aim of welfare work was no longer to correct these circumstances, but to eradicate the racially and politically undesirable, to penalize the weak, and to bolster the strong. "We are intended to be active fighters and not passive sufferers."[268] "The National Socialist state is not a pampered nursery home."[269] Therefore, the work "is principally confined to those who are congenitally sound in health and who are potentially useful members of the community."[270] "It does not give hopeless care which wastes the national wealth on those who are eugenically sick, but cares constructively for those who are eugenically sound."[271]

How many mercy killings which began in 1940 in order to free hospital facilities and food and by what means they were achieved, only the Gestapo knew.[272] The sudden death of many inmates of insane asylums stirred especially the rural population with its conservatism and church loyalty. Insane, aged, physically incurable were "relieved of the burden of life."

[267] Quoted by Erich Hilgenfeldt, "The National Socialist Welfare Organization and the Winter Help Scheme," Bibl. #187, p. 204.

[268] *Ibid.*, pp. 204-05.

[269] Bruno Rauecker (Bibl. #233), p. 36.

[270] Werner Reher (Bibl. #234), p. 8.

[271] Hermann Althaus (Bibl. #303b, II, No. 2), p. 17.

[272] A protest letter of Pastor Braune numbers those whose extermination was considered desirable at 1 million (Alexander Mitscherlich and Fred Mielke, Bibl. #222, p. 107). The final figure of residents of such institutions who were killed was estimated at 200,000. It remained smaller than intended because the leaders of the heads of several religious institutions resisted successfully (*Neuer Westfälischer Kurier*, September 9, 1947). When the pressure of public opinion put an official stop to enforced killings for medical reasons, extermination was based on political and racial criteria.

Physically or mentally defective persons were sterilized.[273] Other infirm people were cared for by denominational institutions which, in order to provide this care, had not been destroyed. The National Socialists detested it, but were afraid of creating centers of epidemics.

The public welfare laws of the Democratic regime were changed only in minor issues. The existing machinery was used without essential transformation, and yet public welfare changed fundamentally in procedure, in motivation, and direction. It was administered not by democratically appointed officers and elected delegates, but by the National Socialist bureaucracy, assisted by appointed counselors. The authorities cooperated, not as formerly with private free welfare organizations, but as with a party institution. Youth welfare was given a different direction by new educational aims. Health welfare was directed toward improving hereditary health. Public welfare was considered not as the first line of help but as the last resort when all other possibilities of private help had failed. The National Socialists declared that one of the fundamental mistakes of the democratic regime was that it had done too much by way of public welfare. Of the former elaborate system of public relief, the National Socialists were interested only in public health and even here prevailingly in eugenics. They improved the care for tuberculous persons and those with venereal diseases. Most other reforms concerned the protection of health by eugenic measures such as marriage consent,[274] for which institutions were established outside the public welfare authorities.

Youth welfare was largely delegated to party agencies such as the Hitler Youth, the League of German Girls, the military formations, since all-em-

[273] Gesetz zur Verhütung des erbkranken Nachwuchses of July 14, 1933 (Bibl. #140, Vol. I, p. 529); amended June 25, 1935 (*ibid.*, Vol. I, p. 773); and February 4, 1936 (*ibid.*, Vol. I, p. 119). Sterilization was stopped by Circular of September. 6, 1944 (*ibid.*, Vol. I, p. 293). However, experiments with sterilization by drugs and X-rays were continued on concentration camp inmates (Mitscherlich and Mielke, *op.cit.*, p. 132ff.).

[274] The rules concerning prohibition of marriage of hereditary unsound persons were never enforced. However, many persons (38 per cent of those who married in 1938) acquired a certificate of hereditary health from the centers for genetic and racial care because they wanted marriage loans. Only 8-9 per cent sought marriage consultation voluntarily ("Der öffentliche Gesundheitsdienst im Deutschen Reich 1938," quoted by Hedwig Wachenheim, Bibl. #263, pp. 21-22). In 1944 the public health offices were ordered to cooperate in a marriage exchange center of the Race Political Office of the NSDAP. The center stimulated correspondence between boys and girls to initiate marriages. The health office had to examine the candidates before they were admitted to the center (Bibl. #346, July 28, 1944, p. 2854).

bracing political indoctrination and military training became their aims. Public and private agencies lost their educational functions. Educational experiments, which the Democratic government had started with children of antisocial behavior, were abolished. The Division of Youth of the National Socialist Welfare Organization assumed the leadership in the remaining non-governmental work. The main legal changes were the introduction of punishment of minor delinquencies of juveniles, reduction of the age limit for juvenile delinquency from fourteen to twelve. Corporal punishment was reintroduced.

General relief was considerably reduced, partly through the abolition of unemployment, partly through the annihilation of unemployables.[275] Until 1942 relief rates were kept on the depression level in spite of the rise in the cost of living; the rates were already called insufficient before the price freeze made increases impossible.[276] As of January 1942 some rates were raised by 15 per cent.[277] However, rates were only directives (Richtsätze) which could be above or below actually paid rates. According to Directives for Genetic Examinations, issued in 1940,[278] families were classified according to their eugenic and social value for the existence and growth of the folk community. The lowest, with antisocial behavior, was excluded from relief. The next lowest, with hereditary diseases, was excluded from marriage loans and children's allowances. The resulting "average" group was entitled to all kinds of grants and allowances and to 15 per cent higher rates of relief (erweiterte gehobene Fürsorge). This regulation created three categories of relief: those who received the old basic rate, those with higher rates, and those receiving the new higher rates. A fourth rate (125 per cent of the new higher rate) and additional advantages were granted to needy war invalids and survivors, social insurance pensioners, and inflation victims.[279]

An innovation was the frequent delegation of investigations to party institutions. Applications of needy persons for public help, guardians, homes for foster children, children reported to criminal courts were frequently not investigated by public social workers but by National Socialist agencies.

[275] The figures for those who received public non-institutional relief were reduced from 1933 to 1939 by 74.8 per cent (Bibl. #153e, 1940, No. 24, p. 552); for those receiving institutional care from 1932 to 1938 by 17.5 per cent.

[276] Hellmut Stadelmann (Bibl. #322).

[277] Hedwig Wachenheim (Bibl. #262), p. 11.

[278] Richtlinien zur Beurteilung der Erbgesundheit of July 18, 1940 (Bibl. #334, p. 1519), quoted by Wachenheim, ibid., pp. 16-17.

[279] Wachenheim, op.cit., pp. 17ff. War invalids received pensions based on the degree of restriction of capacity to work.

While public welfare work was curtailed and the old private organization, insofar as it was not dissolved, came under party jurisdiction, a National Socialist organization was created which was given almost a monopoly in charity work: The National Socialist Welfare Organization (Nationalsozialistische Volkswohlfahrt, NSV).[280] The NSV was made a head organization (Spitzenverband) beside the nation-wide Catholic, Protestant, and Red Cross organizations.[281] Other private organizations were either dissolved or made subcommittees of the NSV. Private organizations that were allowed to continue were not only deprived of public grants they had received formerly but of the right to collect money, food, and clothing.[282] The two Christian organizations were practically restricted to institutional care or care for those who were excluded from public welfare because they were physically or mentally not fitted for the new race. The Red Cross cared for army needs in war time.[283] It maintained hospitals and recreation homes and trained nurses and nurses' aids. Many of the former denominational hospitals, nurseries, kindergartens, were dissolved or withdrawn from the influence of the church and put under party leadership. The NSV appropriated a vast number of services and institutions of the other organizations. It assisted the public authorities by taking care of "valuable" needy persons or by supple-

[280] The NSV, founded in 1932, was established by Decree of the Führer of May 3, 1933 (Bibl. #322, p. 38) as the official party organization for all questions appertaining to social welfare. The administrative Order of March 29, 1935 (Bibl. #140, Vol. 1, p. 502) declared it an association affiliated to the party. Its offices were party bureaus. The NSV was built up according to the organization of the party in blocks, cells, local, county, and district groups. There were 21,619 local groups and 271,487 blocks in 1937 (Josef Zimmermann, Bibl. #270, p. 27). Its chief was Hauptamtsleiter Erich Hilgenfeldt, an officer of World War I, who was subordinated to the Reich Organization Leader and the Treasurer of the party in matters of organization and finance and to the leader of the Party Chancellor in matters of discipline and philosophy (ibid., p. 34).

Membership in the NSV was "voluntary"; however, pressure to join was used in house-to-house canvassing by threat of loss of jobs. Party circulars declared that those who did not join consciously placed themselves outside the folk community (Bibl. #291, December 1935, A, pp. 62-63). Those who tried to leave were accused of sabotage. Similar pressure was used for subscriptions to its periodical, Ewiges Deutschland (ibid., September 1937, A, pp. 88-89). Benefits were refused to those who had not become members of the organization. In April 1937 it claimed a membership of 6,886,000 (Werner Reher, op.cit., pp. 6, 12).

[281] Decree of July 25, 1933 (Bibl. #334, Vol. 1, pp. 977-78).

[282] Collections were regulated by Act of November 5, 1934 (Bibl. #140, Vol. 1, p. 1068) and by Decree of September 7, 1939 (Bibl. #334, p. 1876, b) which made them dependent on permission of the public authorities, except those of the NSDAP, its structural parts and financially affiliated associations.

[283] The Law of December 9, 1937 (Bibl. #140, Vol. 1, p. 1330) made the Red Cross in fact a National Socialist organization under the protectorate of the Führer.

menting grants. Clients of the public welfare departments were frequently placed in NSV institutions.[284]

In addition to assistance of this kind the NSV had its own work, devoted prevailingly to the maintenance of the health of the population. Main social projects were the Assistance to Mother and Child (Hilfswerk Mutter und Kind) and the Recreational Work of the German People (Erholungswerk des Deutschen Volks).

The rural population participated in the latter insofar as peasants became obliged, frequently through strong party pressure,[285] to take in city children without pay, especially when evacuation became necessary for regions endangered by bombing. Some "loyal" farm workers or wives with many children or widows of workers who died in the war were sent to health resorts.

Assistance to mother and child comprised many activities for racially sound expectant mothers and those with children.[286] Except for some help to tubercular mothers, not the sick mothers received help, but those who could be useful to the state; not the infirm child, but the hereditarily healthy child. The project supplied prenatal and maternal advice, given chiefly by nurses in local consultation centers, money, clothing, food, and recreation. Care for youth who could be expected to become valuable members of the community was made the monopoly of the NSV in 1941.[287]

While the cities received the predominant share of most of the welfare work, the country participated in another institution established to make it

[284] The NSV, with its own school of administration and training school for child nurses and for nurses, supplemented the professional staffs of health and child welfare offices by newly trained visiting nurses—all loyal National Socialists. Subordinated to it were a Society of Free Nurses and Nurses' Aides (Reichsbund der freien Schwestern und Pflegerinnen) which replaced more and more denominational nurses in hospitals by party nurses, and an NS Sisterhood (Schwesternschaft) which provided health workers. In some districts public welfare nurses and family social workers were replaced by NSV nurses. Both organizations of nurses were merged in 1942. Besides 34,000 professional nurses, 7,500 kindergarten workers and about 78,500 other paid employees the NSV claimed 1,150,000 volunteer helpers.

[285] Bibl. #291, September 1937, A, pp. 104ff.

[286] Care for babies and their mothers was made over exclusively to the NSV by Decree of October 20, 1941 (Bibl. #334, p. 1900). Public health offices had to yield their infant centers to the NSV. The authority provided examinations; the NSV supervised the treatment through nurses and voluntary helpers. Every baby during its first year was under the supervision of a midwife who was obliged to visit the babies assigned to her by the NSV once a fortnight during the first six weeks, later at least once a month. After one year the supervision passed to a nurse of the NSV (Bibl. #297, January 21, 1943).

[287] The Decree of October 24, 1941 (Bibl. #334, p. 1897) enumerated the functions of the NSV.

possible for mothers to work. All over the country kindergartens and day nurseries were established, amounting in September 1939 to 11,000.[288] About 5,000 of them were harvest kindergartens, with 150,000 openings. Girls of the Labor Service and school children of the League of German Girls helped.

Another party assistance, the Winter Help (Winterhilfswerk des Deutschen Volkes)[289] headed by Hitler, supervised by the Minister of Propaganda, carried through by the Party Office for National Welfare, differed in its organization from all previous institutions in the methods of raising its funds as well as in the type of work done and the aims of the work.

Funds were provided through extra-legal compulsory taxation under party control. The worker had to pay a tax deducted from his pay envelope; farms were assessed according to size to pay contributions. A second type of income was provided by street collections, carried on every Sunday by helpers drawn from different groups: one week party officials paraded the streets with their boxes; the next week actors; then leading representatives of science and art; last, but not least, the school children. Each group tried to surpass the others by utilizing publicity and pressure. These collections were public shows in which children were provided free rides; actors sold their autographs in addition to the badges offered for sale. In addition, money saved by "one-dish dinners" which every household and restaurant had to serve one Sunday a month was donated to the fund. The restaurant received the price of a full meal while serving one dish and delivered the difference to the Winter Help. "This margin is stipulated according to a definite schedule."[290] A lottery was held, selling chances for 50 pfennigs each in restaurants and streets. In spite of ill-will toward this begging, the farmer contributed from his farm produce, housewives had to buy food parcels for the Winter Help, clothes were collected on a large scale and repaired in sewing circles, peasants who refused to deliver potatoes were put under arrest.

The Winter Help received in 1939-1940 681 million Rm. through these means, to which must be added 221 million for the Red Cross and 124 million Rm. for the NSV.[291]

---

[288] Bibl. #153e, 1941, No. 4, p. 71. At the end of 1939 Mother and Child employed 25,000 paid and 3,000 volunteer helpers. There were 7,211 harvest kindergartens for 280,000 children in the summer of 1941 (*Neue Deutsche Zeitung*, July 15, 1942).

[289] Bibl. #140, Vol. I, p. 995; and Decree of March 24, 1937 (*ibid.*, Vol. I, p. 423).

[290] Reher, *op.cit.*, p. 20.

[291] Bibl. #139, 1940, Vol. v, p. 461. In 1942 the income increased by 35 per cent above the previous year to 1.21 billion Rm. 36 per cent of the income represented deduction from salaries and wages at the source. An accounting was never *given of*

Out of this fund needy persons were supposed to get money, food, and clothing. A circular of September 27, 1937, mentioned as groups to be considered among others families of soldiers, seamen, war veterans, survivors of war victims, old people, land helpers, students, migrants, seasonal workers.[292] The card index of indigent persons recorded party membership. There were complaints about unjust distribution.[293]

A by-product of the visits of helpers in private households was the control exercised by the party. The friendly messenger was obliged to see to it that nobody was shirking. In rural districts especially those had to be watched who did not take part in harvest work.[294] Needless to say, all opportunities were used to instill the beneficiaries with the National Socialist world outlook and to check their party loyalty.

In general, National Socialist welfare work functioned in a dual way. Even before the war the NS charity organizations became more and more occupied with helping in the war autarky program by collections of kitchen refuse and clothing, fattening of pigs, etc. During the war their services were concentrated prevailingly on war work, such as distribution of ration cards, evacuation of women and children, providing shelter and food for the bombed out population, cultivation of victory gardens in the conquered

---

how these large sums were used. They amounted to a total of 5,296 million Rm. in nine years at the end of 1942 (Bibl. #297, January 31, 1943). The population believed that much of the money was used for army and party purposes and much squandered. According to official statements the following expenditures were made:

	1936-1937	1939-1940	1940-1941
		(in 1,000 Rm.)	
Benefits in kind	321,843	208,821	289,362
New East territory		26,174	
Mother and Child			
and Reich Mother Service	545,597	353,451	571,320
Health Service	3,000	15,700	20,000
Red Cross and other			
welfare associations	16,500	9,819	3,610
Hitler Youth		2,500	2,750
Operating costs	7,383	25,447	29,127
Total	408,323	641,912	916,169

Source for 1936-1937: Bibl. #153e, 1937, No. 4, p. 700.
Source for 1939-1940: *Ibid.*, 1941, No. 4, p. 71.
Source for 1940-1941: *Ibid.*, 1941, No. 19, p. 370.

[292] Bibl. #291, 1938, No. 1, A, pp. 81-82; Zimmermann, *op.cit.*, p. 106.
[293] Bibl. #291, December 1935, A, p. 54.
[294] Bibl. #345, March 23, 1939, p. 483.

east, and establishment of harvest kindergartens.[295] On the other hand, functions which formerly belonged to public authorities, or to public youth and health offices, were made over to the party agencies. Thus taxes formerly raised for these purposes could be used for war preparation, while unofficial taxation was used for providing welfare money. Welfare work had become a political tool for the specific purposes of the National Socialist state.

[295] According to the Völkischer Beobachter (Bibl. #346) of January 1, 1943, about twenty new fields were taken up by the NSV during the war.

CHAPTER IV

THE LABOR MARKET CONTROL

THE CONTROL of the labor supply for agriculture cannot be isolated from the general labor market policy because it was deeply influenced by urban unemployment in the first period, and by the needs of war preparation and warfare in the following periods. Three stages may be distinguished: (1) the battle against unemployment, 1933-1934; (2) the battle against skilled labor shortages, 1935-1937; and (3) the battle against the general shortage of labor, leading from 1937 without break into the war.

The Battle Against Unemployment

It would be too narrow to characterize the policy of the two or three first years of the regime as designed to reduce unemployment. In fact, the aim was more far-reaching from the very beginning. Labor as an important factor of warfare, the shortage of which had endangered the fighting forces during the last years of the First World War, was to be regulated in its distribution in accordance with the "defense" objectives of a directed economy. Centralization and tightening of control of labor allocation was aimed at during the whole period.[1] Other measures varied according to labor-market conditions: at first a part of them was directed toward reducing the number of unemployed persons by keeping would-be workers away from the labor market—for instance, by marriage loans, various semimilitary and labor services for boys and girls.[2] Many were absorbed by the rapidly growing state and party bureaucracy. The most important measures, however, intended to achieve recovery by rearmament, and succeeded in doing so.

The first reduction of unemployment due to rearmament brought more relief to small towns and to the country than to large cities, more to younger age groups which were depleted anyway by various services. Shortages in

---

[1] The term labor market was dropped. Allocation of labor, Arbeitseinsatz (a military term derived from the verb einsetzen, to set in), was introduced, indicating the part the state was going to play in directing man-power.

[2] In 1935 the Labor and Land Services removed about 395,000 (together with marriage loans about half a million persons) from the labor market (Bibl. #120e, March 21, 1936, Sondernummer, pp. 3-4). Including those removed by military service, the figure reached one million (Bibl. #310, 1938, p. 374).

Unemployed in Agriculture[3]
(in thousands)

			Yearly Average	Total
1933	January	283		6,013
	July	102	160.8	4,464
1934	January	112		3,773
	July	50	66.8	2,426
1935	January	96		2,974
	July	28	52.8	1,754
1936	January	72		2,520
	July	13	33.8	1,170
1937	January	56		1,853
	July	5	18.5	563
1938	January	30		1,052
	July	1.5	8.5	218
1939	January	23		647
	July	1		74

Employees (in Sickness Insurance) in Agriculture[3]
(with Forestry and Fishery)
(in thousands)

		End of June	End of December	
	1934	2,197	2,036	
	1935	2,230	2,044	
	1936	2,253	2,063	
	1937	2,234	2,019	
	1938	2,255	1,949	
	1939	2,256		
July 5	1940	2,009	2,020	October 31
" 31	1941	2,163	2,480	December 31

agriculture coincided with unemployment in industries and cities.[4] Unemployment in agriculture had never been considerable. In January 1933 agri-

[3] Source: figures published in RABl (Bibl. #139).

[4] Of four million unemployed registered in 1933, one million belonged to the eight largest cities. Communities with less than 50,000 inhabitants had 23.8 unemployed to 1,000 inhabitants on March 31, 1934; cities with more than 10,000 inhabitants had 81.3 per thousand; Berlin 100.2, Bibl. #332a (Bibl. #139, 1935, No. 34, pp. 6-7).

culture had 10 per cent unemployed, the total economy 30 per cent. Even 10 per cent seems too high since figures were taken in January. As early as September 1933 the demand for hands for the harvest could not be provided. In the autumn of 1934 the shortage became still more acute.

The reduction of unemployment concerned mostly persons from eighteen to twenty-five years of age whose unemployment was reduced by 67.6 per cent in 1934, while that of employees from forty to sixty years of age decreased merely by 36.1 per cent.[5] This development, as far as it represented real employment and not just new labor services, was the more undesirable since the government intended to train youth for military service. Concentration of unemployed in the cities meant an element of potential unrest and revolt. Therefore the withdrawal of youth from the labor market and closing of big cities against immigration became the first objective.

1. CONTROL OVER FREEDOM OF MOVEMENT IN ORDER
TO PREVENT MIGRATION TO CITIES

As early as May 1934[6] the President of the Reifa was empowered to declare for areas with high unemployment that persons without residence in these sections on the date of enforcement of the law could be employed as manual or nonmanual workers only with approval of the Reifa President. This ruling was subsequently applied to three big cities, and to the Saar district, exceptions granted especially for vocational training.

2. CONTROL OF THE DISTRIBUTION OF EMPLOYMENT AS
BETWEEN AGRICULTURE AND INDUSTRY

The same law of May 1934 empowered the President of the Reifa to prohibit the engagement, without permission, of agricultural workers (e.g. those actually working and those who had been so employed within the last three years, later two) in nonagricultural occupations. These provisions were applied to certain industries which had been inclined to employ unskilled workers from rural areas[7] (mining, building, metal industries, and, concerning girls, the hotel and restaurant service). This power was applied, not rigidly but in an elastic and discriminating manner.[8]

[5] Bibl. #332b (*ibid.*, p. 8).
[6] Gesetz zur Regelung des Arbeitseinsatzes (Allocation of Employment Act) of May 15, 1934 (Bibl. #140, Vol. 1, p. 381).
[7] Order of May 17, 1934 (Bibl. #139, Vol. 1, p. 127).
[8] On November 8, 1934, the director of the Munich employment office reported in the *SP* (Bibl. #338) that only in forty cases had the consent of the Munich office been

Moreover, the President was empowered to require dismissal of such workers. This power remained practically unused in 1934. It was renewed and extended in 1935.[9] Again this power was applied very cautiously. There was no compulsion for the dismissed workers to return to the country. In the period from April 1935 to March 1936, the dismissal of 9,781 men and 5,903 women was ordered from nonagricultural work.[10] In 16,553 cases consent was given to employ former farm people on other work. The low figures for dismissals show that the authorities were afraid of stamping agricultural labor as compulsory labor and thereby making it still less popular. Moreover, farmers would hardly have enjoyed the help of such involuntary workers. The main aim of the orders was to prevent industry from recruiting farm workers and to prevent the latter from looking for employment in industry.

The attempts to persuade unemployed of rural extraction to accept jobs in agriculture met great resistance. The President of the Reifa was compelled to restrict the employment of such persons on public works.[11] Agricultural training courses for unemployed were established.[12]

3. CONTROL OF YOUTH

On August 28, 1934,[13] the President of the Reifa ruled that jobs held by unmarried persons under the age of twenty-five in public and private business with exception of agriculture, forestry, household, and navigation, had to be given up to unemployed elderly salaried employees, especially to fathers of large families. Exempt were married men, those who supported a family, apprentices, veterans of the forces, of the Labor Service and the Land Help

---

asked for (p. 1333). This might be due, in his opinion, either to the fact that employers believe they would not get the permission or to ignorance of the decree.

[9] Act of February 26, 1935 (Bibl. #140, Vol. 1, p. 310); and Circular of March 29, 1935 (Bibl. #139, Vol. 1, p. 120).

[10] Bibl. #139, 1936, No. 34, Beilage, p. 24.

[11] Regierungsrat Dr. Sommer, "Die Regelung des Arbeitseinsatzes in der Landwirtschaft," Bibl. #338, February 7, 1935, pp. 166-67.

[12] Training of Unemployed Workers in Agriculture:

	Participants		Participants
1933-1934	17,040	1936-1937	9,038
1934-1935	13,690	1937-1938	6,277
1935-1936	9,257		

Source: Bibl. #332 (Bibl. #139, 1935, No. 4, p. 25; 1935, No. 35, p. 27; 1936, No. 34, p. 28; 1937, No. 28, p. 35; 1939, No. 3, p. 28).

[13] Bibl. #139, Vol. 1, p. 202; Circular of September 11, 1934 (ibid., Vol. 1, p. 232). The Regulation was supplemented and amended on November 27, 1936 (ibid., Vol. 1, p. 312); March 18, 1937 (ibid., Vol. 1, p. 84); and March 1, 1938 (ibid., Vol. 1, p. 69).

(the two last groups after one year of service), members of SA, SS, steel helmet, and of the NSDAP with low membership numbers. In case employer and employment office could not agree the president of the district employment office decided about the dismissal, with appeal to the President of the Reifa. Subsidies would be granted to make up for lower efficiency of the older employees in the first period. Employers had to obtain permission to engage new employees under the age of twenty-five.[14] Measures were taken to transfer the young employees to agriculture, the Labor Service or similar services, or—not mentioned in the decrees—to military education. Apparently the order which was very unpopular was not rigidly enforced because it resulted in the release of only 130,000 workers from October 1934 to October 1935.[15]

The Battle Against Labor Shortage

I. THE LABOR MARKET AND THE FLIGHT

FROM THE LAND, 1935-1939

Even before the proclamation of the Four-Year Plan in November 1936, the shortage of labor in agriculture had become so acute that special measures were taken to recruit additional labor during the harvest. Only 1,042,300 unemployed were available, on November 30, 1936, for agricultural work, of whom only 17,600 were fully employable, and only 7,900 were employable outside their place of domicile.[16] This meant that the reserve of unemployed labor was practically exhausted. Limited manpower seemed to set bounds[17] to the ambitious autarky program of the Four-Year Plan.

On November 27, 1936,[18] the decrees restricting migration into certain

[14] President Friedrich Syrup, "Die gesetzgeberischen Massnahmen der Reichsanstalt für Arbeitsvermittlung und Arbeitslosenversicherung im Kampfe gegen die Arbeitslosigkeit" (Bibl. #139, 1934, Vol. II, p. 337).

[15] Syrup, "Die Entwicklung des Arbeitseinsatzes," Bibl. #345, July 1938, p. 391. Of 108,000 withdrawn by May 1935, 67,000 had been brought into the Labor Service, 28,063 placed in agriculture as Land Helpers and workers (Bibl. #332b, p. 17).

[16] Bibl. #139, 1937, No. 2, Statistische Beilage, p. 4. At the end of 1936 the Reifa made the first analysis of employability of the unemployed. According to an instruction of the President of October 12, 1936 unemployed were divided into three categories: (1) workers completely employable in their trade, (2) completely employable for work otherwise, (3) not fully employable. The first two categories were subdivided into Ausgleichsfähige, i.e. those capable of accepting work outside their place of domicile and those who were not (Bibl. #332d, #139, 1937, No. 28, p. 17).

[17] Bibl. #345, 1937, No. 5, p. 288. In March 1937 there were 97,000 vacancies in agriculture and only 8,600 fully employable workers available (ibid., No. 6, p. 350).

[18] Bibl. #139, Vol. I, p. 312.

industries and certain districts and directing former agricultural workers back to the country by ordering their dismissal were revoked and not repeated. The reasons were not only that they had resulted in too many breaches of contract and that the government was afraid of frightening more youth away from agriculture,[19] but that industry began to need manpower. Only the legislation conferring the power in question on the President of the Reifa and the restriction of migration to Berlin and Hamburg remained in force.

Farm labor reacted to its regained mobility by an unprecedented flight from agriculture. The census of 1939 records a loss of 1.45 million in agricultural population since 1933. The number of gainfully occupied had decreased by 400,000, which figure included a loss of 643,000 men and an increase of 230,000 women. The decrease in different groups was as follows:

Officials and salaried employees	22,600 (19.5 per cent)
Laborers	421,700 (16.7 per cent)
361,000 men (21.6 per cent) and	60,400 women (7 per cent)
Farmers	217,500 (10 per cent)

while helping members of the family increased by 248,500 (5.5 per cent).[20] The increase in the last group is partly due to a change in statistical methods. The figure is composed of a decrease of men by 105,500 or 10.1 per cent and an increase of women by 353,900 or 10.2 per cent. In fact, the exodus was much greater since alien workers and girls serving their compulsory year were included. An expert of the RN, Guenther Pacyna, estimated that 1.8 million farmers and farm workers left farms between 1933 and 1938.[21] The farm population decreased from 22.8 per cent of the total population in 1925 to 17.7 per cent in 1939, according to an estimate in August 1943 to 16 per cent.[22]

Of 120,000 agricultural laborers in Saxony in 1936 a third had entered industry by the spring of 1939.[23] Württemberg, a state that had always been considered exemplary for its population structure and its combination of agriculture and industry, lost 52,000 family workers and 37,000 non-family

---

[19] Heddy Neumeister, "Landflucht—Unaufhaltsam," Bibl. #139, 1940, Vol. v, p. 431.

[20] Bibl. #153e, 1940, No. 23, pp. 538-39.

[21] Bibl. #321, March 3, 1939. Of the 10.5 million occupied in other than agricultural work, three million were born in the country (Heinz Wülker, "Wie gross ist die Landflucht und was kostet sie?" Bibl. #327, February 1939, p. 90).

[22] Bibl. #321, August 13, 1943.

[23] Bibl. #286, April 21, 1939, p. 1406. In East Prussia 251,000 of the rural population migrated to the cities in 1936 and 26,700 in 1937; 60,000 farm workers, or 14.4 per cent of the total, were lacking in this province in 1938. (Peter Quante, "Bekämpfung der Landflucht," Deutsche Agrarpolitik, February, 1943, pp. 156-57.)

workers or 17.4 per cent of its farm labor between 1933 and 1938.[24] Baden lost 54,785 workers, or 15.2 per cent;[25] Westphalia, 16,425 or 17.7 per cent;[26] Hesse lost 33 per cent of nonfamily workers until 1939, especially in the age groups from twenty to twenty-five;[27] Schleswig-Holstein 14,686 workers or 23.7 per cent;[28] in Lower Saxony only 54 per cent of farmers' children remained in agriculture.[29]

The exodus came from the small farms rather than from large estates. According to an investigation of the RN covering 8,813 farms there was a decline of 28 per cent in the number of adult farm workers in 1938 and 1939 on farms of less than 50 ha., while on farms of more than 100 ha. the decline was 12 per cent.[30] This was due in part to the difficulty experienced by peasants whose land had been taken for military purposes in finding suitable new farms. The small farm, moreover, employed the largest percentage of unmarried servants and these, as a rule, belonged to the age group that had been reduced by the falling birth rate during World War I.

Many factors contributed to the flight from the land. Opportunities for farm workers to migrate to industrial work were better than they had ever been. Industries had been transferred to the country, taking only their skilled workers with them and new industries were being built up in areas far from the cities. With higher wages and shorter hours than those in agriculture, they were attractive to the farm laborers and to those peasant sons and daughters who had no prospects on hereditary farms. Frequently only the wife or husband took up work in industry, while the rest of the family remained on the farm. Industrial workers who lived on a small plot of land and had formerly turned to farm work after their day in the factory now found themselves too tired by longer hours and greater strain to till their land. Some leased their property or gave it up. Others continued to live on

---

[24] Bibl. #220, *Württemberg*, pp. 270-71. Rural exodus was responsible for the loss of population in small communities. Those with fewer than 2,000 inhabitants, which are reckoned as rural, decreased by 960,000 persons, or 4.6 per cent of the population, while cities with more than 100,000 inhabitants increased by 1.3 per cent; those with 50-100,000 by 3.1 per cent; those with 20-50,000 by 6.4 per cent; those with 10-20,000 by 6.5 per cent (Bibl. #153e, 1941, No. 20, p. 374). The distribution of these increases indicates the shift of industry to smaller cities.

[25] *Ibid.*, Carl Brinkmann, p. 249.

[26] *Ibid.*, Friedrich Hoffmann, p. 6.

[27] *Ibid.*, Eduard Willeke, pp. 15, 135, 138.

[28] *Ibid.*, Wilhelm Friedrich Boyens, p. 112.

[29] *Ibid.*, Artur Schürmann, p. 36.

[30] Rudolph Gerhart, Bibl. #321, April 28, 1939, quoted in Bibl. #120b, 1939-1940, NF, No. 1, p. 10.

their holdings and work in the city.[31] Furthermore, military conscription which took the farm boy from his home for two years and familiarized him with town life, often left him reluctant to return to the farm.

Once men had gone into industry, the ensuing overburdening of the peasant women for whom working days of sixteen to eighteen hours were not exceptional, and whom the weight of work made old twenty years ahead of time, became another impetus to migration.[32]

Since most of those who migrated to industry were the young and able-bodied, agriculture was left with an unfavorable age structure. In 1938, 66.8 per cent of all independent farmers in Württemberg were over fifty years of age; of those engaged in industry and handicraft only 30.6 per cent.[33] About 500,000 women over sixty years of age worked full time in agriculture while only 75,000 women in this age group were occupied in industry.[34] On seven peasant farms in Hanover ten workers were employed; seven of whom were from corrective institutions, one sterilized, one feeble-minded, one Russian.[35]

The regime was disturbed. As early as November 1936, on the fourth Reich Peasant Day, a high official of the RN reported that farm workers were almost on their knees pleading to be released for industry. Some obtained physicians' certificates of their incapacity to do farm work.[36] Others *deleted the record of agricultural training from their work books in order* to avoid being sent back to farming.[37] Breaches of contract were the order of the day. It even was admitted that the problem was too serious to blame

[31] Münzinger complained in 1944 that the close connection between industry and agriculture had become a "cancerous growth" for agriculture. "Only the industrial sector has benefited but the Württemberg peasantry has been largely destroyed" (Bibl. #329, *op.cit.*, 1944, Nos. 5-6).

[32] A peasant from the Palatinate said: "One can find one hundred idealists who are ready to die for their fatherland against one who is ready to work unpaid during all his life because nobody can be a hero every day. This is the reason why our peasant daughters do not marry peasants" (Bibl. #286, August 4, 1939, p. 2177). Examination of 200 marriage ads of young peasants in a rural Swabian paper showed that 44.5 per cent received no answer (Dr. Marie Berta von Brand, "Die Landfrau im Reichsnährstand, im weiblichen Bildungswesen und in der Rechtsordnung," in Sering and von Dietze, Bibl. #250, p. 48).

[33] Bibl. #286, August 4, 1939, p. 2178.

[34] Gustav Behrens, "Stillstand der Erzeugungsschlacht?" Bibl. #327, March 1939.

[35] Artur Schürmann, Bibl. #220, p. 31.

[36] Peasant Karl Reichardt, Landeshauptabteilung I, *4. Reichsbauerntag*, Bibl. #275, Vol. 4, p. 251. Reichardt attributed the exodus to the contempt for farm work, monotony, long hours and low wages, and the compulsion laid upon peasant wives to do farm work.

[37] Bibl. #126, 1938, p. 777.

merely the past. On the sixth Reich Peasant Day in 1938 another official reported that in his area there were 620 girls in 1928 who milked cows besides doing housework and only 310 such girls on November 1, 1938.[38] It was mentioned again and again that all means to increase farm labor by special services were merely a drop in the bucket. "The loss of labor from the country is conjuring up the ghost of a decline in agricultural production," said the Minister of Agriculture at the Reich Peasant Day in 1938.[39] "All the advantages of life on the land have been consistently brought to the attention of the German youth during the last few years. Through its compulsory (sic) service on the land, the Hitler Youth Movement has made a reality of the formerly hazy notion of the life on the land. Nevertheless, the flight from the land continued from year to year." "Today agriculture is the only occupation group which shows an absolute drop in the number of hands engaged in it," wrote the *Frankfurter Zeitung*,[40] commenting on the speech of Darré. These trends were directly opposed to the government aim of making Germany agriculturally self-sufficient and to its policy of maintaining the rural population as the "blood source" of the nation.

"A much greater danger is threatening the existence of our nation, mental urbanization (seelische Verstädterung)," said one of the chiefs of the RN. He reported that the rural exodus was more general among the more capable of the younger generation and that tests in elementary schools had shown that the percentage of students migrating to the cities was about twice as high among the gifted as it was among the less gifted. "It is easy to judge which hereditary qualities the German people will have in the future, if the least valuable people remain in the country."[41] The loss of manpower was partly compensated by greater exertion on the part of those who stayed. The health of the remaining youth was reported seriously impaired. "In Saxony of 1,388 applicants to the SS from the rural districts 680 had to be rejected as physically unfit; in a Saxon agricultural school only seven students out of 66 were in good health; four of them came from the city. The others had curvatures of the spine and the chest, flat feet, and other ailments due to overwork."[42]

Not less serious was the economic dilemma. "The outlook seems to be

---

[38] Peasant Gustav Behrens, Reichsobmann, Bibl. #275, Vol. 5, p. 61.

[39] Bibl. #275, Vol. 5, p. 38.

[40] Bibl. #297, November 29, 1938.

[41] Jacobus Hugo de Marees van Swinderen, Reichshauptabteilungsleiter, Bibl. #275, Vol. 5, p. 156.

[42] Gustav Behrens, Bibl. #327, March 1939, p. 153.

sombre," wrote H. Weiss in September 1939.[43] "Either the flight from the land will be stopped—in which case the shortage of industrial workers will be aggravated and industrial development slowed down . . .—or . . . reduction in crops can be expected." From 1938 on, it became increasingly clear that intensive methods of cultivation were being displaced by extensive ones and that the number of workers was not sufficient to maintain the rate of production; the effects of migration could no longer be counteracted by a further increase in productivity. Whenever possible, farmers offered their cattle for sale because there were no cattle tenders, especially dairymen.[44] "The previously attained level of production, especially in stock farming, is endangered," reported the Institute for Business Research in 1939.[45] The reduction of milk cows to the extent of 300,000 or 3 per cent of the milk output and butter production (the latter from 517,000 tons in 1937 to 496,000 in 1938) was partly ascribed to the lack of milkers, according to Darré.[46]

The minister declared in January 1939, at the opening of an agricultural exhibition:[47] "We have to note that according to statistics, Germany's future provisions of beef, milk, butter, pork, and lard are already endangered by the continued flight from the land."

By 1938 the German economy had been pushed close to the limit of its productive capacity.[48] Only 200,000 unemployed were available in July 1938, 23,000 fully employable.[49] Before the outbreak of the war 750,000 farm workers were lacking in Germany.[50]

[43] H. Weiss, "Die Zuspitzung der Landarbeiterfrage—eine Folge der Entwicklung der letzten 50 Jahre," Bibl. #139, Vol. II, p. 330. Weiss concluded that industry should have priority because of its need of specialized workers, while auxiliary agricultural work could be done by workers who did not live in the country and helped only during the season.

[44] A high official in the RN reported that in Mecklenburg he saw one estate of 42½ ha. for which the peasant and his mother had to care without help; they therefore reduced their cows by one half (Gustav Behrens, *op.cit.*, Bibl. #327, March 1939, p. 152).

[45] Bibl. #120f, February 9, 1939, p. 15; *ibid.*, May 23, 1939, p. 51.

[46] Darré, "Die ernährungspolitische Lage," Bibl. #345, 1939, Nos. 1-2, p. 109.

[47] Bibl. #297, January 28, 1939. During 1938-1939 the hog slaughter was 2.7 per cent below the preceding year. The reduction of potato cultivation by 80,000 ha. in 1939 (Bibl. #345, August 1939, No. 16, p. 982), vegetable crops, and of rape were for the same reason. The reduction of potato cultivation was especially undesirable because the potato crop (including utilization in animal stomachs) provided 30 per cent of the food supply of the nation (Herbert Backe, "Der Stand der Erzeugungsschlacht," Bibl. #345, November 1938, No. 11, p. 661).

[48] The employment offices reported 280,000 unfilled vacancies in May 1938, 85,000 of these in agriculture (*Statistische Beilage*, Bibl. #139, 1938, No. 19, p. 2).

[49] Bibl. #338, January 1, 1939, p. 11.

[50] Friedrich Syrup, "Die Etappen des Arbeitseinsatzes," Bibl. #338, January 1939, p. 14.

The measures taken by the government in an effort to maintain the level of production included increased mechanization, the direction of children leaving school into agriculture, mobilization of young persons for Land Services, mobilization of other labor reserves and of alien workers. In addition, subsidies were offered to render farm work more attractive. When all measures failed to check the flight from the land the farm population was immobilized by law. If its effort to halt the rural exodus was a decisive test for the NSDAP as Darré had declared at the sixth Reich Peasant Day,[51] the party failed to pass.

2. MEASURES OF CONTROL

EMPLOYMENT OFFICES. From the beginning the public employment service had been designated as the sole agency for the control of labor recruitment and distribution. In the Reifa the regime took over a coordinated and centralized system which combined placement, vocational guidance, administration of unemployment insurance, work relief, and other related matters. The only change needed was its transformation from an instrument of self-government into a mere government agency. This was done in 1933. All functions of joint bodies were transferred to the presidents of the central, district, and local bodies.[52] The President of the Reifa was given sole power to regulate the distribution of labor.[53] Finally the exclusive right of carrying on employment service, vocational guidance, and placement of apprentices was given to the Reifa.[54] Nonprofit agencies in these fields had to cease working by March 31, 1936, unless they received authorization; if authorized, they were under the Reifa supervision.

---

[51] Bibl. #275, Vol. 5, p. 46.

[52] Decree and Circulars of June 2, 1933 (Bibl. #139, Vol. 1, p. 153); August 24, 1933 (*ibid.*, p. 221); November 7, 1933 (*ibid.*, p. 282); November 10, 1933 (*ibid.*, p. 288); and others. There was no wholesale change of personnel. Friedrich Syrup, a former factory inspector, who had been President of the Reifa since its establishment in 1927, remained as head of the Institute and, after Jews and some Socialists had been purged, many of the former officials also stayed on. Only 3,344 officials of a total personnel of approximately 26,500 were removed or demoted during the "national revolution" according to the *Sixth Report of the Reifa*, Bibl. #332a, p. 39.

[53] Order of August 10, 1934 (Bibl. #140, Vol. 1, p. 786). In June 1935, employment services for Germans seeking positions abroad were concentrated in the Reifa with the intention of preventing labor which might be needed in the country, especially skilled and agricultural labor, from emigration (Decree of June 28, 1935, Bibl. #140, Vol. 1, p. 903).

[54] Act of November 5, 1935 (Bibl. #140, Vol. 1, p. 1281) and Orders of November 26, 1935 (*ibid.*, p. 1361); November 30, 1935 (Bibl. #139, Vol. 1, p. 330), amended March 19, 1936 (Bibl. #140, Vol. 1, p. 195).

Recruitment and placement of migratory agricultural labor lay within the exclusive competence of the Reifa.[55] Any other kind of recruitment, for instance by advertisement, was prohibited. The farmers registered their requirements and the local and district employment offices, in cooperation with the respective peasant leaders, reported the figures of necessary recruitment (for the receiving districts) and possible emigration (for the providing districts) to the central office, which established the balance. The Workers' Central then carried the placement through. Thus a monopoly of placement was established at the end of 1935. Within only two years the placement system had been transformed into a planned system of labor allocation. Close collaboration was established with the military draft boards and with the Secret Police in order to mark politically unreliable people.[56] It was a consistent step when in 1938,[57] the functions of the Reifa were transferred to the Ministry of Labor, of which it became a special department. The President of the Reifa became head of the department as Secretary of State.

After the outbreak of the war the employment service was made responsible for allocation of prisoners of war and workers from conquered countries. Either the latter had to build up their national employment organization under German supervision (in Holland, Belgium, France, Norway, and Denmark) to provide for Germany's manpower needs, or German offices were set up for that purpose.[58]

[55] Order of December 30, 1935 (Bibl. #139, 1936, Vol. I, p. 4). Prior regulation had been by Circular of December 1, 1934 (*ibid.*, 1935, Vol. I, p. 5). Order of December 20, 1934 (*ibid.*, 1935, Vol. I, p. 11). For foreign labor the transfer of all functions to the Reifa had already been established by Decree of January 23, 1933 by the pre-Hitler government.

[56] Bibl. #291, October 1937, A, p. 95.

[57] Decree of December 21, 1938 (Bibl. #140, Vol. I, p. 1892). The Ministry of Labor took over thirteen regional offices (plus the branch offices for Austria and the Sudeten District) and 337 local offices with auxiliary offices and a total staff of 40,000. There were in the Greater Reich in 1941, 468 local employment offices (331 of which were in the old Reich) with 1,300 branches and 23 (16) district employment offices. The Reifa employed 45,000 persons, 13,000 of them in the conquered districts (Beisiegel, "Aufgaben und Leistungen der Arbeitseinsatzverwaltung, Bibl. #139, 1941, Vol. v, p. 492). Since August 1939 the employment offices had become offices of the RTA.

[58] The President of the district employment office Danzig West Prussia, one of the incorporated Polish territories, described the process of establishing these offices in the east as follows: "When on September 1, 1939, the German troops penetrated into the district, the employment office followed immediately behind the fighting troops in order to establish in all important cities offices. . . . On September 3, the employment office Dirschau was established, on the 4th, Stargard, the 8th, Bromberg. Everywhere the following day proclamations in German and Polish language were posted, asking the population to register in the employment office. A few hours later the first gangs of farm workers went to the Polish village or farms reported by German peasants

Dissatisfaction with labor shortage in face of the desperate need to increase production when the German army had suffered severe defeats on the eastern front manifested itself in the "resignation" of Secretary of State Friedrich Syrup in February of 1942. He was succeeded by Dr. Mansfeld, a former lawyer of the heavy industries who frequently had represented the employers' organizations against the trade unions in the courts. During the National Socialist regime Mansfeld had been a high official in the Ministry of Labor. After a two months' tenure in office, Mansfeld was superseded by the party district leader, Fritz Sauckel, as Commissioner General (Generalbevoll-mächtigter) of Man Power, directly responsible to Goering.[59] Sauckel, a ruthless party man, had managed the Gustloff Werke (an armament factory taken away from its Jewish owners) during the National Socialist regime. He had no such experiences in civil service as his predecessors had had. The reorganization deprived the Minister of Labor of his functions in the field of control of wages and of labor recruitment and distribution, and left in his jurisdiction mainly labor protection, social insurance, and preparation of labor legislation. The employment and the wage department with all their subordinate services were placed at the disposal of the Commissioner General who was given wide powers. He was to direct manpower and regulate wages and conditions of employment in Germany and the occupied territories in accordance with the manpower policy.

Sauckel ordered[60] that all manpower direction including placement, vocational guidance, transfer, utilization of foreign labor, and wage control be put in the hands of the agencies of labor supply. No intervention of unauthorized persons would be tolerated. Collaboration with the NSDAP was requested. The district leaders of the party were designated as labor supply deputies for their districts.[61] This measure intended at the same time to tighten party control and to stem the terrific growth of bureaucracy. Labor allocation had to become fanatically National Socialistic, according to Sauckel:

---

as abandoned" (Bibl. #139, 1940, Vol. v, p. 1061). At the end of September there were seventy employment offices in the occupied territories (Minister of Labor Seldte, Bibl. #139, 1940, Vol. v, p. 53). In many cases the employment offices were the first "German authorities, often established while troops were still fighting in the vicinity." By the end of 1942, 286 employment offices, manned by 1,030 German officials, existed in the occupied east (*Deutsche Bergwerkszeitung*, September 4, 1942).

[59] Decree of March 21, 1942 (Bibl. #140, Vol. i, p. 179) and Order of March 26, 1942 (Bibl. #139, Vol. i, p. 257).

[60] Decree of April 24, 1942 (Bibl. #139, Vol. i, p. 258).

[61] Order of April 6, 1942 (Bibl. #139, Vol. i, p. 272); and April 24, 1942 (Bibl. #113 of April 24).

"The unpolitical official, the pure expert, has no place in the National Socialist State."[62] While the first order of Sauckel conveyed the impression that
the powers of the district party leaders would be overriding, a later version[63]
made it clear that their work would be confined to giving political directives.
The presidents of the district employment offices were instructed to provide
the party district leaders with any information they might wish to have and
within the framework of laws and regulations of their usual method of
procedure, to adopt the leaders' suggestions for improvements. Offices of the
RN were to cooperate with them on labor questions.

When experiences of bombing forced decentralization of the machinery
in the course of 1943, the reorganization was used to establish closer collaboration with the party. In November 1942, the party district leaders had been
made national defense commissioners for their districts with the task of
coordinating the war economic policy including manpower. In February 1943,
the employment service and trustee districts[64] were adapted to those of the
economic districts.[65] Before it could be carried out this system was displaced
again in July[66] by one which adapted the regional labor administration to
the party districts. Forty-two district leaders' employment offices (Gauar-
beitsämter) replaced the twenty-two district employment offices (Landes-
arbeitsämter). The placement service thereby became dependent on the party
bureaucracy, a branch of political administration. Offices of the trustees and
the presidents of the district employment offices were officially merged.[67]
Recruitment of foreign workers remained under the supervision of Sauckel,
while their distribution was made over to the Reich Labor Allocation Engineer under the Ministry of War Production (Reichsarbeitseinsatzingenieur).

Following the attempted assassination of the Führer on July 25, 1944,
Hitler subordinated Sauckel to Joseph Goebbels as Reich Plenipotentiary for
the Total War Effort (Reichsbevollmächtigter für den totalen Kriegseinsatz)
under Goering,[68] while both Goebbels and Goering in their turn became

[62] Bibl. #297, September 19, 1942.
[63] Order of May 21, 1942 (Bibl. #139, Vol. 1, p. 272); and July 11, 1942 (*ibid.*, p. 337).
[64] Order of November 16, 1942 (Bibl. #140, Vol. 1, p. 649).
[65] Order of February 27, 1943 (Bibl. #139, Vol. 1, p. 151).
[66] Order of July 27, 1943 (Bibl. #140, Vol. 1, p. 450).
[67] Early in 1944 several district employment offices were coordinated into labor
inspectorates. In August 1944 a Reichsinspection was set up in the Ministry of Labor
under Sauckel, to remove friction in allocation, increase efficiency, and supervise the
enforcement of all orders (Bibl. #139, Vol. 1, p. 281).
[68] Bibl. #140, Vol. 1, p. 161. In a broadcast following his appointment, Goebbels
said: "The party will be the motor of the entire process of reorganization. It will,
from now on, principally serve the task of freeing soldiers for the front and workers

subordinated to all demands of Gestapo Leader Heinrich Himmler, commander of the home front.

THE WORK BOOK. A labor inventory was the second means of control. A complete survey of the available labor power was created by the introduction of the work book (Arbeitsbuch).[69] Beginning with some essential war industries, the compulsion to hold work books was extended to all occupations up to September 1, 1936; in 1935[70] it was introduced in agriculture. In April 1939[71] the exemption for independent gainfully employed persons (except in a few professions), helping members of the family, and highly paid salaried employees was abolished. It was a very unpopular measure which could be enforced only by threat of severe punishment. Alien seasonal workers, school children below fourteen years of age remained exempt. In May 1941[72] alien seasonal workers were included, and in May 1943 all alien workers.[73]

No worker could be employed who did not hold a work book, no employer was allowed to employ a worker unless he held the book. It contained a complete record of the bearer's age, health, marital status, training, former positions held, familiarity with agricultural work, present place of work, date when employment began, type of enterprise, kind of occupation, driver's license, and so forth. No entries were allowed concerning wages, behavior, or efficiency. Yet work books were felt to be warrants since the employee could not conceal a job on which he came in conflict with his employer. Changes of occupation, training, residence, and family status had to be entered by the employer, who kept the book during the period of employment and returned it when the worker left.

The employment office registered all books and copied the records. It had to be notified of every entry. Independent persons had to make entries and notifications regarding themselves. The card index of the employment office thus provided a complete survey of all working persons in the areas and their availability for allocation to different trades. The work book made the

---

for the production of armaments. It will fill this task with its usual energy and with its old revolutionary elan" (Bibl. #346, July 28, 1944).

[69] Law of February 26, 1935 (Bibl. #140, Vol. 1, p. 311); Decree of May 16, 1935 (*ibid.*, p. 602); Order of the President of the Reifa, May 18, 1935 (Bibl. #139, Vol. 1, p. 157); and many Ordinances.

[70] Order of September 14, 1935 (Bibl. #139, Vol. 1, p. 286).

[71] Decree of April 22, 1939 (Bibl. #140, Vol. 1, p. 824).

[72] Decree of May 22, 1941 (Bibl. #140, Vol. 1, p. 288).

[73] Decree of May 1, 1943 (Bibl. #139, Vol. 1, pp. 277, 297).

worker a complete tool of the authority.[74] It was a serious blow to this totalitarian registration when, during the war, the destruction of records by bombing whittled down the mobilization effort and gave workers the chance to evade registration.

3. MEASURES TO PROVIDE LABOR FOR AGRICULTURE

CONTROL AND GUIDANCE OF BOYS AND GIRLS LEAVING SCHOOL. By "guidance" and various services, the regime attempted to plant young people on the land. This seemed desirable since the decrease in the number of young people corresponded to the declining birth rate of the war and postwar years. In agriculture the shortage was especially acute. There were 31 per cent fewer men from sixteen to twenty-five years of age in 1938 than in 1924.[75] Boys leaving school in the old Reich declined from 620,000 in 1934 to 515,-000 in 1944 and were expected to decline to 400,000 in 1947.[76] The number of new entrants in jobs was 41,000 less in 1941 than in 1940, and was expected to fall by another 21,000 in 1942. Moreover, military training reduced the supply of young workers. Before the Second World War more than 100,000 farmers' sons were drafted yearly and had to be replaced for two years by other workers. Boys undertaking gainful employment for the first time turned to agriculture (in the last years, increasingly under compulsion).

New Entrants in Agriculture[77]

	Absolute	*Per Cent*
1922-1927	150,000	25
1934	150,000	29.4
1935	150,000	25.8
1936	130,000	23.2
1937	110,000	20.4
1938	100,000	19.6
1939	100,000	

The percentage remained the same during the depression period. The number of sixteen-year-old boys and girls in agriculture from 1925 to 1938 declined from 144,000 to 63,000, or 56.4 per cent.[78]

---

[74] A valuable addition to the manpower register provided by the work book was the register of enterprises, filed with the employment offices.

[75] R. Bräunnig, "Gesindenot und Bauerntum," Bibl. #296, 1939, Vol. 7, p. 109.

[76] Oberregierungsrat Stets, "Zur Nachwuchsplanung 1941" (Bibl. #139, 1940, Vol. v, p. 482).

[77] Hans Klabunde, "Der Arbeitseinsatz der männlichen Jugendlichen seit dem Weltkriege," Bibl. #273, July 25—August 10, 1939, p. 240.

[78] H. Kaufmann, "Der Nachwuchsbedarf und seine Deckung nach Wirtschaftsabteilungen," Bibl. #338, March 15, 1939, p. 364.

The system of exchange of young for older workers was abolished on December 1, 1936,[79] but permits for the engagement of young workers issued by the employment offices remained obligatory. Apprentices, volunteers, and probationers below the age of twenty-five years were included in the permit system in 1938.[80] Parents or guardians were required to report on all young persons leaving school to the employment offices. A similar obligation was imposed on the school authorities. All young persons below twenty-one years of age who had left school between January 1, 1934, and March 14, 1938, and who had neither taken a job requiring a work book nor were undergoing vocational training or apprenticeship had to register.[81] This opened the way for a complete system of vocational guidance, or direction of young people to whatever occupation seemed desirable. Vocational guidance had been carried through by the Reifa offices in close collaboration with the Hitler Youth. The latter reported to the offices on the "community attitude" of the young people.[82] The methods so far did not provide strict assignment of youth, but left a limited choice. Direction practically became total in 1939, when youth turned away more and more from agriculture. "When industrial works were established in the country, frequently the whole rural youth abandoned agriculture," wrote Walter Stets. "Germany shall not starve because its youth is not inclined to stay in the country. The wishes of young people and their parents are practically unfulfillable."[83] Formal agricultural

[79] Order of the President of the Reifa of November 27, 1936 (Bibl. #139, Vol. 1, p. 312).

[80] Order of March 1, 1938 (Bibl. #139, Vol. 1, p. 69); and a letter of May 15, 1938 (Bibl. #139, Vol. 1, p. 206).

[81] The registration made it possible to recruit 10,000 boys and 14,000 girls who had no occupation (Walter Stets, "Massnahmen zur Nachwuchslenkung," Bibl. #315, 1938, p. 553).

[82] Oberstammführer Ost, "Hitlerjugend und Berufseinsatz der Jugend" (Bibl. #139, 1940, Vol. v, pp. 6off.).

[83] Walter Stets in *Das junge Deutschland* (Bibl. #312), 1939, p. 440. The vocational wishes of the youngster did not conform to the economic needs. One employment office, e.g., reported:

	Choices of Young People	Vacancies
Agriculture	33	280
Mining	41	450
Metal work	418	90
Office work	134	45

Bibl. #291, 1939, No. 2, p. 70. 296,000 girls preferred employment in commerce and offices in 1940, while only 232,000 actually were employed in these occupations. Ministerialrat Stets, "Gesichtspunkte für die Lenkung des weiblichen Berufsnachwuchses" (Bibl. #139, 1941, Vol. v, p. 530).

apprenticeship had been introduced by Orders of October 1, 1937, and Guiding Principles of April 7, 1936[84] as a stimulus for young people to go into agriculture. The scheme provided for a general agricultural instruction on a recognized farm (shortened during the war to two years), concluded by an examination. Periods spent in the Land Service could be deducted. A two years' specialist course (as peasant, milker, poultry raiser, for instance) could follow. To receive a farm worker's certificate the apprentice had to work an additional two years on another farm than the one where he was trained. Older workers could receive the certificate after having worked four years in the last ten years on not more than six farms. The apprenticeship scheme did not achieve any change in education. "Work experience cannot be distinguished from apprenticeship training," wrote the scientific institute of the DAF in 1938, expressing doubts whether the idea had been a wise one to pay higher wages for trained workers which only make farmers employ assistant workers for less wages. So far the scheme had not proved attractive.[85]

From 1938 on a Juvenile Employment Plan was established by the Reifa. The plan was to calculate the number of recruits each branch of occupation ought to receive with due regard to the claims of othe roccupations and the interest of the nation (Nachwuchsbedarf). The plan was gradually worked out and put into operation for the first time in 1941 for boys only.

In distributing the figure of 1.2 million births to the various economic branches according to the census of 1925 and taking the duration of the productive life period in agriculture as forty-six years, the Employment Plan calculated how many young people would be necessary to maintain the working power of agriculture. According to it, the demand for young newcomers for agriculture was to be 22 per cent of the existing number of employed, a total of 186,500, composed of 47,400 independent, 88,300 helping members of the family, 48,900 wage earners, 1,500 salaried employees, and 400 officials.[86]

In 1940 it was calculated that 160,000 male and 150,000 female apprentices would be necessary for agriculture.[87] The Nachwuchsbedarf was estimated as follows:

[84] Bibl. #343, 1937, pp. 543, 549, 551, 555.

[85] Bibl. #310, 1939, Vol. 1, pp. 409, 410.

[86] H. Kaufmann, "Der Nachwuchsbedarf und seine Deckung nach Wirtschaftsabteilungen," Bibl. #338, March 15, 1939, pp. 339ff.

[87] Bibl. #331, December 15, 1940; Bibl. #286, January 17, 1941, p. 618.

  100,000 farmers
   45,000 farm workers
    3,000 milkers and other specialized workers
    1,000 accountants
      700 workers caring for hogs
    8,000 horticulture workers
      800 in agricultural industries
      200 distillers, wine growers, sheep raisers

The plan provided for raising the number of juvenile entrants into agriculture from 100,000 to 115,000 in 1941. The figure actually reached was 110,000.[88] The offices became entitled to refuse permission to enter occupations in which the figure indicated in the plan as desirable had been reached. For instance, only one photographer was admitted in 1941; librarian training was barred.[89] The plan did not apply to girls, although the principles in placing them were the same. They were influenced by various services (especially the Duty Year) to go into agriculture. In 1942-1943 the plan was extended for the first time to the incorporated Polish areas where young people were to be recruited into agriculture and other rural occupations.[90] The plan was gradually to be extended to include all of Greater Germany. The plan was, furthermore, extended to juveniles already in employment who had not had any systematic training.[91] In the autumn of 1940 employers were forbidden to recruit workers in schools. Recruitment of trainees by leaflets, posters, or other means of propaganda required the consent of the employment service.

LAND SERVICES

    A. Land Help (Landhilfe). In this guise, as early as the spring of 1933,[92] a rural aid scheme was introduced and financed by the Reifa. The Land Help

[88] Stets (Bibl. #139, 1941, Vol. v, p. 492; *ibid.*, 1942, Vol. v, p. 540). In 1943 not even 10 per cent of the total of 80,000 required yearly as independent peasants had entered apprenticeship. In July 1944 Dr. Ludolf Haase complained that agriculture could cover its required number of young people by only 60 per cent. "The office greed of young people continues" (Bibl. #346, July 29, 1944). To get the full replacement for agriculture 320,000 boys and girls would have been needed in 1944, but only 222,000 could be won (Bibl. #321, January 26, 1945). For 1945 a claim for 280,000 was established (*Augsburger Nationalzeitung*, January 10, 1945).

[89] Bibl. #297, February 23, 1941.

[90] Order of the German Youth Leader (Bibl. #139, 1942, Vol. I, p. 353).

[91] Bibl. #139, 1942, Vol. v, p. 540.

[92] Decree of March 3, 1933 (Bibl. #139, Vol. I, p. 77); Circular of March 11, 1933 (*ibid.*, p. 87); November 9, 1933 (*ibid.*, p. 282); November 16, 1933 (*ibid.*, p. 295); November 1, 1934 (*ibid.*, Vol. I, p. 268). See also Rudolf Wiedwald, "Ein Jahr Landhilfe," *ibid.*, 1934, Vol. II, pp. 95ff. Circular of November 20, 1934 (*ibid.*, Vol. I, p. 269).

provided subsidies to small and medium-sized peasants for the additional employment of young persons. The farmer had to take the young people into his household and provide food, shelter, and a small wage. Unemployed, racially pure boys and girls, sixteen to twenty-one years of age (later extended to fourteen to twenty-five), selected by the employment offices with the cooperation of the RN, had to bind themselves to remain at least six months. In order to prevent any adverse political influence of urban upon rural youth, the offices were instructed to exclude Communists and those with criminal records. The offices investigated the farm, housing conditions, and type of occupation.

The scheme expanded quickly. From July 1933 until March 1934 an average of 159,000 helpers were employed (123,000 boys and 36,000 girls). For 1934-1935 the quota was fixed at 160,000.[93] The Hitler Youth and the League of German Girls took over the political and physical education of Land Helpers (boys up to nineteen, girls to twenty-two years of age) who had to join the local youth groups. Older people were taken care of by the storm troops.[94]

Land Help was so-called voluntary service. Unjustified refusal, however, resulted in loss of the right to unemployment benefits.[95] At the end of the Land Help period a certificate was provided which helped secure other employment. This was an incentive to accept agricultural work since the helper believed the certificate would give him a claim to better paid work, even in public administration.[96]

Individual Land Help was not a success. The complaints of young people about lodging, food, and treatment were numerous. There were great hygienic, moral, and psychological difficulties in adjustment to such different ways of life.[97] Peasants frequently found that the help was not worth the board. In other cases the young people were used as cheap labor.[98] Turnover was great. In the spring of 1935, therefore, the emphasis was shifted from individual to group help. This shift coincided with that from help for the unemployed to help for farms needing manpower. Consequently, the rule

[93] Bibl. #120a, 1934, Part A, No. 3, p. 104.
[94] Circulars of April 6, 1934 (Bibl. #139, Vol. 1, p. 120); July 9, 1934 (*ibid.*, p. 183).
[95] "From an unfounded refusal must be concluded that he is not at the disposal of the employment office" (Circular of May 7, 1934, Bibl. #139, Vol. 1, p. 120).
[96] This was frequently the feeling of graduates of the other services, too (Max Timm, "Der Arbeitseinsatz in der Landwirtschaft," Bibl. #338, April 4, 1935, pp. 404-05).
[97] Bibl. #338, September 5, 1935, p. 1028.
[98] Bibl. #297, April 25, 1936.

that farmers would be subsidized merely when they engaged labor in addition to the workers ordinarily employed was waived.

Group help was based on an Order of the President of the Reifa[99] that all estates, whatever their size, if approved by the regional or peasant leader, could receive Land Help groups of at least five "Aryan" unemployed boys up to twenty-five years of age with subsidies if no other workers could be provided. The employer had to place at the head of each group a leader who understood farm work and was paid at ordinary rates without subsidy. He was responsible for the vocational, cultural, and political training of the helpers and for the use of their leisure time. Another skilled farm worker had to be provided for every four helpers, charged with the task of developing in them a taste for agriculture. When, in 1936, unemployed boys and girls were no longer available, owing to military and Labor Service, subsidies were no longer granted for individual Land Helpers,[100] but only for groups. The Reifa, however, continued to grant the necessary equipment allowance and traveling costs to young urban people sent to individual farmers, if they were unable to pay it themselves. In 1937 this help was extended to peasants and their children who were to be hired away from small holdings, especially in mountain regions in which the government planned consolidation.

While the original Land Help plan had considered merely the subsidizing of young people, the President of the Reifa in the autumn of 1933[101] extended Land Help to farm worker families. Farmers who employed additionally and housed a worker's family, especially with children of school age, received a subsidy for twelve months (in 1934 extended to two years). Workers who intended to marry could be exceptionally included. A year's contract had to be concluded. No restriction concerning the size of the employing farm was required, but not more than three families were to be subsidized on one farm. This measure intended to stop the development toward shorter contracts in agriculture.[102]

B. *Land Service* (Landdienst). Group help was taken over by the Hitler Youth, to which 90 per cent of German children belonged in 1939, and

[99] March 12, 1935 (Bibl. #139, Vol. 1, p. 104).

[100] Circular of April 3, 1936 (Bibl. #139, Vol. 1, pp. 109ff.).

[101] Decrees of September 28, 1933 (Bibl. #139, Vol. 1, p. 259); November 1, 1934 (*ibid.*, Vol. 1, p. 259); Circular of April 3, 1936 (*ibid.*, Vol. 1, pp. 109, 114).

[102] On April 15, 1935, subsidies were paid for 7,612 families; on April 15, 1935-1936, for 9,000 families; and on April 15, 1937-1938, for 3,800 families (Bibl. #332b, p. 23; Bibl. #332c, p. 24; Bibl. #332e, p. 27).

continued as Land Service with subsidies of the Reifa. At first only boys were sent out, then, after 1936, girls as well. The age range was fourteen to twenty-five. In 1938, 80 per cent were less than sixteen years old. Boys were placed in organized groups of five to fifty, in the first two years only on large estates, later predominantly in village camps from which they were sent to the farms.[103] At first contracts were concluded for the summer (after 1937, for one year), with normal wages and conditions of work. Girls could be trained in groups of four to ten in courses of about eight weeks. They were then placed on peasant farms. Work in the Land Service was taken fully into account in computing time spent on apprenticeship in agriculture. Several special schools were opened for training camp leaders. The aim was also to persuade the young urban people to remain in the country.[104]

Although the voluntary character of the service was constantly stressed in the press, voluntary joining gradually disappeared.[105] The Hitler Youth Year-book spoke of the planned raising of the allocation (Erhöhung des Einsatzes). Thirty Rm. of wages were retained as bail against breach of contract.[106]

Repeated official appeals to use the Land Service only in healthy and selected districts revealed untoward experiences. The authorities demanded that no piece wages be paid[107] and hours should be restricted to fifty-four to sixty. One afternoon had to be set aside to professional and sports training.

During the war the Land Service was used in the conquered territories in

[103] In 1936, 25 per cent were placed in villages; in 1937, 60 per cent; in 1938, 78 per cent; in 1940, 85 per cent (Klaus Danzer, "Landdienst der Hitler Jugend—Idee und Gestalt," Bibl. #139, 1940, Vol. v, p. 236).

[104] In 1937, 1,500 (i.e. about 10 per cent) stayed, and in 1938, 5,200 (29 per cent). Danzer, loc.cit.

[105] Bibl. #291, October 1937, A, p. 136.

[106] Selection became stricter when the Land Service was linked with political aims. On December 17, 1938, an agreement was concluded between the Reich Youth Leader, Baldur von Schirach, and the Reich Leader of the SS and the Gestapo, Heinrich Himmler, which stated that: (1) Land Service is particularly suited to supply the new entrants into the SS; (2) Land Service will therefore select new entrants with particular regard to the physical qualifications and conditions of character demanded by the SS; (3) Land Service will recruit mainly young people who have the definite aim of becoming peasants on their own land (especially soldier peasants, Wehrbauern); (4) all members of the Land Service serving in the SS will be settled on the land after completing the service; (5) all members of the Land Service who fulfill the requirements of the SS will be taken into it after leaving the Land Service (Bibl. #312, 1939, p. 93). In January 1940 an agreement between Hitler Youth and RN reserved for the former the political education, for the latter, the professional (Danzer, loc.cit.).

[107] According to an Order of April 7, 1942, the young people received during the first year 9 Rm. a month plus board and 1.50 Rm. for laundry, and were compensated like farm servants in the second year. Shelter was paid by the Hitler Youth (Bibl. #139, 1942, Vol. I, p. 167).

the east for agricultural and Germanization purposes. In his New Year's message in 1943, Reich Youth Leader Axmann reported that 18,000 young people of both sexes participated in the service in the conquered east; 10 leader schools and nearly 300 youth camps were established.[108]

According to an agreement of the Reich Youth and Reich Peasant Leaders, only the boys and girls needed for leader services (10 per cent) were to be recruited in the country, 90 per cent in the cities.[109]

C. *Land Year* (Landjahr). To overcome the labor shortage even children had to be recruited. The Land Year, beginning Easter 1934 in Prussia,[110] obliged all racially fit German boys and girls who had completed the eighth year of elementary school (usually at the age of fourteen) to a Land Year service of nine months. These children, in groups of thirty each, were to live in camps, ranging in size from 60 to 150 children, under the supervision of young leaders.[111] The Land Year was no "idyllic romance," but was practical experience in farm work where "sweat pours" and the daily bread is earned.[112] The Land Year represented a combination of National Socialist training, physical hardening, and farm work.[113]

Since, owing to the lack of leaders and accommodations, the service could not be carried through completely, it was limited to selected pupils from large industrial centers.[114] During the war it was extended to children from rural areas.[115] A committee composed of representatives of the party, the

[108] *Der Neue Tag*, Prague, January 2, 1943.

[109] *Ostsee Zeitung*, January 28, 1943.

[110] Gesetz über das Landjahr, March 29, 1934 (Bibl. #137, p. 243); and many Ordinances. Bremen, Brunswick, Württemberg, Hesse, the Saar District, and Saxony provided similar institutions by way of administration. The institution gained importance only in Prussia, where 550 camps existed in 1937, while all other regions had only 20 (Rolf Helm, "Landjahr und Bauerntum," Bibl. #327, October 1937, p. 214).

[111] They were supposed to spend half a day in farm work, the other half in political training and sports. The purposes were: to familiarize urban boys and girls with the ideas of blood and soil and bring them back to the purity of existence rooted in the land; to provide help to farmers; to teach youth how to serve for bread; to accustom them to a regime where "military discipline and simplicity determine life" (Bibl. #326, July 1935, Vol. 3, Nos. 13-14, p. 17).

[112] Land Year home leader Fritsche, in *International Education Review*, Berlin, 1935, p. 15.

[113] Educators who came from farms, the Hitler Youth, or elementary school teachers had to participate in a special training course for four weeks in a camp. There were two Reichs-leader schools and two technical training schools. Since educators were badly lacking, exemption from such training was frequently given. Specially fit children were trained as camp sub-leaders in two years, with some additional household training for girls.

[114] Bibl. #326, April and September 1934, Vol. 2, Nos. 8, 18.

[115] Bibl. #324, July 1, 1942.

Hitler Youth, and schools selected the children. They were predominantly allocated in the north and east. These children had some hard experiences because they were physically and emotionally unprepared for the heavy work and the new environment. Lodging in barracks was often primitive, food scarce, the work arduous, the treatment rigorous. The camp life followed military discipline, with many roll calls even during the night. "The soldierly, controlled (straffe und schneidige) bearing of the Land Year boys aroused admiration," wrote a high official of the Ministry of Education.[116] "After eight months the Land Year service child has a clean and soldierly work attitude."[117] The children worked on farms in whatever work was *going on, received instruction in racism,*[118] German history, fabrication of toy soldiers, and rifle practice.[119] The work was supposed to total four hours only. However, a work week of forty-five hours was admitted during the season.[120] Girls' camps established mending meetings for the village and kindergartens. The Hitler Youth took the Land Year camps frequently as centers of their activities.

Land Year children were to be privileged in placement as apprentices, because they were carefully selected and thoroughly inculcated with National Socialist doctrines.[121] The employment offices had to use their influence to keep them in the country[122] when their service ended.

Like all other services, the Land Year changed in character. While in 1934 the intention to bring urban children to the country may have been an important factor, the aim in the course of time became connected with the political aims of the regime. Besides providing labor, the youngsters were to provide National Socialist culture.[123] "The Land Year camp proved to be a folk-political weapon," a "castle of Germandom," the "incorporation of

---

[116] Adolf Schmidt Bodenstedt, "Das Landjahr des Reichserziehungsministeriums, seine erzieherischen und verwaltungsmässigen Grundzüge," Bibl. #335, May 18, 1940, p. 223.

[117] Land Year campleader Emil Häuser, "Erziehung zu handwerklicher Arbeit im Landjahr," Bibl. #287, 1938, Nichtamtlicher Teil, p. 225.

[118] Erwin Gentz (Bibl. #186), pp. 279ff.

[119] Decree of August 12, 1935 (*ibid.*, p. 159). Insurance for possible accidents occurring during rifle practice was provided.

[120] Decree of the Reich Minister of Education, May 3, 1940 (Bibl. #287, 1940, p. 276).

[121] Gentz, *op.cit.*, p. 169; Circular of August 7, 1934.

[122] Only 3-5 per cent of the Land Year children chose agricultural occupation (Bibl. #337, September 23, 1937).

[123] One of the Land Year leaders reported: "Our girls called enthusiastically the attention of the peasant women to the political events of the day. Thanks to constant training in the camps, they could meet all questions, rumors, and doubts in the village." Schmidt Bodenstedt, *op.cit.*, p. 224.

National Socialist character."[124] In 1943 the Minister of Education decreed that work in the Land Year be considered important for the war effort (kriegswichtig).[125]

LABOR SERVICE. Labor Service, introduced by the Democratic government during the depression with the aim of making unemployed youth acquainted with labor, was transformed by the National Socialist government into a semimilitaristic institution.[126] For boys between eighteen and twenty-five years of age the service (Reichsarbeitsdienst, RAD) was made compulsory by law on June 26, 1935.[127] Each year the Reich Chancellor had to fix the quota to be recruited and the duration of their service. The quota was increased from 200,000 in 1935 to 370,000 (including Austria) in April 1939. Until the beginning of the war the duration was fixed at six months. Members of the service received room and board but no salary.

In the first period of the regime the Labor Service was used predominantly for land recovery and land improvements intended to compensate for the loss of land diverted to military purposes. Woods were cleared and leveled, dry land irrigated, dikes built and marshes drained. As labor grew scarce, boys were used as working hands on farms during the harvest. With the beginning of the Four-Year Plan, however, boys were employed more and more at other work until at the outbreak of the war they became an auxiliary

[124] Schmidt Bodenstedt, "Das Landjahr in den eingegliederten Ostgebieten," Bibl. #287, Nichtamtlicher Teil, 1940, p. 131. Fifty camps were established in the conquered Polish territories by order of the Ministry of Education of September 30, 1939. In the Sudeten district ten camps were established (Schmidt Bodenstedt, Bibl. #335, *op.cit.*, p. 224); in the Wartheland, 26 camps for 800 girls and 700 boys; in Danzig West Prussia, 17 for 780 girls, in Ost Oberschlesien, 4 for 100 girls and 120 boys (Schmidt Bodenstedt, Bibl. #287, *op.cit.*, p. 130).

[125] Decree of February 4, 1943 (Bibl. #139, Vol. 1, p. 179).

[126] "The idea of compulsory Labor Service is a logical development and fulfillment of the idea embodied in compulsory education and national military service. Every German must work for his country and fight for the defense of his country. Compulsory Labor Service must become a duty of honor for German youth in the service of the nation. Through the compulsory Labor Service the National Government will have at its disposal a working army that will carry out great public works to serve the economic interests of the nation, as well as its cultural and other public interests," quoted in Fritz Edel (Bibl. #179) pp. 6-8.

[127] Reichsarbeitsdienstgesetz (Bibl. #140, Vol. 1, p. 769). Labor Service became a prerequisite for practically all careers. During the service boys and girls were subject to disciplinary regulations, the breach of which could be punished even by imprisonment. Highest authority was the Reichsarbeitsführer, Reich Labor Service Leader Konstantin Hierl, a former Army Colonel.

to the armed forces.[128] The Labor Service of boys can therefore be considered only partly as measure against labor shortage.

The tabulation of the work accomplished during the years 1935-1937 shows the following:

Distribution of Work Days in Percentage

	1934[a]	From April 1, 1935 to March 31, 1936[b]	From April 1, 1936 to March 31, 1937[b]	From April 1, 1936 to September 30, 1937	1938
Land reclamation	40	54.8	51.8	43.0	55.0
Harvesting	(included in other work)		7.0	33.2	—
Road construction for agriculture	25	13.7	8.5	4.3	15.0
Forestry	10	12.2	16.1	7.4	10.0
Urban settlement		4.0	3.3	1.5	
Rural settlement	8	1.2	1.1	0.5	5.0
Other work	17	14.1	12.2	10.1	5.0
Total	100	100.0	100.0	100.0	90.0

[a] Hellmut Egloff in *Jahrbuch für Nationalsozialistische Wirtschaft*, 1935, p. 149.
[b] Bibl. #153e, 1938, No. 4, p. 126.

While in the first years the RAD had helped only occasionally in harvest work, in 1936 it was ordered to harvest potato crops wherever they were endangered. In 1937 help was granted to all farmers who lacked workers through no fault of their own. Farmers were obliged to pay normal wages. The period of service was prolonged until October 24 in order to bring in potatoes and beet crops.[129] The proportion of land improvement work was reduced[130] in 1937 since more labor was needed for harvest work. From October 1938 on, two-fifths of the yearly complement of boys were to be called during the winter and three-fifths during the summer. Up to then equal numbers had been called up in winter and summer. The change was intended to compensate for the shortage of labor in agriculture and in the building trade. Boys from the country served only during the winter and returned to farm work in summer.

[128] During the war labor service for boys was transformed into basic military training in order to save training time when the boys were turned over to the military forces (Bibl. #317, May 3, 1943; and Bibl. #301, January 16, 1943). The average age of military recruitment was reduced from 19 to 17 (Bibl. #283, August 26, 1944).
[129] Bibl. #338, August 27, 1937, p. 1028.
[130] Decree of November 24, 1937 (Bibl. #140, Vol. 1, p. 1298).

Voluntary Labor Service for girls, reorganized in 1934[181] was open to girls from seventeen to twenty-five years of age with preference given to those between nineteen and twenty-two who were unemployed. Three types of centers were established: (1) centers for domestic work and social work in the neighborhood of towns to train girls from industrial and commercial occupations in domestic work, including gardening and livestock raising on a small scale; (2) rural centers trained girls for country life and for agricultural work and sent groups of about thirty to one farm or to several neighborhood farms; (3) from another type of center, assistance was provided for settlers.

The girls worked about seven hours and received training in National Socialism, hygiene, and sports. In 1937, 80.1 per cent of the girls served in the country, 13.7 per cent in towns, 5.7 per cent in kindergartens, 0.6 per cent in other work, mainly NSV.[132] Their total work was estimated to 150,000 hours of work a day.[133] The total number of leaders and assistants was 2,000. Under an agreement with the Directorate of the RN, concluded in 1937, girls were to serve only to aid the rural population. Their principal duty was to relieve the peasant woman in the home, the garden, the field, or the stable. "Work service for girls is a service of honor to the overburdened women and mothers of the German nation."[134] They were also to be employed in harvest kindergartens.

Lack of leaders delayed making the service compulsory. It was very difficult to provide leaders, since girls used to marry or go into other careers.[135] Many young girls had to be taken after a very short training period. Such leaders were not able to contribute much or exercise educational influence.[136] Up to 1936, the RAD for girls was not larger than 10,000-12,000. About 15,000 farmer

---

[181] Circular of January 27, 1934 (Bibl. #139, Vol. 1, p. 34). On April 1, 1936, the former autonomous organization was incorporated in the Reich Labor Service and detached from the Reifa (Decree of August 15, 1936, Bibl. #140, Vol. 1, p. 633). Its administration was carried out by a directorate through 13 (after the invasion of Austria, 14) branch offices. There were 321 camps in the spring of 1937, with forty girls, including the leader and her assistants, living in each camp.

[132] Bibl. #153e, 1938, No. 4, p. 130.

[133] Else Lüders, "Die Dienstpflicht der Frau," Bibl. #338, November 15, 1938, p. 1352.

[134] Hanna Wohnsdorf-Röbke, "Die Erziehung im Arbeitsdienst für die weibliche Jugend," *International Education Review*, 1937, pp. 285-86.

[135] Girls between 23 and 35 with good party standing were eligible for a leader career. They had to enlist for 12 years, were trained in four to six months in the schools of the Labor Service and could then be gradually promoted to staff leadership.

[136] Oberregierungsrat Helmut Tormin, "Die Zukunft des Frauenarbeitsdienstes," Bibl. #338, September 5, 1935, p. 1033.

families benefited from their work. In 1937 the number was raised to about 16,000; from April 1938 on, to 30,000 with 650 camps; on April 1, 1939, to 50,000. At the outbreak of the war the service for girls was made compulsory and the strength brought up to 100,000,[137] and during the war to 150,000. The lower age limit was reduced to seventeen. Girls working in agriculture were not recruited.[138] In the spring of 1944 compulsory Labor Service, including auxiliary service, was prolonged to one and a half years.[139] In the autumn of 1944 it was ordered that former Labor Service girls could be conscripted again for the Labor Service,[140] to be used especially in air defense.

OTHER SERVICES. Other services which could be used for help in agriculture, especially during the war, were:[141]

A. Youth Service (Jugenddienst)[142] made it the duty of all youngsters between ten and eighteen years of age to serve in the Hitler Youth and League of German Girls and to help according to instructions wherever help was needed, e.g. during the harvest, for the army, collecting garbage, clearing debris. Fines were imposed upon any person who detained the youth from fulfilling his service. Hitler Youth and the League of German Girls were especially used during the war in the conquered east to work on farms of new German settlers, and help to spread Germanization.

B. Auxiliary War Service (Kriegshilfsdienst) was introduced for students of high schools at the outbreak of the war for help in local emergencies. The certificate of graduation (Reife) could be given at the end of the year in spite of the leave from school.

C. Compensation Service (Ausgleichsdienst). Graduates from high schools intending to enter universities had to serve half a year in the Labor Service. For those who were unfit for military and Labor Service the Reich Minister of Education had established compensatory service, carried out by the Reich student leadership. It was rendered prevailingly in air protection and the welfare work of mother and child.

---

[137] Order of September 4, 1939 (Bibl. #140, Vol. 1, p. 1693).

[138] Decree of February 23, 1942 (Bibl. #139, Vol. v, p. 159). By Decree of July 29, 1941, girls became obliged to serve another half year in auxiliary war service on leaving the Labor Service (*ibid.*, Vol. 1, p. 463) and Orders of August 13, 1941 (*ibid.*, p. 491); of February 27, 1942 (Bibl. #140, Vol. 1, p. 95). Assignment to industrial work increased.

[139] Decree of April 8, 1944 (Bibl. #140, Vol. 1, p. 97).

[140] Bibl. #301, October 9, 1944.

[141] Bibl. #139, 1940, Vol. v, pp. 359-60.

[142] Based on Decree of March 25, 1939, for the administration of the Hitler Youth Act (Bibl. #140, Vol. 1, p. 710).

In spite of many adverse experiences, Land and Labor Services—the systematic completion of education in the Hitler Youth—were staged with great skill, with appeal to the longing of youth for activity and adventure. The young people were disciplined in work, and gained a comprehension of farm work and rural life. The constant appeal to nationalism and to the importance of youth for the salvation of the country, the sacrifice needed, the emphasis on the aristocratic character of farm labor did not fail to impress youth. Most of them considered the farm services a challenging sacrifice for the nation. German youth were the most loyal advance guard of National Socialism. Their exalted sense of devotion was utilized for Nazification of older people and Germanization of conquered nations.

But discipline, military drill, hard work, deprivation, and lack of privacy certainly did not appeal to all youngsters. The more intellectual and subtle among them were rebellious. Even in the controlled German press, complaints were heard about overstrain and exploitation. Secret reports stressed the spread of unrest and discontent and how escaping youth was brought back by the police.[143] In the Labor Service, Communist propaganda found a fertile soil.

During the period of democracy, trade unions had carefully watched that boys of the Labor Service did not replace normal workers with cheaper labor. That such misuse spread after control had been abolished was admitted by Reichsleiter Hierl at the party convention in 1937. He said: "There are farmers who seem to consider the Labor Service as an employment office which has to provide them with labor at reduced price or free of charge. In order to prevent them from dismissing their normal workers during the winter because they can use Labor Service during the summer, the Reich should demand payment ruthlessly." Darré expressed himself similarly at the Sixth Reich Peasant Day in 1938 regarding the abuse of the Land Service. "Take care that the peasantdom learns to understand the idealism of youth and proceed ruthlessly against those who consider youth merely convenient cheap labor."[144] The Labor Service for girls remained especially unpopular

[143] Concerning Land Year: Bibl. #291, May and June 1934, A, pp. 28ff.; October, November 1934, A, p. 21; March 1936, A, p. 74; February 1937, A, p. 50; 1938, Nos. 4-5, A, pp. 126-27. About the Labor Service: *ibid.*, October 1937, A, p. 137. That youth service did not improve moral standards may be seen in the rising figures in juvenile delinquency: youth from fourteen to eighteen punished by the regular courts rose from 12,303 in 1934 to 16,872 in 1936, despite increasing employment (Bibl. #153c, 1937, p. 594).

[144] Bibl. #275, 1938, Vol. 5, pp. 47-48.

with parents because boys' camps in the neighborhood gave girls the opportunity to fulfill the Führer's will that they have babies.

Figures for boys and girls in the most important Land Services are given in the accompanying tabulations. In 1938, Austrians were added; in 1939, inhabitants of the Sudeten District; in 1940, inhabitants of the incorporated Polish districts.

Land Helpers[145]

YEAR	April 15	December 15	August 15
1933	16,300	161,961	....
1934	165,000	69,500	....
1935	94,036	81,977	139,232
1936	36,681	31,122	....
1937	35,465	29,870	....
1938	29,286	40,796	....

Land Service[146]

YEAR	Groups	Boys and Girls	
1934	45	500 boys	
1935	240	3,500 boys	
1936	462	6,608 (	900 girls)
1937	1,173	14,888 (3,492	")
1938	1,452	18,000 (6,500	")
1939	1,753	26,016 (12,000	")
1940	....	18,400	
1942	....	30,000 (18,189	")
1943	....	40,000	

Land Year[147]

YEAR	Boys and Girls
1934	22,000 (about 5 per cent of the total number of school graduates)
1936	31,500
1937	28,000
1942	17,000

[145] Bibl. #310, 1938, Vol. i, p. 365. 42,600 individual Land Helpers were allocated in 1937-1938 plus 8,000 group helpers (Bibl. #332e, #139, 1939, No. 3, p. 27).

[146] Klaus Danzer, op.cit. (Bibl. #139, 1940, Vol. v, p. 236), with the two following exceptions: figure for 1940 from Bibl. #312, July-August 1941, quoted in Faschismus (Bibl. #294) 1941, pp. 149-50; figure for 1943 from Bibl. #346, October 11, 1944.

[147] Figure for 1934 from Bibl. #326, September 1934, Vol. 2, No. 18, p. 8; for 1936 from Else Lüders, "Die Dienstpflicht der Frau," Bibl. #338, November 15, 1938, p. 1353; for 1937 from Bibl. #272, May 15, 1939, p. 4; for 1942 (reduced because many leaders were in military service) from Volksrecht, Zürich, December 3, 1942.

Labor Service

YEAR	Boys	Girls
1935	200,000	10-12,000
1939	370,000	50,000
end of 1939		100,000
during the war		150,000

Recruitment of Labor Reserves

I. WOMEN

From the outset, the National Socialist hostility to gainful employment of women, especially of married women, had not included agriculture.[148] There was no need to attack women's work on farms. Since only women in positions desirable for men were to be ousted, drudgery of women on farms was not opposed. Theoretically all women had to be included in the call back to kitchen and nursery. This call, however, was revoked inconspicuously until in 1938 the ideological tenets were completely discarded. Exceptional work permits had been admitted for harvesting work of women receiving marriage loans as early as July 1936.[149] In December 1936[150] the duty for such women to work while their husbands were in the fighting forces or the Labor Service was established. In 1937 the strict prohibition of gainful employment for other women who had received marriage loans had to be made flexible, and was finally dropped.[151]

With the growing shortage of labor, pressure on women to do farm work increased. Since many disliked farm work, appeal for volunteers proved insufficient. The authorities met a resistance against leaving the home, which they themselves had helped to build up. Especially when the work was extended to members of the family, and those who were reluctant to get a work book were prosecuted, women were afraid of becoming "slaves of

[148] Of all women gainfully employed in 1940, 12.6 per cent were in agricultural, 27.7 per cent in domestic, 36 per cent in industry, 23.7 per cent in commercial, technical, and free professions. Land workers numbered 800,000. To them must be added 130,000 girls in Duty Year and Land Service. In forestry 60,000 women were occupied; 40.6 per cent of all working women were below 25 years of age. From 1938 to 1940, women's work in agriculture had increased by 14.3 per cent (Regierungsrat Scharlau, "Der Arbeitseinsatz der Frauen im Kriege" (Bibl. #139, 1941, Vol. v, pp. 89, 93).

[149] Law of July 28, 1936 (Bibl. #140, Vol. i, p. 576); Circular of the same date (Bibl. #139, Vol. i, p. 238).

[150] Circular of December 7, 1936 (Bibl. #139, 1937, Vol. i, p. 24).

[151] November 3, 1937 (Bibl. #140, Vol. i, p. 1158).

the work book." All kinds of incentives were applied. Since wives of soldiers had to be increasingly recruited the government provided in May 1940, that two-thirds of the income did not have to be considered in shortening the benefit to which dependents of the Armed Forces and of party services were entitled (which heretofore had been reduced according to the income from work). For women with children the percentage was higher.[152] Day nurseries and laundries relieved women from child care and household work. Appeals became more and more urgent.

Although conscription was used to recruit women for harvest work, there were complaints during the war that women refused to work because their husbands were earning enough. "For several years we have noticed a definite unwillingness [on the part of women] to do farm work," wrote the *Deutsche Volkswirtschaft* on August 2, 1942. "That is why there is such a large and inexhaustible reservoir among married women." In 1942, therefore, drastic measures were taken.[153]

2. OLD PEOPLE AND INVALIDS

Another group to be drawn back to gainful employment were old age and invalidity pensioners, who during the battle against unemployment had been encouraged to withdraw from the labor market.[154] From 1934 on, all invalidity pensions paid to persons under sixty years of age were reviewed in order to find out whether pensioners had ceased to be disabled. Even though, according to the RVO, invalidity benefits originally were to be paid only to those who could earn less than one-third as normal workers, it was now ruled that working pensioners should not be deprived of their pensions. The government's necessity to repeat in circulars and decrees the promise not to cut invalidity and old age pensions revealed clearly the continuing

[152] Joseph Schlick, "Beobachtungen in der Praxis des Arbeitseinsatzes." Circular of May 23, 1940 (Bibl. #139, Vol. v, p. 434). In the *Münchner Neueste Nachrichten* (Bibl. #317) a woman wrote: "Girls who work during the day in offices and in shops, but so far have used week ends and evenings for themselves; domestic servants who think that they have to use their time off only in entertainments" shall use their spare time to cultivate waste land (quoted in *Das wahre Deutschland*, Bibl. #347, July 1940, p. 8).

[153] The Duty Year for girls, introduced in February 1938, and conscription, introduced for men and women in June 1938, as well as the war measures, will be described below.

[154] "After the induction of the middle age groups the very old workers in the sixth, seventh and sometimes eighth decade form the spine of the working life," wrote *Die Deutsche Volkswirtschaft*, Bibl. #286, in the spring of 1944 (3 Maiheft, p. 423).

distrust of the workers.[155] Pensions which had been discontinued were ordered restored. Entrepreneurs were asked to alleviate the employment of partially handicapped or old workers. According to a declaration of a high official in the Ministry of Labor, one million persons living on pensions had returned to work. During the war even the recruitment of tuberculous persons was regulated.[156]

3. CONVICTS

Convicts were used to enlarge the labor supply. While at first they had been occupied only in fields attached to prisons or within the jails, a decree of the Ministry of Justice of July 23, 1937,[157] encouraged the use of convicts on big estates and in soil conservation. They were allocated in groups of eight to ten men under supervision of prison guards and kept separate from free labor. Convicts serving short terms were allowed to be allocated individually to agricultural work under supervision of the employer. In October 1937 about 15,000 convicts were working in agriculture.

With the growing shortage of labor the Four-Year Plan in 1938[158] opened large employment possibilities for convicts, regardless of length of term or character of crime. All physically fit convicts and persons undergoing preventive detention were to be employed productively on a full-time basis. Work in forests, on moor land, and in agriculture were mentioned. Former agricultural workers were not to be employed on other than agricultural work. Requests for prisoners became so great that in May 1939[159] the Ministers of Justice and Labor restricted the allocation of convicts to work of particular importance to the national economy: first, to defense, and then agriculture, and to melioration. In agriculture they were mainly used in soil conservation and during the harvest. Where they could not be returned to jail for the

---

[155] Act of January 15, 1941 (Bibl. #140, Vol. I, p. 34); Circulars of March 10, 1941 (Bibl. #139, Vol. I, p. 147); November 11, 1941 (*ibid.*, p. 472); July 1, 1943 (*ibid.*, Vol. II, p. 331).

[156] Order of June 8, 1943 (Bibl. #139, Vol. I, p. 379). The Federal Tuberculosis Committee (Reichstuberkuloseausschuss) declared that sufferers from active tuberculosis who . . . do not cough very much and eject only a small quantity of phlegm present little danger of infection under normal working conditions if they observe a strict discipline. All physicians and clinics treating tuberculous patients had to inform the employment office which of the patients were able to work.

[157] Bibl. #139, Vol. I, p. 215.

[158] Circular of the President of the Reifa in conjunction with the Minister of Justice of May 18, 1938 (Bibl. #139, Vol. I, p. 207); and Order of June 7, 1938 (Bibl. #284, p. 887).

[159] Order of May 10, 1939 (Bibl. #284, p. 1918).

night they were housed in special barracks (Gefangenenaussenarbeitslager). They received maintenance from the employer who paid 60 per cent of the normal wage to the government after deduction of cost of maintenance. An Order of December 27, 1940[160] provided that convicts were to be granted wages only if their performance corresponded to the normal work. An efficiency bonus of 10 M. could be granted at the end of the month at the suggestion of the supervisor. Supplementary food rations and shortened prison terms were the incentives to increased production. During the war the employment of young people in reformatories (Fürsorgeerziehung) was stressed.[161]

4. JEWS

Even employment of Jews was permitted after they had been deprived of all possibilities of gainful employment in 1938. In the beginning of 1939[162] business was urged to engage Jewish workers in order to release "German" workers for urgent construction work. Employers giving work to Jews would no longer be penalized. In 1941 compulsion was decreed.[163] However, all rules proved to be preparatory measures for extermination. In 1941 German Jews began to be deported to concentration camps where a small part of the group were forced to work, and a larger number were massacred. During

[160] Bibl. #284, 1941, p. 63.
[161] Circular of March 5, 1943 (Bibl. #139, Vol. i, p. 191).
[162] Bibl. #291, 1939, No. 6, A, p. 76.
[163] Orders of October 3, 1941 (Bibl. #140, Vol. i, p. 675); and October 31, 1941 (*ibid.*, p. 681). Jews were required to accept any work assigned to them by the employment offices. They could not be members of the works community (Circular of June 3, 1940 and Decision of the Federal Labor Court of July 24, 1940, Bibl. #284, p. 1035); Decrees of December 24, 1940 (Bibl. #140, Vol. i, p. 1666 and *ibid.*, p. 681) and could not be leaders or superiors. They received no pay for holidays, in case of sickness, overtime or vacation, no family allowances, no bonuses for childbirth; protective laws and safety rules did not apply to them; there was no protection for young workers, no protection against dismissal (Bibl. #139, 1941, Vol. i, pp. 9, 195, 496); Oberregierungsrat Hans Küppers, "Die vorläufige arbeitsrechtliche Behandlung der Juden" (*ibid.*, 1941, Vol. v, pp. 106ff., 469ff.; and Bibl. #297, November 22, 1941). A special levy of 15 per cent of their wages in excess of 39 Rm. monthly had to be paid. No additional pay (e.g. for days of sickness, old age), no compensation for time lost in air raids was admissible. Labor conflicts were decided by a special judge, nominated for each labor court, without appeal. In occupied Latvia the Jews were not allowed to receive wages, but employers paid a fee to the German authorities (Order of March 19, 1942, Bibl. #289, March 31, 1942). Gypsies were to be treated like Jews. However, there were only 34,000 to 40,000 living in the Reich (Decree of August 7, 1941, Bibl. #334, p. 1443). In the Government General forced labor had been decreed for all Jewish inhabitants from fourteen to sixty years of age as early as December 12, 1939 (Bibl. #344, 1939, p. 246).

the last years of the war the physical extermination of Jews became more important to the authorities than the utilization of their productive capacities.

5. DISABLED SERVICEMEN

Disabled servicemen were retained, usually in their old or related occupation, only exceptionally in a new one.[164] They were entitled to preferential treatment in the labor market. They were placed after medical rehabilitation or, if necessary, after retraining. The old law that employers must reserve at least two per cent of their jobs for veterans and accident victims with more than 50 per cent disability was maintained. Special courses were established for agricultural training of disabled servicemen.[165]

Compulsion to Work

I. INDIRECT COMPULSION MEASURES AGAINST BREACH OF
CONTRACT, SABOTAGE, AND SO FORTH

Before conscription was applied, various indirect means of compulsion had been gradually introduced. When agricultural work was recorded in the work book all other occupations were barred to young workers. As mentioned above, soldiers' wives received benefits only if they were unable to work. From 1935 on, all benefits of the National Socialist Welfare Organization and the Winter Help were made dependent on the condition that all members of the family were at the disposal of the employment offices.[166]

In 1936[167] employers were given the right to retain the work book (necessary for getting another job) of any agricultural worker in case of breach of contract until the date on which the contract would have come to an end if due notice had been given. In such case they had to send the book to the employment office together with the details of the case.[168]

The Wage Order of June 25, 1938, gave trustees of labor the power to punish breaches of contract which, moreover, could be prosecuted as a criminal offense. In November 1938, the RTA for Brandenburg threatened im-

---

[164] Circular of August 7, 1940 (Bibl. #139, Vol. 1, p. 423); and Order of September 18, 1940 (Bibl. #140, Vol. 1, p. 1241).

[165] Decree of May 10, 1940 (Bibl. #139, Vol. 1, p. 350).

[166] Bibl. #315, 1937, p. 117 and Bibl. #291, October 1936, p. 30.

[167] Decree of December 22, 1936 (Bibl. #139, 1937, Vol. 1, p. 13).

[168] The Federal Labor Court decided on September 21, 1938, that the work book could also be retained by the employer if the worker by anti-contractual behavior, for instance, sabotage, caused dismissal without notice. It had to be proved that the worker's behavior was due to a desire to change his job (Bibl. #274, Vol. 34, p. 98).

prisonment for breach of contract and demanded that no worker be hired who was obliged to work elsewhere.[169] After 1940[170] all suits concerning breaches of contract, conscription, or immobilization were to be concentrated in special courts in order to specialize prosecution and judges and to achieve unified decisions. The courts found that breaches had to be punished with imprisonment. In 50 per cent of the cases defenders had been given sentences ranging from two to six months in prison.

After 1940 workers who stayed away from work were to be punished by a corresponding cut in paid holidays.[171] The RTA had to be informed. In July 1942[172] the refusal or delay by a worker to perform any work assigned to him by his employer, including overtime and holiday work, was made punishable as a breach of contract. This included orders to accept transfer to an occupied territory.[173] In case of refusal the worker could be sent to a disciplinary camp.[174] Oversleeping, coming late to work on three occasions, absence from work for a single day without a medical certificate, and refusal to follow orders to move were considered sabotage. Labor trustees instructed employers to impose fines, withhold payment for holidays and children's allowances in cases of unjustified absenteeism. Other punishments for absenteeism were loss of rights to insurance benefits for two weeks,[175] loss of overtime bonus and of holiday bonus[176] if the worker was absent on the day before or after the holiday without excuse. Very elaborate rules about refunding of expenses for the arrest, transportation, and imprisonment of German and foreign workers who were unwilling to work or break their contract indicated frequent offenses.[177] In 1942 the press was full of reports of court proceedings in which workers were sentenced for offenses against work discipline, for inexcused absenteeism, or loafing on the job.

[169] Bibl. #291, 1939, No. 1, A, pp. 18-19.

[170] Order of March 16, 1940 (Bibl. #284, p. 365).

[171] Bibl. #139, 1940, Vol. v, p. 401. For women running their households the cut should be restricted to obstinate cases.

[172] Order of July 20, 1942 (Bibl. #139, Vol. 1, p. 850).

[173] Decree of March 2, 1944 (Bibl. #139, Vol. 1, p. 117).

[174] Bibl. #139, 1942, Vol. 1, p. 385; and Circular, March 2, 1944 (*ibid.*, Vol. 1, p. 117). A Bavarian association established a camp for vagrants in which they were trained on a model farm (*ibid.*, 1940, Vol. 1, p. 580).

[175] Bibl. #346, February 13, 1942 (Bibl. #139, 1940, Vol. v, p. 401; 1941, Vol. 11, p. 80; 1943, Vol. v, p. 16).

[176] A Federal Labor Court decision of June 7, 1941 ordered loss of the Christmas bonus in case of breach of loyalty duties (Bibl. #139, 1941, Vol. 1, p. 340).

[177] Circular of the Minister of the Interior of January 20, 1941 (Bibl. #139, Vol. 1, p. 166).

In 1944[178] the employer was ordered to send investigators to absent workers. If the latter claimed to be sick without medical certificate of incapacity, they could be obliged to make up for the lost working time within the legal limits (including Sunday and holiday without special bonus), or the lost time had to be deducted from vacations. Additional rations were to be cut in case of unjustified absenteeism,[179] conscription allowances (Dienstpflichtunterstützung) to be withdrawn.[180] Youthful loafers could be punished by arrest—in case of repeated offenses, by compulsory education in a reformatory.[181]

At the end of 1944 the courts of the DAF were empowered to deal with breaches of contract. In imposing punishment they were advised to consider the disparagement of money (in an economy in which very little could be bought). Money penalties were to be meted out in such a way as to be considered real punishment.[182]

Since workers frequently claimed to be unfit for farm work when they wished to migrate to industry, physicians were instructed not to help confirm such claims. The *Preussische Zeitung*[183] described as "philanthropy out of place" the willingness of physicians to certify incapacity to do farm work. The association of sick insurance funds, yielding to pressure of the RN, advised its physicians to give such certificates only in the most urgent cases. During the war the right to give such certificates became restricted to physicians employed by the Commissioner General of Manpower.[184] In 1943 employment registration cards had to be presented when women applied for a renewal of their ration cards.[185] However, it was officially denied that ration cards were withheld to enforce registration in 1943. "We have other means of forcing the few scroungers to do their duty. . . ."

[178] Decree of September 23, 1944, zur Sicherung der Ordnung in den Betrieben (Bibl. #139, Vol. I, p. 359).

[179] Decrees of June 19, 1944 (Bibl. #139, Vol. I, p. 245); October 19, 1944 (*ibid.*, p. 390).

[180] June 26, 1944 (Bibl. #139, Vol. I, p. 246).

[181] As a rule, three months of rigid labor education might suffice; if not, it could be prolonged; offenders with criminal tendencies could be imprisoned at the court's discretion. Decrees of December 14, 1943; December 21, 1943 (Bibl. #139, Vol. I, p. 506) and February 10, 1944 (*ibid.*, Vol. I, pp. 116-17); June 19 and 26, 1944 (*ibid.*, pp. 245-46); September 23, 1944 (*ibid.*, p. 359). The purpose of the arrest of offending youth was declared to be "to re-educate him and to force the youth by solitary confinement to consider the results of his misdeeds."

[182] Decree of October 25, 1944 (Bibl. #139, Vol. I, p. 401).

[183] No. 186, 1937.

[184] Decree of January 27, 1943 (Bibl. #278, February 16, 1943).

[185] Bibl. #319, September 19, 1943.

2. CONSCRIPTION OF LABOR

There were four types of compulsory labor services for adults. Labor Service (Arbeitsdienst) of boys and girls which has been discussed above; the Duty Year (Pflichtjahr) of girls; Compulsory Service (Dienstpflicht) to which every employable person was subject; and Emergency Service (Notdienst), ordinarily of short duration, established to meet natural catastrophes and war emergencies (air raids)[186] which was hardly used in agriculture.

The Duty Year (Pflichtjahr). From the very beginning the regime had considered conscription as a means of recruiting labor in case other means proved insufficient. For agriculture this emergency was reached at the end of 1937. In February 1938, when the demand for agricultural labor had risen to 250,000,[187] a year of compulsory labor for women, a so-called Duty Year, was added to the devices to ensure a larger labor supply. The Commissioner for the Four-Year Plan ordered that unmarried women below the age of twenty-five could not be engaged as wage earners or salaried employees in specified industries unless they had previously been occupied for at least one year in agriculture or domestic service. The clothing, textile, and tobacco industries were specified for wage earners (these industries employed one-half of all manual women workers) and all public and private offices for salaried employees.[188] On December 23, 1938,[189] the obligation was extended to any kind of employment. Although the Duty Year remained restricted to girls looking for gainful employment and did not apply to those who could live without earning their living, complete registration of youth made it possible to use pressure. The number of girls serving on it became practically identical with those leaving school.[190] Time spent in the Labor Service, or in agricultural training courses of the Reifa, was at first fully or partly counted against work in agriculture. In 1942 it was announced that Labor Service was not to be reduced if a girl had already done a Duty Year.[191]

Exceptions could be made for girls who were the sole breadwinners of the family or engaged in work of national political importance and for girls

---

[186] Notdienstverordnung of October 15, 1938 (Bibl. #140, Vol. 1, p. 1441); and Decree of September 15, 1939 (Bibl. #140, Vol. 1, p. 1775).

[187] Bibl. #338, January 15, 1939, pp. 81-82.

[188] Decrees of February 15 and February 16, 1938 (Bibl. #139, Vol. 1, p. 46).

[189] Bibl. #139, 1939, Vol. 1, p. 48.

[190] Bibl. #331, March 7, 1943 and Bibl. #283, March 17, 1943. Both newspapers wrote that as early as 1940 90 per cent of all girls below twenty years of age had a work book. The other 10 per cent were students and helping members of the family.

[191] Bibl. #314, July 23, 1942.

working at home in families with four or more children under fourteen years of age, and for those who were physically or mentally incapacitated. Requests for dispensation from this service came mostly from salaried employees.[192] The offices decided prevailingly according to the urgency of the demand for labor. The Duty Year could be served (a) in a free labor contract with wages and social insurance, (b) as household year in the country with free board and pocket money, (c) as agricultural apprenticeship on farms selected by the RN, with a one- or two-year contract, board and compensation, (d) as household apprenticeship with a two-year contract[193] or as Land Service in the Hitler Youth while living in a camp.[194]

At first girls were given the opportunity of going into, besides agriculture, nursing, midwifery, or baby care, in which case the term of the obligatory service was two years instead of one. Girls from rural districts had to remain in the country. The Regulation of December 1938 suppressed the freedom of girls to find positions for themselves.

As a rule their work relations was the labor contract. So great was the danger of exploitation of these girls that the RTA frequently had to remind employers in the first years that the girls were entitled to the same labor conditions as any other women workers and in particular that they must be paid wages as prescribed in collective rules (in distinction to the Labor Service which was supposed to be an educational measure). Housewives were not allowed to call themselves "Duty Year mothers."[195]

During the service, girls were not allowed to attend commercial courses (unless this prohibition would prevent their maintaining previously acquired skills). They were not supposed to distract their attention from their service. The League of German Girls had to take care of them in meetings which were called three to four times a year.[196] Girls were allowed to serve in the Protectorate, although the Duty Year was not introduced in that district.

[192] Erna Hamann, "Der Härtefall im Pflichtjahr der Mädchen," Bibl. #338, June 1, 1938, pp. 921ff.

[193] Bibl. #139, Vol. II, p. 430.
The 44,000 girls who served in 1938-1939 were distributed as follows:

Free labor contract	26,500	Labor service	1,600
Household year	12,000	Land year	1,600
Land service	1,900	Apprenticeship	400

Source: Erna Hamann, "Die Pflichtjahrmädchen in der Landwirtschaft," Bibl. #273, February-March 1940, pp. 28-29.

[194] Regina Frankenfeld (Bibl. #182) p. 75.

[195] Bibl. #297, May 27, 1941.

[196] Circular of May 18, 1940 (Bibl. #139, Vol. I, p. 335).

During the war thousands were sent to the conquered eastern territories. Girls working in nursery schools and kindergartens in the incorporated Polish districts were exempt from the Duty Year.[197]

From February to July 1938 about 30,400 girls were serving their year in agriculture (about 47,000 in domestic service). In the same period of 1939, the figure had risen to some 90,000[198] (127,480 in domestic service).

The Duty Year became thus a great relief for agriculture but remained unpopular, as it was when it started. Mothers did not understand why their daughters had to be trained by another woman.[199] An article in *Das junge Deutschland*[200] declared that the efforts to make girls remain in agricultural or domestic work had not been successful. It appeared that the girls regarded the year as a transition period which entitled them to preferential treatment in other employment. A high official ascribed to unaccustomed living conditions and homesickness the regularly recurring complaints of the girls about inedible food, poor shelter, too heavy work.[201] During the war farmers complained that the families used duty girls to provide food for hoarding.[202] When in 1943 a university professor recommended compulsory service of country-born girls for the postwar period, the periodical *Der Deutsche Volkswirt*[203] referred to the "unfavorable experience made with such rules. Such means will do more harm than be useful."

[197] Circular of August 31, 1940 (Bibl. #140, Vol. 1, p. 487).

[198] "Der Arbeitseinsatz im Deutschen Reich," ed. Hauptstelle der Reifa, December 13, 1938, p. 24. In five years, up to 1943, 1,500,000 girls served their Duty Year, which makes an average of 300,000 a year, about half of whom were allocated to agriculture, half to households of large families (Karla Witt in *NS Landpost*, Bibl. #321, February 5, 1943).

[199] Ida Kisker, "Das weibliche Gesinde in der rheinischen und westfälischen Landwirtschaft." In Sering and Dietze, Bibl. #250, Vol. III, p. 211.

[200] November 5, 1939, quoted in Bibl. #121a, December 1941, p. 636.

[201] Regierungsdirektor Jenzsch, "Der Pflichtjahreinsatz aus einem grossstädtischen Arbeitsamt" (Bibl. #139, Vol. v, pp. 356-57).

[202] The periodical of the SS which, owing to Gestapo affiliation was well informed about the people's troubles and never failed to pillory "undesirable" attitudes, described in detail how a girl tried to avoid the Duty Year. It summarized the measures used in one case: "Two examinations by official physicians, two by private physicians, two Duty Year contracts, two service obligations, four calls to the local police, eight records, one examination of the enterprise, seven reports and interviews in the office, nine letters from persons and agencies, nine telephone calls to the office, four calls by the office, nineteen letters from the father to the office, twenty-two from the office to the father; six assignment cards, in addition to other activities with the trustee and the local community." The case was considered as an example out of many (Bibl. #337, February 3, 1944, p. 5).

[203] March 20, 1943, p. 766.

Compulsory Service (Dienstpflicht). The National Defense Act of May 21, 1935,[204] which applied to men as well as women, had already provided that, apart from the obligation for military service, every German was obliged in the event of war to engage in national service. In 1938 when no labor was available to build the fortifications in the west, the government felt that the time had come to compel labor to take up this work. On June 22, 1938,[205] the Commissioner of the Four-Year Plan ordered the so-called Dienstpflicht, Compulsory Service, for all Germans, "to ensure the labor supply for work of special national importance." The President of the Reifa was empowered to require every employable German man or woman to undertake temporarily work assigned to them or to undergo vocational training. The requisitioned worker received a leave from his former employment. Conscripted labor was used at first for the construction of the Siegfried Wall. Agriculture was deprived of help because the work on the fortifications absorbed in addition to about 400,000 conscript laborers (up to February 1939) about 100,000 members of the Labor Service who might have helped in agriculture.[206]

On February 13, 1939,[207] the Compulsory Service Decree was superseded by a decree bearing the same name. It extended the scope to all persons residing in German territory with the exception of aliens covered by exemption of international treaties or of the recognized rules of international law. Compulsory Service could be required, either temporarily with a leave granted from the former employer, or for an indefinite period. In the latter case the old labor contract was terminated. Since the government intended to maintain the worker's claim to his old job, it was ruled in 1940 that Compulsory Service required "for the duration" or "pending further instructions" was to be considered temporary,[208] and in 1944 that the old employment contract was to be continued.[209]

---

[204] Bibl. #140, Vol. I, p. 609.

[205] Verordnung zur Sicherstellung des Kräftebedarfs für Aufgaben von besonderer staatspolitischer Bedeutung (Bibl. #140, Vol. I, p. 652); and Order of June 30, 1938 (*ibid.*, Vol. I, p. 707).

[206] *Bericht der Reichs-Kredit-Gesellschaft* (Bibl. #333) 1938-1939, p. 55; and Bibl. #120f, February 9, 1939, p. 15. Since the plight of agriculture increased, the Minister of Labor suggested in a Circular of July 9, 1939 (Bibl. #139, Vol. I, p. 321) conscription for sending wives of farm workers who were employed in industry and commerce back to the farm.

[207] Bibl. #140, Vol. I, p. 206; and Orders of March 2, 1939 (*ibid.*, p. 403); September 4, 1939 (Bibl. #139, Vol. I, p. 417); March 14, 1939 (*ibid.*, p. 236).

[208] Circular of October 14, 1940 (Bibl. #139, Vol. I, p. 547); a Circular of February 26, 1941 (*ibid.*, Vol. I, p. 131) ruled that all services were to be considered limited even if the termination could not be fixed in advance. In a Decree of August 5, 1941,

Employers notified the employment office of their labor demand; the offices then investigated to see whether all other possibilities for getting the required labor supply were exhausted, and decided whether to grant or reject the request. The work of the conscripted workers was carried out on the basis of labor contracts. They were allowed to leave their assigned occupation only with the permission of the employment office. Conscription was used to transfer workers from one job to the other. Refusal to obey or incitement to refusal were punishable.

Conscription, at first only cautiously used (in order to keep up workers' morale), had to be gradually increased.[210] The authorities stressed again and again that the summons to service by an employment office was the equal economic counterpart to an order for military conscription. "Arbeitskraft und Wehrkraft sind eins" ("labor force and armed force are one"), said the Minister of Labor.[211]

3. CONTROL OF MOBILITY OF LABOR

In the beginning, the regime intended to do away with the seasonal character of agricultural work, to make it permanent, and to stop migrant labor completely. The RN, the Reifa, and the trustees of labor had to use their influence in this direction. Collective rules provided yearly contracts and bonuses for workers who stayed some years in one job. Documents of honor were granted to such workers. No shortening of the periods of notice prescribed in collective rules was admitted.[212] The President of the Reifa requested heads of agricultural undertakings to employ their workers as much as possible during the winter. Those who dismissed their workers in winter without justification were warned that they would be refused a new

the Minister of Labor demanded the release of women at the end of their term (Bibl. #139, Vol. v, p. 461); however, a Circular of January 14, 1942, restricted release to *those whose personal and social situations so required* (Bibl. #139, 1942, Vol. I, p. 36).

[209] Bibl. #301, January 1, 1945.

[210] According to official statements up to July 1941 a total of about 2.3 million persons had been conscripted. At mid-July 1941, 437,000 men, and 174,000 women were serving, i.e. about 3 per cent of all employed men and 1.7 per cent of all employed women. That 7.8 per cent of all German workers lived separated from their families in October 1942, according to German press news, showed that the figure of Gleichgestellter, i.e. those who were tied up without conscription must have been much larger than those of conscripted workers. In 1940, 10 per cent of all vacancies were filled by the employment office and in 1941, 7 per cent were filled by conscription (Beisiegel, Bibl. #139, 1941, Vol. v, p. 489). In January 1942 the figure was 627,509; 197,372 of them were women (Bibl. #139, Vol. v, p. 284).

[211] Seldte, Bibl. #139, 1941, Vol. v, p. 81.

[212] Bibl. #330, 1937, p. 323.

supply in the season.[213] In fact the shortage of labor made farmers keep workers during the winter whom they formerly would have laid off at the end of the season. This reduced seasonal unemployment of the farm workers and the number of available seasonal workers.

As long as mobility was legally unhampered it had been considerable. In 1936-1937, when the restrictions imposed in 1934-1935 had been removed, the number of farm vacancies filled during the year was more than half a million. However, new restriction started after a short time.

By Order of March 1, 1938,[214] the presidents of the district employment offices were empowered to oblige individual enterprises to employ workers only with the consent of the employment offices in order to prevent pirating of workers, especially from agriculture. The Conscription Decree of February 13, 1939, entitled the Reich Minister of Labor to make the beginning and termination of labor contracts dependent upon the consent of the employment office when such measure seemed desirable on grounds of national policy. The Decree of March 10, 1939[215] made use of this power for agriculture and some war industries. Assisting members of the family were included. The consent of the employment office had to be obtained by employers and employees alike before notice was given "for the mere intention to give notice . . . disturbs work."[216] Permission was not necessary when both parties agreed to dissolve the contract.[217] The worker even in this case had to register with the employment office, which could send him back to the place he left. In spite of this handicap farmers and laborers took advantage of this exception. Moreover, the consent was not required if the worker had been engaged on trial, or if the worker worked only occasionally, merely during the harvest, received little pay, and was therefore not covered by sickness insurance. No consent was needed for young persons of the various services (Land Help, Land Service, Duty Year, etc.) who left at the end of their service.

Engagement of farm workers in other work than agricultural needed the consent of the employment office. Authority was not required for hiring which did not involve transfer of workers to a different branch of production. Thus a farm worker could accept a new job on a farm. If he intended to migrate to industry two permissions were needed, that of the employment

---

[213] Circular of October 20, 1937 (Bibl. #139, Vol. I, pp. 281-82).

[214] Bibl. #139, Vol. I, p. 70.

[215] Bibl. #140, Vol. I, p. 444.

[216] Direktor Timm, "Die Sicherstellung des Kräftebedarfs für Aufgaben von besonderer staatspolitischer Bedeutung" (Bibl. #139, 1939, Vol. II, p. 113).

[217] The Decree of August 11, 1944 (Bibl. #140, Vol. I, p. 176) made the consent of the employment office compulsory for cases of mutual agreement too.

office to which his employer belonged and the office in charge of the employer to whom he wanted to go. To quit without permit would have been a criminal offense. Even mobilized soldiers needed consent of the employment office to give notice while employers were not allowed to give notice to them without additional consent of the RTA.[218]

Thus at the eve of the war the apparatus of labor regulation had become so highly developed that there was little opportunity to escape its meshes. The restriction of "economically unsound fluctuations" had resulted in tying the farm worker to the land, with the power of moving him from one job to the other.

Since complete control of the labor supply had already been established the transition to war policy could be made without a break. When, in September 1939,[219] the termination consent was extended to all employment and apprenticeship, this inclusion of all workers in the mobility restrictions "alleviated the psychological situation in the countryside."[220] Except in agriculture and mining, hiring was made subject to the approval of the employment office (mining, however, with the exception of workers who came from agriculture).

Transfers of workers were used as punishment for grumblers and political "enemies" as in the beginning of the regime. Undesirable persons were punished by transfer to low-paid jobs. As a consequence workers were careful not to disclose dissatisfaction. No appeal, only complaint, was possible against decisions of the employment office. Even for dismissal without notice for important reasons consent was necessary, which, however, could be refused only if absolutely necessary in the interest of allocation of labor.[221]

It appears that, on the whole, complete control of hiring and release, backed by the wage policy of the government, was successfully achieved. Workers were not frozen to their jobs but lost the mobility based on their decision to accept a job or to quit. The right to move the worker was in the hands of the government.[222] The worker was simultaneously mobile, and tied to the job.

[218] Circular of December 12, 1940 (Bibl. #139, Vol. 1, p. 614).

[219] Decree of September 1, 1939 (Bibl. #140, Vol. 1, p. 1685); and Order of September 6, 1939 (ibid., p. 1690); and Order of September 13, 1939 (Bibl. #139, Vol. 1, p. 435).

[220] Heddy Neumeister, "Landflucht—Unaufhaltsam," Bibl. #139, 1940, Vol. v, p. 431.

[221] Decrees of April 19 and 24, 1940 (Bibl. #139, Vol. 1, pp. 251-52).

[222] Attempts of workers to get away from agriculture must have continued because the Frankfurter Zeitung (Bibl. #297) on December 30, 1942 complained: "It is definitely tragic that the flight from the land and farm work has never assumed such proportions as at the moment when the eastern territories demand colossal efforts for their organization."

4. SUMMARY

The attempts of the government to alleviate the shortage of manpower by services and the use of foreign labor did not succeed in closing the whole gap before the outbreak of the war. In Hesse in 1938 only one-third of the manpower which had left agriculture since 1933 could be replaced.[223] In Thuringia the demand for 22,000 workers in 1939 could be only partly filled in the following way:

Recruitment

3,532	Alien workers
3,628	Labor service
3,000	Land service
1,297	Voluntary helpers from industry
2,332	Compulsory " " "
13,789[a]	

In Baden the loss of 54,785 permanent workers could be partly filled in 1938 as follows:

Recruitment of long-term workers

2,000	Alien workers
2,000	Duty year
1,000	Labor service
1,000	Children
200	Land service
6,200	

In addition during the harvest:

1,000	Children
2,450	Labor service
132	SS
4,750	Army
1,500	Voluntary helpers mostly recruited by the NSDAP
500	On leave from industry
35	Students
20	Teachers
25	Prisoners
120	Unemployed
10,532[b]	

[a] Peter Wolf, *ibid.*, p. 162.   [b] Carl Brinkmann, *ibid.*, p. 250.

[223] Eduard Willeke, Bibl. #220, p. 150.

Special War Measures

I. ALLOCATION OF GERMAN MANPOWER

From 1936 on, the shortage of labor during the peak season became so acute that NSDAP, government, and RN appealed to the public for help. Storm troops, civil servants, and workers in their leisure time were urged to help. The Reichsbahn reduced the rate for these helpers.

Germany's entry into the war meant an accentuation of existing difficulties, because men from agriculture formed the nucleus of the fighting forces and children and old men were not equal in efficiency to men in the most productive age bracket. The labor shortage was accentuated by lack of skilled workers for repairing machinery and by a reduction in the number of animals withdrawn for use in the army. Help which town people formerly gave with the harvest was eliminated when authorities prohibited direct contact between producer and consumer in order to prevent hoarding. The first device was for women, children, and old men to perform more and heavier work and to work longer hours. The age for leaving school had already been lowered by a number of ministerial measures in order to secure children for farm work. Now school work was still further reduced. An Order of September 22, 1939,[224] provided that pupils of higher and intermediate schools who had reached sixteen years of age should be employed as auxiliary agricultural workers during the school holidays which could be extended to six months a year. The main holiday period was arranged with due consideration for the requirements of agriculture between May and October. Even children from ten to sixteen years of age could be employed locally on light work outside school hours.[225]

The Reich Student Leader ordered during the summer of 1939 all members of the German Student Body to undertake harvest service. Twenty-five thousand students were mobilized for farm work.[226] In December the Reich Student Leader announced that from January 1, 1940, students would be

---

[224] Children had been largely employed during the harvest in 1938 and had been included in sickness insurance and workmen's compensation.

[225] Similar orders were issued for children's work in 1940-1941. In the Province of Brandenburg alone, 50,000 children helped to bring in potatoes and beets, while 87 Rural Service groups organized 1,200 children for similar work (Bibl. #297, September 8, 1939). An incomplete census counted 350,000 boys and girls working 3.5 million work days during the root crop season, from September 15 to November 15, 1939 (Günter Kaufmann, Bibl. #205, p. 361).

[226] Students had been recruited for harvest work since the fall of 1933 when 1,000 had helped during twelve weeks (Bibl. #338, November 2, 1933, p. 127).

liable to a special labor service during the first three terms. It was to involve help in agriculture and forestry. A special service in the east was introduced, the so-called Grenzlanddienst.

In 1940-1941 the government tried to overcome the shortage of farm labor by employing prisoners of war and other foreign labor. When, however, the alien workers were sent to industry in winter and many of them not returned to farm work in summer, these groups could not provide enough hands for the periods of peak work. On March 7, 1942, Goering, the Commissioner of the Four-Year Plan, therefore decreed the mobilization of all reserves for agriculture.[227] According to the decree, persons living in the country or in country towns who, judging by their age, family obligations, and state of health, could be reasonably expected to carry out agricultural work, could be called upon by the employment office and put at the disposal of the local peasant leader. They were to be assigned to work in agriculture at the customary wage.

The preamble of the decree mentioned expressly wives of farm and industrial workers living in rural areas who were not yet employed in war work. The local peasant leaders were obliged to visit every family and to report to the employment offices on age, marital and health condition, and other obligations of all persons. Women who had to care for large families were to be employed temporarily, others permanently. The employment office had to help place children in nurseries or kindergartens, or with neighbors. Persons who refused to serve were punished and conscripted by way of Compulsory Service. In case failing health was given as a reason, an official physician examined.[228] In order to overcome the fear of women that as owners of a work book they would be liable to unlimited conscription, a work card was substituted for the book in the case of newly employed women. In a Circular of June 2, 1942,[229] the Commissioner General of Manpower enumerated the most important possibilities for recruitment of labor for agriculture and instructed the heads of employment offices to draw up plans for utilizing these reserves. Use of school children was emphasized in the

[227] "Decree concerning the employment of additional labor for safeguarding the food supplies of the German people," March 7, 1942 (Bibl. #139, Vol. i, pp. 120, 134; Vol. v, pp. 167ff.); and Circulars of March 12, 1942 (*ibid.*, Vol. i, p. 134); and May 4, 1942 (*ibid.*, Vol. i, p. 245).

[228] Oberregierungsrat Kaestner, "Arbeitseinsatz in der Landwirtschaft im dritten Kriegsjahr" (Bibl. #139, 1942, Vol. v, p. 170).

[229] Bibl. #139, 1942, Vol. i, p. 254.

first place.[280] Children ten to fourteen years of age were to be employed locally, for not more than six to eight hours a day; boys and girls over fourteen years of age either locally for continuous work or, in emergency, away from home. Wages for boys and girls were 0.30-0.40 Rm. a day with a maximum of 10 Rm. a month, for older girls 10 to 15 Rm.

Another reserve was composed of members of the NSDAP and its associations and structural parts who were obliged to dedicate their weekends "voluntarily" to farm work in compensation for use of clothing and tools. In one district of the state of Saxony, the thirty-two Storms of a local unit of Storm Troops (Standarte) took over the godfathership of one village each. The Storm was responsible for seeing that all labor was done in time by the troopers. In case of need the local peasant leader appealed to the Storm Leader who mobilized his men.[231] Another group was composed of voluntary helpers who worked during their vacations. The Party District Leader of the Saar Territory, for example, suspended vacations for all civil servants in the Westmark until September 1, and obliged them to work three weeks in agriculture.[232] Workers transitionally unemployed because of closing down of their factory, industrial workers on vacation, members of the armed forces, and the police were to be recruited. The NS Frauenschaft, a party association of women called urban women to relieve farm women from cooking and housework.[233] A special appeal was issued to women who, because of the danger of bombing, had migrated to the country.[234] All harvest helpers received additional food rations.[235]

As a result of the campaign,[236] one million workers were recruited from 58,660 communities: 948,000 of them were women; 813,000 of them were

[280] Circular of April 23, 1942 (Bibl. #139, Vol. II, pp. 28off.). On May 22, 1942, the *Frankfurter Zeitung* (Bibl. #297) reported that 500 girls from Berlin High Schools had been sent to Danzig West Prussia to work. In villages five girls were always to work together under a leader who herself was under supervision of the local leader of the League of German Girls. 2,000 to 2,500 girls sixteen to twenty-one years of age and 150 girl leaders were allocated in the east in order to help "in political instruction of the village communities" (Bibl. #139, 1942, Vol. v, p. 142). 17,000 girls were working in kindergartens of the NSV. In the Upper Bavarian hop harvest 5,167 boys and girls were employed, i.e. the total harvest was done by children (Bibl. #317, March 10, 1943). 20,000 students of both sexes, including aliens, were conscripted for eight weeks (1943, nine), but they were not to receive collective rules wages but free board and lodging and pocket money (Bibl. #139, 1942, Vol. I, p. 355; 1943, Vol. I, p. 282).
[231] *Volksrecht*, Zürich, December 3, 1942.
[232] *Brüsseler Zeitung*, May 16, 1942.   [233] *Der Führer*, June 11, 1942.
[234] Bibl. #321, June 26, 1942.   [235] Bibl. #297, May 14, 1942.
[236] Kaestner, "Einsatz zusätzlicher Arbeitskräfte für die Ernährungssicherung," Bibl. #139, 1942, Vol. v, pp. 384-85.

declared employable (einsatzfähig); 718,000 of them (88.3 per cent) came "voluntarily": 50,000 for permanent work (41,000 women and 5,800 men), the others for periods of peak work. About 95,000 persons were conscripted.[237] Von der Decken claimed[238] that Sauckel had succeeded in covering 80 to 100 per cent of the agricultural labor requirements. Transport difficulties, however, had not allowed the fulfilling of demands in all parts of the country.[239]

Still more compulsory measures had to be taken in 1943—at that time not only for agricultural labor. All men from sixteen to sixty-five years of age, and women from seventeen to forty-five, living in the Reich were compelled to "contribute by work and exertion to the war."[240] They were obliged to register in the employment office. Heavy penalties were threatened for failure to do so. Exempt were, among others, men and women who were following a full-time occupation in agriculture, aliens, expectant mothers as well as women with one child below school age or at least two children under fourteen years of age living with them in the same household, and those persons who had already been included in the Decree of March 1942. For recruitment in agriculture, the regulations of 1942 remained valid.[241] All mobilized persons were as a rule to be assigned to one farm. Where many small farms needed laborers and there were not enough draftees to assign at least one to each, draftees were to be grouped in a pool from which the local peasant leaders could assign them to various farms. In order to overcome bitter feelings, it was announced that efficiency wages and bonuses were to be paid.[242] After fifty days of work, higher rations were offered. Workers who did not fulfill their duties would be deprived of their self-suppliers' ration.

It was officially claimed that the demand for labor could be fully satisfied in 1943.[243] Due to the loss of eastern territory, the demand for 1944 was

---

[237] Bibl. #321, June 26, 1942. In 1940 the total number of persons mobilized for sowing and harvest help amounted to 1,236,000; in 1941 to 1,371,000.

[238] Bibl. #286, August 14, 1942.   [239] Bibl. #346, August 12, 1942.

[240] Order of January 27, 1943 (Bibl. #140, Vol. 1, p. 67), repeated on June 10, 1944 (Bibl. #140, Vol. 1, p. 133). The Orders of January 29 and 30 (Bibl. #140, Vol. 1, p. 75) and February 23, 1943 (ibid., Vol. 1, p. 114) aimed at transfer to war essential work. They provided for the closing down or amalgamation of small undertakings in trade, handicraft and industry, and restaurants, in order to release labor. The purged businessmen were promised restitution of their business after the war (in contrast to similar purges in 1938-1939).

[241] Circulars of January 28, 1943 (Bibl. #139, Vol. 1, p. 107); and May 25, 1943 (ibid., p. 326); May 4, 1943 (ibid., p. 282); and July 14, 1943 (ibid., p. 400); July 14, 1943 (ibid., p. 381).

[242] Bibl. #278, May 23, 1944 and Bibl. #286, 1 Juniheft 1944, No. 16, p. 451.

[243] 64 per cent of the additional workers were alien workers (including prisoners)

140,000 less than 1943. Two hundred thousand alien workers who were supposed to return to agriculture from industrial work could not cover the full demand which came to 62 per cent from peasant farms, 38 per cent from large estates.[244] In February, the Commissioner General appealed to all persons not yet in war work to register.[245] Especially, domestic workers and women over forty-five years of age were urged to volunteer even for a few hours daily. Evacuated persons from bombed towns were ordered to do farm work. Mobilization of youth corresponded to that of the former years. The results were unsatisfactory. All manpower reserves seemed to be exhausted.

The attempted assassination of Hitler gave the start for new drastic measures.[246] The shock effect of the so-called generals' plot had to be utilized and, significantly, the Minister of Propaganda was to do it. As Plenipotentiary for Total War Effort, he had the task of rousing the apathetic masses to desperate efforts and to fill the depleted ranks of the fighting and home forces. In a series of decrees,[247] Goebbels immediately started to call up men and women in faked employment (wives in their husband's business, girls in sham clerical jobs). The employment offices were empowered to cancel unsatisfactory labor contracts and to place persons made available in this way at the disposal of the war economy. The registration age for women was raised from forty-five to fifty. The German press frankly admitted that the additions to manpower as a result of this total mobilization could be only limited in number and low in quality, since all reserves had been tapped in 1943. Out of a hundred registrations, forty demanded exemptions and not all were unjustified, wrote the Reich.[248] The press emphasized the moral effect, the elimination of ill-feeling on the part of the drafted workers who saw other women escaping labor duties. Appeals and threats for women to register showed that special difficulties had to be overcome. Women resented being forced to work, and so did their husbands at the front. Women presented medical certificates and wanted to do only office work. The government responded alternately with praise of those who fulfilled their patriotic duties, and punishment of those who evaded registration or work.

---

and 36 per cent (100,000) Germans. Oberregierungsrat Radetzki, "Der landwirtschaftliche Arbeitseinsatz im fünften Kriegsjahr" (Bibl. #139, 1944, Vol. v, p. 197).

[244] *Ibid.*

[245] February 1944 (Bibl. #139, Vol. i, pp. 65, 109); Decree and Circular of June 10, 1944 (*ibid.*, pp. 224-45).

[246] Decree of the Führer of July 25, 1944 (Bibl. #140, Vol. i, p. 161).

[247] Decrees of July 28, 1944 (Bibl. #140, Vol. i, pp. 163-65, 167); July 31, 1944 (Bibl. #139, Vol. i, pp. 270, 309); August 29, 1944 (Bibl. #140, Vol. i, p. 190); and others.

[248] Bibl. #331, August 27, 1944.

Other measures were intended to transfer labor to war-essential work by restricting telephone and telegraph service, simplifying the service of the post office, the Red Cross, the departments of Justice and Finance (the last Prussian ministry, that of Finance, was closed down), the transfer of alien women from domestic to war work, prohibition of repair of watches and clocks without a special permit, the restriction of recreation and cultural life by depriving movies and theaters of their young members and prohibiting all activities not relevant to the war effort.[249] Newspapers by fusion were reduced from 4,900 to 1,500[250] and restricted in volume, and periodicals reduced to one for a field. Manufacture of and trade in luxury goods were prohibited; the number of wholesale and retail dealers was sharply curtailed. Banks and insurance companies, hotels and restaurants were combed out; exhibitions, fairs, and contests were prohibited. Certain high school and university faculties were to combine, or suspend activity. University students (with the exception of those who had studied several terms in technical fields important to the war effort, injured war veterans who were too incapacitated to work, and war widows) as well as students in the upper classes of the high schools, were systematically drafted[251] for war work. To pacify the army, which accused party officials of being shirkers, even the NSDAP was combed out. All transfers were achieved by conscription.

It is doubtful whether agriculture profited by these measures. Many of the transferred workers merely replaced those inducted into the armed forces. "All dispensable workers have been rushed to the frontier to help build fortifications, and therefore harvest work has slackened," wrote the *National Zeitung*, Essen, on September 24, 1944. The Home Army (Volkssturm),[252] formed in October 1944, of all able-bodied men between sixteen and sixty for the defense of the home soil, absorbed manpower which might have been used for farm work; prolongation of hours in industry and business had a similar effect. An additional strain by the military training for the Volkssturm which was supposed to occupy half a day on Sundays was imposed upon people who had already spent themselves to the point of physical exhaustion. This could not but impair work efficiency. Sauckel himself in a programmatic speech, admitted that women from forty-five to fifty years were the only reserve and that increase in production could be achieved

[249] Bibl. #346, August 12, 1944, and Bibl. #283, August 25, 1944.
[250] Bibl. #346, September 9, 1944.
[251] Bibl. #283, September 9, 1944.
[252] Decree of the Führer of October 18, 1944. The Home Army members were considered soldiers during their service (Order of February 1943, Bibl. #321, March 5, 1943; Bibl. #283, October 20, 1944).

merely by increasing efficiency.[253] No expansion of alien labor force was possible in the period of defeat. In February 1945 women were summoned for auxiliary work with the Volkssturm.[254]

Another means of providing labor was by farm patronage, ordered by the RN. The farmer, exempt from military service, was not only obliged to work his own farm, but to assist and advise in the management of neighboring farms whose owners were serving in the armed forces. The patron-manager had to do the work himself where women were too old or sick, but they did not receive pay.[255] A peasant frequently had to manage two or three farms in addition to his own.

The patron was obliged to supervise the farm daily, to take care of the utilization of the output, to pool tools and machines. The local peasant leader in collaboration with the local advisers found out which farms needed help and proposed the patron. Then an arrangement was concluded which had to be confirmed by the county peasant leader.[256]

2. ALLOCATION OF ALIEN LABOR

In spite of their promise to abolish alien labor made before their rise to power and despite their disinclination to lose currency,[257] from 1937 on the regime had to take steps to bring foreign agricultural workers to the country.[258] After the outbreak of the war the problem of labor shortage was solved

[253] Bibl. #301, November 22, 1944.   [254] New York Times, February 13, 1945.
[255] Bibl. #297, March 3, 1943.
[256] Similar forms of neighborhood help were the so-called Ortsdreieck (Village triangle), composed of the local party leader, the mayor, and the local peasant leader and the Kriegshöfegemeinschaft (war farm community) established in Austria in the autumn of 1944. The latter united several farms which had no substitute for the inducted farmer, and were put under the supervision of an efficient farmer by the Ortsdreieck. The patron farmer could run these farms either together with his own or separately, or rent them temporarily. He was especially responsible for a rational use of manpower and implements (Bibl. #346, October 21, 1944).
[257] Every foreign worker meant a loss of 350 Rm. a year in foreign exchange (Friedrich Syrup, "Der Arbeitseinsatz in Deutschland," Bibl. #338, February 1, 1938, p. 136).
[258] Foreign workers employed in German agriculture:

1933-1934	44,645	1936-1937	64,976
1934-1935	51,992[a]	1937-1938	121,638[c]
1935-1936	53,653[b]	1939	216,045[d]

Not included in these figures is the large amount of workers introduced from Austria and Czechoslovakia after the annexation of these countries.
[a] Source: Bibl. #332b, p. 24.
[b] Source: Bibl. #332c, pp. 32-33; Bibl. #332d, p. 39.
[c] Source: Bibl. #332e, p. 31.
[d] Source: Bibl. #341b, 2. 183,133 of them were farm workers; 10,015 independent; 21,680 helping members of the family; 1,217 salaried employees (Bibl. #341b, 2, p. 58).

by the large-scale utilization of civilian labor from conquered countries and employment of war prisoners.

PRISONERS OF WAR.[259] While the High Command of the Armed Forces retained ultimate authority allocation was entrusted to the employment service.[260] Allocation officers (Arbeitseinsatzoffiziere) were attached to each prison camp. They cooperated with the nearest employment office. Each camp included about 10,000 prisoners. Upon arrival prisoners were interviewed, classified according to occupation, and grouped into labor commandos of ten, which were used as a mobile corps to work on several farms in the same village. Undertakings wanting to employ prisoners applied through their local employment office to the department of placement of the camp which decided in each case. Legal relations existed merely between camp and employer, not with the prisoner.[261]

In April 1940 Polish prisoners were occupied as follows:

	Per Cent
Agriculture	90.8
Forestry	1.7
Land improvement	1.4
Industry	6.1[262]

Following the invasion of Western European countries 360,000 prisoners from these countries were put to work, 53 per cent of them in agriculture, 47 per cent in industry,[263] since it was advisable to use available skills.

A Circular of the Ministry of Labor of October 7, 1940,[264] repeated in the following years, obliged employment offices to investigate whether prisoners of war were occupied according to their skill and if not, to transfer them.

[259] As early as autumn 1939 more than 261,000 Polish farm workers could be occupied. The figure of prisoners of war, was estimated to amount to three million in late 1941. Although since that time more prisoners were taken, the total number decreased because many prisoners were transferred to civilian labor status in Germany in order to release prison guards; some died and some were exchanged. *The International Labour Review* (Bibl. #121a) gave the figure of 1,750,000 for 1943 (September 1943, p. 317).

[260] The employment of prisoners was regulated in a series of decrees and circulars, summarized, July 10, 1940 (Bibl. #139, Vol. 1, p. 384).

[261] Decree of March 20, 1942 (Bibl. #139, Vol. 1, p. 208); Bibl. #297, May 11, 1942.

[262] Regierungsrat Holk, "Der Einsatz von Kriegsgefangenen in Arbeitsstellen (Bibl. #139, 1940, Vol. v, p. 354).

[263] *Ibid.*, p. 355.

[264] Bibl. #139, Vol. 1, p. 531. Circular of May 27, 1942 (Bibl. #139, Vol. 1, p. 288). Priorities in 1940 were fixed in the following way: (1) agriculture, (2) forestry, (3) land improvements, (4) to (8) others, (9) building for agriculture, (10) turf production.

The offices were instructed to transfer labor not needed in agriculture during the slack season to other occupations and to return them later to seasonal work,[265] so that during the season again 65-70 per cent could be occupied in agriculture.

By Circular of May 8, 1941,[266] it was ordered that all prisoners of war from the southeast, even those from other vocations, were to be used at first in agriculture. Only if they belonged to scarcity vocations (Mangelberufe) such as metal work and mining, could they be returned to these occupations from agriculture immediately after the spring work had been completed. In the autumn of 1941, of 1.5 million prisoners, half were engaged in agriculture and forestry.[267]

FOREIGN CIVILIAN WORKERS. The second class of alien workers were civilians from conquered countries. The National Socialist government could use labor in a twofold way: to make the conquered country work for the Reich, or to dispatch foreign workers to the Reich. Both methods were used.[268]

There were two groups of foreign workers in German agriculture, those who by incorporation ceased to be aliens, and those who remained aliens. The official announcement enumerated as "nonaliens" besides the inhabitants of Austria, Sudetenland, Memel, Danzig, Western Poland, Alsace-Lorraine, Eupen, Malmedy and Moresnet, the following: inhabitants of Luxembourg and the Protectorate (Bohemia Moravia) and the repatriated Folk Germans from Bessarabia, Bukovina, Galicia, Estonia, Latvia, Volhynia, South Tyrol.[269] Part of these workers belonged to invaded and conquered countries. The others had "come home to the Reich" according to treaties concluded with their respective countries.[270]

---

[265] Circular of October 9, 1940 (*ibid.*, Vol. 1, p. 532).

[266] Bibl. #139, Vol. 1, p. 217.

[267] Beisiegel, *op.cit.* (Bibl. #139, Vol. v, p. 490).

[268] In March 1942 the *Vierjahresplan* (Bibl. #345), reported that 14 per cent of all Belgian workers (270,000) were already in the Reich and that more than 50 per cent worked immediately in the German interest in Belgium.

[269] Bibl. #286, May 30, 1941, p. 1261.

[270] Workers were deported not only to Germany but from one occupied country to another. Italians, Slovenes, Dutchmen, Belgians, and Frenchmen were sent into the Government General, Poles and Dutchmen into France, Poles and Russians into Norway (Bibl. #286, July 17, 1942). The huge migration movement inspired the *Schwarze Korps* (Bibl. #337, July 9, 1942) to a note, "The East is the Future, German Heerfahrt": "We who came here were Germans, Netherlanders, Flemish, Swedes, Norwegians, Danes. On the stops of our trip we met Italians, Spaniards, Slovaks, Hungarians, Croats, Frenchmen, Rumanians, Finns, the troopers and shield bearers of the European knights. SS men of the Greater German Division, we are standing shoulder to shoulder in this land, in our East."

A. Recruitment, Allocation, and Amount of Foreign Labor. From all occupied territories a large number of workers were recruited by various devices. These included: (1) "Voluntary" enlistment by promises of increased pay and rations; for nonpolitical prisoners awaiting trial, exemption from prosecution; exemption from taxes; and other inducements. Volunteers at first had a choice among different regions, later they were allocated to a certain place of work. (2) Indirect compulsion by withholding unemployment benefits and food rations from those who refused to go. Unemployment was created by closing down restaurants and shops not necessary to the war effort. (3) Direct compulsion: In the occupied countries (with exception of Denmark), from compulsory registration in public employment offices with the help of work books, combing out of workers, to labor service of young people and general conscription, control of change of jobs, all devices of the control of the labor market were employed. Arrest and enlistment of idlers and manhunts were used especially in the east where no pretense at legality was made. In the Government General "often entire city districts or villages were surrounded by Gestapo agents and all the people found in the districts were rounded up and taken to labor camps or sent to Germany. Often quotas were imposed on municipalities and the communities were made responsible for the required number of laborers to be supplied for emigration to Germany.[271] Even night raids were utilized to get Polish workers. In Prague in 1942 restaurants were raided and all visitors not in war work were sent to Germany. (4) Compulsion against the occupied, allied or neutral countries was used by threatening to withhold food and fuel supplies from occupied countries unless labor was sent. There were other threats against allied or neutral countries. With the Axis states or others under German influence, agreements[272] were concluded to provide "guest workers." The countries found German demands very burdensome.

Differentiations made in the beginning by showing more consideration for northern and western workers were reduced, partly because of the resistance in the privileged countries, partly because of the manpower shortage. Transfer of foreign labor from the occupied countries to the Reich took place more and more by forcible methods. Compulsion, however, alternated with inducements. Sauckel himself admitted that "out of 5 million foreign workers who had arrived in Germany not even 200,000 came voluntarily."[273] Deportation

---

[271] Simon Segal (Bibl. #248), p. 164.
[272] Italy, Slovakia, Croatia, Hungary, Rumania, Spain, and Bulgaria.
[273] Bibl. #227, Part II, p. 314.

of workers to Germany was a method of removing the temptation to revolt in the homeland by holding alien workers as hostages in Germany. Refusal to follow the draft or help members of the family to evade it was heavily punished (even by expropriation) and could be considered sabotage. For the Eastland (Lithuania, Latvia, Estonia) the stages were described as: registration, collection in camps, physical examination (after which those unfit were sent home), political test, transportation in caravans by foot to the railway station, then in freight cars into the Reich.[274] On arrival they were put into camps, whence they were distributed to various farms.

A correspondent described in the *Sozialistische Warte*[275] in June 1940 a typical street scene in an agricultural town in Württemberg where Polish workers had been brought into the market place for farmers to choose laborers. The Poles were grouped together; they could not speak German and had no interpreters. The farmers went among them and chose them like cattle. If it happened that one farmer chose the husband and another the wife, the Poles made frantic attempts to disclose their relationship. Later, however, it was discovered that separation of families impaired performance, and special regulations provided that families be allocated together.[276]

The great influx of foreign workers began after autumn of 1941.[277] By June 1942 the number of aliens from twenty-one nations acknowledged to be working in the Reich in agriculture had jumped to 1.9 million. At that time almost one quarter of the total number of workers in the Reich were aliens.[278] In July more than 2 million aliens were working on farms,[279] in 1944 more than 2.4 million (including Austria and Sudetenland).[280]

---

[274] Bibl. #278, September 14, 1942.

[275] *New Statesman and Nation*, June 29, 1940, p. 791. For Bavaria, see Bibl. #317, August 5, 1942.

[276] Decrees of November 21, 1942 (Bibl. #139, Vol. 1, p. 550); April 21, 1943 (*ibid.*, Vol. 1, p. 301); August 30, 1943 (*ibid.*, Vol. v, p. 424).

[277] In the winter of 1940-1941, the number of foreign agricultural workers added during the war was officially given as follows:

Polish civilians	469,000
Other aliens	92,000
Prisoners of war	650,000
Released Polish prisoners of war	180,000
Total	1,391,000

Source: Bibl. #153e, 1941, No. 5, p. 100. These figures were an understatement. They did not include an unknown number of citizens of incorporated areas, resettlers and other aliens who for biological reasons were claimed to be Germans.

[278] *The Economist*, London, June 13, 1942, p. 830; and Bibl. #297, August 4, 1942.

[279] In the beginning of 1944, according to an estimate of the International Labour Office, the total number including 2 million prisoners of war was approximately

In the fall of 1940 the government changed its policy with regard to the type of job to be assigned to foreign workers. Poles and other Slavs were to be used in agriculture while Scandinavian, Dutch, French, and Belgian workers would be assigned primarily to mining and industrial enterprises. The allocation to industry of workers whom the National Socialists considered racially superior and to agriculture workers considered racially inferior was in strange contradiction to the National Socialist tenet of the elevated status of the tiller of the soil.

A priority list for the employment of workers from conquered countries was issued in the autumn of 1942.[281] Foreign manpower was to be used in the first place to meet important wartime requirements of the German troops, occupation and civil authorities. Thereafter came the requirements of food supply and agriculture. In the fourth place, labor had to serve needs of undertakings producing goods for the German population. Civilian industries of the occupied countries could employ the remaining labor pool. Since that time all pretense of voluntary recruitment was stopped. Foreign workers had a work book like German workers and their employment was controlled by a National Register.

B. *Contracts of Work.* Contracts were at first concluded for six months with the understanding that the worker could return home at the expiration of this period. Actually, however, he was not allowed to return. The contractual period was later extended to cover the duration of the war. Or it was stipulated that a certain percentage of the wage would be paid only after renewal of the contract. There were statements that foreign workers would be kept indefinitely if needed. Workers frequently did not understand the contracts they signed, or found their contracts altered after they had left for Germany.

8,670,000. These figures refer to a larger area than the Reich of 1939 (Bibl. #121a, October 1944, p. 469). A high official in the Ministry of Expellees gives the figure of foreigners in Germany at the end of the war as 9,259,000 (Werner Middleman, Bibl. #221, April 27, 1953, p. 5). According to official German figures, about 65 per cent of the total number of foreign workers were drafted in Poland and Soviet Russia. The next largest quota, 18 per cent, came from Holland, Belgium, France. Czechoslovakia and Italy together contributed 10 per cent (Karl Brandt and others, Bibl. #170, p. 615).

[280] German official statistics compiled by US Strategic Bombing Survey (*Monthly Labor Review*, February 1946, p. 195). Although the number of foreign workers in agriculture was rising, the proportion of farm to industrial workers was falling.

[281] Decree of August 22, 1942 (Bibl. #139, Vol. 1, p. 382). The decree applies also to prisoners of war employed in occupied countries.

As soon as the worker was assigned to work in Germany his ration card was canceled and a new one provided at the place of destination. Once on the job, the worker was obliged to stay. Only well certified diseases or, in case of women, pregnancy, could bring about the return to the home country. Leaving without consent of the authorities brought heavy penalties. A tight network of controls enforced these regulations. Foreign workers were largely employed in national groups.

C. *Productivity of Work and Slavization.* Although the employment of war prisoners and civilian workers from occupied countries had gone a long way toward ostensible aid in coping with the problem, the labor shortage was not fully offset. Foreign labor was only a poor substitute for German labor, although the difficulties met in industries were still greater, because the division of labor which assigned Slavs to agriculture provided the latter with the more docile labor type. Workers who were involuntarily employed by the oppressor of their country, separated from their families, in alien surroundings, were not overexerting themselves. Many of them lacked the skill, intelligence, and education of the German worker. They were not used to German methods of work and were incapable of doing much without detailed direction. Livestock, which requires trained and experienced help, especially was endangered. Difficulties of understanding the language slowed their work down.[282] Farmers complained that they were not permitted to keep the worker who had become used to the work and whom they had clothed and fed but that these workers were transferred to industry at the end of the season. Regulations were prescribed for minimum output. The reasons for failure to achieve the minimum amount were investigated. Disciplinary measures to induce laborers to work were warnings, fines, deduction from

[282] According to an estimate of the Berlin Commissioner of Prices dated March 2, 1942, the deficiencies of war prisoners on building work was as follows (normal = 100):

	Per Cent		Per Cent
French	80-90	Serbs	60-70
Belgians	75-85	British	45-55
Poles	65-75	Russians	40-50

Quoted in *Fascism*, November 18, 1942, p. 161. On January 13, 1944 the *Schwarze Korps* (Bibl. #337) complained that employers demanded two to three foreign workers to replace one German. The periodical added: "If someone claims that he needs three Russians for one German, one must answer that the Soviets hardly had been able to display their amazing armament power with such lack of efficiency." A study of the Labor Research Institute of the DAF which in 1942 investigated 3,671 workers in 19 industrial establishments, found that eastern workers reached about 80 per cent of the performance of German workers (Bibl. #139, 1944, Vol. v, p. 226).

leaves of all time lost.[283] Employers were instructed to forward to the Gestapo information concerning foreigners' disloyalty to their work. In case sabotage or unwillingness to conform was suspected or the conduct was "contrary to duty," the worker could without trial be sent to a concentration camp; even death sentences were inflicted. Sabotage (although not frequent in agriculture),[284] and carelessness showed that the use of aliens from the conquered countries was far from profitable.

With German youth trying to get away from agriculture and more and more foreign workers recruited for it, the danger arose that German soil might be tilled only by foreigners. In some parts of Germany aliens ran the farms. In a broadcast address the Minister of Labor said on October 22, 1940: "We must never reach a point where mining and agriculture become occupations for foreign workers." "The present large-scale employment of foreign workers in our agriculture can be only an emergency measure that must never be allowed to become a permanent state of affairs. After the war, the most that could be allowed would be the employment of foreigners in compact groups on large estates in building or on specific industrial jobs. The employment of such workers in family undertakings and on hereditary farms must be ruled out."[285] "The soil belongs in the long run only to the people who are employed on it. No national economy is sound which cannot dispense with the help of foreign workers."[286] "To do nothing, to make money, and to let others do the work would become a base ideal disrupting our people," wrote the *Frankfurter Zeitung*.[287] Those who believed in blood and soil, in the National Socialist promise of an increase in the dignity of farm work, were deeply disappointed.[288]

[283] Order of February 20, 1943 (Bibl. #139, Vol. I, p. 196).

[284] A circular issued by Himmler, the Gestapo Chief, showed that sabotage occurred in agriculture, too. The circular drew attention to the measures for safeguarding the German harvest against damage by fire, and demanded the immediate denunciation of all persons who intentionally or carelessly exposed the harvest to fire.

[285] Bibl. #139, 1940, Vol. v, p. 519. On October 25, 1941, the *RABl.* wrote: "The solution of keeping the youth of the countryside in the countryside and of provoking an outward flow of young persons from the city to the country is definitely a matter of eminently political and social significance" (Vol. v, pp. 540ff.).

[286] Syrup in Bibl. #139, July 15, 1941.   [287] August 14, 1940.

[288] In the Völkischer Beobachter (Bibl. #346), a peasant complained that replacement of German labor brought a sharp decline in the morals of the farm population. "That farm work has sunk to second-rate work for which foreign workers are collected because it is not good enough for his own workers" "embitters the heart of the farmer." He said that farm children continued to desert farm work. Colonization of conquered countries was useless (quoted by the *Christian Science Monitor*, October 13, 1942). In fact, Eastern Germany was Slavicized.

CHAPTER V. CONCLUSION

NATIONAL SOCIALISM had come into power with a well defined romantic agrarian program. De-urbanization and repopulation of rural districts were to restore physical and mental health of the degenerated nation and provide a sound breeding place for the future generation. Rootedness in the soil, stabilization instead of mobility, security of land tenure, would result in a new aristocracy of blood and soil, the rise of a peasant class of highest prestige. The Hereditary Farm Law was to achieve the "denomadization" of the soil by securing ownership and inheritance to racially pure men who—together with their wives—would comply with the childbearing demands of the party.

As systematic as the program seemed to be, it soon showed its inner contradictions, especially when the other aims: self sufficiency of food supply and preparation for war are added. The luxury of a peasant system which was to represent the new elite had to be sacrificed to the food needs of a nation planning for war. The promise to develop the human side of agriculture came into conflict at first with the aims of agricultural autarky which favored large scale farming, later with the aims of maximum autarky of the total national economy. Agriculture had to become more and more mechanized and industrialized and peasant farming suffered correspondingly. Even before the war men on the farms were drawn into the armament industries and replaced by women and foreigners. The nostalgia for the pre-industrial, pre-capitalistic, pre-market age, the hatred for the "pavement" had no practical result. The demands of war industry proved more persuasive than the ideological requirements of blood and soil. No regime succeeded in depleting the farm population and strengthening urbanization so much as the National Socialists did with their program of re-agrarization. To acquire new holdings by conquest, proved to be easier than to fill with German farmers the empty space from which the natives had been expelled. Hitler's prophetic words at the harvest festival in 1933 seemed to come true: A ruined peasantry cannot be reborn.[1] In spite of its proclamation favoring private ownership, totalitarian planning and the intention to secure racial purity and political reliability of peasants, led to property restrictions which transformed the free farmer into an employee of the state who paid for a small improvement in security with regimentation and impairment of his freedom to act. The peasant who was to return to a life with old costumes, sagas and

---

[1] Speech on the Bückeberg on October 7, 1933, Bibl. #198, Vol. 1, pp. 872-73.

folktales—became in fact subjected to the modern machinery of a vast organization. He who was to be liberated from the market, had to follow the command of public authorities. He paid with loss of property rights and the insecurity of a constant change of policy in opposite direction according to the interests of the party or war needs.

It was symptomatic of the breakdown of the romantic plans that in May 1942 the Minister of Agriculture and Reich Peasant Leader R. Walther Darré who stood for a mystic peasant agriculture and who since 1930 had been head of the agrarian machinery of the party resigned and that the responsibility for directing agricultural policy was transferred to the party office. The Minister of Agriculture was merely to give effect to the party's policy which at that time concerned war needs only.

The agrarian institutions of National Socialism, RN, the system of regimentation, the hereditary farm scheme were wiped out after the breakdown of the regime as if they never had existed.

The labor policy of the regime tried to overcome the antagonism of capital and labor by abolishing the independent organizations of employers and employees by forcing both into one organization which served mainly propaganda purposes. The paternalistic relationship of the works community with leaders and followers to be established on estates remained without significance on farms with their traditional labor relations. Labor lost interest in labor courts because collective disputes were suppressed and the settlement of individual disputes was delegated to other agencies, such as the Labor Front, the trustees of labor and employment offices.

Protective legislation was not without progressive features. Protection of women during pregnancy and after childbirth was an innovation for agriculture where so far no prohibitions of work or protection against heavy work for women had existed. A further achievement was the generalization of the claims to paid vacations, for adults as well as for young people, although restrictions had to be imposed at the end of the war. New was the general recognition of paid absences due to reasons of illness or death in the family, birth of a child, moving, or by reasons of civic duties. Of course well intended rules were not enforced when manpower shortage compelled the government to exact the last ounce of working strength from people. There were also contradictions in social policy, e.g. when the patriarchal desire to increase wages in kind and the economic request for efficiency wages clashed. In such cases the romantic wish such as for wages in kind had to yield. Nor could the objective of maintaining wage rates on the same level be achieved in spite of the complete control of mobility of labor. Consequently the differential between the agricultural and industrial wages widened. Compared with the exploited foreign worker, however, the German farm worker was still a privileged group.

An innovation also were family allowances and other privileges granted to large families, although these measures as so many others were distorted by restrictions to racially sound and bodily fit families who were loyal to the regime. In sickness insurances large families were freed from paying fees, again restricted to hereditary healthy families. Unpopular were the racial prejudices and political requests attached to nearly all benefits the regime had provided. Sickness insurance had become useless for those who were afraid of being stigmatized as hereditary poor stock. Tight supervision of physicians who were supposed to give the certificate to work at the earliest possible date after the sickness did not improve the doctor-patient relationship; nor did the restriction of the free choice of physician. It was a good measure to include permanently incapacitated persons in sickness insurance, but undesirable that persons who had proved inimical to the regime were deprived of their pensions. The German worker—so proud of his social insurance—disliked the clear intention of the National Socialists to transform the system into one of general assistance, without legal claim, with the threatening introduction of the means test. Wherever a step was made which might have been in the right direction, such as in housing, settlement of landless workers, the condition to select families with many healthy children or procreative faculties, marred the measure. Assistance to mother and child helped the mother who could be useful to the party or the hereditary healthy child, while infirm mothers and children remained without help.

This kind of discrimination culminated in welfare work which intended to help only the strong, to penalize the weak, and to eradicate the racially and politically undesirable person or family. That families were classified according to their eugenic and social value for the folk community and that the lowest were excluded from relief, that inmates of insane asylums were eradicated, aroused deep concern especially in the rural population which still had religious ties. The delegation of welfare tasks to a party organization strengthened the political domination in this field.

Party promises to the farm workers were not fulfilled. Werner Willikens,[2] a member of the Reichstag, and Friedrich Hildebrandt,[3] a member of the

[2] Werner Willikens (Bibl. #266), pp. 61ff.
[3] Friedrich Hildebrandt (Bibl. #194).

Mecklenburg Diet, had formulated the party platform before the NSDAP came into power: equal real wages of farm workers and industrial workers, a worker's share in output, a ten-hour day, promotion by settlement, no wage earning by wives, no employment of foreign workers, pension funds for farm workers. The worker's share in output and his pension did not considerably increase; nor did he reach the industrial worker's real wage. He had to work longer hours and his wife had to toil harder. He had no chance to settle in his own country.

Restrictions of mobility, introduced for agricultural workers as early as 1934, although very cautiously applied, were felt as discrimination by the farm worker and resulted in a flight without precedence when the restrictions were removed, two and a half years later. The regime was unable to stop the exodus and had to see how the most able workers, the "blood source" of the nation, were attracted by industry, while agriculture's productivity suffered correspondingly.

Hardly had the mobility of farm workers been restored when, in March 1938, new restrictions intended to prevent pirating of workers from agriculture. Their engagement in other than farm work again needed government consent. Thus the farm worker became tied to the land with the possibility of moving from one farm job to the other. When after the outbreak of the war in September 1939 the restrictions of mobility were extended to all working people, the psychological situation for the farm worker was somewhat relieved.

The worker, tied to farming, found himself in some kind of state of feudalism. He was serf in relation to the state, free worker in his relation to his employer. The latter acted as functionary of the state and was supposed to be paternalistic to his workers. In distinction from medieval feudalism, the worker was not a fixture on the particular farm, not dependent on the character of his master, but was bound to official consent for changing employers. Labor market control already in peace time was directed exclusively by military needs, indicated by the concentration of labor administration, by the public monopoly of placement, the work book, compulsory direction and total control of the change of jobs.

Socially the worker had gained by the levelling down of higher classes, the disappearance of the "bourgeois," the creation of groups of outcasts, such as Jews, enemies of the state and foreign workers. He advanced in prestige as "German" labor, and like the peasant was glorified in pictures, books, movies, on the stage. The farm worker, however, as "production soldier" could not lose the feeling of inferiority. The soldier, the engineer, the skilled industrial worker, proved more indispensable for warfare. In reversing the former progress from status to contract, the National Socialists, by stressing the public character of the job, strengthened a development from contract to status.[4] The farm worker lost his right of coalition and of collective bargaining and all other achievements of the revolution of 1918. His standard of living was threatened again by foreign labor, although the government felt responsible for keeping labor, as a valuable instrument of production, in good physical condition, as well as in good morale. Controlled in his work, he was not free in his personal life. But control of income, of mobility and living, loss of freedom, were not characteristics of only one class in National Socialist Germany. It was the fate of the nation.

Since Hitler, in the divided Germany the traditional problems of farm labor have largely disappeared.

Agricultural conditions in East Germany have been patterned after the Russian, and in this conquered country more rigidly so than in the other satellite states.[5]

In West Germany, middle and small sized family farms prevail and—with a few exceptions—they are fenced in between industrial areas. The conditions of farm labor are not, and never have been there, a serious problem. Like all National Socialist laws, those governing agriculture and the people engaged in it have been eliminated. Certain reforms have been introduced with the aim of bringing the working and living standards of farm labor closer to those of industrial workers.

[4] Ernst Fraenkel (Bibl. #25), p. 135.
[5] Wunderlich, *Farmer and Farm Labor in the Soviet Zone of Germany*, New York, 1958.

BIBLIOGRAPHY

Parts I, II: Introduction and Period of Democracy

a) Books

1. Aereboe, Friedrich. *Agrarpolitik*. Berlin, 1928.
2. ———. "Der Einfluss des Krieges auf die landwirtschaftliche Produktion in Deutschland," Carnegie Endowment for International Peace, Division of Economics and History, *Wirtschafts- und Sozialgeschichte des Weltkrieges*, deutsche Serie No. 4. Stuttgart, Berlin, Leipzig, 1927.
3. *Arbeitsrecht und Arbeiterschutz*. Die sozialpolitische Gesetzgebung des Reichs nach dem Stande vom August 1924. Berlin, 1924.
4. Asmis, Walter. *Der landwirtschaftliche Arbeitsertrag nach bürgerlichem und Gemeinderecht*. Merseburg, 1909.
   Baade, Fritz. See #112h.
   Das bäuerliche Erbrecht. See #149b.
5. *Der Bauer ist kein Spielzeug*. Festschrift für Dr. Ernst Mayer. Langensalza, 1932.
6. Becker, Friedrich. "Die Kriegsmassnahmen zur Hebung der landwirtschaftlichen Produktion im Amtsbezirk Heidelberg." Doctoral dissertation, Heidelberg, 1917.
7. Beckmann, Fritz and others (eds.). *Deutsche Agrarpolitik im Rahmen der inneren und äusseren Wirtschaftspolitik*. Im Auftrage des Vorstandes der Friedrich List Gesellschaft. Teil 1, *Die Lage der deutschen Landwirtschaft und die Gestaltung der agrarpolitischen Einzelmassnahmen*. Berlin, 1932.
8. Behrens, Franz. *Gewerkschaftliche Selbsthilfe der Landarbeiter*. Berlin, 1919.
9. Bergmann, Mauricy; Schleiter, Franz; Wickel, Heinrich. *Handbuch der Arbeit*, 3. Abt., *Die Koalitionen*. Jena, 1931.
   Bernier, Wilhelm. See #112 h,1 and #112 o.
   Böker, Hans. See #121b,3.
10. Borsig, Ernst von. *Reagrarisierung Deutschlands*. Jena, 1934.
11. Braun, Otto. *Von Weimar zu Hitler*. 2nd ed., New York, 1940.
12. Brecht, Arnold. *Federalism and Regionalism in Germany. The Division of Prussia*. New York, 1945.
13. Brentano, Lujo. *Über Anerbenrecht und Grundeigentum*. Berlin, 1895.
   ———. See also #114.
   Brugger, Peter. See #105g.
   Bülow, F. W. von. See #121b,3.
   Carver, Thomas Nixon. See #26.
14. Clapham, J. H., and Eileen Power (eds.). *The Cambridge Economic History of Europe from the Decline of the Roman Empire*, Vol. 1, *The Agrarian Life of the Middle Ages*. Cambridge, 1941.

15. Chemnitz, Walter. *Die Frauenarbeit im Kriege*. Berlin, 1926.
16. Cohnstaedt, Wilhelm. *Die Agrarfrage in der deutschen Sozialdemokratie von Karl Marx bis zum Breslauer Parteitag*. München, 1903.
   Damaschke, Adolf. See #124.
17. David, Eduard. *Sozialismus und Landwirtschaft*. Leipzig, 1922.
18. Delbrück, Hans. *Die Polenfrage*. Berlin, 1894.
19. Dierkes, Johannes and Erwin Rawicz. *Taschenbuch für die Sozialpolitik*. München, 1930.
20. Dietz, Johann Friedrich. *Das Dorf als Erziehungsgemeinde*, 2nd ed., Weimar, 1931.
21. Dietze, C. von. *Die ostdeutschen Landarbeiterverhältnisse seit der Revolution*. Berlin, 1922.
   ———. See also #149d.
22. Doegen, Wilhelm. "Die feindlichen Kriegsgefangenen in Deutschland," in Schwarte, M., *Der grosse Krieg 1914-1918*, Vol. 10, Leipzig, 1923.
23. Falke, Friedrich. *Die Landflucht und ihre Ursachen und Wirkungen*. Leipzig, 1929.
24. Fallada, Hans. *Bauern, Bomben, Bonzen*. Berlin, 1931.
   Feige, Georg. See #147.
25. Fraenkel, Ernst. *Military Occupation and the Rule of Law. Occupation Government in the Rhineland 1918-1923*. Oxford, 1944.
26. Fuchs, Carl Johannes. "The Epochs of German Agrarian History and Agrarian Policy," in Carver, Thomas Nixon, *Selected Readings in Rural Economics*. Boston, 1916.
27. Fuhrmann, Hans. "Die Versorgung der deutschen Landwirtschaft mit Arbeitskräften im Weltkriege." Doctoral dissertation, Würzburg, 1937.
28. Goltz, Theodor Freiherr von der. *Die ländliche Arbeiterfrage und ihre Lösung*, 2nd ed., Danzig, 1874.
29. ———. *Geschichte der deutschen Landwirtschaft II*. Stuttgart, Berlin, 1903.
30. *Great Britain*. Final Report, Agricultural Tribunal of Investigation. London, 1924.
31. Grünberg, Karl. *Agrarverfassung. Begriffliches und Zuständliches. Grundriss der Sozialökonomik*, Part 7. Tübingen, 1922.
32. Hainisch, Michael. *Die Landflucht*. Jena, 1924.
33. *Handwörterbuch der Staatswissenschaften*, 4th ed., Jena, 1923-1929.
34. Heberle, Rudolph. *From Democracy to Nazism: A Regional Case Study on Political Parties in Germany*. Baton Rouge, 1945.
35. Heiligenthal, Roman. *Staat und Siedlung. Karlsruher akademische Reden*. 1932.
   Helmerking, Wilhelm. See #112n.
   Hering, Franz. See #112k.

36. Hofer, Max. *Die Lohn- und Tarifpolitik des Zentralverbandes der Landarbeiter.* Berlin, 1926.

37. ———. *Die Lebenshaltung der Landarbeiter. Wirtschaftsrechnungen von 130 Landarbeiterfamilien.* Berlin, 1930.

38. Hohlfeld, F. *Deutsche Reichsgeschichte in Dokumenten 1849-1934,* 2nd ed., Berlin, 1934.

39. Holzapfel, W. *Siedlungsgesetzgebung.* Berlin, Leipzig, 1920.

40. Hucho, Wolfgang. *Die Naturalentlohnung in der deutschen Landwirtschaft.* Berlin, 1925.

Kamm, Walter. See #152.

41. Kiesenwetter, Otto von. *Fünfundzwanzig Jahre wirtschaftspolitischen Kampfes.* Geschichtliche Darstellung des Bundes der Landwirte. Berlin, zum 18. Februar 1918.

42. Knapp, Georg Friedrich. *Die Bauernbefreiung und der Ursprung der Landarbeiter in den älteren Teilen Preussens.* Leipzig, 1887.

43. ———. *Die Bauernbefreiung in Österreich und Preussen.* Einführung in einige Hauptgebiete der Nationalökonomie. München, Leipzig, 1925.

44. Koeth, Oberst. "Die wirtschaftliche Demobilmachung, ihre Aufgabe und ihre Organe," *Handbuch der Politik,* ed. Gerhard Anschütz and others. 3rd ed., Berlin, Leipzig, 1921.

45. *Die Kreditlage der deutschen Landwirtschaft im Wirtschaftsjahr 1932-1933* (and later), ed. Deutsche Rentenbank-Kreditanstalt (Landwirtschaftliche Zentralbank), Berlin.

46. *Kriegsgefangene Völker,* Vol. 1. *Der Kriegsgefangenen Haltung und Schicksal in Deutschland,* ed. Wilhelm Doegen, im amtlichen Auftrage des Reichswehrministeriums. Berlin, 1919.

47. Krünitz, Johann Georg. *Ökonomisch-technologische Enzyklopädie oder allgemeines System der Staats-, Stadt-, Haus- und Landwirtschaft.* Berlin. Started to appear in 1773.

48. Kusiewicz, Stanislaus T. *Le problème de l'émigration polonaise en Allemagne.* Paris, 1930.

Kwasnik, Walter. See #112m.

49. *Die Landschule,* ed. Geschäftsführender Ausschuss des Deutschen Lehrervereins. 1926.

50. *Um die Landschule.* Karl Eckhard and Stephan Konetzky (eds.), im Auftrage des Zentralinstituts für Erziehung und Unterricht. Langensalza, 1931.

51. *Das landwirtschaftliche Bildungswesen in Preussen.* Denkschrift des Ministers für Landwirtschaft, Domänen und Forsten. Berlin, 1929.

52. League of Nations, Economic Committee. *The Agricultural Crisis,* Vol. 1, Geneva, 1931.

Ley, Norbert. See #105d.

53. Luetgebrune, Walter. *Neu-Preussens Bauernkrieg. Entstehung und Kampf der Landvolkbewegung.* Hamburg, Berlin, Leipzig, 1931.
    Marckmann, Ernst. See #105b,2.
54. *Material for a Study of Germany's Economy, Currency and Finance.* By Order of the German Government, Berlin, 1924.
55. Mattes, Wilhelm. *Die Bayerischen Bauernräte.* Stuttgart, Berlin, 1921.
    Migration Laws and Treaties. See #121b,4.
56. Milhaud, Edgard. *La Démocratie socialiste allemande.* Paris, 1903.
57. Morier, R. B. D. "The Agrarian Legislation of Prussia during the Present Century," *System of Land Tenure in Various Countries,* ed. J. W. Probyn. London, 1876.
58. Muncy, Lysbeth Walker. *The Junker in the Prussian Administration under William II. 1888-1914.* Providence, R.I., 1944.
59. Münzinger, Adolf. *Der Arbeitsertrag der bäuerlichen Familienwirtschaft.* Eine bäuerliche Betriebserhebung in Württemberg. Berlin, 1929.
60. Naumann, Werner. "Der deutsche Arbeitsdienst; eine historische kritische Darstellung seiner Ideengeschichte und praktischen Verwirklichung." Doctoral dissertation. Jena (1934 ?).
    Niehaus, Heinrich. See #105b,1.
61. Padberg, Kurt. *Die Soziallasten der deutschen Landwirtschaft. Deutscher Landwirtschaftsrat,* No. 30. Berlin, 1932.
62. Polenz, Wilhelm von. *Der Grabenhäger,* 3rd ed., 2 vols., Berlin, 1903.
63. Preussisches Ministerium für Landwirtschaft, Domänen und Forsten (ed.). *Die deutsche ländliche Siedlung. Formen. Aufgaben. Ziele.* 2nd ed., Berlin, 1931.
64. Puttkammer, Ilse von. "Die Landarbeiterfrage in Pommern." Doctoral dissertation, Heidelberg, 1929.
65. Quante, Peter. *Die Flucht aus der Landwirtschaft.* Berlin, 1933.
66. Radetzki, Werner. *Die inländischen landwirtschaftlichen Wanderarbeiter Deutschlands.* Breslau, 1930.
67. Raupach, Hans, and Peter Quante. *Die Bilanz des deutschen Ostens.* Kitzingen-Main, 1953.
68. Rawicz, Erwin. *Die deutsche Sozialpolitik im Spiegel der Statistik.* München-Gladbach, 1929.
69. Reichsbauern- und Landarbeiterrat. *Durch Not zur Einheit.* n.d.
70. Reichsverband der deutschen land- und forstwirtschaftlichen Arbeitgebervereinigungen, *Zusammenstellung der wichtigsten Tarifbestimmungen aus den vom Reichsverband erfassten landwirtschaftlichen Tarifverträgen für das Jahr 1920.* Berlin, 1921.
71. Roeber, Gustav. "Die deutsche Landarbeiterfrage nach dem Weltkriege." Doctoral dissertation, Hamburg, 1931.

72. Rumpf, Fritz. "Die Wandlungen von Zielsetzung und Methode." Doctoral dissertation, Königsberg, 1935.

73. Schmidt, Georg. *Sozialdemokratie und Landwirtschaft.* Berlin, 1920.
———. See also #112e.
Schmitt, Julius. See #112d.

74. Schmoller, Gustav. *Umrisse und Untersuchungen zur Verfassungs-, Verwaltungs- und Wirtschaftsgeschichte.* Leipzig, 1898.

75. Scholz, Hans. "Die Organisation der technischen Nothilfe und ihre volkswirtschaftliche Leistung." Doctoral dissertation, Köln, 1938.
Seiff, Rudolf. See #105a.

76. Sering, Max. "Die agrarische Grundlage der Sozialverfassung," *Probleme des deutschen Wirtschaftslebens.* Deutsches Institut für Bankwissenschaft und Bankwesen. Berlin, Leipzig, 1937.

77. ———. (ed.) *Deutsche Agrarpolitik auf geschichtlicher und landeskundlicher Grundlage,* unter Mitarbeit von Heinrich Niehaus und Friedrich Schlösser. Leipzig, 1934. (See also #250.)
———. See also #105e and #149a, 149b, 149c.

78. Simon, Helene. *Landwirtschaftliche Kinderarbeit.* Berlin, 1925.

79. Skalweit, August. *Die deutsche Kriegsernährungswirtschaft.* Carnegie Endowment for International Peace, Division of Economics and History, *Wirtschaft- und Sozialgeschichte des Weltkrieges,* deutsche Serie, No. 5, ed. James T. Shotwell. Stuttgart, Berlin, Leipzig, 1927.

80. ———. *Agrarpolitik.* Berlin, Leipzig, 1924.

81. Specht, Fritz and Paul Schwabe. *Die Reichstagswahlen von 1907.* Berlin, 1908.
Statistisches Jahrbuch. See #153c.

82. Tirrell, Sarah Rebecca. *German Agrarian Politics after Bismarck's Fall: The Formation of the Farmers' League.* New York, 1951.

83. Wangenheim, I. Freiherr von. "Die landwirtschaftliche Besiedlung in Vergangenheit und Zukunft." *Veröffentlichungen des Königlich Preussischen Landes-Ökonomie-Kollegiums,* No. 13. Berlin, 1913.

84. Weber, Max. *General Economic History.* New York, 1927.

85. ———. "Die ländliche Arbeitsverfassung." *Gesammelte Aufsätze zur Sozial- und Wirtschaftsgeschichte.* Tübingen, 1924.
Weigmann, Hans. See #105f.
Wirtschaft und Statistik. See #153e.

86. Wittich, Werner. *Epochen der deutschen Agrargeschichte. Grundriss der Sozialökonomie,* Part 7, 3rd Book. Tübingen, 1922.

87. Wolf-Stettin, Johannes. *Die Landarbeiterfrage,* 2nd ed., Berlin, 1924.

88. ———. *Reichslandarbeiterbund, Kampforganisation oder Wirtschaftsbund.* Berlin, n.d.
Wollenweber, Heinrich. See #105c.

89. "World Agriculture," an International Survey. London, 1932.

90. *Wörterbuch der Volkswirtschaft*, 2nd ed., Jena, 1906-1907.
91. Woytinsky, Wladimir. "Die Tarifverträge in Deutschland Ende 1929," *Gewerkschafts-Zeitung* (#119) Sonderheft 1, 1930.
92. Wunderlich, Frieda. *German Labor Courts*. Chapel Hill, 1947.
93. ———. *Labor under German Democracy. Arbitration 1918-1933*. Social Research Supplement No. 2. New York, 1940.
94. ———. *Versicherung, Fürsorge, Krisenrisiko*. Leipzig, 1932.
95. Wygodzinski, Willy. *Die Landarbeiterfrage in Deutschland*. Tübingen, 1917.
96. *Zehn Jahre christlich-nationale Landarbeiterbewegung 1913-1923*. Berlin, 1923.
97. *Zehn Jahre Preussisches Landwirtschaftsministerium 1919-1928*. Denkschrift des preussischen Ministers für Landwirtschaft, Domänen und Forsten. July 1929, Berlin.
98. Zentralinstitut für Erziehung und Unterricht, Berlin, *Das deutsche Schulwesen, Jahrbuch 1930-1932*. Mit Unterstützung des Reichsministeriums des Innern. Berlin.

b) Series, Periodicals, Newspapers

99. *Allgemeine Schweizer-Zeitung* (Der Schweizer). Fachzeitschrift der Vereinigten Stallschweizer Verbände Deutschlands, Plauen.
100. *Die Arbeit*, Zeitschrift für Gewerkschaftskunde, Politik und Wirtschaftskunde, Berlin.
101. *Archiv für angewandte Soziologie*, Berlin.
102. *Archiv der Landarbeiterfrage*. Erste Sonderreihe des Jahrbuchs für Wohlfahrtsarbeit auf dem Lande. Berlin, 1919.
103. See PART III, *b) Series, Periodicals, Newspapers*, #275.
104. Ausschuss zur Untersuchung der Erzeugungs- und Absatzbedingungen der deutschen Wirtschaft (Enquete Ausschuss). Verhandlungen und Berichte des Unterausschusses für Landwirtschaft, II. Unterausschuss, Berlin.
104a. Vols. *2-4. Landwirtschaftliche Buchführungsergebnisse*, 1927-1929.
104b. *7. Untersuchungen über Landarbeiterverhältnisse*, 1929.
104c. *10. Das ländliche Siedlungswesen nach dem Kriege*, 1930.
104d. *12. Die Verschuldungs- und Kreditlage der deutschen Landwirtschaft in ihrer Entwicklung von der Währungsbefestigung bis Ende 1928*, 1930.
104e. *14. Das landwirtschaftliche Bildungs- und Beratungswesen in Deutschland*, 1930.
105. *Berichte über Landwirtschaft*, ed. Reichsministerium für Ernährung und Landwirtschaft. Sonderheft, Neue Folge. Berlin.
105a. Nos. *3-4*. Seiff, Rudolph. *Die Kleinbauerngebiete, die wirtschaftliche*

| | | *und soziale Bedeutung der Zeitpacht in der deutschen Landwirtschaft.* 1926. |

105b.   *13. Untersuchungen des Deutschen Forschungsinstituts für Agrar- und Siedlungswesen,* ed. M. Sering and others. *Die zweckmässigen Betriebsgrössen in der Landwirtschaft.* 1929.

105b,1.   Niehaus, Heinrich. *Die landwirtschaftlichen Betriebsgrössen und ihre Mischung in ihrer betriebs- und volkswirtschaftlichen Bedeutung, dargelegt an den Verhältnissen im Fürstentum Osnabrück.*

105b,2.   Marckmann, Ernst. *Das Betriebsgrössenproblem in den Holsteinischen Elbmarschen unter Berücksichtigung der verschiedenen Betriebsformen.*

105c.   *44.* Wollenweber, Heinrich. *Auswirkungen der Siedlung I; Bausteine zum Siedlungsproblem. Ländliche Siedlung und Bevölkerung.* 1931.

105d.   *48.* Ley, Norbert; Eilmann, Friedrich; Magura, Wilhelm. *Auswirkungen der Siedlung II*; Siedlung und *Siedlungsverfahren.* 1931.

105e.   *50.* Sering, Max, and others. *Die deutsche Landwirtschaft unter volks- und weltwirtschaftlichen Gesichtspunkten.* 1932.

105f.   *97.* Weigmann, Hans. *Auswirkungen der Siedlung; Bausteine zum Siedlungsproblem, Part V; Siedlung und sozialer Aufstieg der Landarbeiter,* 1934.

105g.   *121.* Brugger, Peter. *Der Anerbe und das Schicksal seiner Geschwister in mehreren Oberämtern des Württembergischen Oberlandes,* 1936.

106. *Blut und Boden,* Berka.

107. *Der Deutsche.* Tageszeitung für deutsche Volksgemeinschaft und für ein unabhängiges Deutschland, Berlin.

108. *Deutsche Allgemeine Zeitung,* Berlin.

109. *Deutsche Arbeit.* Monatsschrift für die Bestrebungen der christlich-nationalen Arbeiterschaft, Berlin.

110. *Deutsche Rundschau,* Berlin.

111. *Der Deutsche Volkswirt,* Berlin. See also #286.

112. Deutscher Landarbeiterverband, Berlin, *Schriften*:

112a.   Nos. *3. Materialien zur Beurteilung der kommunistischen Agitation unter den Landarbeitern und Kleinbauern,* 1919

112b.   *5. Geschäftsbericht des Deutschen Landarbeiterverbandes für die Jahre 1914-1919,* 1920.

112c.   *8. Niederschrift von der zweiten Generalversammlung des Deutschen Landarbeiterverbandes, 16 bis 21 Februar 1920,* 1920.

112cc. *12. Niederschrift der Verhandlungen auf der Konferenz des Verbandsvorstandes mit Gauleitern, 1921.*

112d. *13.* Julius Schmitt. *Tarifverträge in der Landwirtschaft, 1922.*

112e. *14.* Georg Schmidt. *Die gewerkschaftliche Entwicklung und ihre Lehren, 1922.*

112f. *16. Bericht des Verbandvorstandes über die Verbandsarbeit in den Jahren 1920 bis 1922,* Niederschrift von der dritten Generalversammlung des Deutschen Landarbeiterverbandes, 17 und 18 September 1923. 1923.

112g. *17. Bericht des Verbandsvorstandes über die Verbandsarbeit in den Jahren 1923 bis 1925,* Niederschrift von der vierten Generalversammlung des Deutschen Landarbeiterverbandes, 15 bis 18 März 1926. 1926.

112h. *18.* Fritz Baade, *Die wirtschaftliche Lage der Landwirtschaft.*

112h,1. Wilhelm Bernier, *Die Lohnfrage in der Landwirtschaft.*

112h,2. Walter Kwasnik, *Sozialpolitik und Landwirtschaft.* 1927.

112i. *19. Die wirtschaftliche Lage der Landarbeiter und Landarbeiterinnen in Deutschland.* 1928.

112j. *23. Industrielöhne für Landarbeiter.* 1929.

112k. *24.* Franz Hering, *Die Landarbeiter und ihre Gewerkschaften.* 1929.

112l. *25. Bericht des Verbandsvorstandes über die Verbandsarbeit in den Jahren 1926 bis 1928.* Niederschrift von der fünften Generalversammlung des Deutschen Landarbeiterverbandes, 2 bis 6 Juni 1929. 1929.

112m. 20 & 27. Walter Kwasnik, *Der Reichslandarbeiterbund und seine Unterverbände sind keine wirtschaftlichen Vereinigungen im Sinne der arbeitsrechtlichen und wirtschaftspolitischen Gesetzgebung.* 1928, 1930.

112n. *30.* Wilhelm Helmerking, *Untersuchungen über die vergleichsweise Höhe der Landarbeiterlöhne in Deutschland vor und nach dem Kriege.* 1931.

112 o. *32.* Wilhelm Bernier, *Die Lebenshaltung, Lohn-und Arbeitsverhältnisse von 145 deutschen Landarbeiterfamilien.* Ergebnisse einer Erhebung des Deutschen Landarbeiterverbandes in der Zeit vom 1 Juli 1929 bis 30 Juni 1930. 1931.

112p. *34. Die wirtschaftliche Lage der Landwirtschaft und der Landwirte in Ostpreussen.* 1932.

113. *Deutscher Reichsanzeiger und Preussischer Staatsanzeiger,* Berlin.

114. *The Economic Journal,* London.

  Vol. 8. Brentano, Lujo. *Agrarian Reform in Prussia.* 1897.

  Enquete Ausschuss. See #104.

115. *Entscheidungen des Reichsarbeitsgerichts und der Landesarbeitsgerichte,* ed. Georg Flatow and others. Mannheim, Berlin, Leipzig.

116. *Entscheidungen des Reichsgerichts in Zivilsachen,* by the Mitglieder des Gerichtshofs und der Rechtsanwaltschaft. Berlin, Leipzig.

117. *Frankfurter Zeitung,* Frankfurt a.M.

   Gesetzsammlung. See #137.

118. *Gewerkschafts-Archiv.* Monatsschrift für Theorie und Praxis der gesamten Gewerkschaftsbewegung, Jena.

119. *Gewerkschafts-Zeitung,* Organ des Allgemeinen Deutschen Gewerkschaftsbundes, Berlin (Until 1919, *Korrespondenzblatt der General Kommission der Gewerkschaften Deutschlands;* from 1920 to 1923, *Korrespondenzblatt des Allgemeinen Deutschen Gewerkschaftsbundes*).

120. Institut für Konjunkturforschung, Hamburg, Berlin.

120a.   *Vierteljahrshefte zur Konjunkturforschung,* A und B.

120b.   *Halbjahrsberichte zur Wirtschaftslage* (formerly Part B, Text).

120c.   *Vierteljahrsbericht zur Wirtschaftsforschung* (formerly Part A).

120d.   *Statistik des In- und Auslandes* (formerly B, Statistics).

120e.   *Wochenbericht*

120f.   *Weekly Report of the German Institute for Business Research.*

121. International Labour Office, Geneva.

121a.   *International Labour Review.*

121b.   *Studies and Reports.*

121b,1.   *Series K,* Nos. *9. Vocational Education in Agriculture.* 1929.

121b,2.   *11. Collective Agreements in Agriculture.* 1933.

121b,3.   *12.* Böker, H. and F. W. von Bülow. *The Rural Exodus in Germany.* 1933.

121b,4.   *Series O,* No. *3. Migration Laws and Treaties.* 1928.

122. *Jahrbuch des Allgemeinen Deutschen Gewerkschaftsbundes,* Berlin.

123. *Jahrbuch der Berufsverbände im Deutschen Reiche.* Sonderhefte zum Reichsarbeitsblatt: Nos. 25 (1922); 30 (1925); 36 (1927); 52 (1930).

124. *Jahrbuch der Bodenreform,* ed. Adolf Damaschke, Jena.

125. *Jahrbücher für Nationalökonomie und Statistik,* Jena.

126. *Juristische Wochenschrift,* ed. Deutscher Anwaltverein, Leipzig, Berlin.

127. *Der Landarbeiter,* Nachrichtenblatt des deutschen Landarbeiterverbandes, Berlin.

128. *Landarbeiter-Archiv,* Deutscher Landarbeiterverband, Berlin.

129. *Der land- und forstwirtschaftliche Arbeitgeber,* Nachrichtenblatt des Reichsverbandes der deutschen land- und forstwirtschaftlichen Arbeitgebervereinigungen, Berlin.

130. *Landwirtschaftliche Jahrbücher,* Zeitschrift für wissenschaftliche Landwirtschaft, Berlin.

131. *Ministerialblatt der Handels- und Gewerbeverwaltung* (Prussia), Berlin.

132. *Ministerialblatt für die Preussische Innere Verwaltung,* Berlin.
133. *Ministerialblatt der Preussischen Verwaltung für Landwirtschaft, Domänen und Forsten,* Berlin.
134. *Ministerialblatt des Reichs- und Preussischen Ministeriums des Innern,* Berlin.
135. *Mitteilungen der Deutschen Landwirtschafts-Gesellschaft,* ed. Direktorium, Berlin.
136. *Naumburger Briefe,* Artamanenhefte. Naumburg, Leipzig.
137. *Preussische Gesetzsammlung* (before 1907, *Gesetzsammlung für die Königlichen Preussischen Staaten*), Berlin.
138. *Protokoll der Verhandlungen des Kongresses der Gewerkschaften Deutschlands.*

138a.	*2.* Breslau, 1895	Hamburg, 1895
138b.	*11.* Leipzig, 1922	Berlin, 1922
138c.	*12.* Breslau, 1925	Berlin, 1925
138d.	*13.* Hamburg, 1928	Berlin, 1928
138e.	*14.* Frankfurt a.M., 1931	Berlin, 1931
138f.	*15.* Berlin, 1932	Berlin, 1932

139. *Reichsarbeitsblatt,* Amtsblatt des Reichsarbeitsministeriums und der Reichsarbeitsverwaltung, Berlin.
139a. *Die Tarifverträge im Deutschen Reich.* Sonderhefte zum Reichsarbeitsblatt.
Der Reichsbauerntag. See Part III, #275.
140. *Reichsgesetzblatt,* ed. Reichsministerium des Innern, Berlin.
141. *Der Reichslandarbeiterbund,* Zentralorgan der wirtschaftsfriedlichen nationalen Landarbeiter, Berlin.
142. *Reichsministerialblatt der Landwirtschaftlichen Verwaltung,* ed. Reichs- und Preussisches Ministerium für Ernährung und Landwirtschaft, Berlin.
143. *Reichssteuerblatt,* ed. Reichsfinanzministerium, Berlin.
144. *Reichsverband ländlicher Arbeitnehmer, Geschäftsbericht,* Berlin.
145. *Die Rundschau.* Zeitung für das schaffende Landvolk. Reichsverband ländlicher Arbeitnehmer, Berlin.
146. *Schmollers Jahrbuch für Gesetzgebung, Verwaltung und Volkswirtschaft im Deutschen Reiche,* Leipzig.
147. *Schriften des betriebswissenschaftlichen Ausschusses des land- und forstwirtschaftlichen Arbeitgeberverbandes für die Provinz Schlesien,* Breslau.
Heft 5. Feige, Georg. *Arbeitseinkommen und Arbeitsverbrauch auf 168 ober- und niederschlesischen Betrieben im Jahre 1926.* 1927.
Schriften des Deutschen Landarbeiterverbandes. See #112.

148. *Schriften der Gesellschaft für Soziale Reform*: Vol. *58, Das Recht der Organisationen im neuen Deutschland.* Jena, 1917.
Schriften des Deutschen Landarbeiterverbandes. See #112.

149. *Schriften des Vereins für Sozialpolitik.*

149a.   Vols. *56.* Sering, Max. *Die innere Kolonisation im östlichen Deutschland.* München, Leipzig, 1893.

149b.   *61.* Sering, Max. *Das bäuerliche Erbrecht.* München, Leipzig, *1895.*

149c.   *178.* Sering, Max, and Constantin von Dietze (eds.). *Die Vererbung des ländlichen Grundbesitzes in der Nachkriegszeit.* Part 1, München, Leipzig, 1930.

149d.   *182.* Dietze, C. von. *Die deutsche Wirtschaftsnot und die ländliche Familie.* München, Leipzig, 1931.

150. *Soziale Praxis* (subtitle changes), Berlin.

151. *Sozialistische Monatshefte*, Berlin.

152. *Sozialwissenschaftliche Abhandlungen*, Karlsruhe.
No. *4.* Kamm, Walter. *Abgeordnetenberufe und Parlament. Ein Beitrag zur Soziologie des Parlamentarismus.* 1927.
Statistisches Jahrbuch. See #153c.

153. Statistisches Reichsamt, Berlin (formerly Kaiserliches Statistisches Amt).

153a. *Einzelschriften zur Statistik des Deutschen Reichs*: No. 35, *Verbrauch und Einkommen in der Steuerwirtschaft.* 1937.

153b. *Statistik des Deutschen Reichs:*

153b,1. *Berufs- und Betriebszählung vom 12. Juni 1907.* Vol. 212, 1909.

153b,2. *Volks-, Berufs- und Betriebszählung vom 16. Juni 1925, Landwirtschaftliche Betriebszählung.*

153b,3. Vols. *410. Personal, Viehstand, Maschinenverwendung.* 1929.

153b,4.   *412,* Part II. *Die Landwirtschaft im Deutschen Reich.* Textband, 1931.

153b,5. *Volks-, Berufs- und Betriebszählung vom 16. Juni 1933.*

153b,6. Vols. *453. Die berufliche und soziale Gliederung der Bevölkerung des Deutschen Reichs.* 1936.

153b,7.   *459. Die land- und forstwirtschaftlichen Betriebe nach Betriebsgrösse, Besitzverhältnissen und Viehhaltung.* Einführung; Zahl und Fläche der Betriebe; Besitzverhältnisse. 1936.

153b,8.   *460. Bodenbenutzung in den land- und forstwirtschaftlichen Betrieben.* 1937.

153c. *Statistisches Jahrbuch für das Deutsche Reich.*

153d. *Vierteljahrshefte zur Statistik des Deutschen Reichs.*

153e. *Wirtschaft und Statistik*, Stuttgart.

154. *Stenographische Berichte über die Verhandlungen des Reichstages*, Berlin.

Vierteljahrshefte zur Statistik des Deutschen Reichs. See #153d.

155. *Vorläufiger Reichswirtschaftsrat, Drucksachen,* Berlin.
Wirtschaft und Statistik. See #153e.

156. *Wirtschaftsdienst: Weltwirtschaftliche Nachrichten,* ed. Hamburgisches Weltwirtschafts-Archiv, Hamburg. See also #286.

157. *Wirtschaftskurve mit Indexzahlen der Frankfurter Zeitung,* Frankfurt a.M.

158. *Zeitschrift des Deutschen Landwirtschaftsrates* (Neue Folge der Zeitschrift für Agrarpolitik), Berlin.

159. *Zeitschrift für Agrarpolitik.* Organ des Deutschen Landwirtschaftsrats (title varies), Berlin.

160. *Zeitschrift für die gesamte Staatswissenschaft,* Tübingen.

161. *Zeitschrift der Landwirtschaftskammer Niederschlesien,* Breslau.

162. *Zeitschrift des (Königlichen) Preussischen Statistischen Landesamts,* Berlin.

163. *Zentralblatt für die gesamte Unterrichtsverwaltung in Preussen,* ed. Ministerium für Wissenschaft, Kunst und Volksbildung, Berlin.

164. *Zentralblatt der christlichen Gewerkschaften Deutschlands,* ed. Gesamtverband, Berlin.

PART III: THE PERIOD OF NATIONAL SOCIALISM

a) Books

165. *Akademie für Deutsches Recht, Jahrbuch.* Berlin.
Althaus, Hermann. See #303b.

166. Axmann, Artur. *Der Reichsberufswettkampf.* Berlin, 1938.

167. Backe, Herbert. *Das Ende des Liberalismus in der Wirtschaft.* Berlin, 1938.

168. ———. *Um die Nahrungsfreiheit Europas.* Leipzig, 1943.
———. See #300a.

169. Bargel, Richard. *Neue deutsche Sozialpolitik.* Berlin, 1944.
Baynes, Norman. See #198.

170. Brandt, Karl, in collaboration with Otto Schiller and Fritz Ahlgrim. *Management of Agriculture and Food in the German-occupied and other Areas of Fortress Europe. A Study in Military Government,* Vol. 2, *Germany's Agricultural and Food Policy in World War II.* Food Research Institute, Stanford, 1953.

171. Brecht, Arnold. *Federalism and Regionalism in Germany. The Division of Prussia.* New York, 1945.

172. Burgdörfer, Friedrich. *Der Geburtenrückgang und die Zukunft des Deutschen Volkes.* Berlin, 1929.
———. See also #340.
Clauss, Wolfgang. See #277b.

173. Darré, R. Walther. *Neuadel aus Blut und Boden.* 18.-23. Tausend, München, 1934.

174. ———. *Im Kampf um die Seele des deutschen Bauern.* Berlin, 1934.

175. ———. *Das Bauerntum als Lebensquell der nordischen Rasse,* 6th ed. München, 1937.

Decken, Hans v.d. See #277a.

Decker, Will. See #303d.

Deutsche Arbeitsfront, Arbeitswissenschaftliches Institut. See #310.

176. *Deutsche Sozialpolitik, Bericht der Deutschen Arbeitsfront,* Zentralbüro, Sozialamt. Berlin, 30 Juni 1936 bis 31 August 1937; 1 Januar 1938 bis 31 Dezember 1938.

177. Dickinson, Robert E. *The Regions of Germany.* London, 1945.

178. Drescher, Leo. *Entschuldung der ostdeutschen Landwirtschaft, auf Grund einer Untersuchung von Osthilfe Entschuldungsbetrieben.* Im Auftrage der Bank für deutsche Industrieobligationen. Berlin, 1938.

179. Edel, Fritz. *German Labor Service.* Berlin, 1937.

180. Engel, Hans und Eckert, J. *Die Sozialversicherung im Dritten Reich.* Berlin, 1937-1938.

181. Feder, Gottfried. *Hitler's Official Program and Its Fundamental Ideas.* London, 1934.

182. Frankenfeld, Regina. *Das Pflichtjahrmädel auf dem Lande.* Ein Leitfaden. Berlin, 1943.

183. Franz, Heinz. "Der Mensch und die Siedlungsbewegung." Doctoral dissertation, Heidelberg, 1937.

184. Frase, Robert. "A Study of Labor Market Control," *Public Policy* (A Yearbook of the Graduate School of Public Administration), Harvard University, 1940, eds. Friedrich, C. J. and Edward S. Mason, Cambridge, 1945.

185. ———. *The Administration of Unemployment Insurance and the Public Service in Germany.* Social Science Research Council. January, 1938.

186. Gentz, Erwin. *Das Landjahr.* Eberswalde, n.d.

187. *Germany Speaks.* By 21 Leading Members of Party and State, with a preface by Joachim von Ribbentrop. London, 1938.

188. Gnisa, Helmut. "Die Anwendung und Auswirkung der neuesten Agrarpolitik und Marktordnung im Kreise Geldern." Doctoral dissertation, Köln, 1938.

Goodrich, Carter. See #204.

189. Hamburger, L. *How Nazi Germany has Mobilized and Controlled Labor.* Washington, 1940.

190. ———. *How Nazi Germany has Controlled Business.* Washington, 1943.

191. Hedemann, Justus Wilhelm. *Die Fortschritte des Zivilrechts im 19. Jahrhundert,* Part II. Berlin, 1935.

192. Heiden, Konrad. *A History of National Socialism*. A translation made from *Geschichte des Nationalsozialismus* and *Geburt des Dritten Reichs*. New York, 1935.

193. Hesse, K. (ed.). *Kriegswirtschaftliche Jahresberichte*. Hamburg, 1936.
Hierl, Konstantin. See #300f.

194. Hildebrandt, Friedrich. *Nationalsozialismus und Landarbeiterschaft*. Nationalsozialistische Bibliothek, No. 17. München, 1931.

195. *Hitler Calls This Living*. By a member of the German Freedom Party. London, 1939.

196. Hitler, Adolf. *Mein Kampf*. New York, 1940.

197. ———. *My New Order*, ed. Raoul de Roussy de Sales. New York, 1941.

198. ———. *The Speeches of Hitler April 1922-August 1939*, ed. Norman H. Baynes. New York, 1942.
Högel-Wertenson, Marie. See #210.

199. Holt, John Bradshaw. *German Agricultural Policy 1918-1934. The Development of a National Philosophy toward Agriculture in Postwar Germany*. Chapel Hill, 1936.

200. Huber, E. R. *Die Gestalt des deutschen Sozialismus*. Hamburg, 1934.

201. Jacoby, Gerhard. *Racial State, the German Nationalities Policy in the Protectorate of Bohemia-Moravia*. Institute of Jewish Affairs of the American Jewish Congress and World Jewish Congress. New York, 1944.

202. *Jahrbuch für Nationalsozialistische Wirtschaft*, ed. Otto Mönckmeier. Stuttgart, Berlin, 1935; München, 1937.

203. *Jahrbuch für Sozialpolitik*, ed. Ludwig Münz. Leipzig, 1937.

204. Jasny Philippi, Marie. "Some Hints from Foreign Experiences: Germany," in Carter Goodrich and others, *Migration and Economic Opportunity*. Philadelphia, 1936.
Jeserich, Kurt. See #300e.

205. Kaufmann, Günter. *Das kommende Deutschland. Die Erziehung der Jugend im Reich Adolf Hitlers*. Berlin, 1943.
———. See also #303c.

206. Kelley, Douglas M. *22 Cells in Nuremberg. A Psychiatrist Examines the Nazi Criminals*. New York, 1947.

207. Koeppen, Anne Marie (ed.). *Das deutsche Landfrauenbuch*, mit einem Geleitwort von Reichsbauernführer R. Walther Darré. Berlin, 1937.

208. *Kreditlage der deutschen Landwirtschaft im Wirtschaftsjahr 1933-1934*, ed. Deutsche Rentenbank Kreditanstalt, Berlin 1935; for 1937-1938, *ibid.*, 1939.
Kulischer, Eugene M. See #305b.

209. Lamartine, P. Yates. *Food Production in Western Europe*. London, New York, 1940.
Lammers, H. H., and Hans Pfundtner. See #300.

210. Laupheimer, Gertrud und Högel-Wertenson, Marie. *Die vorstädtische Kleinsiedlung in der Mark Brandenburg und in der Grenzmark.* Berlin, 1935.

211. Ley, Robert. *Durchbruch der sozialen Ehre.* Berlin, 1935.

212. Lohr. *Das Landjahr.* Eberswalde, 1937.

213. Lorenz, Robert. "The Essential Features of Germany's Agricultural Policy from 1870 to 1937." Doctoral dissertation, New York, 1941.

214. Marrenbach, Otto (ed.). *Fundamente des Sieges. Die Gesamtarbeit der Deutschen Arbeitsfront von 1933 bis 1940.* Berlin, 1941.

215. Maunz, Theodor. *Die Enteignung im Wandel der Staatsauffassung.* Freiburg i.B., 1936.

216. Mehrens, Bernhard. *Die Marktordnung des Reichsnährstandes.* Berlin, 1938.

217. Merkel, H. und Wöhrmann, O. *Deutsches Bauernrecht.* Leipzig, 1936.

218. Meyer, Konrad (ed.). *Landvolk im Werden,* 2nd ed., Berlin, 1942.

219. ———. *Die Arbeitsverfassung in Gefüge und Ordnung der deutschen Landwirtschaft. Gemeinschaftsblatt des Forschungsdienstes.* Berlin, 1939.

220. Meyer, Konrad and Thiede, Klaus (eds.), with cooperation of Udo Froese. *Die ländliche Arbeitsverfassung im Westen und Süden des Reiches, Beiträge zur Landfluchtfrage.* Heidelberg, Berlin, Magdeburg, 1941.

221. Middleman, Werner. *Die internationale Flüchtlingsfrage.* Bad Homburg and Berlin, 1953.

222. Mitscherlich, Alexander and Fred Mielke, *Doctors of Infamy: The Story of the Nazi Medical Crimes.* New York, 1949.

223. Molitor, Erich. *Deutsches Bauern- und Agrarrecht.* Leipzig, 1936.

224. Nathan, Otto. *The Nazi Economic System.* Durham, N.C., 1944.

225. Neuling, Willy. *Neue Deutsche Agrarpolitik.* Tübingen, 1949.

226. Neumann, Franz, Behemot. *The Structure and Practice of National Socialism.* London, New York, Toronto, 1942.

227. *Nuremberg Proceedings. The Trial of German Major War Criminals.* Proceedings of the International Tribunal sitting at Nuremburg H. M. S. O., Part II. London, 1946-1950.

228. Oermann, J. *Die arbeitsrechtliche und die steuerrechtliche Behandlung der Ostarbeiter.* Berlin, 1944.

229. Oppenheimer Bluhm, Hilde. *The Standard of Living of German Labor under Nazi Rule.* Social Research Supplement V, New York, 1943.

230. Pfundtner, Hans, Reinhard Neubert and F. A. Medicus. *Das neue deutsche Reichsrecht,* Vol. IV: *Sozial- und Arbeitsrecht,* 1933ff.

231. Pihl, Gunnar T. *Germany in the Last Phase.* New York, 1944.

232. Pritsch, Erich and Gustav Mitzschke. *Verordnung zur Sicherung der Landbewirtschaftung vom 23 März 1937.* Berlin, 1937.

233. Rauecker, Bruno. *Social Policy in the New Germany.* Frankfurt a.M., n.d.
234. Reher, Werner. *Social Welfare in Germany.* Berlin, 1938.
235. *Reichsnährstandsgesetze,* ed. Wilhelm Saure. Berlin, Leipzig, 1935.
236. Reinke, Helmut. *Der deutsche Landarbeiter. Sein Kommen und Werden.* Berlin, 1936.
237. Reischle, Hermann and Wilhelm Saure. *Aufgaben und Aufbau des Reichsnährstandes.* Berlin, 1934.
    Reischle, Hermann. See also #300b and #303a.
238. Rosenberg, Alfred (ed.). *Wesen, Grundsätze und Ziele der National-sozialistischen Deutschen Arbeiterpartei.* München, 1930.
239. Rumpf, Fritz. "Die Wandlungen von Zielsetzung und Methode der Agrarsiedlung." Doctoral dissertation, Königsberg, 1935.
240. Saure, Wilhelm. *Das Reichserbhofgesetz.* Berlin, 1933.
241. Schechtmann, Joseph B. *European Population Transfer, 1939-1945.* New York, 1946.
    Schmeer, Rudolf. See #300d.
242. Schmid, Edmund. *Die deutsche Siedlung im Ersten, Zweiten und Dritten Reich.* Nationalsozialistische Bibliothek No. 48. München, 1933.
243. Schmidt, Friedrich and Hermann Bellinger. *Die Kleinsiedlung.* Hand-bücherei des Wohnungs- und Siedlungswesens No. 14. Eberswalde, Berlin, Leipzig, 1936.
244. Schmietendorf, Karl Heinz. *Das Eigentum am Erbhof: Der neue Eigentumsbegriff des bäuerlichen Rechts und sein Verhältnis zum Eigentumsbegriff des B.G.B. Beiträge zum Bauern- und Bodenrecht,* ed. Wilhelm Saure. Reichsnährstandsverlagsgesellschaft. Berlin (1935?).
245. Schubnell, Hermann. *Der Kinderreichtum bei Bauern und Arbeitern. Untersuchungen aus Schwarzwald und Rheinebene.* Freiburg i.B., 1941.
246. Schürk, Josef. *Die Neuordnung der Enteignungsentschädigung.* For-schungsstelle für Siedlung und Wohnungswesen an der Universität Münster, Materialsammlung No. 24. Münster, 1937.
247. Schultze, Joachim H. *Deutsche Siedlung. Raumordnung und Siedlungs-wesen im Reich und den Kolonien.* Stuttgart, 1937.
248. Segal, Simon. *The New Order in Poland.* Research Institute on Peace and Postwar Problems of the American Jewish Committee, New York, 1942.
249. Seldte, Franz. *Sozialpolitik im Dritten Reich, 1933-1938.* München, Berlin, 1939.
250. Sering, M. and C. von Dietze (eds.). "Die Frau in der deutschen Land-wirtschaft," *Deutsche Agrarpolitik: auf geschichtlicher und landes-kundlicher Grundlage,* Vol. 3, Berlin, 1939.

251. Seydewitz, Max. *Civil Life in Wartime Germany*. New York, 1945.
252. Siebert, Wolfgang. *Das Deutsche Arbeitsrecht*. Hamburg, 1938-1939.
  Singer, H. W. See #292.
253. *Der Sinn des Gesetzes zur Ordnung der Nationalen Arbeit*, ed. Reichs-arbeitsministerium, Berlin, 1934.
254. Sperlich, Otto. *Arbeitslohn und Unternehmergewinn in der Kriegs-wirtschaft*. Hamburg, 1938.
255. Spiegel, Henry William. *Land Tenure Policies at Home and Abroad*. Chapel Hill, 1941.
  Stadelmann, Helmut. See #322.
256. Stremme, H. and E. Ostendorff. See #328.
257. Syrup, Friedrich. *Der Arbeitseinsatz und die Arbeitslosenhilfe in Deutschland*. Berlin, 1936.
  ———. See also #300c.
258. *Das Taschenbuch Schönheit der Arbeit*, ed. Anatol von Hübbenet. Berlin, 1938.
259. Taylor, John W. *Youth Welfare in Germany*. Nashville, Tenn., 1936.
260. U.S. Foreign Economic Administration. German Food Self Sufficiency and Landed Estates, Reports of the Technical Industrial Disarmament Committees, No. 23, September 5, 1945.
  Verbrauch und Einkommen in der Steuerwirtschaft. See #341a,1.
261. Vogt, Wolfgang. "Wandlungen im Rechte der Enteignung." Doctoral dissertation, Köln, 1937.
262. Wachenheim, Hedwig. *Relief in Nazi Germany and the Future*. 1944.
263. ———. *Public Health Administration in Germany 1919-1945*. Institute of World Affairs, New School for Social Research, New York, 1945.
264. *Wege zur neuen Sozialpolitik* (Arbeitstagung des Sozialamtes der Deutschen Arbeitsfront vom 16 bis 21 Dezember 1935), ed. Franz Mende. Stuttgart, Berlin, 1936.
265. Weigmann, Hans. *Politische Raumordnung; Gedanken zur Neuge-staltung des deutschen Lebensraumes*. Hamburg, 1935.
266. Willikens, Werner. *Nationalsozialistische Agrarpolitik*. München, 1931.
267. *Wir schaffen. Jahrbuch des B.D.M.*, München, 1940.
268. Wolter, Joachim. "Die Mecklenburgische Landbevölkerung und ihre Einstellung zur nationalsozialistischen Agrarpolitik." Doctoral dis-sertation, Rostock, 1935.
269. Wu, Schautan. "Der Aufbau des Reichsnährstandes und dessen erzieher-ische Einflussmöglichkeiten auf Bauerntum und Volkstum." Doctoral dissertation, Berlin, 1938.
270. Zimmermann, Josef Franz. "Die NS-Volkswohlfahrt und das Winter-hilfswerk des Deutschen Volkes als die vom Hauptamt für Volks-wohlfahrt der Reichsleitung der NSDAP betreuten Sozialgemein-schaften des Dritten Reiches." Doctoral dissertation, Würzburg, 1938.
  Zypries, Gertrud. See #303e.

b) Series, Periodicals, Newspapers

(Those cited in Parts I and II of this Bibliography are not repeated if they continued under the same name after 1933).

271. *Der Angriff.* Tageszeitung der Deutschen Arbeitsfront, Berlin. (1945 amalgamated with *Berliner Illustrierte Nachtausgabe*).

272. *Arbeitertum.* Blätter für Theorie und Praxis der nationalsozialistischen Betriebszellen Organisation, Berlin (Subtitle changed to Amtliches Organ der Deutschen Arbeitsfront einschliesslich NS Gemeinschaft Kraft durch Freude).

273. *Arbeitseinsatz und Arbeitslosenhilfe.* Fachzeitschrift für Arbeitseinsatz und Lohnpolitik, Arbeitsvermittlung, Berufsberatung, unterstützende und wertschaffende Arbeitslosenhilfe, Arbeitsbeschaffung, Berlin.

274. *Arbeitsrechtssammlung, Entscheidungen des Reichsarbeitsgerichts und des Reichsehrengerichtshofes, der Landesarbeitsgerichte, Arbeitsgerichte und Ehrengerichte,* eds. Hermann Dersch and others, Berlin.

275. *Archiv des Reichsnährstandes. Der Reichsbauerntag,* ed. Reichsnährstand. Vols. 1-5, Berlin, 1934-1938.

276. *Badisches Gesetz- und Verordnungsblatt.* Karlsruhe.

277. *Berichte über Landwirtschaft,* ed. Reichsministerium für Ernährung und Landwirtschaft. Sonderheft, Neue Folge. Berlin.

277a.　　Vols. *138.* Decken, Hans v. d. *Entwicklung der Selbstversorgung Deutschlands mit landwirtschaftlichen Erzeugnissen.* 1938.

277b.　　　　*148. Die Deutsche Landwirtschaft.* Deutsche Wiedergabe des Sonderheftes der italienischen Zeitschrift L'Italia Agricola, mit einem Geleitwort vom Reichsbauernführer R. W. Darré, ed. Wolfgang Clauss. 1939.

278. *Berliner Börsenzeitung.* Tageszeitung für Politik und Wirtschaft, für Wehrfragen, Kultur und Unterhaltung, Berlin.

279. *Berliner Lokal-Anzeiger,* Berlin.

280. *Berliner Tageblatt,* Berlin.

281. *Der Betrieb.* Führer und Informationsorgan der NSBO, Berlin.

282. *Deutsche Agrarpresse.* Zeitschriftenkatalog für die Fachpresse in der Land- und Forstwirtschaft sowie für die übrigen Gebiete des Reichsnährstandes, Berlin.

283. *Deutsche Allgemeine Zeitung,* Berlin.
Deutsche Arbeitsfront. See #310.

284. *Deutsche Justiz: Rechtspflege und Rechtspolitik* (formerly *Justizministerialblatt*). Amtliches Blatt der deutschen Rechtspflege, ed. Reichsjustizminister Franz Gürtner, Berlin.

285. *Deutsche Landwirtschaftliche Presse,* Berlin.
Deutsche Sozialpolitik. See #176.
Die Deutsche Sozialpolitik. See #315.

286. *Die Deutsche Volkswirtschaft.* Nationalsozialistischer Wirtschaftsdienst, Berlin (during the war, in Kriegsgemeinschaft mit *Der Deutsche Volkswirt*, #111, und *Wirtschaftsdienst: Weltwirtschaftliche Nachrichten*, #156).

287. *Deutsche Wissenschaft, Erziehung und Volksbildung.* Amtsblatt des Reichs- und Preussischen Ministeriums für Wissenschaft, Erziehung und Volksbildung und der Unterrichtsverwaltung der anderen Länder, Berlin.

288. *Deutsche Zeitschrift für Wirtschaftskunde*, Leipzig.

289. *Deutsche Zeitung im Osten*, Riga.

290. *Deutsches Recht.* Zentralorgan des Nationalsozialistischen Rechtswahrerbundes, Berlin (united with *Juristische Wochenschrift*).

291. *Deutschland Berichte der Sopade*, Prag (later called *Deutschland Berichte der Sozialdemokratischen Partei Deutschlands, Paris*).
    Deutschlands Wirtschaftliche Lage. See #333.

292. *Economic Journal, London.* Nos. 1-12. December 1940 to June-September 1944. Singer, H. W. "The German War Economy."

293. *Entscheidungen des Reichserbhofgerichts*, ed. Beamtete Mitglieder des Gerichtshofs, Berlin.
    Deutsche Sozialpolitik. See #176.

294. *Faschismus.* Tatsachen über die Diktaturen. Internationale Transportarbeiter-Föderation, Kempston, Bedford, England.

295. *Foreign Agriculture.* United States Department of Agriculture, Office of Foreign Agricultural Relations, Washington, D.C.

296. *Forschungsdienst.* Organ der deutschen Landbauwissenschaft, ed. Konrad Meyer, Neudamm, Berlin (continues as the *Deutsche Landwirtschaftliche Rundschau*).

297. *Frankfurter Zeitung*, Frankfurt a.M.

298. *Freude und Arbeit.* Offizielles Organ des Internationalen Zentralbüros Freude und Arbeit, Berlin.

299. *Gesetzsammlung für den Freistaat Hessen.*

300. *Grundlagen, Aufbau und Wirtschaftsordnung des nationalsozialistischen Staates*, eds. H. H. Lammers and Hans Pfundtner, Vol. III, Berlin, 1936.

300a. Nos. *48.* Backe, Herbert. *Agrar- und Siedlungspolitik.*

300b. *49.* Reischle, Hermann. Der Reichsnährstand und seine Marktordnung.

300c. *50.* Syrup, Friedrich. *Arbeitseinsatz und Arbeitsbeschaffung.*

300d. *51.* Schmeer, Rudolf. *Aufgaben und Aufbau der deutschen Arbeitsfront.*

300e. *58.* Jeserich, Kurt. *Sozialpolitik.*

300f. *59.* Hierl, Konstantin. *Arbeitsdienst.*

301. *Hamburger Fremdenblatt.* Reichsausgabe der Kriegsarbeitsgemeinschaft Hamburger Zeitungen, Hamburg.

302. *Hessische Landwirtschaftliche Zeitschrift.* Amtsblatt der Landwirt-schaftskammer für den Volksstaat Hessen, Darmstadt.

303. Hochschule für Politik, Berlin. *Schriften Abteilung II.*

303a. Nos. *1.* Reischle, Hermann. *Die Deutsche Ernährungswirtschaft.* 1935.

303b. *2.* Althaus, Hermann. *Nationalsozialistische Volkswohlfahrt.* 1935.

303c. *3-4.* Kaufmann, Günter. *Der Reichsberufswettkampf. Die be-rufliche Aufrüstung der deutschen Jugend.* 1935.

303d. *14.* Decker, Will. *Der Deutsche Arbeitsdienst.* 1937.

303e. *17.* Zypries, Gertrud. *Der Arbeitsdienst für die weibliche Jugend.* 1938.

304. *Informationsdienst, Mitteilungen der NSBO-Pressestelle,* ed. Heinrich Muchow. Berlin.

305. International Labour Office, Montreal. *Studies and Reports.*

305a. Series C, No. *25. The Exploitation of Foreign Labour by Germany.* 1945.

305b. Series O, No. *8.* Kulischer, Eugene M. *The Displacement of Popu-lations in Europe.* 1943.

306. *International Review of Agriculture.* International Institute of Agriculture, Rome.

307. *International Transport Workers' Federation, News Service,* London.

308. *International Yearbook of Agricultural Statistics.* International Institute of Agriculture, Rome.

309. *Internationale Zeitschrift für Erziehung (International Educational Review),* Berlin.

310. *Jahrbuch* 1937ff. Deutsche Arbeitsfront, Arbeitswissenschaftliches Insti-tut, Berlin (Jahrbuch DAF).

311. *Jahrbuch des Reichsarbeitsdienstes,* Berlin, 1936ff.

312. *Das Junge Deutschland.* Amtliches Organ des Jugendführers des Deutschen Reichs. Sozialpolitische Zeitschrift der deutschen Jugend, Berlin.

313. *Knickerbocker Weekly, The Netherlands Magazine,* New York.

314. *Kölnische Zeitung,* Köln a.Rh.
Lammers, H. H. and Hans Pfundtner. See #300.

315. *Monatshefte für NS Sozialpolitik,* ed. Franz Mende, Stuttgart and Berlin (merged in 1944 with *Soziale Praxis* and *Soziale Zukunft* under the title: *Die Deutsche Sozialpolitik*).

316. *Monthly Bulletin of Agricultural Economics and Sociology,* Interna-tional Institute of Agriculture, Rome.

317. *Münchner Neueste Nachrichten,* München.

318. *Die Nationale Wirtschaft,* Berlin.

319. *National Zeitung*. Organ der nationalsozialistischen Arbeiterpartei, Essen.

320. *National-Zeitung*, Basel.

321. *Nationalsozialistische Landpost*. Parteiamtliches Organ des Reichsamtes für das Landvolk der Reichsleitung der NSDAP, Hauptblatt des Reichsnährstandes, Berlin.

322. *Nationalsozialistische Volkswohlfahrt e.V., Schriftenreihe*: München No. 6. Stadelmann, Helmut. "Die rechtliche Stellung der N.S. Volkswohlfahrt und des Winterhilfswerks des Deutschen Volkes," Berlin, 1938.

323. *Nationalsozialistisches Jahrbuch*, ed. with the cooperation of the Hauptparteileitung der NSDAP, München.

324. *Neue Zürcher Zeitung*, Zürich.

325. *Neues Bauerntum*, Berlin-Dahlem.

326. *News in Brief*. Reports and documents on contemporary Germany, published by the Deutscher Akademischer Austauschdienst, E.V., Berlin.

327. *Odal*. Monatsschrift für Blut und Boden, Berlin (until 1934: *Deutsche Agrarpolitik*, Monatsschrift für Deutsches Bauerntum).

328. *Petermann's Mitteilungen aus Justus Perthes Geographischer Anstalt*, Ergänzungsband 50, No. 228. Stremme, H. und E. Ostendorff. "Die bäuerliche Siedlungskapazität des Deutschen Reichs." Gotha, 1937.

329. *Raumforschung und Raumordnung*. Monatsschrift der Reichsarbeitsgemeinschaft für Raumforschung, Heidelberg, Berlin.

330. *Recht des Reichsnährstandes*. Zeitschrift für Bauern- und Bodenrecht, ed. Reichsnährstand, Berlin.

331. *Das Reich*, Deutsche Wochenzeitung, Berlin.

332. Reichsanstalt für Arbeitsvermittlung und Arbeitslosenversicherung (*Reifa Report*):

332a.	6. *Bericht* für 1 April 1933 bis 31 März 1934, *RABl.* 1935 No. 4
332b.	7. " " 1 " 1934 " 31 " 1935, " 1935 " 35
332c.	8. " " 1 " 1935 " 31 " 1936, " 1936 " 34
332d.	9. " " 1 " 1936 " 31 " 1937, " 1937 " 28
332e.	10. " " 1 " 1937 " 31 " 1938, " 1939 " 3

Der Reichsbauerntag. See #275.

333. Reichs-Kredit-Gesellschaft, Aktiengesellschaft, Berlin. *Deutschlands Wirtschaftliche Lage. Halbjahresberichte*. *Report: Germany's Economic Situation* (title changes).

334. *Reichsministerialblatt für die innere Verwaltung*, Berlin.

335. *Reichsverwaltungsblatt*, ed. A. Mirow and others, Berlin. *Reifa Report*. See #332.

336. *Rural Sociology*, devoted to scientific study of rural life. Official organ

of the Rural Sociological Society. Published by the North Carolina State College of Agriculture and Engineering, University of North Carolina, Raleigh, N.C.

337. *Das Schwarze Korps.* Zeitung der Schutzstaffeln der NSDAP, Organ der Reichsführung SS, Berlin.

338. *Soziale Praxis.* Zeitschrift für Aktienwesen, Gesellschaftsrecht und Sozialpolitik, Berlin (see also #315).

339. *Sozialistische Warte.* Blätter für kritisch aktiven Sozialismus, Paris.

340. *Staatsmedizinische Abhandlungen,* Vol. 8, Burgdörfer, Friedrich. *Aufbau und Bewegung der Bevölkerung.* Leipzig, 1935.

341. Statistisches Reichsamt, Berlin:

341a. *Einzelschriften zur Statistik des Deutschen Reichs:*

341a,1.   Nos. 35. *Verbrauch und Einkommen in der Steuerwirtschaft.* 1937.

341a,2.   42. *Die Besteuerung der Landwirtschaft.* 1941.

341b. *Statistik des Deutschen Reichs:*

341b,1.   Vols. 530. *Der Steuerabzug vom Arbeitslohn im Jahre 1936.* 1939.

341b,2.   552. *Die Bevölkerung des Deutschen Reichs nach den Ergebnissen der Volkszählung 1939,* Heft 5. *Die Ausländer im Deutschen Reich,* 1943.

342. *Südost Echo,* Wien.

343. *Verkündungsblatt des Reichsnährstandes,* Berlin.

344. *Verordnungsblatt des Generalgouverneurs für die besetzten polnischen Gebiete.*

345. *Der Vierjahresplan.* Zeitschrift für nationalsozialistische Wirtschaftspolitik. Amtliche Mitteilungen des Beauftragten für den Vierjahresplan, Ministerpräsident Generalfeldmarschall Goering, Berlin.

346. *Völkischer Beobachter,* Kampfblatt der nationalsozialistischen Bewegung Grossdeutschlands, Berlin.

347. *Das wahre Deutschland.* Auslandsblätter der Deutschen Freiheitspartei, London.

348. *Die Weltwoche.* Unabhängige Schweizerische Rundschau, Zürich.

349. *Die wirtschaftspolitische Parole,* ed. Hermann Reischle.

350. *Zeitschrift der Akademie für Deutsches Recht,* ed. Reichsminister Hans Frank, München, Berlin.

351. *Zeitschrift für Geopolitik,* ed. Karl Haushofer, Berlin.

INDEX

9 780691 625843